Out of the Horrors of War

POLITICS AND CULTURE IN MODERN AMERICA

Series Editors: Margot Canaday, Glenda Gilmore, Michael Kazin, Stephen Pitti, Thomas J. Sugrue

Volumes in the series narrate and analyze political and social change in the broadest dimensions from 1865 to the present, including ideas about the ways people have sought and wielded power in the public sphere and the language and institutions of politics at all levels—local, national, and transnational. The series is motivated by a desire to reverse the fragmentation of modern U.S. history and to encourage synthetic perspectives on social movements and the state, on gender, race, and labor, and on intellectual history and popular culture.

Out of the Horrors of War

Disability Politics in World War II America

Audra Jennings

PENN

UNIVERSITY OF PENNSYLVANIA PRESS

PHILADELPHIA

Published by
University of Pennsylvania Press
Philadelphia, Pennsylvania 19104-4112
www.upenn.edu/pennpress

Printed in the United States of America on acid-free paper
10 9 8 7 6 5 4 3 2 1

Library of Congress Cataloging-in-Publication Data
ISBN 978-0-8122-4851-7

For my parents and grandparents

Contents

Introduction

In early 1943, Mildred Scott, who was in her early thirties and living in Dallas, Texas, at the time, came across a pamphlet for a new organization—the American Federation of the Physically Handicapped (AFPH). Intrigued by what she had read, she wrote for more information and eventually joined the organization, whose emblem promised "Justice," "Opportunity," "Unity," and "Equal Rights." Her own experiences had taught her that people with disabilities could not expect opportunity, equal rights, or justice in the same way able-bodied individuals could. Growing up in Cecil, Pennsylvania, just outside Pittsburgh, disabled by polio and one of seven children, she rarely felt "different" or "looked upon as a 'novelty.'"[1]

That changed shortly before she graduated from high school, when she learned that she would be denied the career path of the women she "knew and admired best." Her home state, like many others, banned people with visible disabilities from teaching. Scott attended a teachers college but could not get a job as a teacher. Eventually, she landed work as a stenographer with the U.S. Bureau of Mines, a job that would ultimately take her to Dallas, but she would later say that her experience searching for "what I might do" taught her that people with disabilities needed to work for better laws and greater opportunity. Discovering that she was legally barred from following her ambitions, and experiencing what must have been a difficult search for some other path, surely made the AFPH commitment to ending "all unfair discrimination against the employment of otherwise qualified but physically handicapped applicants" particularly appealing.[2]

For a while, Scott did little beyond joining the fledgling organization, which by the following year already boasted forty-five lodges and an extensive at-large membership.[3] As a member, however, Scott began to receive mailings from the AFPH. She grew increasingly interested in the organization that she would later describe as "pioneering in a virtually unknown field." When she moved to Washington, D.C., after having saved money to return to school, Scott began volunteering with the AFPH in the evening, learning more about the organization, its aims, and its agenda. She decided to invest her "time and money into [the AFPH] instead." Later, Scott recalled that she "had never met anyone before who was so convinced and determined that there must be a real program for the Nation's millions of handicapped, and, a militant organization to back it up," as Paul Strachan, the organization's founder and president.[4]

A man with impressive government and union connections from his days as an organizer and legislative representative for the American Federation of Labor (AFL), Strachan had founded the AFPH to improve the economic and social lot of disabled Americans. Chartered in Washington, D.C., in 1942 as a nonprofit, educational, and beneficent organization, the AFPH grew out of Strachan's personal experiences of being "broke and dependent" after an automobile accident and several prolonged illnesses, and his vivid memories of how disabled World War I veterans had been cast aside once the embers of war and victory celebrations had faded.[5] Eventually, Scott's determination and commitment grew to match Strachan's. She began working for the AFPH full-time as the national organization's secretary. Scott described the AFPH as full of "faith and hope," working "for things that are right and just," and her own activism as working toward "a program which someday would bring about better conditions for the handicapped and the members of their families."[6]

In discovering that Pennsylvania law prevented her from fulfilling a calling toward which she had worked and for which she felt able, Mildred Scott began to understand that society imposed limits on her beyond any physical limitation associated with her disability. Disability was imbued with social consequences and meaning that extended far beyond the lasting physical, mental, or intellectual consequences of disease, accident, or birth defect. Scott's personal experiences speak to this larger story, not just of the organization she helped to run, but of American society, law, and the state. Disability is, and has always been, evolving, defined variously by religious leaders, physicians, policymakers, philanthropists, social workers, and disabled people themselves. Scholars in the fields of disability studies and history have come to understand disability as a social construction and a powerful tool for understanding relationships of power and systems of exclusion. Disability studies scholar Rosemarie Garland-Thomson maintains "that disability, like femaleness, is not a natural state of corporeal inferiority, inadequacy, excess, or a stroke of misfortune. Rather, disability is a culturally fabricated narrative of the body."[7] In the 1940s, AFPH members, like Scott, began to recognize and confront socially constructed narratives of disability that limited their participation in the workforce and their lives as citizens.

The AFPH enabled members to look beyond individual struggles and identify a broader pattern of disability exclusions that belied narratives of individual failure and faults. More than an end to disability discrimination, AFPH leaders and members imagined a society in which state policy made possible disabled individuals' full participation in civic life. While its demands changed over time, the AFPH sought a range of federal services to facilitate the employment of people with disabilities, advocating for greater access to government employment, employment placement assistance, and legislation requiring employers to hire people with disabilities. The organization further called for a federal pension program for people with disabilities years before Congress extended social insurance to disability or aid to people with disabilities beyond blindness, which had been written into the original Social Security Act. AFPH activists demanded improved access to health care and education, increased building access, better safety and hygiene programs, and federally funded research on various disabilities and potential treatments. Moreover, they envisioned a state in which people with disabilities participated in the development and administration of the policies that would shape their lives.[8]

As a national, cross-disability social movement organization, the AFPH represented something new. The AFPH pulled thousands of disabled citizens—civilians and veterans with a range of physical disabilities—into the national political arena, demanding equal access to economic security and its corollary, economic citizenship, where older organizations had grown around a single disability, a local community, or military service.[9] AFPH leaders claimed that all Americans with disabilities had much in common. Indeed, AFPH chapters facilitated a more universal notion of disability as members' interactions with one another sensitized them to the challenges of others' disabilities. These interactions fostered a sense that disability exclusions transcended the specific type of disability or the way it was acquired and that only national activism and federal action could create a better situation. Beyond its disabled constituents, the organization won the powerful support of labor leaders in the AFL, Congress of Industrial Organizations (CIO), United Mine Workers of America (UMWA), International Association of Machinists (IAM), and other unions.[10]

This vision had its limitations. As the organization's name suggests, AFPH leaders and members imagined a society and state accessible to people with *physical* disabilities. Furthermore, members and leaders often claimed rights on the basis of their mental abilities. The distinction is significant. Historian Douglas C. Baynton has demonstrated that disability served as a powerful tool to "justify inequality" in American history. In the nineteenth and early twentieth centuries, he maintains, disability shaped arguments for slavery, against women's suffrage, and for immigration restrictions. Essentially, these arguments pointed to socially constructed narratives of physical and mental frailties and deficiencies of African Americans, women, and certain ethnic groups to protect the institution of slavery and guard against expanding the boundaries of citizenship. Instead of challenging exclusions based on disability, he argues, social movements for greater equality have often refuted their association with disability.[11] When AFPH members emphasized physically disabled people's mental ability, they reified the notion that at least some kinds of disability justified exclusion, even as they sought to create an accessible state and dismantle, or at least reframe, disability exclusions.

Disability placed AFPH members outside what historian and legal scholar Barbara Young Welke calls the "borders of belonging." Welke argues that throughout the long nineteenth century, notions of ability and disability, alongside race and gender, infused the law "with legal consequences of inclusion and privilege or exclusion and subordination."[12] Scholars have shown that state growth in the twentieth century both reflected and reinforced gendered, racial, and class-based hierarchies. Indeed, twentieth-century state growth expanded the systems of exclusion rather than constricting them as state efforts to police homosexuality helped to construct a "homosexual-heterosexual binary" that like gender and race would shape access to the rights of citizenship.[13]

I argue that ability and disability—the (dis)ability binary—continued to shape the ways Americans defined and codified the rights of citizenship; notions of fitness, dependency, and entitlement; and the responsibilities of the state to its citizens in the twentieth century. Mildred Scott and the AFPH more broadly encountered state policy built around the idea that disability represented a problem to be solved and disabled individuals others who needed to be excluded, contained, or aided because they could not fulfill the social and economic roles defined by their gender and class.

In the midst of dramatic economic, social, and political change of the late nineteenth and early twentieth centuries, disability inspired and framed significant state growth.[14] At the turn of the century, workplace accidents annually killed or at least temporarily disabled one worker in every fifty.[15] American workplaces were the most dangerous in the industrialized world, with risk of injury, disability, and death so high as to inspire comparisons to warfare.[16] The rising human toll of industry informed Progressive Era reformers' desire to ease the plight of workers and curb the excesses of industrial capitalism. Between 1910 and 1925, all but five states adopted workers' compensation laws that mandated financial restitution for injured workers. Historian John Fabian Witt argues that these efforts to cope with the carnage of American industry transformed the legal system with "new ideas and institutions organized around risk, security, and the actuarial categories of insurance" that would offer Americans disabled at work new rights but also frame social policy and the rise of the administrative state in the first four decades of the twentieth century.[17]

As the terrifying rate of industrial accidents, a new wave of immigrants, who were viewed as physically, mentally, and morally suspect, World War I, and successive polio epidemics repeatedly brought disability into focus, Americans adopted a range of strategies to address what they perceived as a growing problem. At its most grim, the response to this growing awareness of disability gave rise to policies of involuntary institutionalization and sterilization targeting individuals deemed "feebleminded," immigration restrictions, and anti-begging ordinances that banned individuals who were "diseased, maimed, mutilated, or deformed in any way, so as to be unsightly or disgusting" from being seen in public.[18]

The federal government had always provided some sort of compensation to disabled veterans through "invalid" pensions, but by the early twentieth century the veteran pension system contributed to the sense of crisis around disability. By 1915, Civil War pensions cost the nation more than two hundred million dollars a year. In costs and loss of productivity, the Civil War pension system embodied what proponents of a new system would call "war's waste." During World War I, progressive reformers transformed the veteran pension system. With the War Risk Insurance Act of 1917, they attempted to provide financial security for disabled veterans who faced systematic discrimination in the labor market and veterans with more severe disabilities who were unable to work. Equally as important, the federal government instituted a system of medical rehabilitation, and later vocational rehabilitation, for veterans injured in combat. Through rehabilitation, reformers sought to salvage disabled men and equip them to become productive citizens once again.[19]

Congress extended vocational, but not medical rehabilitation, to civilians "disabled in industry or otherwise" in 1920 with the Industrial Rehabilitation Act, or Smith-Fess Act.[20] The administration of the civilian rehabilitation program reflected and supported a particular understanding of citizenship, belonging, and workers. Women, people of color, and people with the most severe disabilities were typically excluded, with the average rehabilitation recipient being a thirty-one-year-old white man. Moreover, the U.S. Office of Education that ran the program, designed to return disabled men to productive labor, required that rehabilitation caseworkers be "physically capable."[21] The desire to rehabilitate disabled individuals built on changing notions of dependency, which scholars Nancy Fraser and Linda Gordon have demonstrated, grew increasingly stigmatized during the late nineteenth and early twentieth centuries. The rehabilitation movement's emphasis on work suggests that disabled dependency had also grown increasingly problematic. Work served as the defining characteristic of male citizenship, and willingness to work divided the deserving from the undeserving poor. In this framework, rehabilitationists, as historian Brad Byrom suggests, viewed disabled dependents as "the antithesis of American citizenship."[22] Finding ways to put disabled men to work would push back this unspoken challenge to American citizenship while also solving the economic problem of supporting disabled Americans.

In 1952, AFPH vice president J. Rosemond Cook, Jr., wrote that the AFPH had been born amid "the troubles and terrors" of World War II—a moment of promise and consequence for disabled people.[23] The war, I argue, made disability particularly visible to policymakers and infused it with greater consequences for the nation and a new sense of urgency. It also enabled the rise of a national, cross-disability social movement by creating a new sense of what was possible for people with disabilities.

The necessities of war brought the New Deal promise within the reach of disabled people. While recovery proved elusive during the 1930s, the New Deal, through a stunning array of legislative and executive actions, fundamentally changed Americans' expectations of the federal government. President Franklin D. Roosevelt engaged the federal government in an unprecedented effort to provide Americans with direct relief, jobs, and long-term protection against the uncertainties of unemployment, old age, and widowhood. In 1941, he equated the health of a nation with its ability to provide: "Equality of opportunity for youth and for others. Jobs for those who can work. Security for those who need it."[24]

Yet during the Depression years that New Deal promise—of opportunity, work, and security—was empty for many Americans. New Dealers drew a line between those who should have the guarantee of work and those who could not or should not work, and thus receive aid, by legislating the promise of work to some and relief to others. The drawing of this line, in many respects, had little to do with the individual's desires or citizen status and more to do with prevailing notions about the "appropriate" structure of families, men's and women's roles within the family, race, and class. In this dichotomy of work and relief, which political scientist Barbara J. Nelson argues created a "two-channel welfare state," able-bodied white men should be guaranteed work, and others with no breadwinner to rely upon should receive aid.[25] By instituting these divides, the New Deal intensified the already profound cultural meanings assigned to work and dependence. Moreover, exclusion from work had growing repercussions as New Deal policy linked social rights such as old age pensions and unemployment insurance to work.[26] Furthermore, as Fraser and Gordon have shown, the New Deal further heightened the stigma attached to aid and dependency. Whereas work entitled citizens to the benefits of social insurance, relief, or unearned aid, carried with it the indignities of means and morals tests and supervision.[27] Scholars have built on, extended, and critiqued this model, providing a more nuanced view of the state's inclusions and exclusions.[28] Examining how the state managed disability enriches this conversation. Disability is simultaneously another binary in a matrix of inclusion and exclusion and yet transcends the typical boundaries of inclusion and exclusion, cutting across distinctions based on race, gender, and class. Disability shaped work-earned entitlements, veterans' benefits, and the aid programs most often considered welfare.

Despite President Roosevelt's own disability, the New Deal state had both reflected and reinforced notions of fitness for employment that drew on assumptions that disabled people could or should not work. The Social Security Act provided grants to the states to support relief payments to needy blind citizens and increased funding for the civilian rehabilitation program. With the Aid to the Blind program and an expansion of rehabilitation policy, the New Deal underscored disabled people's exclusion. Even in rehabilitation, a program designed to help people with disabilities return to work, the state marked disabled people as others who required aid, instruction, and assistance—presumably from an able-bodied individual—to work. Essentially, the program sought to help the individual conform to social expectations, leaving intact and perhaps even fortifying able-bodied privilege.

U.S. involvement in World War II necessitated state action to draw the New Deal promise within reach for disabled Americans. While the nation's factories took up the task of supplying Allied troops with the tools of war, millions of young men left the factory floor and headed to the front lines. Labor shortages rapidly replaced unemployment as the economic concern of the nation, and the need for workers pushed the federal government to develop policies to support and encourage the employment of people with disabilities. Just as the needs of the wartime economy challenged gendered and racial prescriptions about work, physical fitness as an abstract prerequisite for work fell by the wayside, and a vast majority of the nation's factories put disabled workers on their payrolls.[29]

World War II catalyzed disability activism by facilitating the dramatic influx of people with disabilities into the workforce, fostering a sense that individual rights were at the heart of American identity, and linking war work and volunteer activities on the home front to victory. In the context of the war and fascism, American patriotism focused around a notion of individual rights. Those rights set the United States and Americans apart from their enemies, and those rights fueled the drive to protect and celebrate the nation and became central to how Americans understood citizenship and what it meant to be an American. As people with disabilities responded to the nation's call for manpower, many gained opportunities that had been closed to them before the war. Alone, this experience might have shifted disabled individuals' expectations for the postwar economy and of the state, but wartime propaganda infused this working experience with deeper meaning. In linking war work and volunteerism with victory and patriotism, propaganda suggested that people with disabilities who had helped on the home front were serving the nation, helping to protect a range of rights, not all of which people with disabilities could themselves enjoy.

World War II also created an acute public awareness of disability. Everywhere, it seemed, the nation confronted disability. Reflecting on his experience managing the nation's draft, Major General Lewis B. Hershey, director of the Selective Service System, painted a grim portrait of the physical and mental condition of the nation. More than five million young men had been found physically, mentally, or emotionally unfit for service—a fact Hershey believed "should give citizens of America cause for alarm." World War II, and the need for soldiers and laborers, served as a lens that brought disability into clear focus. "It is quite useless," Hershey said, "to talk of democracy and the acceptance of equal obligation by all our citizens when a very considerable proportion of these citizens are unable to carry out their civic obligations."[30] Hershey's bleak testimony not only suggests the persistence of (dis)ability in defining citizenship but also the way the war made disability visible and rendered it urgent.

With the grim realities discovered by the Selective Service, labor campaigns that drew hundreds of thousands of disabled Americans into the workforce, an astonishing accident rate that produced each year during the war on the home front more than two million workplace accidents that caused at least a temporary disability, and the specter of the disabled veteran, the war provoked a new and powerful awareness of disability.[31] In 1945, a House joint resolution suggested that the "problem" of disability would "be more severe at the conclusion of World War II than at any other period in the history of our country."[32] Policymakers understood disability as a "problem" because of its perceived power to disrupt and strain the structures and relationships that tied citizens to the state—employer and employee, husband and wife, and family and child. AFPH leaders recognized the potential of this visibility and urgency. Indeed, AFPH president Strachan often pointed to insight he had gained during World War I from a fellow organized labor legislative representative that unions would secure gains in disability policy only when "the horrors of disablement" of the war were fresh in people's minds.[33]

The history of the AFPH challenges existing narratives of the disability rights movement and our understanding of twentieth-century American social movements. I join with numerous scholars whose work, as historian Felicia Kornbluh has described it, "interrupts a metanarrative of civil rights struggles in the twentieth century that begins with the movement against legal Jim Crow and extends chronologically to the women's, LGBT (lesbian, gay, bisexual, transgender), environment, and disability movements, with the latter usually treated as though it began in the 1970s."[34] Like historian Jacquelyn Dowd Hall, who argues for a "long civil rights movement" to more accurately describe the African American civil rights movement, I argue disability activism has a long history. And like the African American civil rights movement, the politics of World War II and the New Deal shaped the disability rights movement.[35]

AFPH leaders understood coalition building as a vital tool in enacting their vision for an accessible state, and the organization recruited the support of organized labor. The AFL, CIO, UMWA, IAM, and other unions helped to finance the AFPH and provided it with organizational and legislative support. Working-class members' networks at the local level and Strachan's connections from his work as a labor organizer helped to facilitate the disability rights-organized labor coalition, but the ties between movements ran deeper. As AFPH leaders and members cultivated the support of organized labor, they tapped into a deep history in which disability and safety concerns helped to fuel union organization and a sense that disability itself was a working-class problem, often caused by dangerous workplaces and a lack of health care. In their interactions with the AFPH, organized labor leaders drew connections between the AFPH agenda and labor's broader vision for the state and democracy. The AFPH agenda offered a concrete link between traditional union concerns about health and safety and newer goals of expanding the protections offered by the welfare state and helped focus labor's attention on both union and nonunion disabled people.[36]

Wartime necessities drove the Roosevelt administration and Congress to expand disability policy. In the postwar period, however, the sense of crisis surrounding disability remained. Both AFPH members and liberal policymakers sought to channel that feeling of crisis. Disability figured in President Harry S. Truman's Fair Deal vision from his earliest articulations of his domestic agenda. To ensure "health security for all," he called for social insurance to cover disability and sickness, national health insurance, government-sponsored medical and scientific research, federal funding to build health care facilities, and greater attention to public health. But his Fair Deal was larger than disability. It represented a commitment to a wider vision of economic security through full employment, affordable housing, and a higher minimum wage and civil rights.[37] Postwar liberals who supported the Fair Deal agenda argued that the prevalence of disability and the conditions that disabled people faced justified a wide sweep of Fair Deal aims, but they supported disability activists' arguments that the federal government needed to do more to make the promise of the New Deal accessible to people with disabilities. This ongoing sense of crisis around disability and the AFPH campaign for greater opportunities drew numerous voices—members of Congress, disabled people, organized labor leaders, physicians, a growing number of experts who claimed specialized knowledge in the field of disability, and leaders in the Department of Labor (DOL), Federal Security Agency (FSA), and the rehabilitation bureaucracy—into a national dialogue about disability and policy in the postwar state. Many questions emerged in this debate. Did the problems people with disabilities faced stem from discrimination or problems inherent in the individual? Should experience of disability or expert knowledge guide policy? Should it focus on providing jobs or medical support? Both AFPH leaders and experts in the field of rehabilitation offered answers to these questions that would ultimately shape the future of U.S. disability policy. Throughout much of the 1940s and 1950s, the AFPH sought to make the state, economic security, and citizenship accessible, but the horrors of war that had created a space for disability activists to be heard also lent weight to the authority of a growing body of professionals who claimed expertise over disability and people with disabilities. As postwar policymakers sought to extend disability policy and the welfare state more generally, they had to navigate a growing gap between disability activists' demands and the prescriptions of disability experts.

The chapters that follow, organized in a roughly chronological order, trace the story of the AFPH—its claims, demands, and vision as well as its efforts to translate its vision into action, policy, and change. But they also tell a broader story about the growth of the disability rights movement; how policymakers, bureaucrats, activists, physicians, and a range of professionals grappled with disability during World War II and the immediate postwar years; how the (dis)ability binary continued to define citizenship; and how disability intersected with liberal policymakers' postwar vision for an expanded welfare state.

Chapters 1 and 2 focus on the moment of World War II. Chapter 1 examines how disabled Americans fought to contribute to victory and for greater opportunities to participate in the growing prosperity on the home front during World War II. It also illustrates how the needs of the wartime economy and disabled veterans led the Roosevelt administration and Congress to push businesses to employ disabled workers and develop policies to facilitate disabled people's entry into the workforce as well as disabled veterans' integration into the peacetime economy. Chapter 2 focuses on the House of Representatives' two-year investigation on aid to people with disabilities, beginning in August 1944. The subcommittee that led the investigation interviewed disability activists, government officials, organized labor leaders, physicians, and employers.[38] The AFPH, which had fought for the investigation, used the hearings to highlight the failings of federal disability policy and the discrimination that disabled people faced on the job market and in education.

Chapter 3 turns to the reconversion moment. It examines how postwar anxieties contributed to the growth of the AFPH. As the organization worked to expand its base, leaders worked to foster unity and community and develop coalitions to put political weight behind the AFPH objectives. The chapter also analyzes how the policies put in place during World War II shifted in the postwar era. Chapters 4 and 5 focus on specific AFPH initiatives—National Employ the Physically Handicapped Week (NEPHW), the President's Committee on NEPHW, and the AFPH legislative campaign to overhaul federal disability policy generally, but rehabilitation policy more specifically. Chapter 5 also examines the organization's coalition with the labor movement that drew on union concerns about health and safety and labor's postwar vision for a more robust welfare state. Chapter 6 analyzes the AFPH's final years and disability policy under the Eisenhower administration.

A Note on Sources

No central collection of AFPH papers exists. In an effort to reconstruct the history of the organization and trace the contours of the state's relationship with disability, I have drawn on a diverse range of previously neglected primary sources. Taking a broad view of state action, I analyzed both the creation of disability policy on the legislative side and its administration on the executive side. I drew on the *Congressional Record* and legislative hearings as well as archival research at the National Archives and the Harry S. Truman and Franklin Delano Roosevelt Presidential Libraries. I examined the organizational papers of the DOL, the FSA, the President's Committee on Employment of the Physically Handicapped, the Office of the Surgeon General of the Army, and the Veterans Administration; the papers of both presidents Truman and Roosevelt; and the papers of numerous government officials. In the absence of central collection of AFPH papers, these federal sources offer a window to the organization's activities because of its strong ties to the DOL, participation in the President's Committee, and continual interaction with a number of federal officials. The AFL, CIO, and a number of other unions provided much of the funding and legislative support that made the AFPH campaign for disability rights possible. As a result, the George Meany Memorial Archives and the Walter Reuther Library offer rich resources about the activities of the AFPH and its relationship with organized labor. Two small collections of AFPH newsletters and magazines at the New York Public Library and City College of New York, respectively, provide a more nuanced picture of the AFPH. Various government publications, contemporary periodical literature, newspapers, union publications, and professional journals complement these archival sources.

Chapter 1

Salvaging People: Disability in a Nation at War

In December 1942, the *New York Times* ran the thirty-first installment of its annual public appeal, "New York's 100 Neediest Cases," in which the *Times*, in partnership with eight relief organizations, sought contributions to "lift the Neediest out of despair." As in other years, the *Times* sifted the lists of partner organizations to discover the one hundred neediest cases, individuals worthy of aid—"good people, brave people, people overwhelmed by conditions beyond their control." The newspaper sought to answer the question its readers would surely ask: how "in these days of public relief and war employment" are there still individuals in need of aid? Even amidst wartime prosperity and with a system of public relief, the *Times* responded preemptively, there "is a kind of sorrow that knows no season." These "neediest cases" fell into "a No-Man's Land of human needs in which public relief does not operate," and where the prosperity ignited by war industries did not touch.[1]

Ideas about worthiness for assistance, shaped by social and class values, gendered thinking, notions of dependency, and thoughts on poverty no doubt informed the selection of these cases as the "neediest" in the city. In the calculus of need, however, the limits of public relief weighed heavily. Permanent and temporary disability and ill health sat at the heart of seventy-seven of the one hundred cases and cast a shadow across nearly every case, as relief workers feared that poverty, stress, emotional turmoil, and poor housing would wreck the health and threaten the sanity of even those regarded as fit. That disability and illness figured so prominently on the list suggests that both shaped the no man's land where public relief did not function or failed the individuals it sought to assist. For example, nineteen-year-old wheelchair user Jack B., case five among the neediest one hundred, needed hospitalization and special treatments for a bone disease that affected his legs before he could be eligible to participate in a job-training program for disabled individuals. Medical treatments and training for Jack B. were well beyond the financial means of his widowed mother, whose income barely met day-to-day expenses. Jack B.'s situation was typical among people with disabilities in the early 1940s. In fact, the federal-state rehabilitation program that existed to provide the type of training Jack B. needed to land a job often required clients undergo medical treatments, yet until 1943 federal law prevented the program from paying for those treatments. The New Deal had instituted new forms of aid for people with disabilities, including offering public relief for impoverished blind citizens, expanding funding for the federal-state rehabilitation program, and providing medical services for children with disabilities through the Social Security Act. Yet, as story after story in the *Times* attested, these policies only scratched the surface of need. Ill health of any family member could disrupt a home, exhaust a family's savings, lead to spiraling debts, and require treatments many families simply could not manage.[2]

As the *Times* acknowledged, Americans, engaged in a global war, confronted a vastly different economic situation in 1942 than they had only a few years before. By December 1942, U.S. participation in World War II had transformed the nation's economy, its society, and its citizens' lives. Even before the United States declared war in 1941, unemployment lines had begun to disappear as the nation supplied the industrial and agricultural needs of its British and Soviet allies. In the wake of the December 1941 Japanese attack on the U.S. naval base at Pearl Harbor that drew the nation into war, military spending exploded. In the first half of 1942, the military issued over one hundred billion dollars in purchasing contracts. Gone were the days of desperation and deprivation that characterized the Depression years. Employment and consumption shot upward, with American purchases of books, jewelry, records, cosmetics, and more at new highs during the war. The wartime economy facilitated the creation of seventeen million new jobs, and these new jobs paid well, including frequent overtime work.[3]

In the best of situations, the necessities of war constrained the prosperity it created. The federal government called on Americans to conserve, sacrifice, and work when and where they were needed in service to the defense of the nation. Production restrictions and efforts to conserve narrowed consumer options, even changing fashions, with hemlines moving upward and double-breasted suits and trouser cuffs disappearing. The federal government limited the construction of homes and banned the manufacture of automobiles for private use. The transition from supplier to combatant created new burdens for the expanding economy as the war campaign not only heightened production needs but also drew millions of young men out of the workforce and into the military. The nation now confronted a new economic crisis—labor shortages.[4]

For people with disabilities, wartime prosperity was not always easily accessed, and the sacrifices demanded by the war often weighed heavily on them. Services to disabled children slowed as care providers joined the armed forces, the U.S. Children's Bureau and the state programs it funded encountered "spiraling costs," transportation to clinics and other care facilities became more difficult to arrange, and production restrictions limited the availability of assistive devices and braces.[5] Gas and tire rationing made it difficult for people with mobility impairments to work, as accessible public transportation was decades away.[6]

At the same time, however, the war rendered disability legible to policymakers in new and powerful ways. The desperate need for workers forced the federal government to develop and expand policies to bring disabled citizens into the workforce. The speed of production, the massive growth of industry, the dangers inherent in war production, and the influx of unseasoned workers and new machinery combined to produce an explosion of industrial accidents, swelling the ranks of disabled citizens and increasing the need for disability services. The draft heightened the sense that disability presented a problem that must be solved for the success of the war as physical inspection of the nation's men provided concrete evidence of the extent of disability in the United States. Moreover, policymakers were painfully aware that the war itself would create disability. Indeed, in a message to Congress in October 1942, President Roosevelt, himself an ever-present reminder of the threat of polio, pointed out that military casualties were already on the rise and predicted that "the tremendous strides in medical science during the past two decades" would mean that a great number of men would survive battle wounds and return home disabled.[7] Finally, people with disabilities clamored to participate in the war effort and the growing prosperity around them.

These realities produced a wave of disability activism during the war. The American Federation of the Physically Handicapped (AFPH) was founded in 1940 and chartered in August 1942 as a nonprofit educational and beneficent organization in Washington, D.C., just months before the *Times* published its appeal.[8] During the early years of the war, the AFPH demanded that the federal government facilitate disabled people's entry into war work by pushing for expanded services from the federal-state rehabilitation program, the U.S.

Employment Service, the U.S. Civil Service Commission, and the War Manpower Commission (WMC). Moreover, the organization demanded that people with disabilities have a say in shaping federal disability policy. While the AFPH represented something new—a national organization recruiting members across the spectrum of physical disabilities, civilian and veteran alike—older organizations built around the shared experience of a specific disability or military service also pushed for greater access to wartime prosperity and new services to promote equality and opportunity. The politics of aid, work, and representation inspired the National Federation of the Blind (NFB), a national social movement organization of blind Americans, also founded in 1940.[9]

As disability activists clamored for inclusion in the drive to defend the nation, in the prosperity the war created, and in the promises of the New Deal state, policymakers sought to address a cluster of issues—the need for military personnel, the shortage of workers, and how to provide services for disabled veterans.[10] Disability cut across these issues. Drawing disabled Americans into the workforce could potentially free able-bodied men for military service and help solve the chronic labor shortages. Yet the spiraling accident rate on the home front compounded the labor problem. The factors that had created a no man's land in public relief, where people like Jack B. fell through the cracks, and the discrimination that people with disabilities faced on the job market, complicated policymakers' efforts to bring disabled citizens into war service and encouraged the federal government to rethink disability policy in the context of war.

A Disability Rights Wartime Agenda

During the same month that the AFPH received its charter, Nazi forces unleashed an offensive on the city of Stalingrad, initiating a grueling months-long battle that would break the German offensive in the Soviet Union. Meanwhile, the first U.S. bombers launched attacks in continental Europe. In the Pacific in August 1942, U.S. forces landed on the island of Guadalcanal, continuing the shift from defensive to offensive that began with the Allied victory at Midway in June. On the home front, disruption reigned. Millions of men and women moved for military service and better job opportunities. Housing grew scarce in military and industrial centers. Labor shortages helped to drive this mobility and scarcity, as labor needs drove wages up and drew a more mobile population. In this context, employers and the federal government struggled to reduce turnover and recruit new workers.[11]

The need for labor and the nation's call for its citizens to sacrifice in the name of democracy precipitated a civil rights moment. African Americans had already demonstrated that discrimination was vulnerable to attack in the context of a war against fascism. In 1941, African Americans wrested important victories against racism in the form of Executive Order 8802, banning discrimination in defense employment, and the Fair Employment Practices Committee, charged with enforcing the order. This success came when A. Philip Randolph, leader of the African American union the Brotherhood of Sleeping Car Porters, threatened a march on Washington to protest segregation in the military and racial discrimination in defense employment. The threatened march was just the beginning of a larger campaign against racism at home in the context of the war abroad. Randolph and other activists leveraged the tight labor market and international reputation of the United States in negotiations with the White House.[12] Ultimately, the need for labor would expand employment opportunities for people of color and women, and would provide opportunities for people with disabilities as well.[13]

Even before the organization secured its charter, the AFPH articulated an activist agenda that, like the civil rights movement, linked its campaign for greater rights for people with disabilities to the war effort. For example, AFPH founder Strachan appealed to Congress in May 1942 "not only to save scrap, but save and utilize men and women who have been, are, or may be scrapped by reason of disability."[14] In August 1942, the AFPH National Council slammed the federal government for its failure to fully utilize citizens with disabilities in war production. Despite pronouncements from the WMC, the Federal Security Agency (FSA), and the Civil Service Commission, the council's report concluded, efforts to aid citizens with disabilities and draw on their work for national defense had yielded "far more promises than performance."[15]

In a series of articles that appeared in the *Congressional Record* in April and May 1942, Strachan outlined a broad political agenda for the new organization—one that emphasized jobs and the war emergency. He declared that people with disabilities represented "a valuable and worth-while reservoir of hitherto almost untapped strength" to bring to the problem of labor shortages. He pointed out that while the nation saved aluminum, rubber, and oil, among other materials, little effort had gone toward "saving and utilizing men." Strachan proposed five key initiatives that would form the core of the AFPH wartime agenda and that, he argued, would better serve a nation at war: expansion of the federal-state rehabilitation program, a federal agency for people with disabilities, a national education campaign focused on employment of people with disabilities, special consideration in public employment, and a national advisory council.[16]

For people with disabilities, the federal-state rehabilitation program represented an unrealized promise of inclusion and opportunity. Strachan cited Division of Vocational Rehabilitation statistics that nearly 800,000 Americans became permanently disabled each year, including congenital and disease- and accident-related disabilities. Yet, he pointed out, "despite all the effort and hullabaloo," only around 30,000 individuals a year were rehabilitated, leaving "a huge army—approximating 770,000—for which there has been no rehabilitation."[17] In 1942, when Strachan penned his recommendations, the rehabilitation service was rapidly proving it was ill equipped for the war. One commentator in the field described the civilian rehabilitation program at the time as "beset by limitations" and "groping for a sound operational basis."[18] Indeed, before 1943, the program had served fewer than 210,000 people over the course of twenty-three years. State agencies had considerably limited financial and personnel resources. In 1942, most agencies had fewer than ten rehabilitation professionals; ten states employed just one. California, the largest state program at the time, employed thirty-seven people, not including clerical workers.[19]

The Smith-Fess Act of 1920, which had established the civilian rehabilitation program, defined the end goal of rehabilitation as making disabled individuals "fit to engage in a remunerative occupation."[20] In the shared federal-state administration of the civilian program, the U.S. Office of Education established standards, policies, and procedures for states; monitored state plans and their use of federal funds; and sponsored research in the field of rehabilitation. In turn, states handled the actual business of rehabilitating people with disabilities and promoting the program. The Office of Education required states to develop and maintain their own administrative structures and to work with other federal, state, and private agencies to rehabilitate clients. Ultimately, the Office of Education determined that the main job of the rehabilitation program would be to "eliminate or ameliorate" the underlying causes that made people with disabilities "unemployable," which, the agency concluded, were linked to "loss, impairment, or lack of" physical function or skill and "loss of morale."[21]

According to Office of Education guidance, the rehabilitation process began with case workers considering an individual's background and personality and then helping the individual secure any treatments that might create "improvement in the individual's physical fitness." Next, case workers selected a vocational goal for the individual and the most appropriate training to meet that goal. The Office of Education advocated that case workers utilize the placement assistance of other agencies but warned that job placement and follow-up with rehabilitants was a duty that should not be ignored as the goal of the process was to ensure that people with disabilities secured employment at "self-supporting" wages—a warning that suggested that rehabilitation case workers were sometimes more focused on the process of rehabilitation than the job placement at the end. The case workers, or field agents, that rehabilitation applicants encountered had a college education and experience in vocational rehabilitation, education, personnel management, or other relevant work, a requirement that could be waived with one to two years of graduate education. Beyond being "aggressive" and "energetic," the Office of Education recommended that case workers be "physically capable," suggesting that people with disabilities who sought assistance from the civilian rehabilitation program would most likely encounter an able-bodied individual who would assess their eligibility; suggest treatments, procedures, or aids; determine vocational goals for them; and set out a rehabilitation program they should follow.[22]

Between the actual provisions of the law and the policies of the Office of Education, the rehabilitation program faced significant financial limitations. Funds could not be used for medical, surgical, or hospital care or on stipends to support rehabilitants during their training. Despite the designs of World War I orthopedic surgeons who sought to extend their authority into the field of vocational rehabilitation, Congress had implemented a clear separation between medical and vocational rehabilitation. It did so initially in its program for veterans, vesting the U.S. Army Medical Department with control over medical rehabilitation and the Office of Education with control over the vocational element until the 1921 establishment of the Veterans Bureau, the forerunner to the Veterans Administration (VA). This separation of the medical and vocational aspects of veterans' rehabilitation shaped the provisions of the civilian program and would continue to do so until 1943.[23]

Federal funds also could not be used as capital for people with disabilities to launch businesses, and the agency explicitly banned the use of federal funds for the purchase of wheelchairs or for the repair or replacement of artificial limbs originally purchased by the rehabilitation program. Instead, federal funds paid for state administrative costs, tuition for training and educational programs, medical examinations to determine eligibility and "feasibility" for rehabilitation, and, in cases where funds could not be obtained through other sources, prosthetic devices and medical assistance in fitting them. The Office of Education, however, recommended that state rehabilitation programs carefully consider whether to purchase artificial limbs for rehabilitants, weighing the decision between the "urgency of need," the "substantiality of results," and the availability of other funds for the device.[24]

In the context of civilian rehabilitation, eligibility did not guarantee services, and before 1943, personal or family financial resources were almost always required for assistance. To be eligible for assistance, an individual had to be "unable because of a permanent physical handicap to earn a livelihood." The agency maintained, however, that "such factors as advanced age, degree of physical disability, attitude of mind, or social status, sometimes make it inadvisable, uneconomic, or impossible to" rehabilitate an individual. "Feasible" applicants had disabilities that would still allow them to be trained and placed in full-time jobs. They were "mentally competent" and not in need of "constant supervision." Their attitude suggested that they would "get along with others," indicating "promise of cooperation" both through the rehabilitation process and in later employment situations. Feasible applicants had to have means for supporting themselves and their dependents during the rehabilitation process. Finally, an individual's feasibility hinged on the availability of training programs in the area.[25]

Given these constraints, the AFPH's Strachan argued that expanding rehabilitation alone would not yield a program that could effectively "conserve and develop" the human resources people with disabilities could bring to the war effort or meet the social and economic needs of people with disabilities in the postwar period. Legislating more rehabilitation, a "slow" process of training and education, Strachan insisted, would take too long to meet wartime labor needs. Additionally, he pointed out that various proposals in Washington to expand the program contemplated doubling funding, a prospect he felt fell short of meeting war needs or adequately serving people with disabilities but supported nonetheless.[26]

Strachan viewed establishing a federal agency for people with disabilities, either through legislative or executive action, as vital in achieving the organization's most ambitious aims of ending disability discrimination in employment and education and promoting a comprehensive federal disability policy that would ensure people with disabilities could access opportunity and security. In this first articulation of a goal that would shape the organization's agenda throughout its existence, Strachan argued that federal programs dealing with disability should be consolidated in an agency that would collect information about disability and disabled citizens' welfare, research and publicize the types of employment in which they could excel, encourage equal employment in private industry, and help facilitate rehabilitation and job placement. Moreover, he asserted that people with disabilities should themselves control disability policy, suggesting that they staff the agency. When Strachan first described the proposed agency, he envisioned a bureau in the FSA, forerunner to the Department of Health, Education, and Welfare. Since its creation in 1939, the FSA had housed the Office of Education and the civilian rehabilitation program along with the Employment Service, Social Security Board, and the U.S. Public Health Service. As the AFPH and civilian rehabilitation developed during the war and postwar period, the organization would eventually seek a home for its proposed agency in the Department of Labor (DOL).[27]

In Strachan's view, public education, built around a coalition effort, would be necessary to effect the changes the AFPH envisioned. He described efforts to enlist "every group at interest" in a national education campaign that would incorporate the press and radio. Strachan argued that few beyond people with disabilities understood the problems they faced and the significance of those problems to the nation. Through a national public education campaign, he believed "it would be thus possible to reach down into the subconscious minds of the average man and woman, and vividly portray just what the relation of the physically handicapped is to them as individuals." In particular, he emphasized that such a campaign could highlight the fact that, if the majority of people with disabilities were "put to work," tax burdens would be lightened for everyone and the nation's productivity would increase—a key point given the realities of labor shortages.[28] As part of this public education campaign, he called for the establishment of a "National Employ the Physically Handicapped Week." Like his broader plans for public education, Strachan envisioned a cooperative effort that would engage political groups, women's organizations, disability organizations, veterans' associations, and industrial, business, labor, education, civic, and religious leaders along with stage and screen stars.[29] In a national education campaign that sought to make other organizations and the public more generally understand disability as a problem that mattered to them and employment opportunities as the solution, Strachan recognized an opportunity to build coalitions and support for the AFPH agenda and to reach and organize a broader range of people with disabilities.

While employment broadly defined animated the AFPH agenda, the organization paid special attention to government employment. Strachan called on the Civil Service Commission and state-level commissions to establish special divisions for people with disabilities and to give them "special consideration" for public employment. For this effort to be successful, he proposed that the Civil Service Commission launch a study of government employees to determine how many, where, and how effectively people with disabilities were engaged in public service work.[30]

Finally, Strachan suggested extending this research on a much broader scale, and including people with disabilities in the process, to develop effective policies to benefit people with disabilities. He proposed a national advisory council, including disabled people and representatives of their organizations, to expand the employment of people with disabilities and the range of vocational options available to them, by studying employment patterns, vocational instruction, and existing laws and by providing legislative recommendations.[31]

At the heart of the organization's short- and long-term goals was a demand to make the New Deal's promises of economic security, opportunity, and work accessible to people with disabilities. In this promise of work and economic security, AFPH leaders saw the path to full citizenship. The organization's emphasis on public education and its specific legislative proposals grew out of the central idea that the state had a responsibility to make its promises a reality for people with disabilities. The AFPH demanded that the state facilitate disabled citizens' inclusion in the promise of the New Deal through a range of policies that would support their access to the workplace. Over time, the organization's agenda would include better educational opportunities, health care, improved medical treatments, and physical access to public spaces.

AFPH organizing efforts hinged on the notion that personal experience of disability was necessary to form effective and just disability policy. Members, therefore, had a unique service to offer the nation. More than just demanding that their experiences and opinions be taken into account, the AFPH imagined a disability bureaucracy staffed as much as possible by people with disabilities themselves. In this context, the AFPH campaign represented both an implicit and explicit challenge to a range of experts who claimed authority in the field of disability services.

The organization drew on the patriotic fervor of the war to justify their demands, highlighting notions of freedom, justice, national defense, and victory, casting disability rights as imperative to the moral and actual survival of the nation. Strachan claimed that improving disabled people's lives and prospects, bringing them into the workforce, and expanding federal programs were "vitally important to the continuance of our Nation as the citadel of freedom and social justice to the individual."[32] He argued that in the United States it was the "human beings who compose our citizenry" that formed the "first, and last, lines of defense" and "conserving and developing" that resource was as central to victory as it would be to postwar economic and social stability.[33]

Strachan pointed out that it cost $500 per year to support an unemployed disabled adult, whereas $300 spent on rehabilitating that person would make that person self-supporting. Recognizing and facilitating the productive capacity of people with disabilities could save the state money otherwise spent on the care of those individuals. He further emphasized that the national significance of disability grew each day with war production, as the ranks of disabled Americans swelled at an enormous rate because of accidents and disease. According to Strachan, 460 million man-days had been lost to industrial accidents as compared to 30 million lost to strikes.[34] The comparison was a pointed one as growing antistrike sentiment, particularly after a series of coal strikes the following year, led Congress to curb organized labor's power with the Smith-Connally Act, passed over the president's veto in 1943.[35] In demonstrating that industrial accidents far overshadowed the problem of strikes in undermining defense production, Strachan sought to position disability as an issue that was central to the war effort and deserved congressional attention.

Indeed, the home front was a dangerous place. In June 1942, William A. Irvin, head of the National Safety Council's War Production Fund to Conserve Manpower, declared, "One of the most destructive attacks on our nation last year was not made by a foreign enemy. The attack came from within, and left in its wake 102,500 dead—more than twice the 49,475 killed in the AEF [American Expeditionary Forces] ranks during World War I. Moreover, it left 350,000 persons permanently disabled and inflicted 9,000,000 other lesser casualties."[36] Irvin's figures paint a broad portrait of accidents on the home front, including those that happened on the factory floor and highways and in homes and recreation. Still, wartime production exacted a heavy toll. Safety director at Pullman Company and member of the DOL National Committee for Conservation of Manpower in War Industries Harry Guilbert reported that industrial accidents in 1941 had killed enough draft-aged men to fill two full army divisions. Prior to World War II, industrial accidents typically claimed 16,000 lives and disabled, at least temporarily, around 1.5 million annually. Over the course of 1940, that figure shot up at least 10 percent. Data from early 1942 suggested that the situation had grown much worse. In Illinois, monthly figures pointed to a 20 percent increase in fatal accidents from 1941 to 1942.[37]

According to the Bureau of Labor Statistics, the rate of disabling and deadly industrial accidents would remain above two million per year for the duration of the war. In 1943, the worst year for industrial workers on the home front, over 128,000 Americans died or developed a permanent disability and another 2.28 million experienced a temporary disability because of a workplace accident.[38] In July 1942, Louis F. Buckley of the Bureau of Employment Security wrote that the war created a disastrous cluster of unsafe conditions through "the speeding up of production, employment of inexperienced help and women, long hours, expansion into two or three shifts leaving little time for maintenance work, hasty renovation of old machinery and crowding in of new machinery, the opening of long-closed factories and of new ones planned in haste, and the use of poisonous chemicals."[39]

Activists Emerging from the Human Scrap Pile

The goals, strategy, connections, and style of the AFPH drew on the personal history of Paul Strachan. The organization's founder and president had had more than his fair share of "hard knocks," as one journalist phrased it. The hardest, perhaps, came in a deadly automobile crash in November 1929. Strachan, thirty-seven, was driving with his father in East Point, Georgia, just southwest of Atlanta. According to a witness, despite attempts to warn them, neither man saw the switch engine and line of railway cars until it was too late. The accident at the railroad crossing killed his father and left Strachan injured. Newspaper coverage of the incident reported that he was "badly bruised and cut." Later accounts described more extensive injuries and a long recovery. Strachan emerged from the accident with a broken spine. At fifty-five, he reported that he had spent seven years of his life in and out of the hospital because of the accident, operations, and a host of other illnesses. Childhood diphtheria had damaged his hearing in one ear, and as a younger man, he had had a brush with death during the Spanish influenza pandemic. Later, he came down with amoebic dysentery from drinking polluted water. By the post-World War II period, Strachan was deaf and anemic; had chronic heart, kidney, and sinus troubles; had had a double hernia; and walked with a cane.[40]

Strachan described his activism as "born of personal experience, as one 85 percent physically disabled, and who, because of that disability was cast upon the human scrap pile, despite a fierce and intense desire to live, to work, and to achieve." Beyond his personal experience, he rooted his activism in "vivid and poignant recollections" of disabled veterans being "pushed around and ignored as soon as the parades stopped and the bands no longer played" and of other disabled individuals "who were the discards of society."[41] Strachan challenged what he termed an "unreasoning, unjust prejudice against millions of Handicapped people." Questioning the injustice he perceived around him, he asked, "Why cannot Industry, and the public, generally, realize that we, too, aspire to the comforts, the feeling of security that comes from fair recognition of our rights, as citizens, and our needs, as Handicapped?"[42]

Strachan's colorful past took him across the country, gave him access to government officials and labor leaders, provided connections in Hollywood, and helped him to develop a magnetic personal style and a skillset well-suited to launching a movement. Born in Perry, Michigan, in February 1892, Strachan grew up in Michigan and Georgia. He learned an important skill early in life—typing—most likely from his father, who was a journalist. By age sixteen, he had left school and was working as a stenographer at a law office. From there, he took to traveling, pursuing a host of jobs that took him around the world. He claimed to have prospected for gold in Alaska and worked as a stevedore, sailor, and steamship agent.[43]

Strachan moved to Washington, D.C, during World War I and would eventually find work in the Bureau of War Risk Insurance. The bureau initially insured ships and crews navigating the Atlantic war zone but grew dramatically with the War Risk Insurance Act, which issued payments to servicemen's dependents during and in the immediate years following World War I. This work led Strachan to become active in the National Federation of Federal Employees, serving as a legislative representative and general organizer as well as a consultant on federal employees to Samuel Gompers, president of the American Federation of Labor (AFL). From 1917 to 1922 and intermittently after 1931, he worked for the AFL, helping to organize the American Federation of Government Employees, of which he was still a member in the 1950s, and assisting several other unions, including the Post Office Clerks. His work in the Bureau of War Risk Insurance and the labor movement led to an interest in vocational training, which inspired him to help Arthur Holder of the International Association of Machinists (IAM) and the AFL on federal vocational education initiatives.[44] His own experience as laborer, labor organizer, and labor lobbyist as well as his knowledge about and interest in vocational education and rehabilitation not only shaped the rhetoric, tactics, and demands of the movement he led but also solidified ties between organized labor and the disability rights movement.

During the 1920s, Strachan held a range of positions in the burgeoning film industry, experience that helped him cultivate a dynamic personal style and a new set of personal connections. By 1924, he had returned to Georgia and was living in Atlanta and working as a salesman for First National Pictures, which would later merge with Warner Brothers. Later in the decade, he worked for Pathé Exchange. At various points, he would describe himself as a film salesman, press agent, theater operator, producer, tour manager, and correspondent for theatrical papers.[45] His work in the film industry gave him the skills to captivate an audience, sell an idea, and promote a cause.

Strachan's life again shifted course in the aftermath of his 1929 accident. He was unable to work and moved with his family from Georgia back to the Washington, D.C., area to live with relatives, relying on his wife's income and shelter and support from her relatives until the family could get "back on their feet."[46] Strachan worked intermittently with organized labor during the 1930s. A family member reflected that "life was a struggle" during the Depression for the Strachans.[47]

That struggle was compounded in 1931. While traveling and doing organizational work for the AFL, Strachan stopped at a hotel in Chicago. Somewhere along the way, he drank polluted water and developed amoebic dysentery, which began a nearly ten-year period of chronic illness, as no effective treatment for chronic dysentery existed. By the time he checked into Johns Hopkins for "a long siege" and a new treatment in 1940, Strachan had lost a tremendous amount of weight and developed pernicious anemia and an enlarged pericardium. He had also lost his hearing, which at the time, he thought, was perhaps a temporary side effect of one of his ailments or the many treatments he had tried. The hearing loss, however, was permanent.

Strachan described his health as having declined to the point "where there seemed no hope." He suggested that the famous insurance market "Lloyd's [of London] would not have given less than 1000 to 1 odds that I would survive even the treatment." His family's finances had also suffered from his inability to work. He wrote that for "several years" he "was confined to bed, and unable to move," a condition that had left him and his family "completely broke."[48]

Strachan's treatments at Johns Hopkins did not cure all that ailed him, but he regained nearly fifty pounds. Still, he was, as he described it, "obliged to live, of course, on a most rigid dietary regimen."[49] It was during this stay at Johns Hopkins that Strachan would become committed to disability rights. In 1940, he developed the plan for the AFPH though the organization did not take off until 1942. In the meantime, he eked out a living doing research, writing, and performing some legislative work, while investigating disability issues in his free time.[50]

Strachan approached the National Association of the Deaf (NAD) in 1941, seeking information and offering his service to the organization. A group of Gallaudet University-educated deaf leaders had founded the NAD in 1880 to represent the interests of deaf Americans and to address discrimination against deaf citizens nationally. Initially, Strachan suggested that the organization needed representation in Washington, writing to NAD president Tom L. Anderson that he had scoured House and Senate documents but could not find any pending proposals to advance the welfare of deaf Americans where he had found many for blind people. Also, in searching for organizations he might devote his time and expertise to, none of his Washington acquaintances pointed to the NAD.[51]

At first, NAD leaders seemed receptive to Strachan. Anderson responded to Strachan's original inquiry, "We need such a man as you in Washington, the worst way." He also noted that the organization did not have the finances "to pay for help of the sort we really need." Anderson outlined two key areas in which the NAD hoped to gain ground in the national political scene. The organization wanted Congress to establish a "Bureau for the Welfare of the Deaf" in the DOL, and it hoped to end arbitrary restrictions that civil service positions be filled by hearing individuals. Strachan responded with a good deal of insider knowledge, critiquing the NAD's present strategy and suggesting more fruitful paths that ranged from rewriting the bill to placing the proposed bureau in the FSA, recruiting different sponsors, and pushing simultaneously for legislative and executive action. He also wrote that he was willing to work to demonstrate his abilities and perhaps position the organization to afford a Washington office in the future.[52]

The relationship soured shortly after it began. Strachan overwhelmed NAD leaders with lengthy letters and plans for legislative, organizational, and fundraising drives.[53] After numerous exchanges and a meeting with NAD leaders, Strachan developed a two-part plan. The first part contained his recommendations for amending the NAD's bureau proposal and pushing for its enactment. His suggestions ranged from working with all groups who might benefit from the bureau's services, including hard-of-hearing and deafened individuals, to launching an all-out education and publicity campaign to secure support from the general public. The second part of his plan focused on the development of a "Washington Service Bureau." This bureau would essentially be a national lobbying office that would push for favorable legislation and provide information to members about Civil Service examinations, government programs and jobs, members' "rights, privileges, and prerogatives, as citizens of the United States," and recourse when confronting discrimination. Strachan suggested that the NAD launch a membership campaign, expand its membership to include individuals "Deaf in whatever degree," and develop new types of memberships to encourage donations. He also advised that the NAD should consider offering other services such as sick, death, and hospital benefits.[54]

Anderson responded with a mixed assessment. He reported that he and other NAD leaders were generally behind his plans for revising and securing the passage of the welfare bureau bill but strongly against the Washington Service Bureau. Anderson conveyed other board members' assessment that "Mr. Strachan undoubtedly isn't familiar with the great multitude of the deaf," in that he seemed to think that the rank and file could be roused into action through the Washington Service Bureau when the board knew "they raise the devil about the NAD because the NAD doesn't get jobs for them, although that has never been the NAD objective." Essentially, NAD officers proposed to use deaf leaders, working to stimulate interest in wider society, to replace Strachan's plan for rank-and-file action. Still, the NAD hoped to hire Strachan if he would "work along the lines indicated in Part I alone" and agree to "certain control over [his] activities."[55]

Strachan took offense and fired off an angry nine-page letter. He defended the need for a legislative office and took issue with NAD leaders' characterizations of rank-and-file members. While Anderson and others felt that members would not get behind action and the Washington Service Bureau,

Strachan argued that many average deaf people felt "THAT THEIR OWN LEADERS, BY THEIR LACK OF ACTION, ARE THE BOTTLENECKS" (emphasis his). He also claimed that the key to ensuring members' access to jobs was through government action. Strachan wrote that it was a "fatal mistake" to assume that passing any law would solve the problems of deaf Americans. Instead, he asserted that any law would be just the beginning of the work. Strachan took particular exception to Anderson's desire to exert "control" over his efforts, writing, "if you talk to responsible people in any such fashion as this, they will promptly tell you to go to Hell!" Further, Strachan questioned "the 'intent,' interest, and enthusiasm necessary on the part of NAD officers to make an effective campaign." He concluded that he was "deeply interested in helping the Deaf, in fact, ALL the Physically Handicapped" and vowed to continue working with or without the NAD. Ultimately, he suggested means by which he would be comfortable working with the NAD, but the damage was done. Anderson replied, "The utter impossibility of our expecting to come together in a common understanding of all the angles presented by the project you ask the NAD to sponsor, by mail, grows more and more apparent with each slap you choose to deal out to me and my responsible associates when we attempt to exercise a reasonable degree of restraint, or present our viewpoint." The correspondence continued for another month, but it was clear that Strachan and the NAD were on radically different pages.[56]

Strachan's communication with the NAD hinted at the strategies he would employ in the AFPH and revealed the temper that would get him, and his organization, into trouble. The experience also shaped his opinion that people with disabilities lacked "the means and the leadership to come forward and properly present their cases for public consideration." His opinion notwithstanding, a number of organizations had long represented disabled constituents, including the NAD.[57] New Deal, wartime, and postwar politics grew that number.

Another long-standing organization was the Disabled American Veterans (DAV), founded in 1920 by disabled World War I veterans, who were troubled by the lack of available services and the inefficiency, lack of coordination, and confusing mountains of paperwork required for the services that did exist.[58] During World War II, the organization aimed to "preserve America's freedoms," "equalize burdens and profits of war," and improve the lives of "America's disabled defenders." DAV leaders sought to do this by pushing for growth of the military, efficient mobilization of labor on the home front, limits on wartime profits, greater pay for servicemen and women during and after service, disability insurance, and more thorough medical record keeping by the various branches of the armed services. Disabled veterans, the DAV maintained, needed the organization. It sought to expand what would count as a service-connected disability, increase the benefits disabled veterans received, soften VA guidelines for determining disability, harshen the punishment for feigning disability to gain benefits, expand vocational training and job placement programs for disabled veterans, extend hospital care for individuals with service- and nonservice-connected disabilities, expand the number of VA facilities, and provide greater financial support to the dependents and widows of disabled veterans.[59]

Growth of the New Deal state spurred the organization of the NFB in 1940. At the state level, blind activists had fought for pensions and other aid programs for blind citizens throughout the late nineteenth and early twentieth centuries. These successes, in part, led New Deal policymakers to include Aid to the Blind in the Social Security Act of 1935. Moreover, Congress passed a series of laws that aimed to create employment opportunities for blind citizens. Blind activists, whose efforts had been focused at the state level, shifted strategy to the national level. The new organization's president, Jacobus tenBroek, criticized the "intolerable authoritarian arrogance" of the Social Security Board and insisted blind people had to organize nationally to protect blind people's interests. The NFB objected to nonblind professionals' authority over programs for blind Americans and demanded representation for blind people. The organization also fought against employment discrimination.[60]

These disparate organizations would push for a broad range of goals during World War II and the immediate postwar years, but greater employment opportunities, particularly amid the war-fueled job boom, would be a shared priority for disability activists. These organizations would also all demand a role for disabled people in the development and administration of disability policy. Taken together, these organizations would seek to channel the promise of the war moment to gain access to full citizenship.

Wartime Federal Disability Policy

As disability rights activists responded to the changing political landscape, policymakers confronted new realities that would make disability more visible and the problems that activists sought to address more pressing. In March 1942, John J. Corson, director of the Employment Service, declared that recruiting and placing the 10.5 million additional workers who would be necessary to meet the production demands of the war that year was "the biggest job of its kind ever imposed on a democracy."[61]

By early 1942, the nation faced the difficult dilemma of growing the size and strength of the armed forces and meeting the ever-increasing production demands to outfit these new soldiers, sailors, and marines and our Allies with the tools of war. Before Pearl Harbor, the navy and marine corps relied on recruits, and the army had nearly drafted the 900,000 men it sought for preparedness. Overnight, military needs exploded and Selective Service, or draft, calls followed suit. Indeed, the army had called for 20,000 men in December 1941, but by December 1942 the monthly call came in at almost 500,000. Roughly a year after Pearl Harbor, President Roosevelt ended voluntary enlistment to allow local Selective Serve boards to determine where best a man might serve the nation—in the military or on the home front. In 1943, the Selective Service aimed to bring the size of the army to 7.7 million, the navy to 3.6 million, and the marine corps to 500,000. The process of drawing millions of men into the armed forces—hundreds of thousands of women also volunteered—shrank the labor pool, compounding the complex problem of making the materials of war. Indeed, even before Pearl Harbor, the demands of producing for the Allies and preparing for the possibility of war had created labor difficulties. As early as May 1940, FSA official Wayne Coy warned President Roosevelt, "The expansion of war industries is already creating local shortages of skilled labor." By 1942, Corson emphasized the need for workers on the nation's farms and in defense production. He also outlined the need for new thinking—drawing older and disabled individuals and people of color into the workforce, for example. So acute was the need for defense workers, Corson explained, that people would be shifted away from unnecessary jobs into war production.[62]

The process of drafting men for military service also brought the extent of disability in the nation into focus. In September 1941, Lewis B. Hershey, director of the Selective Service System, wrote to Eleanor Roosevelt, "The operation of Selective Service during the past twelve months has uncovered certain practical problems that are matters of the gravest concern to our Nation." He noted that members of the Selective Service System had "been deeply concerned because of the numbers of men who do not meet the physical and mental standards prescribed by the Army." Hershey felt that many could be rehabilitated for military service while "undoubtedly many of the others can be brought to a physical standard which would make them far more efficient as citizens of this nation."[63] As Hershey's letter suggests, the draft made disability more visible and imbued it with greater consequence.

The need for labor on the home front and soldiers on the frontlines, many of whom would become disabled at work or in combat, shaped the federal government's response to disability during the war. Within days of the December 1941 attack on Pearl Harbor, President Roosevelt wrote to FSA head Paul McNutt, instructing him to work with various federal agencies to develop a plan for expanding vocational rehabilitation. Roosevelt hoped that the rehabilitation program could be retooled to both meet the needs of the disabled soldiers the war was sure to create and contribute to solving the nation's man- and womanpower crisis.[64] McNutt responded quickly, meeting with officials from the military, VA, Selective Service System, War Production Board, DOL, Public Health Service, Office of Education and Division of Rehabilitation, and American Red Cross, among other agencies and groups. By February 1942, he had developed a plan to intensify the use of disabled workers in war industry and put some of it in motion.[65]

The slow pace of the rehabilitation process, the fact that officials did not know the extent of disability in the nation, the rehabilitation program's reliance on matching dollars from the states, and the lack of trained rehabilitation caseworkers made McNutt's task all the more difficult. In 1941 and 1942, the service rehabilitated only 15,000 to 20,000 persons each year and placed just one in three clients in a job. Furthermore, McNutt recognized that the lack of knowledge about U.S. disabled citizens contributed to the difficulty of developing an effective plan. He admitted that he could not estimate "with any degree of accuracy" the number of disabled individuals of appropriate age who could benefit from rehabilitation. The Employment Service estimated that some 20 percent of its four million applicants had some sort of disability that contributed to their unemployment. Public Health Service data suggested that four million Americans had a permanent physical disability.[66]

Ultimately, McNutt concluded that the program's reliance on states' matching dollars and the lack of caseworkers meant that it would be impossible to provide rehabilitation for every disabled citizen who could benefit from the service and be fitted for war work. Indeed, drafted individuals who were deemed not fit or able to be made fit for military service had already enhanced the pool of potential clients. McNutt predicted that military causalities and the explosion of industrial accidents would increase the existing caseload by up to 300,000 in the coming year alone. In early 1942, around 100,000 Americans were at some stage in the rehabilitation process, and McNutt believed that "possibly 150,000 additional persons can be accepted for direction toward and into war industry during this calendar year, though not all of these can be conditioned to stable and useful war work." Still, he argued, many others could be placed directly into work. Regardless of the number of disabled citizens and the increase in disability, the fact that state rehabilitation agencies employed only about three hundred caseworkers in early 1942 limited the speed and size of potential growth. Moreover, any growth depended on federal dollars. Historically, the federal government had matched state contributions, but as McNutt pointed out, growing the program was "war service" and that growth could not wait for additional state appropriations, as many state legislatures would not be in session.[67]

Despite these limitations, McNutt crafted a plan that would maximize rehabilitation's potential for wartime aims. He worked with the National Labor Supply Committee of the Office of Production Management to develop a plan "to secure the widest possible acceptance by war industry of handicapped persons directly into plants for pre-job training or initiation into the job at once." Then, he argued that the Employment Service, "because of its wide acquaintance with workers, employers, and labor market conditions," must be central to the effort. He mandated that the agency, then part of the FSA, work with the rehabilitation service to place into jobs clients who had been rehabilitated and disabled individuals fit for direct employment. For individuals not quite ready for direct employment, McNutt suggested that the federal government encourage trade schools to accept disabled applicants, and he called on the rehabilitation program to intensify training courses to make them shorter and speed the entry of clients into the workforce. To support these efforts, he proposed to grow the rehabilitation workforce, recruiting and training the caseworkers needed to meet the war emergency.[68]

McNutt argued that the federal government would have to increase appropriations for rehabilitation and that amendments to the Vocational Rehabilitation Act would be necessary "to provide a broader base for emergency purposes." Because of the constraints related to federal-state matching appropriations, he called for additional federal funding during the war, $500,000 for fiscal year 1942 and a budget of $25 million for 1943. Beyond these increased appropriations, McNutt maintained that the law governing rehabilitation needed adjustments. In particular, he saw medical services and prostheses as "essential" to an expanded rehabilitation program. While those services were available to injured soldiers, sailors, and marines through the army, navy, and VA, the rehabilitation program could not yet provide medical care.[69]

McNutt's work with the National Labor Supply Committee yielded a concrete policy designed to promote the employment of people with disabilities in war industries. In January 1942, the committee issued a policy statement that advocated hiring people with disabilities for war work, a policy they believed would release physically fit men for military service and provide more laborers for war industries. Committee members, however, remained mindful of the postwar potential of such a policy, writing that disabled war workers might "supply experience that will facilitate the adjustment" of future disabled veterans. The National Labor Supply Committee billed hiring disabled workers as "a patriotic service." Whether officials genuinely believed in the postwar value of this particular war effort or they simply sought to draw on the patriotic pull of disabled veterans, it is certain that committee members believed that disabled citizens would need assistance to become workers.[70]

Echoing the thinking McNutt had presented to President Roosevelt, the National Labor Supply Committee tasked the Employment Service with the greatest responsibility in the campaign to convince employers to hire disabled workers. The committee called for the Employment Service to establish specialized services, work more closely with the rehabilitation program, and foster relationships with disability-focused private agencies, drawing on their expertise. Furthermore, the committee instructed Employment Service officials to analyze the work of disabled citizens to determine the types of war work that could be accomplished safely and productively by people with different types of disabilities.[71]

Beyond the Employment Service, the committee directed numerous government programs and urged private agencies to expand services for people with disabilities and focus their efforts around war production. Members of the committee outlined their aim to persuade industry and organized labor of the virtue of employing disabled individuals in war work and asked regional, state, and local labor committees to do the same. The committee advised rehabilitation officials to "intensify" their efforts to bring more people with disabilities into the war labor market and called on the Public Health Service to locate public and private agencies able to provide surgical or medical services to ready people with minor disabilities for war work. Finally, it asked private agencies to focus their energies on the immediate goal of preparing disabled citizens to contribute to the war economy. Within days of issuing this new disability policy, the War Production Board absorbed the Office of Production Management, but McNutt had gained the War Production Board Labor Division's approval of the policy and goal of convincing industry to hire disabled workers.[72]

In early February 1942, McNutt reached out to governors to secure their cooperation in utilizing disabled workers and to inform them that the FSA was developing plans to expand vocational rehabilitation at Roosevelt's prompting. McNutt asked each governor to assist, as the actual work of rehabilitation happened through state agencies with both federal and state funds. He told governors that the rehabilitation training programs operated by their states would need to be faster and more intensive and that the links between rehabilitation and Employment Service offices shored up. Moreover, McNutt explained that he had directed the Employment Service to give the matter "special attention" and instructed his regional officers of the Vocational Rehabilitation Division to work with officials and rehabilitation organizations in each state. Finally, McNutt suggested that governors could offer "a signal service to the necessitous business of mobilizing all our manpower for the winning of this war" by making citizens of the state aware of available rehabilitation services, ensuring that disabled service members received "special consideration" by state rehabilitation offices, encouraging the government-funded vocational training programs in the state to recruit and accept disabled trainees, and making employers and agencies in the state aware of "the responsibility we have for the full utilization of the services of these handicapped workers as a very necessary element in our war effort."[73]

On 12 March, President Roosevelt referred McNutt's proposal and his request to work for additional appropriations to the director of the budget for comment, but McNutt pressed the matter. At the end of March, he wrote the president, "War production is waiting on us in specific locations. The handicapped clientele is marking time." In just under two months since he had written to the state governors, McNutt could report significant progress on making the rehabilitation service war ready, noting "rehabilitations and placements have been stepped up, but the limit possible within existing funds has been reached." By 1 March, 27,000 eligible citizens had registered for rehabilitation, more than had been rehabilitated in any single year before the war, and 7,000 additional people had been referred for rehabilitation in the first two weeks of March, the result of McNutt's efforts to create synergy

Figure 1. War workers install control wires on a BT-13A Valiant airplane. The photograph highlighted the man's short stature as he worked from inside the small space of the aircraft, next to an average height woman. Courtesy of the Franklin D. Roosevelt Presidential Library and Museum.

Figure 2. Polio survivor Robert H. Drake, photographed in 1942 by the U.S. Office of War Information, operated a drill press in a factory that produced airplane motor parts. The photograph visually recorded Drake's disability by including his crutches in the background. Photograph by Ann Rosener. Courtesy of the Library of Congress Farm Security Administration—Office of War Information Photograph Collection.

between the rehabilitation program and the Employment Service, the Selective Service System, the Red Cross, and state workers' compensation commissions. McNutt reminded the president that hundreds of disabled veterans were among those who would be waiting for service if additional appropriations were not secured. Finally, he wrote that he would request a small amount of money "to meet the present and pressing emergency" from the Bureau of the Budget until Roosevelt had decided on how he wanted to approach the broader program. The president signed off on the temporary funding, but the Bureau of the Budget requested more time to study McNutt's original proposal.[74]

In July, the Bureau of the Budget and the FSA presented Roosevelt with a concrete plan for new rehabilitation legislation. The plan called for an office of rehabilitation to be housed in the FSA that would be charged with

Figure 3. Photographed by the U.S. Office of War Information in 1942, Belva Fletcher, on the left, and Henriette Furley painted airplane engine parts at the Maryland League for Crippled Children. The original caption noted Fletcher's progressive paralysis and Furley's need to stand at work because of arthritis. Photograph by Ann Rosener. Courtesy of the Library of Congress Farm Security Administration—Office of War Information Photograph Collection.

rehabilitating disabled civilians for the manpower crisis, providing rehabilitation for civilians injured in civil defense, and addressing the needs of injured veterans. The plan contemplated offering services to veterans as the VA no longer offered the vocational rehabilitation services that had been available to World War I veterans, and the civilian rehabilitation program offered the only publicly funded vocational rehabilitation services in the nation at the time. The administration's proposal added "medical services and physical repair, prosthetic appliances and mechanical aids," to the civilian rehabilitation program's pre-war services of job training, education, and counseling. The Bureau of the Budget and the FSA proposed to maintain the existing federal-state funding system but aimed to address the reality that states had "unequally developed" programs by giving the FSA the authority to supplement matched funding with federal dollars to strengthen rehabilitation programs in states with underdeveloped rehabilitation agencies.[75] The Bureau of the Budget cautioned Roosevelt against delay, as "the question of seeking additional emergency funds will continue unabated." McNutt and budget officials feared that the process of seeking funds would lead to "piecemeal modification of the present legislation" and could "render more difficult the adoption of a sound permanent program." Moreover, they pointed out that Congress had taken up the issue and that several "inadequate bills" had been proposed.[76]

Indeed, labor shortages, the increased visibility of disability, pressure from disabled veterans for greater employment opportunities, and the need to provide rehabilitation for injured soldiers from the present conflict had pushed Congress into action. Members of both the House and Senate introduced numerous bills, ranging from initiatives to expand Social Security to increased appropriations for the rehabilitation program in 1941 and 1942.[77]

In 1941, Representative Graham Barden (D-NC) had introduced rehabilitation legislation promoted by the National Rehabilitation Association. Founded in 1923, the National Rehabilitation Association, a professional society that represented the interests of workers within civilian rehabilitation, had struggled to keep the program on sure financial footing. While the civilian rehabilitation program had remained small, the organization had grown and positioned itself to play an increasingly important role on the federal legislative front in the 1940s. In 1941, the organization hired an executive director and set up a national office, allowing the National Rehabilitation Association to advocate for growth of the rehabilitation program. Barden's bill would have increased federal funding for rehabilitation, established a federal office for the program in the FSA, provided rehabilitation for disabled soldiers, expanded the range of services the program could provide, and eased the financial burden on states by reducing states' matching responsibilities to one dollar for every two spent by the federal government and making the federal government responsible for costs incurred in rehabilitating soldiers and federal employees. While nothing came of his first rehabilitation bill, Barden would continue working on the rehabilitation question, and his initial thoughts on rehabilitation had been shaped by professionals in the field.[78]

Barden's next rehabilitation bill was the product of the conferences, research, and planning led by the FSA following the president's request that the agency develop a plan to expand rehabilitation. In August 1942, Barden and Senator Robert La Follette, Jr. (PRG-WI) introduced identical rehabilitation bills in the House and Senate. La Follette, a member of the Senate Committee on Education and Labor, had sponsored with Barden legislation to increase rehabilitation appropriations earlier in the year.[79]

In proposing that the FSA be in charge of veterans and civilians vocational rehabilitation, Barden's second rehabilitation bill, in line with McNutt's plans for expanding rehabilitation, ruffled feathers in the VA and did not gain the Bureau of the Budget's approval. In early October 1942, General Frank T. Hines, head of the VA, weighed in on the Barden and La Follette bills, arguing that the VA handled all services for veterans, ranging from hospital care to pensions and other benefits, except employment placement. He told the Senate subcommittee, chaired by La Follette, that the La Follette bill did not have the official backing of the administration and that veterans' organizations wanted veterans' rehabilitation to be handled by the VA. Hines agreed with the veterans' organizations, noting that the VA already assessed veterans' disabilities and had the necessary information about disabled veterans to develop a training plan. He concluded, "We also know his history pretty well and we should be in a position to at least guide him to the right place for training." Hines, however, danced a fine line in the hearing, as it was clear that the broader Roosevelt administration favored a plan that would prevent duplication and waste. Despite Hines's call for VA authority in veterans' matters, he argued that the federal government "should not, under any circumstances, duplicate training facilities that now exist." Instead, he maintained that the VA should have the authority to determine whether existing rehabilitation programs were appropriate for individual veterans, "rather than to have some other agency decide that," the other agency, of course, being the FSA. Essentially, Hines argued that the VA should certify a veteran's disability and eligibility for services, develop a plan for rehabilitation, but utilize existing rehabilitation and vocational programs to carry out the actual training.[80]

Disabled veterans were more direct. Millard W. Rice, national service director of the DAV, expressed concerns that having disabled veterans rehabilitated by the FSA would set a dangerous precedent of veterans receiving medical care and vocational assistance outside of the VA, arguing that "it might well be the first step in a gradual and logical absorption of the VA into the Federal Security Agency." Rice maintained that war-disabled individuals should "be kept in a class separate and apart and that they should be treated separate and apart through the Federal agency, which has been designated by Congress to attend to veterans' matters." He referenced "the chaos and confusion that existed following the First World War," prior to the establishment of the VA when five different federal agencies administered some element of veterans' benefits. Indeed, he argued that the very conditions that La Follette's bill would re-create had spurred the founding of the DAV. Rice maintained, "The war-disabled veterans should be required to go to only one Federal agency to find out what they are entitled to, as to all benefits, from the Government, on the basis of their status as war-disabled veterans with service-connected disabilities." Moreover, returning veterans, he pointed out, may not wish to return to their home states, that they would be a more mobile group, moving in search of opportunities. The VA would be better equipped to handle a population no longer rooted in a single place.[81]

On the other side of the coin, McNutt argued for a single rehabilitation program for all disabled citizens. He maintained that one of the central difficulties of expanding rehabilitation to meet wartime needs would be in recruiting trained rehabilitation counselors. "This shortage," he concluded, "will be particularly serious if two agencies are separately established." McNutt suggested that no proposal for rehabilitation, whether for civilians and veterans or veterans alone, would establish new training facilities. Instead, rehabilitation programs would use existing training schools and programs. He noted, "It is, of course, a matter of judgment for the Congress as to whether there shall be an integration of training facilities by one Federal agency or by two Federal agencies." Downplaying the degree to which a universal rehabilitation program would dispense veterans' benefits, McNutt suggested, such a program would merely be guaranteeing veterans access to a program open to all disabled citizens even if a veteran's home state had exhausted annual appropriations or lacked appropriate facilities for the individual's training plan. But he conceded that the VA should determine eligibility for veterans with service-connected disabilities to "do away with any argument that might come afterward" and noted that training allowances legislated for these disabled veterans would be handled by the VA. Finally, McNutt argued that establishing separate programs for veterans and civilians would "unquestionably hamper the rapid and effective development of the general rehabilitation program which is today so vital."[82]

While they were not on the same page about the particulars, McNutt and Hines agreed that the need to expand rehabilitation was a pressing problem. McNutt argued that the need for labor on the home front demanded the "immediate expansion" of the national rehabilitation program, "not as a social gain, but as a wartime necessity." He referenced the "startling increase in disability"—the threat of civilian casualties in a total war and the reality that the army was discharging thirty-five hundred soldiers a month for disability and that industrial accidents on the home front were mounting in the war economy. Finally, he asserted that rehabilitation, in expanding the nation's manpower, represented "a direct contribution to wartime activity."[83] Unlike McNutt, Hines's commitment to rehabilitation focused on the nation's responsibility to its soldiers and the need to incentivize work over pensions. He maintained that the nation needed a program "to fit [disabled veterans] for gainful employment" and that the lure of a pension should not be greater than the incentive "to complete training and get into employment."[84]

The need for workers, and soldiers, had grown to such a degree that President Roosevelt spent considerable time on the problem in a fireside chat just days after McNutt and Hines testified before La Follette's subcommittee. Roosevelt noted that the nation was "becoming one great fighting force," with each individual—whether a soldier, sailor, or worker—"playing an honorable part in the great struggle to save our democratic civilization." He said that the war was being fought "in airplanes five miles above the continent of Europe" and "in mines deep down in the earth of Pennsylvania or Montana." The president painted war production as a central part of the war effort and necessary for victory, yet millions of new workers were needed. Essentially, the fate of the nation hinged on the intertwined problems of developing the nation's fighting force and producing the weapons and food necessary for victory. A coordinated policy and sacrifice on the part of many, he suggested, would be required. Workers should no longer follow their whims about where to work, employers needed to think of the larger picture when hiring, war-focused production had to replace nonessential work, and more men had to be freed for military service by using "older men, and handicapped people, and more women, and even grown boys and girls, wherever possible and reasonable." Roosevelt called on Americans to report to the Employment Service to find out where their "skills and labors are needed most" and to be referred "to an employer who can utilize them to best advantage in the war effort."[85]

Disabled people themselves also expressed their desire to participate in the war effort. The War Production Board, and its predecessor agencies, received around a thousand letters a week from disabled people and friends and family members arguing that the nation, in the midst of war, needed to do more for disabled Americans so that they could do more for their country. Leonard Outhwaite specialized in services for individuals who were difficult to place in jobs, including people with disabilities, for the War Production

Board. He would later say that the letters that flooded his office suggested that disabled Americans and the people closest to them "felt that they were entitled to" rehabilitation, that "it was the responsibility of the Federal Government in time of war to do something more for them."[86]

Both the AFPH and NFB wrote to the Senate committee considering the La Follette measure, urging policymakers to consider the opinions of disabled Americans in their deliberations on rehabilitation policy. The NFB opposed the bill and chastised the committee for failing to include the organization in hearings. The organization argued, "The National Federation of the Blind, consisting of associations of the blind in the several States and being the only national organization of the blind, feels that it has more to contribute in the consideration of such legislation than any other group." The organization maintained that rehabilitation should be administered by the DOL, using the Employment Service for placement. Any placement that happened through the rehabilitation program on its own, the organization asserted, would "probably consist of placing the blind in [sheltered shops]." Moreover, the NFB lambasted the bill's reliance on "the sixteenth century pauper-law principle of individual need," maintaining that "however broadly and literally Congressmen may construe the principle of individual need, our experience has shown that this concept in the hands of administrators and social workers has been narrow, restricted, and even niggardly." Indeed, blind people's experience with public assistance informed the NFB's stance on the La Follette bill. In arguing against FSA leadership of rehabilitation, NFB leaders wrote that the Social Security Board and FSA had "forced a reduction of the standards of public assistance in many States" and had "saddled on the blind of the Nation a demoralizing and humiliating budgetary system by which social workers tyrannize over the lives of the blind." This perceived tyranny led the NFB to call for "standards, principles, policies, limitations or control upon those who are to administer it" and a policymaking board with blind representatives not selected by the individuals who run rehabilitation. Finally, the NFB argued that the bill should mandate the employment "of a proportion of administrative and clerical workers and of practically all placement workers from among the blind," declaring that "justice would require that the blind be given employment in an agency for their benefit and much of the work of such an agency could be done properly only if people with experience of blindness were included on the staff."[87]

The AFPH, still in its early days of organizing and seeking the backing and membership of disabled veterans, wrote to the Senate Committee on

Education and Labor in support of VA control of veterans' rehabilitation. Moreover, the organization used the hearings to reassert its critique of "the lack of intelligent planning" by the federal government to utilize disabled workers' labor. The AFPH's national council argued that disabled Americans could and should be used to release physically fit individuals for military service or other war work "requiring full physical strength." In particular, the AFPH offered a scathing critique of the WMC, the FSA, and the Civil Service Commission, noting that while the FSA sought to take credit for the growing number of disabled individuals in the workforce, the trend was the result of the labor crisis and not due to any "particular effort or design" of the FSA. Despite pressure from the AFPH and other disability rights organizations, the AFPH claimed, Civil Service Commission officials "still stubbornly refuse to map out and put into operation a practical program." Additionally, the council accused the commission of perpetrating "a fraud upon the handicapped," by encouraging disabled individuals to take the civil service examination but then refusing to hire them on the grounds of disability.[88]

The AFPH outlined eight key demands in its correspondence with the committee. The organization called for Congress to pass National Employ the Physically Handicapped Week, legislation that had been introduced by Representative Jerry Voorhis (D-CA) and Senator Richard B. Russell (D-GA), and to launch an investigation to gather information about the nation's response to disability in order to develop "proper and feasible remedies" for the problems confronting disabled Americans and the nation. The national council suggested that such an investigation should result in legislation that "would render more effective service to the handicapped on a scale commensurate with the real size of the job, instead of the 'piddling' methods now generally observed." Additionally, the AFPH demanded a Federal Bureau of Welfare for the Physically Handicapped, staffed as much as possible by disabled citizens, to serve the nation's disabled population and greater services for people with disabilities in the Civil Service Commission and Employment Service. The AFPH called for "an all-out program of complete education, rehabilitation, including all essential medical care, and appliances, and placement in employment of the physically handicapped." Finally, the AFPH's national council staked a claim for the right of disabled individuals to shape their own destinies, arguing that government, at all levels, and private service providers should "afford the physically handicapped representation in all matters in which their interests are at stake."[89]

While the NFB and AFPH's concerns did little to shape the direction of federal efforts to expand rehabilitation, VA and veterans' objections did prompt a rethinking. Initially, Barden had been working with the legislative counsel of the House of Representatives and the FSA drafting counsel. Given the disagreements between the FSA and the VA, the Bureau of the Budget brought in Outhwaite from the War Production Board and Dr. Floyd W. Reeves, a University of Chicago professor who held numerous federal positions during the Roosevelt administration, including a position with the National Resources Planning Board, to study the rehabilitation problem and work with attorneys from the FSA and the VA in drafting legislation. As Barden put it, the Bureau of the Budget "was not in line with me, and I was not in line with the Federal Security, and the veterans were not in line with anybody right at that particular time." Barden's third rehabilitation bill would be the "result of many, many conferences and the ideas of all being shaken down and worked out."[90]

In January 1943, Barden and La Follette introduced new bills that left the VA administrator in control of veterans' rehabilitation, in an attempt to address veterans' criticisms. Still, the bills mandated that the VA "as far as practicable, utilize training provided under approved State plans"—essentially the VA would provide medical rehabilitation and assign veterans to rehabilitation training provided by states through the existing, civilian rehabilitation system.[91]

The change did little to halt veterans' protests. Senator Joel Clark (D-MO) argued the bill's history had to be considered. In its initial form, he said, it "absolutely and boldly raped the Veterans' Administration of any jurisdiction over veterans' rehabilitation." Clark's use of the imagery of rape suggested both the gravity of veterans' objections and their outrage at being stripped of their privileged identity as veterans and the powerlessness that being treated as ordinary citizens would entail. Given the bill's initial stance on the VA's role in rehabilitation, Clark maintained that he and other veterans "feared that if the two problems are linked together"—the need for veterans' rehabilitation and an expanded civilian program—"there will be a repetition of such an attempt."[92]

The DAV, the American Legion, and the Veterans of Foreign Wars (VFW) all denounced the bill. Omar B. Ketchum, national legislative representative of the VFW, explained that his organization had no objection to civilians receiving rehabilitation, but that they were "unalterably opposed" to the idea that a single bill could address the needs of veterans and civilians. American Legion members flooded Congress with a wave of opposition letters. Senator

Clark, himself a World War I veteran, complained that the bill tangled "the special rights of the veterans" with the question of the federal government's obligation to civilians. For their part, Representative Barden and Senator La Follette argued that a program that addressed the needs of both civilians and veterans made sense given the vital link between military success and industrial production. The labor of disabled civilians, they maintained, would be necessary for victory, but this labor would be lost without an expanded rehabilitation program. Moreover, in a total war, the nation had to be ready to rehabilitate men and women injured on the battlefield and home front by enemy attack or on the production lines. Finally, they sold the new rehabilitation program as a cost-saving efficiency measure, reasoning that a single rehabilitation bill would reduce waste and duplication and save money. Efficiency, savings, and arguments that workers were as necessary to victory as soldiers, however, did not convince a Congress wary of any action that might be construed as threatening "the special rights of veterans." In the end, La Follette and Barden removed the provisions for dealing with veterans' rehabilitation from their bills. The House and the Senate passed a separate veteran rehabilitation bill in March, which the president quickly signed into law.[93]

When the House and the Senate returned to the issue of civilian rehabilitation, the question of veterans' rights continued to impede progress. Barden and La Follette had removed the major provisions for veterans from the measure, but Barden sought to ensure their access to the civilian program in case they did not qualify for VA assistance, which would be the case for veterans with disabilities not certified as service-connected. He sought to compel states that accepted federal funds through the civilian program to cooperate with the VA if the agency wanted to use their services in rehabilitating veterans. Ketchum argued that veterans were being used "for sugar-coating purposes and to gain support of the bill by appearing to favor veterans." He charged that the bill referenced veterans twice unnecessarily, once giving the program authority to work cooperatively with the VA to support veterans' rehabilitation and again by opening the program to veterans with disabilities not connected to service-related injuries. As citizens, disabled veterans not eligible for services from the VA would be eligible for rehabilitation through the civilian program, whether they were referenced in the bill or not. Ketchum concluded if the sponsors wanted to serve veterans, they would give them preference in obtaining services. Short of that, he argued, they should not be mentioned at all. Representative William Jennings Miller (R-CT), a disabled World War I veteran, pointed out that state directors of the civilian program "would like by hook or by crook to bring under their control the training of disabled veterans" to make the task of securing state appropriations easier. After much debate and further evidence of the displeasure of veterans' organizations, Barden yielded and removed veterans from the bill entirely.[94]

Aside from the jurisdictional controversy over veterans, several congressmen raised questions over states' rights and on federal spending. In the 1940s, policymakers marshaled states' rights arguments both to push back against the tremendous growth of the federal government under the New Deal and defend the South's Jim Crow system. In the case of rehabilitation policy, both sides of the states' rights coin mattered. In anticipation of states' rights-based opposition to any federal expansion of disability policy, many supporters of the bill offered arguments that sought to distinguish the program from New Deal social policy and reassure states' rights proponents. As Committee on Education members from both sides of the aisle argued for the bill on the floor of the House, Representative George Dondero (R-MI) noted that he, like Barden who chaired the committee, believed the measure was "a States' rights bill." Another committee member, Representative Charles Vursell (R-IL) argued, "When this bill came to us it had a good many ideas promulgated there that drifted away from the protection of the States. During some 30 days the 21 members of this committee attempted at all times to curb the power of the Government, not to extend bureaucracy but to retard its onward march in this country." Vursell also claimed that the bill represented "legislation of economy," in that it would position disabled people "to get off the financial back of the National Government," a prospect that would have resonated with policymakers frustrated with New Deal state growth. Physician and committee member Walter Judd (R-MN) addressed concerns about extending aid programs and increasing national dependency, fears that shaped New Deal opposition. He distinguished rehabilitation, which would help disabled people "to acquire productive capacity or earning power, so they can be independent and self-sustaining" from programs that would make people with disabilities "objects of charity," which would cause them to lose "self-respect" and become "victim[s] of pauperization and paternalism."[95]

Still, the assurances did not stop questions about how the bill might change the relationship between states and the federal government. Representative Henry O. Talle (R-IA) questioned whether the bill's liberalization of federal funding—the federal government covered all administrative costs, while states received one-to-one matching grants for other costs—would "deprive the States of any power they now have." William Blackney (R-MI) expressed concern whether the bill grew out of "the apparent policy on the part of the Federal Government to encroach on the educational policies of the States." Others criticized the fact that the committee had removed the limit on federal funding in the original act.[96]

An amendment to ban discrimination "on account of race, creed, or color" in the program, proposed on the House floor by Earle Willey (R-DE), shone light on the other side of the states' rights coin. Representative John E. Rankin (D-MS), himself having led the charge against the bill on veterans' issues, railed, "this amendment would just kill the bill. If the gentleman wants to destroy this legislation, that is the way to do it." Barden also objected to the amendment claiming, "There has never been the slightest inference of any discrimination." He argued that legislating protections for African Americans would unfairly portray the program as discriminatory. Debate over the amendment was short, and it failed to pass. But the response to the amendment revealed how the fight for states' rights was also about protecting the South's system of separate and unequal. Despite these challenges and questions, the bill passed both the House and Senate in June, and President Roosevelt signed the bill into law in July 1943.[97]

Taken together, Public Law 16, which established the new veterans' vocational rehabilitation program, and the Barden-La Follette Act, aimed at addressing key war crises, discharging the debt owed to disabled veterans, and addressing the country's labor shortage. Moreover, rehabilitation had the potential to extend the New Deal promise of opportunity, employment, and security to Americans with disabilities. Yet, by separating veterans as a special class of citizens, these laws perpetuated divides in disability policy based on how, and whether, one earned access to federal assistance.

Vice Admiral Ross T. McIntire, Surgeon General and Chief of the Bureau of Medicine and Surgery of the Navy, argued that the VA rehabilitation program sought to help the disabled veteran understand that "he should be a useful citizen and make his way, earning his living," instead of existing on a pension. The program worked to give the veteran the tools to become that productive citizen.[98] On the whole, Public Law 16 aimed to make veterans with service-connected disabilities employable. To be eligible for services under the new law, veterans had to have served after the attack on Pearl Harbor, been honorably discharged, and have a disability from or aggravated by service that limited the individual's vocational prospects. Any injury or aggravation of an injury sustained during VA occupational training counted as a battle injury for pension purposes. The VA provided counseling, drawing on veterans' previous education, experiences, disability, wishes, and available programs. It then assigned veterans to training courses at universities and other educational facilities and used on-the-job-training programs offered by businesses; however, the VA limited educational funding to four years. During their time in a rehabilitation program, veterans received an eighty-dollar a month pension, with increases for married veterans and those supporting children or parents. Veterans could also receive pay through on-job-training programs, provided that a veteran's combined pension and training pay did not exceed the typical pay for fully trained individuals in the veteran's field. Additionally, the VA covered the cost of tuition, books, supplies, and equipment, while disabled trainees could receive loans of up to one hundred dollars for incidental expenses not covered by the program. Veterans who completed rehabilitation training received additional financial support for two months as they looked for jobs.[99]

The Barden-La Follette Act sought to prime the civilian rehabilitation program to contribute to the pressing needs of the wartime economy. In so doing, however, policymakers put in motion a longer-term transformation of the program that would contribute to the growth of the disability rights movement. The expanded civilian rehabilitation program aimed to provide "all services necessary to render disabled persons capable of engaging in remunerative employment, or of becoming more advantageously employed, on a normal competitive basis." The pressing needs of the wartime economy led lawmakers to liberalize services available to disabled citizens, allowing federal funds to be used for "the physical reconstruction of the handicapped so that they can as nearly as possible approximate normal work capacity." It also extended rehabilitation to people with mental illness and intellectual disabilities and made psychiatric care available both to people with mental disabilities and those "with physical disabilities complicated by the presence of psychiatric difficulties."[100]

War needs also encouraged policymakers to shift more of the financial burden for the program to the federal government. They removed the fixed ceiling on federal appropriations, and the federal government covered all state administrative costs, which essentially meant that the federal government paid the full cost of providing vocational guidance and counseling. Medical and training costs were shared on a matching basis—one federal dollar for every state dollar, except in specific cases where the federal government committed to covering the full cost: civilians disabled in the conflict, including merchant seamen, and federal employees injured on the job. The day-to-day business of rehabilitation remained with the states, and states continued to place individuals accepted for rehabilitation into existing training programs through public and private schools and in on-the-job training programs with established companies. Medical services were to be obtained through local physicians.[101]

The civilian program worked closely with the Employment Service; state education, welfare, agriculture, and workers' compensation agencies; "Crippled Children's Societies"; the American Red Cross; and a range of community members and service organizations, from doctors to churches, to identify potential clients. An applicant would receive medical examinations "to determine eligibility and to link his capacities with the physical demands of jobs" and "a vocational diagnosis" after completing various aptitude tests and interviews to determine past education, work experiences, and interests. Throughout the process, rehabilitation workers sought to help the client "understand his assets and liabilities, the causes of his present problems, and the steps necessary to correct these difficulties." "Physical reconstruction," if it would significantly reduce the individuals "employment handicap," followed for individuals deemed eligible and feasible for rehabilitation. Medical rehabilitation services could include a wide range of medical, psychiatric, surgical, convalescent, hospital, and dental care; therapy; and prosthetics, drugs, and other medical supplies. Once "physical reconstruction" was complete, clients pursued training, and rehabilitation counselors assisted them with job placement.[102]

Rehabilitation represented a medical- and means-tested form of aid. Applicants had to be disabled enough that rehabilitation would "reduce substantially or eliminate the employment handicaps" and yet able-bodied enough that physicians viewed their physical and mental condition as "relatively stable and remediable." Essentially, rehabilitation was not meant to provide "long-term care for chronic illness," and indeed, hospital care was limited to ninety days. Disabled people's attitudes also figured into the determination of eligibility and feasibility. As Michael J. Shortley, director of the new U.S. Office of Vocational Rehabilitation (OVR), put it, "there must be a sense of directed objective, which is 'hope' expressed in another way." All those determined to be eligible received counseling, training, and placement at no cost. Financial need opened the door to medical services, financial support during rehabilitation, and assistance with supplies and other training materials.[103]

While disability activists demanded the right to shape federal services, the OVR instead turned to a range of professionals for advice in developing the expanded program. The office established two new advisory committees. The first, the National Rehabilitation Advisory Council, was "composed of outstanding representatives of business and industry, labor, education, medicine, services to the blind, social welfare, and other interests closely allied to the problems of rehabilitation." The second, the National Professional Advisory Committee, brought physicians more directly into the program. This committee advised "on matters of professional policy in the general operation of the program" and provided "technical recommendations for physical restoration services."[104] Though this expanded program offered disabled citizens greater services and opportunities, the fact that it reified the power of medical professionals and ignored disabled citizens' calls for the right to shape its administration would contribute to the growing wave of disability rights activism.

World War II was a moment of promise and consequence for people with disabilities. The booming war economy breathed life into the New Deal promises of opportunity, security, and work for people with disabilities. Indeed, people with disabilities clamored to work, serve the nation on the home front, and contribute to victory, and policymakers worked to secure them space in the wartime economy. Rehabilitation and a host of federal efforts to bring disabled people into the workforce represented a federal promise of inclusion—the promise of salvaging people.

In seeking to shore up the gaps in the no-man's land of state and federal aid policy that made it difficult for people with disabilities to contribute to the war effort, however, policymakers set in motion a medicalization of disability policy. More than additional funding, World War II rehabilitation policy redefined the program, opening the door to a range of medical services to support the transformation of dependents to workers.

In the short term, the rehabilitation bureaucracy would focus on immediate results, growing the wartime workforce. In the long term, the growth of the rehabilitation bureaucracy would further mark people with disabilities as others. Individuals who sought rehabilitation would encounter a growing body of experts who would dictate the terms of their inclusion into the workforce and the broader boundaries of citizenship. Physicians and a range of rehabilitation experts would increasingly claim expertise over people with disabilities, arguing that disabled people needed their specialized knowledge, and presumably their supervision, to be prepared for and placed in jobs. Moreover, much as Strachan had predicted, the Barden-La Follette Act never came close to covering the gap.

Both the promise and consequence of the war would explode into the disability rights movement. In the years to come, AFPH members and leaders along with other disability activists would fight to shine a light on that no-man's land of public aid that had shaped "New York's 100 Neediest Cases" and colored the realities of everyday life for Americans with disabilities. They would demand that the state make full citizenship accessible to people with physical disabilities through a range of policies that would support disabled people's access to the workplace, better educational opportunities, health care, and improved medical treatments as well as their physical access to public spaces. Further, disability activists would demand that people with disabilities define and shape these policies, challenging the growing authority of a range of experts in the rehabilitation bureaucracy.

Chapter 2

From the Depths of Personal Experience: Disability Activists Demand a Hearing

In 1946, at congressional hearings demanded by the American Federation of the Physically Handicapped (AFPH), Margaret Nickerson Martin, a national vice president of the organization, argued that the AFPH platform represented "a sincere endeavor by handicapped people to raise the level of their own group to that of 'people.'" She lamented the common inclination to assume people who did not "have their full quota of physical equipment" were "mentally disabled, or at least incapable." Martin placed this desire for the recognition of disabled individuals' personhood in a longer history. Arguing that while society no longer killed disabled people, she asserted that Americans—and American governance—did so figuratively. "But we do forget them, willfully," Martin claimed. "We burn them at the stake of public opinion when we throw the stigma of charity at them and expect them to smile and thank us for it." She described the "wasted existence" of individuals whose disabilities prevented any independence in the existing legal and social framework and individuals "thrown upon the unwilling care of relatives" or institutionalized and who lacked real control over their lives, bodies, and choices. She argued that the AFPH agenda could allow these individuals to bring "real worth and value to society."[1]

Martin testified before the House of Representatives Subcommittee to Investigate Aid to the Physically Handicapped, a subcommittee of the Committee on Labor. The two-year investigation sought, as its chair Augustine B. Kelley (D-PA) put it, to determine the scope of disability in the United States, where disabled Americans lived, how best "to group and classify" them, the causes of various disabilities and "the means to cure or alleviate them," best practices in education and job training for people with disabilities, and "an over-all program for assistance to this enormous segment of our population."[2] The AFPH had fought for the subcommittee as an opportunity for disabled individuals to share their "own story." Just days before the investigation began in late August 1944, Paul Strachan told AFPH members at the organization's second biennial convention, "we will tell our own story, and we will tell it from the depths of our personal experience with our afflictions and with the difficulties we have encountered in meeting the problems of economic life, and participating, if we could, on equal footing with the non-handicapped."[3] The investigation represented the AFPH's first victory in Congress. Over the course of two years, the subcommittee amassed a substantial record of the problems people with disabilities encountered and the types of federal, state, and local aid they received. It interviewed disability activists, employers, government officials, physicians, social workers, and labor leaders and collected thousands of pages of testimony.[4]

Through the AFPH, members developed and articulated, at these hearings, a critique of the ways that the American state and American society privileged able bodies and excluded disabled ones. By insisting that Congress listen to their stories and the organization's agenda, AFPH members transformed personal experiences into political action. As Martin's testimony suggests, the AFPH argued that federal policy, or the lack of coordinated federal policy, prevented disabled individuals from controlling their lives, their bodies, and their destinies, from making contributions to society, and from being recognized as full citizens. Martin, like many activists in the AFPH, demanded recognition of much more than the humanity of people with physical disabilities. In framing the AFPH's proposals for federal action as an attempt to elevate the status of physically disabled individuals "to that of 'people,'" she sought a place for disabled individuals as citizens and contributing members of the national body.[5]

Through the AFPH, disability activists came to the realization that the shared challenges that prevented their full participation in the economic and civic life of the nation extended beyond the personal and were changeable—essentially, that the meaning, privileges, and exclusions tied to (dis)ability were not fixed. Activists drew links to other social movements that had shown identities to be more fluid. For example, Martin reminded congressmen of their colleague who had recently said "brains had no sex." She argued, "Well, neither have they physical attributes which inhibit them because their owner happens to sit in a wheelchair." She claimed, "In the past humanity has been roughly divided into classes or categories: people, women, idiots, and the handicapped—in that order." For Martin, society had begun to rethink the position of women and people of color, and it was now "the handicap's [*sic*] turn."[6] By drawing connections between disability, gender, and race, Martin tied disability to broader social change and emphasized that the realities people with disabilities faced could be changed.

In 1944, the year the congressional investigation on aid to the physically handicapped began, President Roosevelt argued in his State of the Union address that Americans had "accepted as self-evident" a new series of rights, among them "the right to a useful and remunerative job," "the right to earn enough to provide adequate food and clothing and recreation," "the right to adequate medical care and the opportunity to achieve and enjoy good health," "the right to adequate protection from the economic fears of old age, sickness, accident, and unemployment," and "the right to a good education."[7] Roosevelt deemed these rights "a second Bill of Rights." As the speech suggested, New Deal and wartime policy had led citizens to look increasingly to the federal government to guarantee access to opportunity. The right to earn a living, to work, and to a broadly defined sense of security emerged as an entitlement of citizenship—one that was, as scholars have shown, mitigated by race, gender, and sexuality.[8]

For people with disabilities, the war played an important role in creating a new sense that these rights were also theirs to claim. The House investigation and national news coverage of the home front shone a light on disability employment practices during the war. Wartime employment opportunities helped to ignite disability rights activism and the AFPH. Hiring practices that aimed to cope with labor shortages and make space for disabled veterans, along with the state's efforts to encourage and facilitate those practices, created a new sense of what was possible. World War II policy and employment realities suggested the state could make the New Deal promise and protections of Roosevelt's Second Bill of Rights accessible to Americans with disabilities. Numerous federal agencies worked with employers across the country to create new opportunities and find new ways to utilize the skills of people with disabilities. Those efforts, the jobs that grew out of them, and the meaning invested in those jobs created a new sense of rights. The AFPH grew out of and channeled those new expectations.

But even with wartime employment opportunities, those rights remained an unrealized promise for many people with disabilities. As AFPH members would work to demonstrate to the subcommittee, the patchwork of state and federal laws designed to improve the status of disabled Americans left large gaps of discrimination and need. Even as the New Deal and World War II fundamentally altered Americans' expectations for the federal government, people with disabilities remained on the margins, underserved and classed as dependents. Through their interactions with the subcommittee, AFPH members sought to demonstrate how people with disabilities had been excluded from the promises of employment, security, and opportunity.

New Deal policy had tied access to security and the rights of citizenship to work.[9] In this context, disabled people's ability and right to work became central to AFPH arguments for inclusion and demands for state action. Access to work and state support of that access cut across much of the AFPH agenda. Work could secure for members greater access to economic security and health care. Improved access to education, expanded rehabilitation services, medical treatments, and physical spaces could mean greater employability. The emphasis on productive capacity and work stood in direct opposition to charity. Indeed, Martin linked charity to stigma and a figurative death. In essence, people with disabilities had become objects of charity because they were assumed to be unable to work without assistance. The connection reified the notion that people with disabilities were not citizens. Instead, charity marked people with disabilities as others, whose bodies prevented them from contributing to the national body. As AFPH members translated their personal frustrations and those of their fellow members into an agenda, a social movement, they demanded that the state recognize and facilitate their full citizenship by supporting their access to employment, rather than consigning them to charity—a prospect they viewed as dehumanizing. The realities of discrimination, economic marginalization, and failing policy would both foster and shape the AFPH and disability activism more broadly in the mid-twentieth century.

In the Context of War

The AFPH grew rapidly as people with disabilities sought opportunities to contribute to the war efforts on the home front, participate in the prosperity fueled by the war economy, and claim rights from the state as it sought their service in meeting the production needs of war. Between August 1942 and May 1945, the organization grew from the small, committed group who founded it and secured a charter to an organization with around 2,000 dues-paying members. The AFPH had established some sixty chapters and recruited members in every state before the war ended.[10]

As Martin's testimony suggests, the AFPH represented people with *physical* disabilities. The distinction helped to define the movement's strategies, claims, and goals, and perhaps limited its transformative potential. In arguing for people with physical disabilities' working and citizenship capacity, members often highlighted their abilities in comparison to people with intellectual disabilities. In so doing, they defined their citizenship claims in opposition to people with intellectual and cognitive disabilities, implying that the exclusion of one group was unjust and the other just. Historian Douglas C. Baynton maintains, "When categories of citizenship were questioned, challenged, and disrupted, disability was called on to clarify and define who deserved, and who was deservedly excluded from, citizenship."[11] AFPH members did not fully challenge a system of exclusion based on disability. Instead, they challenged a system of exclusion based on *physical* disability.

In 1944, Strachan told members that organization was the key to progress for people with disabilities and countering the "political indifference and ignorance on the part of the great mass of people." He warned against focusing too much attention on local issues. Organizations of people with disabilities, he argued, floundered when "they persist in seeing things only in their immediate neighborhood; they persist in thinking entirely in terms of local problems; we must think in terms of the Nation."[12] As Strachan's speech suggests, the AFPH's developing agenda sought to position disability as a national problem—no longer a problem solely of families, communities, charities, and local and state governments but one of national significance requiring federal action.

Organizationally, the AFPH drew on that message of the importance of national politics, tapped into existing, local networks of people with disabilities, and worked to broaden and politicize those networks. For example, participants in a swimming class for disabled men and women at the Harrisburg, Pennsylvania, Young Women's Christian Association had formed a club, the Keystone Arrow Club, in the spring of 1941. In May 1943, a national AFPH officer attended a club meeting, and the group that had begun around a swimming class voted to become an AFPH chapter. The national AFPH's presence at that May 1943 meeting drew George Lehr, Jr., to the event. Lehr, a disabled veteran of World War I, served as personnel director of Pennsylvania's Bureau of Motor Vehicles, and through his status as a disabled veteran, his involvement in the new Harrisburg AFPH chapter would expand the group's organizational reach to include disabled veterans and government networks.[13]

In other cases, the AFPH offered a national network for local disability organizations already politically and economically engaged. Harold J. McMahon of Buffalo, New York, would become a national vice president of the AFPH, but his organizational work in Buffalo, before and after the AFPH was founded, had primed the city's residents to be active members in a national movement. McMahon's personal experiences shaped his work in Buffalo. As a young man he had developed osteomyelitis, a bone infection, and lost his left leg above the knee and a bone in his left arm; he also nearly lost his right leg. After recovering, McMahon worked in the printing trade, holding numerous positions from work in the composing room to sales. During World War I, he worked in a war plant outside of New York City. McMahon convinced his employer that other people with disabilities could meet the factory's labor demands, and the factory eventually hired sixty disabled workers. After the war, McMahon returned to the printing industry. A few years later, however, he visited the plant where he had worked during the war to discover that all the disabled folks he had worked with there had "been discarded and replaced by able-bodied people." That experience stuck with McMahon, but another sharpened the feeling that he had to do something to improve the opportunities for people with disabilities. He recalled seeing a bread line in Philadelphia in 1930 and realizing that nine of the thirty people in line had visible disabilities. That breadline, he later said, represented a truth he had known for some time: "the handicapped worker is always the last hired and the first fired." McMahon decided that freedom from charity and public aid would come through organization of businesses owned by people with disabilities.[14]

Even as defense industries expanded and industry faced labor shortages, McMahon moved forward with his plan to establish a factory managed and run by disabled people, noting "I could not help but believe that these handicapped boys and girls who had been hired in defense plants would be the first to be dismissed as soon as war production ceases." He also recognized that many disabled people remained unemployed even as factories were desperate for workers. The war economy presented both challenges and opportunities for McMahon's idea. Regulations designed to increase defense production limited available materials for consumer goods, but because many factories had shifted from consumer to defense production, there was an opening in the market. In the summer of 1942, he launched the Toymakers Guild, a division of his broader company, Handicapped Persons Industries, Inc., to produce wooden toys. McMahon recruited other successful disabled individuals to serve on the board, ranging from teachers to a master watchmaker, a housewife, and a defense worker. The group designed toys, produced samples, and secured $100,000 in orders at a toy fair in New York City.[15]

McMahon and the board of Handicapped Persons Industries, Inc., employed individuals from the relief rolls, all deemed not feasible for rehabilitation by the civilian rehabilitation program. The first twenty-one people he hired had spent a combined total of 125 years existing on meager public aid and private charity. Handicapped Persons Industries, Inc., paid workers full wages, despite the fact that the Fair Labor Standards Act allowed employers to pay people with disabilities less than the minimum wage. McMahon also ensured that his employees had access to Social Security benefits and were paid time and a half for overtime work.[16] Through Handicapped Persons Industries, Inc., and McMahon's organizing efforts, Buffalo's disabled citizens had already begun to demand something more than charity, and the AFPH's message of justice, opportunity, and equal rights found an eager constituency.

By the end of 1942, the AFPH's national campaign for legislation was underway. In June 1942, Representative Jerry Voorhis (D-CA) had introduced a joint resolution to establish National Employ the Physically Handicapped Week (NEPHW), Strachan's plan for a formal public education campaign.[17] The AFPH had also begun the drive for a federal investigation of the needs of Americans with disabilities and the aid programs that benefitted them. Voorhis told AFPH members that such a committee "would be the means of focusing public attention" on the problems people with disabilities faced, reveal their needs, and contribute to "the formulation of a national policy." Additionally, the organization had begun to develop plans for a federal agency for disabled individuals, a federal ban on employment discrimination, representation in government agencies serving people with disabilities, and mandates for special services through the U.S. Civil Service Commission and U.S. Employment Service.[18] By 1944, the AFPH had found sponsors for four different bills. In the House, the AFPH got two different bills introduced: one, instructing the Committee on Labor to "investigate, survey, and develop a national program for all the physically handicapped," and another that would have established a personal catastrophe loan system. The organization succeeded in finding sponsors in both the House and Senate for bills to establish NEPHW and to create a division in the Employment Service for disabled job seekers.[19]

The House of Representatives voted to launch the AFPH proposed investigation in June 1944. The resolution directed the Committee on Labor "to conduct thorough studies and investigation of the extent and character of aid now given by the Federal, State, and local governments and private agencies to the physically handicapped" and "employment opportunities" to "aid the Congress in any necessary remedial legislation." It gave the committee and any subcommittees it formed the power to subpoena records, hold hearings, compel testimony, and access Selective Service System, War Manpower Commission, and Bureau of the Census records.[20]

As chair of the Committee on Rules, Representative Adolph Sabath D-IL) introduced the measure for consideration, noting his support and that he had "received a very large number of communications, telegrams, and resolutions from nearly every section of the United States favoring the passage of this worthy resolution." While promoted by Democrats, Republicans, including the minority leader Joseph Martin (R-MA), also expressed approval. The AFPH figured in the discussion on the House floor. Henderson Carson (R-OH) contended, "It is imperative that we immediately plan a national program to provide a cushion against the unhappy days of post-war chaos and possible unemployment and want which a large number of these people have experienced in the past." He noted that people with disabilities "are patriotic in the extreme," having committed "to all war activities." Carson's words were shaped by his personal connection to the AFPH. He was an honorary member of the organization and knew one of the national vice presidents well, both hailing from Canton, Ohio.[21]

Committee on Labor member Richard J. Welch (R-CA) argued that the investigation would focus on "the human rights of physically handicapped individuals" and that Congress "should give them fair consideration." Representative Kelley, who would chair the committee, said that Congress confronted "an astonishing lack of knowledge" on the problems that contributed to the unemployment of people with disabilities. Without an investigation, he maintained, Congress would not have the information necessary "to deal with the problem." Beyond the question of rights, members of the House repeatedly referenced labor shortages and the need to assist disabled veterans, as Jennings Randolph (D-WV) phrased it, "fit themselves into our peacetime day-by-day economy."[22]

The House Committee on Labor established a subcommittee to conduct the investigation, which lasted from August 1944 until June 1946. In 1944, Randolph, Welch, Thomas E. Scanlon (D-PA), Stephen A. Day (R-IL), and Joseph Clark Baldwin (R-NY) formed the subcommittee with Kelley serving as the chair. After the 1944 election, the subcommittee grew to seven members, and Ellis E. Patterson (D-CA), William J. Green, Jr. (D-PA), and Sherman Adams (R-NH) replaced Scanlon and Day. The subcommittee conducted twenty-five hearings, focusing on aid to amputees; blind, deaf, and "spastic" individuals; as well as people with poliomyelitis, tuberculosis, orthopedic disabilities, cancer, and epilepsy. The hearings examined conditions in New York City, Pittsburgh, Detroit, and Philadelphia and studied disability through the lenses of accident prevention, monopolies and advertising, international activities, Library of Congress programs, drug addiction, employment, federal aid, rural conditions, coordination of federal programs, federal employment for blind individuals, and maternal and child health. The subcommittee also held hearings on the AFPH's proposed federal agency.[23]

When Personal Became Political

Through the AFPH, the mosaic of members' individual struggles to access health care, education, rehabilitation services, employment, and a broad range of physical spaces formed a broader picture of state and social failures. Members who lacked familial or community support existed on the margins of society and faced the threat of being placed in institutions. All these factors led to chronic fears, and regular experiences, of economic insecurity. By demanding a federal investigation and sharing their stories, members transformed their personal experiences of discrimination, exclusion, and frustration with a lack of services into a collective, political statement.

Civilian rehabilitation policy was central to the critique offered by AFPH members. In many ways, it came to represent a broad range of social and economic problems people with disabilities often faced and the failures of government policy to address these issues. Like many AFPH members, McMahon had been deemed a poor candidate for rehabilitation because his disability was too severe when he sought assistance in the 1920s. His own experiences, and those of other disabled members of the Buffalo community, many of whom worked with or for him at Handicapped Persons Industries, Inc., led him to conclude, "Entirely too many physically handicapped individuals are being considered not feasible for rehabilitation." One of his secretaries, who had "a progressive paralysis," had been denied rehabilitation, and when the counselor who had rejected her visited her home a year later, he did not believe her mother's report that she was working. Like his secretary, more than half McMahon's employees had been refused rehabilitation. Through his own business and connections in the community, McMahon tried to demonstrate that the rehabilitation program rejected many people who could be successful workers. He hired thirty-three workers with disabilities and placed another fifteen with other firms in just one year.[24]

AFPH member Edith Povar of Dorchester, Massachusetts, wrote to Strachan, asking him to share her experience with rehabilitation with the subcommittee. She concluded that the program was all "politics and red tape." Povar wrote, "They said I had the mental ability to hold a position but because I was a spastic they could not help me." Having a form of cerebral palsy, despite being "able to get about well" and not having impaired speech, meant that rehabilitation counselors deemed her not feasible for the program.[25] Warren D. Wright of Rockwell City, Iowa, had a similar experience of being too "seriously handicapped" for rehabilitation. He wrote the subcommittee that "for every person they are able to help in any way, there are many more for whom they can do nothing." In rehabilitation, Wright saw a stymied path to the opportunities "most of us are interested in—to be able to be more independent from our family, and to work out some method of making our own living, not to mention medical aid, or better health."[26]

Beyond the rejections, McMahon complained that rehabilitation officials in Buffalo refused to work with other agencies and were out of touch with the realities people with disabilities faced in the community. McMahon reported being "astounded" by a wartime press release from the head of the Buffalo rehabilitation office, which claimed that, if one thousand disabled individuals came to the office for rehabilitation the next day, he could place them in jobs. For McMahon, the announcement was startling because the Erie County Welfare Council and the Employment Service had a backlog of disabled job seekers and the rehabilitation director had not taken "the time to call either one of these other two agencies." Further, he claimed that the rehabilitation program directly undermined the work of the Employment Service as some employers had been led to believe that they should not hire disabled individuals through the Employment Service unless the rehabilitation program approved the applicant.[27]

Other AFPH members complained about the "superior and patronizing attitude" of rehabilitation counselors, who, they believed, understood little about the labor market, job training, or job placement. "There is a tendency," Margaret Nickerson Martin argued, "of certain groups working with handicapped people to feel that their exposure to the upper brackets of learning, their attainment of certain educational set standards, entitles them to a private halo, which they wear very straight upon their heads." J. A. Strohmeyer, a national vice president and leader in the AFPH in Chicago, suggested that the individuals involved in the rehabilitation program were "more interested in gratuities and cheap publicity for themselves than for common-sense aid to the physically handicapped."[28]

Rehabilitation counselors made judgments about the possibilities and fitness of the individual to work. Rejection meant that the counselor deemed the individual unfit for work and that reasonable educational, medical, and vocational help would not make the person employable. The gap between the number of cases registered and the number of individuals rehabilitated was wide. In 1944, the first year of the investigation, the civilian rehabilitation program registered 269,960 cases but rehabilitated only 43,997 persons, only 16 percent of those who applied.[29] These figures indicate, at least in part, that the very agency charged with preparing and placing people with disabilities in employment found employment potential in only a small percentage of the disabled individuals it encountered.

Rejection meant that the sole federal agency that served disabled people's interests had deemed them unemployable, cutting them off from the resources that might have improved their employability and access to social resources and civic life. Rejection from rehabilitation equaled rejection from the opportunity to secure the full rights and benefits of citizenship, let alone any sense of economic security. Pauline Solomon, who served as financial secretary of one of the Washington, D.C., AFPH chapters, described people with disabilities as being "unfairly condemned to a life of idleness and despair because of injury or disease which we do not have the means to remedy."[30]

Rejection from rehabilitation often spelled dependence on charity or family, or even institutionalization. A disabled resident of Whitinsville, Massachusetts, wrote, "It is unfair that we should be the responsibility of charitable organizations and the burdens of relatives or family however willing or able they are to stand the financial strain which is always great to all but the very rich." A disabled person who was rejected from rehabilitation "does not want or expect his or her family to give up comforts or convenience that should normally be their's [*sic*] to give them to him. A person cannot feel anything but a burden under such circumstances."[31]

The vocational rehabilitation program provided the only broad-based form of aid for adults with disabilities, but families played an integral role in closing the gaps in social services. Families provided not only the first defense against poverty and need but also the safety net when the rehabilitation program failed people with disabilities. The absence of family resources could spell disaster for a person with a disability. The failures of the rehabilitation service and welfare policy cemented disabled people's dependent status. George Booth wrote, "I was refused any public assistance other than the county home for the poor." At sixteen, he began work in the mines, but he fractured his pelvis in an automobile accident. After nearly two years in the hospital, Booth continued to use a crutch for mobility. His mother died during the Depression, leaving his aging father to support him and three young children. Booth tried to work and helped care for his younger brothers, but his father struggled to make ends meet on a public works project wage. Booth applied for relief because he was unemployed, but he was told that "if my father refused to keep me I should sue him for nonsupport." The response from relief officials made clear that Booth, who was in his twenties at the time, was regarded as a dependent. His disability negated his previous working history and blocked him from accessing the protections against uncertainty that the New Deal had created.[32]

The gaps in New Deal protections also shaped Mildred Willis's life. Living in Otwell, Indiana, Willis depended on her sixty-one-year-old father for support. At forty, she had "been bedfast 23 years with tuberculosis of the bone." Her father's ill health prevented him from working on a regular basis, and the cost of her care, which required dressing her hip each day, was becoming a greater burden on the family. Willis's father did not yet qualify for Social Security, and the program did not yet provide financial assistance to people with disabilities beyond Aid to the Blind. Willis eked out an existence selling greeting cards, but she reported growing difficulties in making ends meet as more organizations sold cards and others could be purchased at stores. She described others in her situation who were able to get bedding or other minor assistance from a charity organization, but Willis wrote that they needed "other things just as bad and all the time."[33]

The availability of family resources and willingness to expend them on a disabled relative could mean the difference between living in an institution and receiving an education, between confinement and mobility. Children with physical disabilities, without family support, might have been institutionalized in state or county homes for the "feebleminded" or aged. Adults with disabilities who were unable to secure employment and without family support also feared being institutionalized. Susan Polk Graves of St. Louis, Missouri, wrote the subcommittee that she was "handicapped by spastic paralysis to the extent that I cannot even sign my own name, dress, or feed myself; I do not walk alone, either." She described the "dreadful situation" common when a person, like her, with cerebral palsy, "is left alone in the world or for some reason cannot be cared for in his own home, he is sent to State institutions for the feeble-minded, regardless of his intelligence."[34] Ultimately, without family support or the assistance of rehabilitation or charities, the economic marginalization of people with disabilities could end in their institutionalization—a dreaded fate.

Members' testimony emphasized that difficulties in finding employment were a critical component of their economic marginalization. For example, Charles J. Hobbins, an AFPH member from Pennsylvania, had worked for much of his life but had nearly always struggled to find employment. An accident at age twelve resulted in the amputation of his left arm at the elbow and a right arm that was "pretty badly crippled." He reported that he had been told time and time again that workers' compensation laws in Pennsylvania prevented employers from hiring "a crippled person."[35] Likewise, Helen J. Apgar of St. Louis, Missouri, wrote to the subcommittee about the difficulties she and other disabled people faced on the job market. She had found work during the war, a job she hoped "to hold" with the transition to peace, "but during the depression," she wrote, "I was laid off because they could have their choice of healthy and better-looking girls who were willing to work for low wages." Apgar had fractured her back as a toddler, which resulted in "some deformity" of her spine. "The personnel heads," she noted, "take one glance at a crippled person and say: 'The job has been filled,' 'No more applications are being taken.' Nine out of ten offices have told me that (when same firms have advertisements in the next day's paper)." Apgar opined that if disabled people were "too 'terrible' to stand seeing around, then the healthy taxpayer should give them a pension to live on." She concluded, "The poor injured returning veterans certainly have my sympathy if they meet the cool atmosphere I come up against time after time in job hunting."[36] Cynthia May Lurie of Arlington, Virginia, criticized employers for their attitude toward her disability. She noted, "Some of those who interviewed me asked me if I had a warm home and plenty to eat. After telling them I did, they couldn't understand why I wanted to work." Still other employers, she argued, "treated me as though I was out of my mind and would rush me out of their office at the beginning of the interview."[37]

AFPH members and other people with disabilities who wrote to the subcommittee described experience after experience of informal, yet widespread, employment discrimination. The employers they encountered rarely explained that they were passing on an individual because of a disability, but instead rushed through interviews or told disabled applicants the position had been filled, while continuing to advertise for employees. Employers routinely blamed insurance companies for their refusal to hire people with disabilities, insisting that insurance rates would be higher if they did so or that insurance policies were unavailable for disabled workers. Insurance companies, however, claimed that employers misinterpreted their policies and were unnecessarily restrictive in their hiring policies when it came to disabled individuals. For example, one insurance company reported, "Some employers assume that physical examinations are had for the purpose of discrimination." In reality, the company required the examinations prior to employment to protect employers from paying for existing injuries.[38] Whether employers or insurance companies were actually to blame, people with disabilities often heard that ineligibility for insurance or high rates prevented their employment.

Educational inequality often exacerbated the difficulties that AFPH members and other disabled Americans experienced as they searched for work. A lack of educational opportunities was central to AFPH testimony before the subcommittee and its broader developing agenda. Representing the AFPH committee of the deaf, Alan B. Crammatte pointed out that "schools for the deaf provide an elementary education or less for their students, plus a few years (3 to 7) of vocational education, for 2 to 4 hours a day, and necessarily at an elementary school level." This level of education, Crammatte asserted, prepared deaf children "for little other than menial labor."[39] AFPH leaders shared with the subcommittee a 1944 report produced by the organization's national leadership council that emphasized widespread educational failures. The report suggested that many states had been "remiss in their scrutiny of services to handicapped children, especially in relation to school set-ups." It noted the need for better facilities, instruction, and teachers. Of particular concern to the members who drafted the report was the fact that disabled children were often "being taught by second-rate teachers who are not—sad to relate—deemed of sufficient quality, in several instances, to teach in nonhandicapped schools."[40]

Indeed, disabled children and young adults encountered considerable barriers to obtaining an education. Before Congress enacted the Education for All Handicapped Children Act of 1975, public schools could deny children access to education based on their disabilities. Most states maintained separate, residential facilities for blind and deaf children, where they were educated away from their homes and families.[41] Still, the availability of instruction through special classes or schools was woefully inadequate. In 1937, the U.S. Office of Education estimated that of the approximately two million disabled children in the country only one in every ten benefited from a special education program.[42] Access to public or special schools for children with physical disabilities largely depended on the city and state the child lived in, the individual child's disability, family resources and advocacy, and decisions of school administrators. For example, Melvin E. Schoonover, AFPH member and editor of the *Shut-In's Companion*, wrote to other AFPH members, "The shut-in fraternity as a whole probably constitutes the largest single unit of illiterate and semi-literate persons within our national community." He claimed that "very few" homebound people with disabilities were "able to complete even grammar school." Schoonover concluded, "It seems foolhardy to refuse to the shut-in what is compulsorily given to others."[43]

While white children with disabilities encountered serious barriers to their education, the conditions African American children with disabilities faced were worse. Writing for the *Journal of Negro Education* in 1937, educator James A. Scott argued that blind and deaf African American children had the greatest access to education, but that even the education that these children received was "distinctly inferior." Many southern states maintained completely separate schools for blind and deaf African American children, while others provided instruction for African American pupils in segregated classes within the states' blind and deaf schools. Scott declared, "Practically no effort is made to enforce compulsory attendance laws for either Negro blind or deaf pupils." Moreover, he maintained that in the South public education programs for white children with other physical disabilities were "practically non-existent," and conditions were much worse for African American children. Finally, Scott contended that racial discrimination against African American children with disabilities also extended to some programs in the North. On the whole, racial discrimination dramatically reduced the already slim educational opportunities open to children with disabilities, and in most cases, the institutions open to African Americans suffered from chronic underfunding, with the quality of instruction falling far below what was available to white children.[44]

People with disabilities also faced considerable barriers to higher education. For example, Lurie told the subcommittee that she had tried for more than a year to attend college, applying for admission to several schools. Lurie complained, "Not one of these colleges would accept me because of spastic paralysis." At least one of the schools was direct about rejecting Lurie because of her disability. The dean, Lurie reported, thought that the school would be too crowded for her and "feared that I would not fit into the college due to the fact that all of my classmates would be physically fit and I would be the only one handicapped."[45] As late as 1949, an effort to find a college or university to accept a group of disabled students, mostly veterans, who had been attending the temporary Galesburg campus of the University of Illinois, yielded telling results. Of the approximately 150 schools contacted, fifteen expressed a willingness to admit the students but only four could offer an accessible campus.[46]

The quality and availability of prosthetic limbs and mobility aids, necessary for many people with disabilities to gain an education or employment, figured prominently in disability activists' testimony—both on the military and civilian side. Like members of the AFPH, veterans and the organizations that represented them used the House investigation to draw attention to the difficulties that they faced. As early as 1942, the American Legion had begun a campaign to pressure the government to conduct research into better prosthetics. During the war, the Army Medical Corps alone performed successful amputations on roughly 14,000 soldiers. Amputees overwhelmed the system caring for them. Early in the war, the army provided initial treatment for its amputees who were then transferred to the VA for further care, rehabilitation, and training. By 1943, the army—soldiers suffered the bulk of injuries during the war that required amputations—had to offer definitive care for its amputees, as the VA could not handle the influx of patients. The army established special amputation centers in seven army hospitals across the country that produced limbs and provided surgical and medical care and rehabilitation. Army limbs were meant to be temporary to facilitate adjustment, while the VA would provide permanent, commercially manufactured limbs after discharge. The army struggled to meet the demand for limbs with a limited number of trained prosthetic device makers and technicians. The results were troubling to soldiers who were issued these prostheses. Moreover, once discharged, veterans relied on the VA for future prostheses, follow-up care, and maintenance, repair, and replacement of artificial limbs. Veterans applied for services at a local field station but might be referred to one of the VA's twelve amputation centers. The VA contracted with private manufacturers to provide limbs for veterans, which typically narrowed the choices available to them. The surgeon general of the army worked with the National Research Council to launch a study of artificial limbs that resulted in the establishment of a permanent National Research Council committee on the development of better prostheses in 1945, but the effort came too late to stave critique.[47]

In 1945, Lieutenant Sol Rael, who had received medical care and an artificial limb at Walter Reed General Hospital in Washington, D.C., told subcommittee members that his prosthetic was "crude and out-moded and definitely a throw-back to horse-and-buggy days." He reported, "There was no question in my mind when I received my prosthesis that I was greatly disappointed and disillusioned in seeing what a hackneyed article it really was."[48]

Veterans expressed frustration about the utility and fit of their new limbs and the process they had to go through to get assistance from the VA. After losing a limb in an explosion in northern Africa in July 1943, Robert L. Rogers was shipped home to receive treatment at Walter Reed. His leg was amputated about five inches below the knee, but once he began walking with his prosthetic, his stump opened up. After four surgeries and over a year in Walter Reed, Rogers still had constant troubles with his leg and was waiting for a new socket and a new leather foot to give him greater function. He argued that the army's legs were improperly fitted and made of poor quality materials—materials so cheap that a limb maker had told him his leg was not worth "two hoots in hell."[49]

For men like Rogers, who depended on their earnings to make ends meet, replacing an ill-fitting or low-quality limb with personal funds was out of the question. Taking time away from work to travel to the VA for repairs and to apply for a new limb had costs as well. The VA had determined that Rogers's artificial leg should be repaired and not replaced; consequently, Rogers had to go to the VA repeatedly and wait. He had to wait for repairs. He had to wait for the VA to decide that he was eligible for a new limb. He even had to wait for new crutches. When his army-issued crutches broke, he went to the VA to request a new pair. Fortunately, Rogers was able to borrow a pair from the dispensary at his job as it took over two months for his VA crutches to arrive. All of the waiting had profound consequences for Rogers. He had difficulty working, shifting from job to job in hopes of finding something that would not set off the pain, and as a result, he struggled to make a living.[50]

According to Rogers, disabled veterans were tired of waiting and tired of having their situation ignored. He said that the public face of army amputation centers was a farce. When they photographed men walking and dancing, he claimed, it was after only a few steps and not "after he had walked 20 steps" or after the dance when "he has hopped . . . into the corner or goes hopping downstairs to get his crutches." Just as the pain made Rogers "hate to walk," it made him, and others like him, question the government that had sent them to battle. "These derned legs," he cried, "I do not know what is wrong, the Government is supposed to be trying to do so much for us, and they are not doing a darned thing."[51] A DAV representative told the committee that developing better artificial limbs was necessary to pay back "an undischarged war debt."[52]

The difficulties disabled soldiers and veterans faced with their prosthetic limbs were amplified in the civilian sector. When a member of the subcommittee asked Dr. Charles M. Griffith, medical director of the VA, how a civilian might fare in purchasing an artificial limb, he replied, "If he does not have a private doctor or an orthopedist to help him, God have mercy on him."[53] Griffith described the exact situation of many civilians. Representing the AFPH committee of the amputees, Agnes Schnaus, a national vice president of the organization, reported, "As it stands, anyone can set themselves up as a maker and fitter of surgical appliances and the appliance fitter can go about his business any way he sees fit." In these circumstances, she concluded, "there is nothing to prevent the public from being sold misfit appliances."[54]

F. A. Tingley, who on hearing that the House was investigating artificial limbs wrote to the subcommittee, had personally experienced what the AFPH committee of the amputees had described. In his letter, Tingley complained, "I have never in all my life seen any industry or business where there was so much abuse as there is in the artificial limb business." He had worn a below-the-knee prosthetic leg for almost thirty years and in that time purchased eleven prostheses. He explained that he had been forced to travel to a "strange city" to purchase his limb. Once he arrived after a long train ride, he had difficulty finding the limb factory. He waited for days for service, having trouble finding a place to eat and sleep. Finally, a company official told him his leg would be shipped to him. When the leg arrived, well over a month later, he found that he could not "possibly wear it for 5 minutes." In the end, Tingley had no recourse to get his money back or a better-fitting limb.[55]

Beyond discomfort and prostheses that did not fit, the cost associated with artificial limbs could be prohibitive. It was not just the limb itself that made prosthetic devices so expensive but also the wool socks that covered the stump, replacement parts, and repairs.[56] In 1945, prices for prosthetic limbs from J. E. Hanger, a national prosthetic device-making company, ranged from $325 for an above-the-knee "Dural" light metal leg with a metal socket, to $100 for a partial willow hand. Any needed extra features, like braces, upped the cost.[57] When measured against the fact that local assistance payments to disabled people averaged between three hundred and five hundred dollars annually in 1944, the cost of obtaining and maintaining a prosthetic limb could be far too much for an unemployed disabled person without additional family resources or state assistance.[58] Indeed, even with assistance, the costs often remained too steep. An employer had promised Hobbins better prospects if he acquired a prosthetic arm that would allow him to carry a briefcase and hold a pad to write. He had applied for assistance in purchasing a prosthetic limb from the rehabilitation program but had been told that the agency would pay only $100 toward the $250 device.[59]

People with disabilities faced similar difficulties in obtaining other assistive devices such as wheelchairs. John Carncross, a friend of AFPH leader Martin, could not walk and did not own a wheelchair. Instead, his brother pulled him to school in a wagon, and he used a stove caster to move himself about the house.[60] Still, wheelchairs and mobility aids also had their limits because of the physical barriers built into everyday living. Medical professionals, and people with disabilities themselves, sometimes spoke of being "confined to a wheelchair."[61] In this context, it was not actually the wheelchair that confined its user but the built environment. Decades before any state would mandate that public buildings had to be accessible to people with disabilities and long before curb cuts that enabled wheelchair users to maneuver from the street to the sidewalk without assistance were commonplace in cities, people with disabilities who could afford prosthetic devices and mobility aids encountered physical barriers that both negated the benefits of their assistive devices and limited their full participation in society and the economy.[62] For example, AFPH member Emerson Wickert, who was born with club feet and "marked scoliosis," normally got around with a back brace and crutches, but as a child in the 1920s, he needed further assistance to make it to school each day. Typically, his father carried him or classmates dragged him in a sled or pushed him in a wheelbarrow.[63]

The AFPH moved beyond critique and used the subcommittee's investigation as an opportunity to present the organization's agenda. In December 1944, Schnaus called for the adoption of a "long-range program" for citizens with disabilities. Despite the opportunities defense production had created for them, Schnaus remained skeptical of the future. She warned that disabled people feared that "much of the present good work will be abandoned when this war ends, and the handicapped . . . will lapse into their former state of being regarded with indifference, suspicion, and distrust of their working capacity, to say nothing of intensification of their economic and social needs." Building on Strachan's earlier proposals, Schnaus suggested that Congress establish a federal agency for people with disabilities, staffed as much as possible by disabled citizens, to offset this potential postwar disaster for people with disabilities. The AFPH's proposed agency would have sweeping authority over disability policy and be charged with meeting the medical, educational, training, and employment needs of the nation's disabled citizenry. Moreover, the primary goal of the agency would be to work for the "Abolition of all unfair discrimination against the employment of otherwise qualified but physically handicapped applicants."[64]

In addition to these broad goals, Schnaus outlined the AFPH's short-term goals. The organization continued to demand that the Civil Service Commission appoint people with disabilities and that the Employment Service expand its services for people with disabilities, along with appropriations to support those efforts. The AFPH insisted that industry "provide adequate, suitable employment for the handicapped whenever possible." It also called for congressional action to further develop the federal rehabilitation program, provide greater services for disabled children through the U.S. Children's Bureau, facilitate additional research on disabling conditions and treatments through the U.S. Public Health Service, and determine the full scope of disability in the United States by initiating a survey to be conducted by the U.S. Census Bureau and the Public Health Service.[65]

AFPH activists argued both that they were entitled to equal opportunities for work and that guaranteeing those opportunities made fiscal sense. Hobbins told the subcommittee, people with disabilities should "be pardoned for believing that they are entitled to equal opportunities within reach of their abilities." He argued that gaining admission "to the ranks of the producing population" alone would not ensure disabled people's access to "full economic rights." Instead, he maintained that people with disabilities had to have a "voice in bringing about the reform. Our voice will be a still small one, like the voice of conscience, but it definitely belongs." He believed that disabled people's "economic emancipation" would best be achieved by having people with disabilities direct and provide government disability services.

Moreover, he argued that opportunities for work would mean the difference between full citizenship and "segregation and subsidization of the handicapped as an inescapable burden on society."[66]

That same year, Strachan told AFPH members at the organization's convention, "there can be no welfare of the people unless they are physically able to lift up their heads and assume their share of the country's burdens." For him, the AFPH did "not want charity," but instead, the organization claimed, "for those who need it, assistance as a matter of right, as a part of their citizenship."[67] Strachan's speech emphasized the group's central demand—one that members emphasized to the subcommittee repeatedly—that the broader welfare of the nation would be served by recognizing, supporting, and facilitating the full citizenship of people with disabilities.

Industry and the Disabled Citizen and Soldier

Disability activists' demands for economic rights and successful veteran and civilian rehabilitation hinged on employers' willingness to hire disabled workers. The Subcommittee to Investigate Aid to the Physically Handicapped and American magazines and newspapers captured a new climate of employment opportunity for people with disabilities. World War II labor shortages and the powerful patriotic sentiment for returning disabled veterans encouraged many employers to rethink who was "fit" to work and in what jobs. With production, profits, and victory on the line, employers and disabled workers found creative ways to capitalize on disabilities.

Concern for disabled veterans figured prominently in employer efforts to find space for disabled workers.[68] The plight of the disabled veteran captured the nation's attention and pulled at Americans' heartstrings. As Harold Russell, disabled veteran and Academy Award-winning actor for his role in 1946's *The Best Years of Our Lives*, put it, "The war gave a fillip to interest in the problems of the handicapped. Workers were needed regardless whether they were physically perfect. . . . Then returning war veterans added the dash of sentiment that was needed to keep up the interest in the handicapped."[69] This concern prompted the Bulova Foundation to establish the Bulova School of Watchmaking to train disabled veterans in watch making and repair. When program representatives appeared before the subcommittee, the school was on track to enroll its first two classes in January 1945. "We felt that it was our duty," said Arde Bulova, trustee of the Bulova Foundation, "to do whatever our facilities permitted to show our appreciation for the sacrifices so willingly made by our coworkers and their fellow servicemen."[70]

Officials at the Bulova Foundation coordinated with the VA, War Manpower Commission, and War Production Board to build a program that would benefit the most disabled veterans. Bulova's research revealed that many servicemen would suffer from injuries that would leave their hands and sight unimpaired; therefore, Bulova officials believed that they could help even gravely injured veterans to become "skilled artisans." The essence of the Bulova plan was to train disabled veterans at its new training facility on Long Island and find them jobs in their home communities through Bulova product distribution agencies. After disabled veterans' needs had been met, officials at Bulova planned to use their school to train disabled civilians. For Bulova, the program represented an important "contribution to the economic advancement of all" and to the maintenance of "public stability," releasing families and communities from the weight of caring for people with disabilities.[71]

Other programs designed to bring people with disabilities into the workforce further blurred the boundaries between companies, communities, and the state. Dr. H. A. Vonachen, medical director of the Caterpillar Tractor Company in Peoria, Illinois, reported to the subcommittee that Pearl Harbor and concern for the "great number of boys coming back from service with handicaps" brought the problem of disability into focus for his company. Personnel employees analyzed all Caterpillar's jobs to determine which positions disabled workers could fill. By 1945, people with disabilities made up 10 percent of Caterpillar's workforce, and Vonachen emphasized that Caterpillar's statistics counted only individuals with serious disabilities, not someone "with a finger off or some other minor defect." This success and the realization that the problem of disability was too big for Caterpillar alone to solve led officials to launch an ambitious community-based organizing drive called the Peoria Plan.[72]

Caterpillar built broad-based community support for a program to increase the employment of people with disabilities in the area by contacting other businesses and industries through the Peoria Manufacturers' Association and the Association of Commerce, building ties to military, religious, and community organizations, and reaching out to the American Federation of Labor and the Congress of Industrial Organizations. Some eighty-four organizations in Peoria joined the program and pooled resources to hire a job counselor to survey employment opportunities for people with disabilities in the area. As disabled veterans began to return home, the community expanded the program, bringing community and government resources together. Officials in the War Manpower Commission, Employment Service, Selective Service System, and VA participated in the program, offering disabled participants additional counseling services. Vonachen emphasized that the program was one of community education and action.[73]

Ford Motor Company, which had previously extended a successful campaign to hire disabled World War I veterans into a sustained program to employ disabled workers, found more to do during World War II. In the interwar years, Ford had commissioned surveys and began hiring the same percentage of disabled workers as there were disabled people in the communities surrounding its plants. While it is important to note that Ford's "medical cases" included people with dermatitis, acne, and nasal conditions, anyone whose physical or mental health varied from a strictly defined normal, the company also hired blind workers, epileptics, and amputees. During World War II, Ford expanded its progressive disability policies again. The company established Camp Legion, a five-hundred-acre facility in Dearborn, Michigan, to train disabled World War II veterans for employment. At Camp Legion, Ford provided disabled soldiers with room and board, training, and a stipend of three dollars a day. Veterans could stay at the facility, "growing strong, preparing themselves for more skilled jobs," until they were "mentally, physically, and skillfully ready to take a job." In October 1944, Ford representatives reported that the company employed 11,300 people with disabilities.[74]

Other employers turned to disabled workers only when faced with labor shortages. An official with L. A. Young Spring & Wire Company testified that the company never exerted much effort to look for employees before the war, but with the war, many of their employees joined the armed forces or went elsewhere. Labor shortages and high turnover forced the company to rethink the physical requirements for each job. Of the company's 2,500 employees, between 150 and 200 had disabilities. Like many firms, L. A. Young Spring & Wire found ways to turn disabilities into advantages for the company. "Not long ago," a company official remarked, "we had an example, where the foreman complained of one of his sweepers talking too much and bothering the rest of the help. Fortunately, we had a deaf mute come in and we put him to work on that job. The job is done, and the man is satisfied, and it is something he can do. This is typical of what is going on out there."[75]

The L. A. Young Spring & Wire official was not exaggerating. To facilitate the influx of hundreds of thousands of disabled workers, factories and businesses had to be flexible, and at times creative, about how work would be accomplished and who could do that work. This flexibility often led disabled workers and employers to find more efficient production methods and jobs that were better suited for disabled workers than their able-bodied peers. For example, health magazine *Hygeia* printed an in-depth story about North American Aviation's "Salvage Board," which had led the plant to hire over five hundred disabled employees. North American employed deaf people to work in riveting areas and other noisy places in the plant. In one area, described as "the most vicious assailant of the human ear in the entire plant," deaf people worked "serenely," while hearing individuals could work there for no more than two hours at a time.[76]

Echoing the folk wisdom that informed many employers' placement programs for people with disabilities, Edsel Ford wrote in the *Saturday Evening Post*, "Indeed the loss or impairment of a sense or limb is often compensated for by increased abilities with the remaining senses or limbs."[77] Journalist Enid Griffis claimed that blind people could outperform sighted individuals in a range of jobs requiring a delicate sense of touch. She told the story of a young blind man in Connecticut who inspected shells at an armament factory. For almost a year, Griffis wrote, the man had maintained a perfect inspection record, and "not one bad shell has slipped through his sensitive fingers."[78] *Business Week* took this logic one step further claiming that deaf workers had "accident-protection" because they were not easily distracted and could "detect faults in the operation of a machine by its vibration."[79] *Science Digest* confirmed the report, adding that deaf workers were "particularly well equipped to do work requiring great concentration."[80]

Journalists and commentators carefully described the otherness of disabled workers. For example, Margaret Stedman, author of *Hygeia*'s article on the disabled workers at North American Aviation, devoted considerable space to the appearance of a man who worked on the electrical systems of the North American planes. She recounted how the man vanished from his high stool during a break, emerging from the other side on a scooter. Describing the worker as "half a man," Stedman wrote, "His back is thin and deformed; both legs are withered, shapeless things below the hips." Ultimately, both the man's appearance and his ability "to do a man's work" seemed to have fascinated Stedman.[81] She was by no means exceptional. A certain level of curiosity and incredulousness informed much of what journalists wrote about disabled workers during the war, whether about individuals' bodies or their abilities to work.

Even narratives of dependability and efforts to "sell" disabled workers were tinged with a fundamental otherness. For example, *Science Digest* suggested that disabled workers had lower absentee rates because they were "less prone to the morning after payday hangover" and that people with disabilities made "the most punctual employees; shunning crowds in the plant or in public transportation systems."[82] Underlying this praise for disabled workers was the belief that people with disabilities did not participate in normal social activities and circles. It is unclear if the isolation hinted at here was the product of people with disabilities avoiding their able-bodied peers or ostracism. What is clear, however, is that many Americans perceived people with disabilities as social outsiders.

As journalists and other commentators sought to capture the human feelings behind wartime employment shifts, two important themes emerged—the significance of work to identity and an overwhelming desire to contribute to the war. A longtime blind employee at Ford Motor Company told Edsel Ford, "No one will ever know—unless he has been through it himself—what the employment manager really said to me when he told me to 'report Monday.' He told me I was still useful to this world and to myself; that I could mix with my fellow men on some basis of equality." The man linked his happiness, his future, and his sense of worth and equality to employment.[83] War propaganda that emphasized the need for all Americans to contribute to victory heightened the connection between work and self-worth. In 1944, a twenty-two-year-old wheelchair user confessed to journalist T. Otto Nall that war work had changed his life. "Until I found work sorting airplane rivets," he lamented, "I felt that I wasn't doing my part in the war effort." But, his new job had given him the opportunity to serve his country, and he proudly proclaimed, "I'm a war worker in a wheel chair."[84]

The process of reshaping notions of fitness for work created considerable opportunities for disabled Americans to live and work in more equal conditions. The 160 disabled men and women who worked at one of the sheltered workshops run by Brooklyn Bureau of Social Service in December 1941 are instructive here. Rejected by industry and unable to find work outside the sheltered shops, these 26 blind people and 134 people with orthopedic disabilities worked under the guidance and watchful gaze of counselors and social workers. Just three and a half years later, on V-E Day in May 1945, two-thirds of the people who had worked in Brooklyn's sheltered workshops worked in regular industry. In 1944, counselors at the Brooklyn shops found a list of people with disabilities "for whom [they] had had no hope" before the war. That summer twenty of those thirty-six people had "regular jobs with good wages."[85]

A comparative study of disabled and able-bodied workers led by the Bureau of Labor Statistics (BLS) suggested that disabled people made dependable workers. The BLS poll of three hundred businesses, employing a total of 63,382 people with disabilities, found that disabled workers were, on average, as efficient as their nondisabled counterparts and less likely to have accidents at work. The survey found less turnover and better attendance among the disabled workers than among the able-bodied employees.[86] Supervisors at Vultee Aircraft confirmed BLS findings in an article for *Nation's Business*, commenting about the quality of work and regularity of attendance that could be expected from disabled workers.[87] Lockheed Aircraft official R. A. Von Hake said that his disabled employees were "hard-hitting, dependable and capable." He noted, "They seem determined to compete with or excel the physically normal workers and they put in extra effort."[88] An awareness of how precarious these wartime employment gains were likely contributed to this effort to be efficient and dependable.

The numbers tell a dramatic story. Placements of disabled workers through the Employment Service rose from a mere 27,700 in 1940 to nearly 300,000 in 1944, a remarkable jump. The rate remained high in 1945, when 297,000 people with disabilities found jobs through the Employment Service. In total, the agency placed over three-quarters of a million disabled men and women in jobs during the war.[89] These figures by no means tell the entire story, as they exclude those who found jobs through personal connections, their own initiative, or employer recruitment outside of Employment Service channels. All told, 83 percent of the nation's factories had disabled workers on their payrolls during the war.[90]

The Committee's Findings

In October 1946, the Subcommittee to Investigate Aid to the Physically Handicapped issued a twenty-page report summarizing its findings and recommending sweeping changes in federal disability policy. Subcommittee members concluded "that the extent and character of aid now given by the Federal, State, and local governments, and by private agencies to the physically handicapped is inadequate, haphazard, and unevenly diffused." The report shone a stark light on the no-man's land in which Americans with disabilities existed in the 1940s. "Down the list of disabilities and diseases," it argued, "this is the story: Not enough." The subcommittee uncovered a lack of schools for disabled children, teachers for disabled individuals confined to their homes, occupational therapists, vocational training, "satisfactory" prostheses or facilities to train amputees to use them, wheelchairs, reading material available to blind Americans, bedding for individuals who were unable to leave their beds and living in poverty, preventative medicine and disease screening, facilities for patients with tuberculosis and rheumatic fever, and "well-run sheltered workshops." Moreover, the subcommittee wrote that a wide range of assistive devices were "provided or not provided in a helter-skelter fashion, depending upon the resources and imagination of local and private agencies, and upon the eligibility of the person to receive" assistance from the rehabilitation program. "The existing inadequacies," the subcommittee maintained, "place a great burden of bitterness, sorrow, pain, waste, ignorance, insecurity, idleness, hopelessness, and death upon the physically handicapped and their families."[91] Indeed, the investigation had done exactly what disability activists had hoped. It made public and political the personal suffering caused by policy failures and social neglect.

By the time that the subcommittee had issued its report, the war was over and gone was the justification that serving disabled citizens would contribute to victory. The nation, instead, occupied the difficult liminal space between war and peace. In that space, just days after Japan's formal surrender on 2 September 1945, President Truman outlined his postwar agenda, eventually known as the Fair Deal—an agenda he hoped would continue the prosperity of the war, ward off a return of the dark days of the Depression, and offer Americans further security against uncertainty. He maintained that the federal government had a responsibility to ensure full employment, reiterating Roosevelt's 1944 assertion that work was a fundamental American right. Importantly, he called for federal mechanisms to ensure this right for all Americans, regardless of race, religion, or color. Among the twenty-one points that formed this first articulation of his domestic agenda, Truman called for affordable housing, medical and scientific research, and a higher minimum wage. In November 1945, Truman offered a more detailed program to provide "adequate medical care" and "security against the economic effects of sickness." To achieve "health security for all," Truman urged Congress to provide financial support to build health care facilities, expand public health, particularly maternal and child health, programs, provide federal grants to support medical education and research, and expand the nation's social insurance system to provide health care and sickness and disability benefits.[92]

The subcommittee's recommendations affirmed and extended Truman's vision for greater security and prosperity in the postwar world. In 1946, Democrats controlled the House and consequently the subcommittee. Moreover, of its Republican members, Richard J. Welch would distinguish himself from the majority of congressional Republicans in the coming years for his support of organized labor and the administration's efforts to protect and extend New Deal programs.[93] As a result, the subcommittee linked the fate of disabled Americans to many of these Fair Deal goals, suggesting that people with disabilities, "as much as any group in the community, would benefit from full employment, adequate health and hospital services, broadened social security, and well-financed and well-planned educational systems." While during the war policy makers argued that victory necessitated disability services, in the postwar period, Democrats began to argue disability justified the need for broader social insurance and greater government services.[94]

Still, the subcommittee called for congressional action to reorganize disability services, expand existing programs, and establish several new programs. It envisioned executive reorganization as the first step in providing better and more accessible services to people with disabilities. In line with Truman's proposals for the Federal Security Agency (FSA), the subcommittee suggested that conferring department status on the FSA and placing it in charge of the broad range of "health, welfare, education, and social-insurance programs" would help to centralize disability services and prevent the need for disabled citizens to go from agency to agency in search of assistance. The report noted the need for a representative of this broader agency in each community or county to ensure awareness of disability services as well as their accessibility. The subcommittee reasoned that an executive department charged with administering the broad range of services important to disabled citizens would promote efficiency and reveal programmatic failures. When rehabilitation failed, the subcommittee suggested, public assistance needs would increase. Likewise, rehabilitation applications would indicate when preventative programs were failing.[95]

The subcommittee proposed that the Office of Vocational Rehabilitation, renamed the "United States Service for the Handicapped" to reflect a broader mission, serve as the cornerstone of an expanded range of services for disabled Americans. Rehabilitation, the subcommittee concluded, reached just "a fraction of those who would benefit," even with the expansion of the program under the Barden-La Follette Act of 1943. The program, while valuable and important, served such a small portion of the people who needed assistance that the subcommittee judged it "entirely inadequate in terms of the real needs of the disabled." Appropriately advertising the program would make the gap between the availability of services and the need for them all the more apparent. Moreover, the subcommittee argued that access to services should not be dictated by the ability to engage in employment. Instead, rehabilitation should be expanded and made "available generally to the physically handicapped," with "a much wider range of services." The subcommittee suggested reworking the financing of disability services, maintaining federal and state shared responsibility but introducing a system of variable grants to enable the program to grow in states with underdeveloped rehabilitation programs. Further, the subcommittee recommended appropriations to support rapid growth. While the AFPH called for a survey through the census to clarify the extent of disability in the nation, the subcommittee disagreed, arguing that the cost of such an endeavor would outweigh the benefits. In particular, the subcommittee noted that existing data had not been fully analyzed for information about disability, including the 1936 national health survey and data from the Selective Service System. These sources already offered "unmistakable evidence" of the extent of disability. It was clear to the subcommittee that disabled Americans numbered in the many millions and there was "no danger of too rapid expansion, or overexpansion, in services to the physically handicapped."[96]

The subcommittee's recommendations for new and expanded services fell into seven broad categories: employment support, health care, education, social insurance, protection from fraud, disability prevention, and research and professional training. Disabled people's testimony and letters led the subcommittee to conclude, "The need which the physically handicapped feel most keenly themselves is for employment. They yearn to become independent, to produce something of value to society, and to take a normal place in industrial and commercial life of the Nation." The subcommittee identified "public prejudice" as an important obstacle in meeting this need. While the report noted that the war and the efforts of various federal agencies had "diminished slightly" the prejudice disabled people faced on the job front, data from the Employment Service suggested that discrimination remained. In March 1946, 6.4 percent of the job seekers who registered with the Employment Service had disabilities, yet they received just 3.1 percent of the jobs.

Moreover, by the end of April, 261,697 disabled veterans remained unemployed and were seeking Employment Service assistance. As an example of the prejudice people with disabilities encountered that informed their employment situation, the subcommittee pointed out that some visitors to the World's Fair in New York City in 1939 "were afraid to shake hands with the blind workers" engaged in one exhibit. Addressing prejudice against disabled workers, the subcommittee argued, would be essential for disabled people "to be granted the opportunity for normal lives." Consequently, it recommended that federal agencies providing services to disabled Americans should also "devote a portion of their efforts to the removal of psychological and emotional barriers which exist in the public mind and hinder the friendly acceptance of physically handicapped people for their own worth." Further, the subcommittee suggested that part of the broader role of an expanded Office of Vocational Rehabilitation should be to engage in public education on behalf of people with disabilities.[97]

The subcommittee argued that the state should lead the way in creating employment opportunities for people with disabilities in federal employment by directing the Civil Service Commission to "redouble its efforts to place physically handicapped persons in Federal work," be flexible about examination policy, and "check any prejudice against the physically handicapped which may come to its notice." Additionally, subcommittee members concluded small businesses and factories would need support in placing disabled workers and that assistance should come from specialists in the Employment Service who were trained in "selective placement." To support these efforts, the subcommittee called for increased funding for the Employment Service to expand the number of job placement personnel trained to work with disabled applicants.[98]

Based on the testimony and evidence they received, the subcommittee estimated that about 20 percent of disabled Americans would need more extensive services and "special facilities." Still, the subcommittee argued that all but 2 percent of that remaining group could be employed either in the broader workforce or in sheltered workshops if given proper services. The report maintained that sheltered workshops had "definite value in the rehabilitation of the disabled." These workshops, members wrote, could provide disabled workers "a hardening before returning to normal working hours and conditions" and "a place of work, and a means to a more normal life, for those who are so severely disabled that they cannot compete in the regular labor market." The subcommittee recommended that vocational rehabilitation legislation be amended to provide sheltered work for those who would benefit from it.[99]

The subcommittee tempered its support of sheltered workshops with recommendations for their careful regulation. The subcommittee noted that federal funds should support only those sheltered workshops that had "medical supervision" and were "free of substandard labor practices, which have too often prevailed in the operation of sheltered workshops." Further, subcommittee members argued that the federal government should protect people with disabilities from workshops that failed to meet minimum standards and engaged in exploitative practices.[100] The subcommittee's stance likely drew in part on the National Federation of the Blind (NFB) testimony during the investigation. Representing the organization, A. L. Archibald complained that many sheltered workshops exploited blind labor, offering low wages and "very poor working conditions," and disregarding labor laws that protected sighted individuals.[101]

In the area of health care, the subcommittee called for more hospitals and medical and rehabilitation facilities and "a national system of prepaid medical care," which it argued would reduce the prevalence of disability by fostering "early diagnosis and treatment of crippling and disabling diseases." Access to health care, the subcommittee maintained, would be particularly vital in meeting the needs of that 20 percent of disabled citizens who required specialized services. For them, the subcommittee recommended extending the kind of intensive care "widely used and observed in the programs for the rehabilitation of servicemen in Army and Navy hospitals during the war." The subcommittee noted the scarcity of these services, which meant that even disabled people of significant means could not always access them. Consequently, the subcommittee called on Congress to extend the Hill-Burton Act to rehabilitation centers. Passed earlier in the year, the Hill-Burton, or Hospital Survey and Construction, Act provided federal grants for the construction of hospitals. The report also indicated the need for convalescent care facilities and facilities to screen workers and children for diseases, such as tuberculosis and cancer.[102]

The investigation revealed a dearth of educational services for disabled children and adults as well as for parents of disabled children. The subcommittee found that less than 10 percent of the children who needed specialized educational services received them. State educational officials reported a lack of funding and trained personnel as well as difficulties "in bringing together enough pupils in one place to justify special classes." The subcommittee concluded that colleges and universities were "not often receptive to the applications of some of the more severely handicapped." Moreover, it heard numerous complaints that deaf African Americans had been denied admission to Gallaudet University and that many white deaf students from the West also faced difficulties earning a college education.[103]

To rectify the lack of educational opportunities, the subcommittee offered several proposals. It suggested extending federal funding through the Office of Education to expand educational opportunities for disabled children and called on the agency to provide leadership to encourage the states to develop and offer better educational services. The subcommittee argued that either Gallaudet grow to meet the needs of qualified deaf college applicants, white or black, or an additional deaf college be established. Subcommittee members contended that disabled people, aside from deaf individuals, could and should be served by "regular" universities and colleges and that these institutions needed to be a focus of the larger campaign to reduce prejudice through education. Additionally, the subcommittee recommended that the Library of Congress expand its program for providing reading materials to blind individuals, both in its offerings and audience. The subcommittee envisioned opening services to a broader audience of disabled Americans, including young people and people whose disabilities made it physically difficult to read a book. Finally, it called on the Children's Bureau to develop educational materials for new parents of disabled children and parents of children recently disabled.[104]

The subcommittee concluded that without significant family resources homebound disabled individuals would have "meager" lives, but it viewed educational opportunities as an important component of the needed remedy. Despite the fact that these individuals would likely never be employed, members of the subcommittee suggested that the federal-state program provide services to better the lives of both homebound children and adults. As their happiness depended more on "the pleasures of the mind than any other group," the subcommittee argued that these individuals should have access to library services and teachers.[105]

While the subcommittee noted that another House committee had been charged with examining Social Security law, members felt it important to indicate "the need is great" among disabled individuals for expanded Social Security. The subcommittee insisted, "When accident or disease strikes down the wage earner, whole families are made destitute." Moreover, Social Security provided no assistance to physically disabled people, apart from blind individuals, despite their "desperate need" for the support. Concretely, the subcommittee recommended that those who could not work should receive financial assistance, that workers in sheltered shops should get financial support to help them make ends meet, and that provisions for Aid to the Blind should "be liberalized" and recipients "relieved of the burden of perpetual supervision of the intimate details of their living."[106]

The subcommittee also stressed the importance of trade regulations for drug and assistive device producers to ensure that medicine and these devices were "readily available to people who need them, and at prices which are reasonable and fair." Furthermore, the subcommittee suggested that the Federal Trade Commission (FTC) needed additional staff to protect "the suffering public" from advertising for false cures for deafness and cancer and the Antitrust Division of the Department of Justice needed resources to ensure that monopolies did not distort the prices of drugs and assistive devices.[107]

Conditions uncovered by the subcommittee surrounding the manufacture and provision of artificial limbs had been so bad and the pressure from disabled veterans and other disabled citizens so strong that members did not wait until issuing their final report to take action. The subcommittee issued an early and separate scathing report, condemning the "shocking examples" they had seen of low-quality prostheses, poor methods of providing and fitting those appliances, and unnecessary bureaucracy that veterans had to navigate to receive a working, well-fit, quality prosthetic. Kelley, who authored the report, argued that the limitations it set on how often, where, and at what cost veterans could obtain prostheses "condemn[ed] the veteran who is badly fitted to needless and inexcusable pain and inconvenience." The subcommittee urged the VA to relax its strict regulations in relation to prostheses, making it easier for men to obtain better prosthetics and repairs on the ones that they already had. Kelley suggested that the Public Health Service supervise research efforts because of the VA's lack of experience managing research.[108]

Kelley also focused attention on the artificial limb industry, maintaining "there is little substantial difference in the limbs being made and furnished veterans now and those made at the close of the Civil War." Barbers and beauticians, he pointed out, faced greater regulation than artificial limb makers. The subcommittee prompted the FTC to develop a trade-practice code for the industry and encouraged the Federal Bureau of Investigation to investigate the industry's violations of antitrust laws.[109]

The subcommittee's call to action produced results. In 1945, the Justice

Department indicted approximately three-quarters of the artificial limb industry for antitrust violations, claiming that members of the Association of Limb Manufacturers of America had fixed prices. The Justice Department charged that these manufacturers had agreed to submit identical, artificially inflated prices to the VA when it collected its annual bids and to charge higher prices to veterans who approached them directly. Finally, the indictment alleged that the manufacturers of artificial limb parts had refused to sell to government agencies that provided limbs for free. The Justice Department secured convictions in 1946, but the U.S. Court of Appeals reversed these convictions the following year.[110] Despite this reversal, the investigation and prosecution brought attention to the industry and demonstrated that veterans, the public, and the government would not tolerate abuses of the nation's former and current servicemen.

A public lashing in Congress and in the press pushed the VA into action. It began funneling existing research monies in the agency to the Committee on Prosthetic Devices, ultimately investing a million dollars a year in research in what would become a permanent piece of the VA budget. Additionally, it adopted a policy of veteran participation in its research efforts. The VA hired Walter Bura, an engineer and amputee, to run its prosthetic program and simplified the repair process by negotiating maintenance and upkeep into all of its new contracts with manufacturers. It also began to push manufacturers to agree to offer repairs on limbs made by other companies. Further, the VA planned to open orthopedic shops in each of its general hospitals to service veteran amputees and to pay for their travel expenses to one of these shops.[111]

As important as providing services to disabled individuals was, the subcommittee argued that the prevention of disease and disability should be "the cornerstone of any future program." The subcommittee determined that children in public schools should be screened and treated for hearing and vision difficulties. Because these services were nonexistent in many states, the subcommittee proposed federal grants to ensure that all children received "at least this minimum health service." Childhood malnutrition caused by "poverty and ignorance" gave rise to disease and disability; consequently, the report recommended that the school lunch program be continued and expanded "so that there is available to every school child in the Nation, at least one well-balanced hot meal per day." In the calculus of disability, the issues of maternal and child health were important enough that the subcommittee issued a separate report on the topic, concluding, "The toll of blindness and hearing loss because of inadequate care in cases of common childhood diseases is tragic and wasteful in terms of production, money, and misery." While the subcommittee determined that expanding the availability of preventative medicine was beyond the scope of its investigation, it resolved, nonetheless, that preventative medicine must be addressed in "any program which aims at raising the national level of physical fitness, saving lives, and conserving physical function."[112]

The subcommittee offered strong words on the issue of accident prevention, noting that the Committee on Labor had twice issued reports to the House on "this tragedy and waste." It noted the "shameful record" that 16,000 Americans had died at work, another 96,000 became permanently disabled, and over two million acquired temporary disabilities in 1944 alone. The subcommittee's investigation supported the findings of the broader Committee on Labor that "there are too many accidents; they happen, largely, for reasons we know how to control; we are paying many times more through death, lost wages, public assistance, workmen's compensation, insurance premiums, illness, and suffering than it would cost to keep most of the accidents from happening." The subcommittee concluded, "It is contrary to common sense to spend an average of $300 to rehabilitate a physically handicapped worker who need not have become handicapped if a few dollars had been spent on a safety program to prevent his injury—leaving out of the account the value of human life, happiness, health, the costs of compensation, hospitalization, and medical care." The subcommittee suggested that Congress adopt a workers' safety measure sponsored by Mary Norton (D-NJ), who chaired the Committee on Labor. The bill, which was ultimately defeated, would have provided federal funding to state labor departments for worker safety programs if they met minimum standards set by the federal Department of Labor.[113]

The subcommittee's calls for services and prevention tied into its recommendations for expanded opportunities for professional training and research in the field. The subcommittee pointed to the need for more training programs for doctors, dentists, and therapists who would serve people with disabilities and suggested that rehabilitation legislation be amended to allow the Office of Vocational Rehabilitation to train new professionals in the field. The subcommittee linked quality services with training and research, arguing that federal disability services were "at such an immature level" that research was needed to develop better programs and approaches to address the needs of Americans with disabilities. The subcommittee called on the Office of

Education to encourage research and efforts to improve teaching and training methods for people with disabilities. Moreover, the subcommittee determined that research would be necessary to better understand various diseases and disabilities, more effectively prevent accidents in America's homes and on its farms and roads, and develop better means of preventing, curing, and treating disease and disability. To realize this goal, the subcommittee suggested that the Public Health Service be charged with research on "health and disease" and that it "be authorized to make use of universities, State agencies, and other mediums of research, and should be provided liberally with funds for such work."[114]

The subcommittee noted that its own efforts to conduct research in the field of disability services had been made difficult by the field's narrow focus on American efforts. It condemned the lack information available in the United States about disability services in other nations and the lack of translated materials in the field. In particular, the subcommittee had hoped to study disability policy in Denmark, where the government reportedly offered "remarkably fine service" to its disabled citizens, and England, which had instituted a mandatory quota for the employment of disabled workers, but it did not have the funds to complete these studies and could find little material in English about Danish disability service programs. The subcommittee recommended greater international cooperation on issues of disability to ensure a sharing of "knowledge and experience."[115]

Taken as a whole, the subcommittee's report demonstrated sensitivity to the concerns of people with disabilities and openness to the demands of disability activists. The report responded to AFPH activists' key demand for employment with broad recommendations for facilitating greater employment opportunities. It gave considerable attention to reinventing the rehabilitation program to address activists' concerns that the program excluded too many disabled applicants and that disability services more broadly lacked coordination. The subcommittee's report reflected agreement with activists that educational opportunities must be enhanced and sheltered workshops regulated. It also lent support to activists' demands for pensions and the NFB contention that the administration of the means-tested Aid to the Blind led to unnecessary professional supervision and suppressed blind people's ability to accept work.[116] The subcommittee's work to make prosthetics better and more widely available offered the clearest example of its responsiveness to disabled citizens' concerns, particularly those raised by disabled veterans.

Yet the report also revealed a clear sense that subcommittee members viewed physicians, educators, rehabilitation counselors, professional service workers, and researchers as critical to meeting the needs that disabled citizens articulated. Indeed, the subcommittee advocated for more experts, as well as more training for them, and greater funding for them to provide a wider range of services. These two trends—a serious consideration of disability activists' concerns and a push for greater professional services—represented an important tension that the disability rights movement would increasingly confront. In making disabled people's needs visible, AFPH members and other disability activists shone a light on disability and the inadequacies of the present system. The AFPH and other organizations would offer solutions—often at odds with professionals in the field, but in the realm of disability, policy makers often turned to physicians and other professionals in the field for answers. Those answers often conflicted with the disability rights agenda of the day.

The AFPH's interactions with the subcommittee sought to call attention to the need for federal action to end employment discrimination and improve federal services to better meet disabled people's medical, educational, training, and employment needs. Members' statements and letters revealed a growing conviction that the state should make the promise of work and economic security accessible to them. Just as World War II fostered the growth of the civilian rehabilitation program and new employment opportunities for people with disabilities, it also created a space for the AFPH. The wartime climate of opportunity for work, employer flexibility about physical requirements, and federal interventions to facilitate employment opportunities created new expectations among disabled people who, like the majority of Americans, increasingly viewed federal promises of work and financial security as rights that the state should protect.

Members' stories—the ones the AFPH urged them to tell from the depths of personal experience—highlighted the ways in which these rights remained unrealized for people with disabilities. In doing so, they insisted that the state both recognize and facilitate their citizenship. In addition to demanding new policies as a matter of right—an entitlement of citizenship—AFPH members and leaders framed their demands in the interest of the nation, arguing that ensuring disabled people's access to employment would save tax dollars, increase the national wealth, and reduce the burden on families, communities, states, and the nation.

The subcommittee's investigation contributed to a growing awareness of disability. Hundreds of thousands of disabled veterans, millions of workers injured on the home front, millions of young men found unfit to serve, and hundreds of thousands of disabled war workers rendered disability both visible and urgent. Indeed, a sense of urgency infused the AFPH in its early years as disabled Americans looked to the future with considerable hope and uncertainty. Policymakers' fear that the United States confronted a crisis of disability created a space for the voices of disabled citizens to be heard. Yet as the war came to a close, policymakers and disability activists could no longer claim that victory necessitated addressing the needs uncovered in the subcommittee's study. Instead, disability itself would become a call to action for policymakers and a justification for proposals to extend the protections of the welfare state—a much more divisive proposition. Moreover, activists' success in highlighting the problems people with disabilities faced did not guarantee that policymakers would turn to them for solutions.

Chapter 3

Toward a New Freedom from Fear: Disability and Postwar Uncertainty

In 1946, Howard F. Nolan wrote a passionate plea in support of the American Federation of the Physically Handicapped (AFPH) legislative agenda to Representative Augustine B. Kelley (D-PA), who chaired the House of Representatives Subcommittee on Aid to the Physically Handicapped. A resident of the Home for Incurables in Philadelphia, Nolan had been a wheelchair user since age fourteen and spent much of his life in hospitals or other institutions because of arthritis. His letter, as much a prayer as a political appeal, called for "justice," particularly for the three million disabled men and women who were considered unemployable. Nolan demanded, "Give us the right to live, and the means to live and the desire to live." He asked, "Why are there so many agencies, providing so little service, with such a constant insufficiency of funds? Where is our 'freedom from fear'?" Nolan wrote that Kelley's committee, and Congress as a whole, represented a jury that would decide the fate of millions of "condemned" Americans. "What," he asked, "is the verdict? To continue to suffer endless, unnecessary misery as long as they shall live, or by act of Congress in the year 1946, to be relieved of that suffering insofar as the law and man's humanity to man makes it possible?"[1]

In his letter, Nolan described his conversion from patient to activist, writing that from the moment that he had learned of the AFPH plan for a federal agency and a broad range of federal services for disabled people, "almost nothing else has existed for me." Nolan placed his conversion experience and the demands of people with disabilities in the context of President Roosevelt's 1941 State of the Union address, in which he sought to convince war-wary Americans of the dire need to support democracies around the world fighting World War II and called on Americans to ensure "a world founded on four essential human freedoms"—freedom of expression, freedom of religion, "freedom from want," and "freedom from fear." In "freedom from fear," Roosevelt called for a more secure world community, in which nations would be safe from the kind of military aggression that threatened the survival of democracies around the globe in 1941.[2] Nolan, however, argued that disabled people's "freedom from fear" would come when Congress took action to prevent and cure "all of those crippling and wasteful diseases" and establish an agency to serve people with disabilities, armed "with a power equal to the destructive power of that same atom."[3]

The AFPH served as a catalyst for Nolan's conversion from patient to activist, but World War II inspired and shaped this conversion. Americans emerged from the war victorious, with what one historian has called "grand expectations" for the postwar world—expectations for prosperity, a government committed to ensuring that prosperity, a safer world, and continued medical and scientific triumphs.[4] Still, fear and uncertainty tinged those "grand expectations" in 1946. Americans feared that the prosperity of the war years would give way to a return of the dark days of the Great Depression when military spending dried up and soldiers returned home in search of work. Between V-E Day and V-J Day, aircraft and armament factories and shipyards cut half their workers, and the federal government cancelled orders worth thirty-five billion dollars after the Japanese surrender. Within a month of victory in Europe, the military began discharging service men and women, releasing nine million Americans from military service in the space of a year—individuals who would all return home in search of work. Prices and unemployment surged, with 2.3 million Americans out of work in 1946, up from one million in 1945. Moreover, the ubiquitous overtime of the war disappeared. Many of the people who had answered the nation's call for workers but were perceived as a temporary fix to a wartime problem—women, African Americans, people with disabilities, and older Americans—felt the sting of unemployment first. The number of women workers declined to 16.8 million in 1946 from the wartime peak of 19.1 million.[5]

American life in 1945, while significantly better than the Depression years, looked very different than it would just five, ten, or fifteen years later. More than twenty-five million Americans lived on farms with no electricity. Fewer than half of Americans lived in cities or towns with more than 10,000 residents. As late as 1950, 38 percent of American families had never watched a television program. Young and old alike listened to singers such Frank

Sinatra, the Andrews Sisters, and Bing Crosby. Americans flocked to the movies but rarely ate dinner out.[6]

The end of various wartime restrictions began a transformation of American life. The high wages, abundant overtime, and controls on consumer production of the war meant that Americans had saved billions of dollars—dollars they would spend on consumer goods in the postwar period. Businesses used wartime profits to convert war plants and build new factories. Americans bought 11.6 million televisions, twenty million refrigerators, and 21.4 million automobiles between 1946 and 1950. Gone too were the restrictions on travel and gasoline rationing.[7]

Federal policy helped to ensure that those "grand expectations" would become a reality for many Americans. U.S. aid helped Europe rebuild and also enabled European consumers to purchase American goods, further boosting the U.S. economy. The Servicemen's Readjustment Act of 1944, or G.I. Bill of Rights, provided veterans with funding for education and job training, low-interest home and business loans, and unemployment compensation to facilitate their readjustment to civilian life.[8]

Still, uncertainty would remain. The cost of living grew faster than wages throughout the postwar period. By the end of the 1940s, roughly one in three Americans lived in poverty. Moreover, despite Roosevelt's hope that U.S. engagement in the war would produce a "freedom from fear," the war gave way to a new and powerful international fear—Soviet and communist expansion. The glow of victory faded rapidly as the Soviet Union made clear that it would retain control of Eastern Europe. By 1947, the United States committed itself to containment of the Soviet threat. The U.S. government provided aid around the world, established alliances, and sought to control access to atomic weapons in an effort to contain the spread of communism. At home, these efforts translated into an eruption of anticommunism in the late 1940s. The Red Scare extended from the Federal Employee Loyalty Program of 1947 that scrutinized federal employees' actions and associations to congressional efforts to hunt out communists and purges of radicals in a wide array of American organizations. Red Scare fears and purges often failed to distinguish between active communists and those who had simply been critical of American policy. In this new Cold War atmosphere, fear flourished, repressing debate and criticism, especially on the left.[9]

The expectations and the fear provided fertile ground for movements committed to social justice. In 1945, nearly 22 percent of all American workers were union members. Despite the Red Scare purging of radicals, unions remained an important force in American politics, pushing liberals toward the left. Still, unions would face significant roadblocks as they fought to improve the living and working conditions for all working Americans in the postwar years, including growing antiunion sentiment in the Republican Party and among southern Democrats.[10]

Around a million African Americans had served in the military during the war, but those who returned to the South, where the majority of African Americans continued to live in the 1940s, encountered fierce racism, legal segregation, discrimination in almost every aspect of life, and widespread poverty. But increasingly African Americans, particularly veterans, would challenge Jim Crow. Membership in the National Association for the Advancement of Colored People had grown from 50,000 to 450,000 during the war, and African American activists founded the Congress of Racial Equality to combat racism with direct action. Moreover, some 2.5 million African Americans left the South in search of better economic opportunities in the 1940s and 1950s.[11]

Women also fought for greater opportunities during the war and sought to maintain and expand those opportunities in the postwar period. Even amidst postwar layoffs women's postwar participation in the workforce was greater than it had been in 1940, and by 1947, the number of women in the workforce would begin to rise again. During the 1940s, numerous women's organizations fought for greater equity, including the American Association of University Women, the National Federation of Business and Professional Women's Clubs, the National Council of Negro Women, and the National Women's Trade Union League. The number of women serving in state legislatures grew during the war. In 1945, 288 women held office in various state legislatures compared to just 144 in 1941. At the national level, women were more likely in the 1940s to gain election, and reelection, to Congress in their own right, rather than to be appointed to fill a vacant seat, as they had been in previous decades. With few exceptions, these women worked to end legal and social discrimination against women and advocated greater opportunities for women. They pushed for equal pay, fought for child care, and sought to protect Women's Bureau funding.[12]

New expectations and postwar uncertainty also fueled the AFPH and converted thousands of Americans with disabilities to activists who would demand change. Just as the war raised expectations that the federal government would support disabled people's access to employment, education, and health care, the AFPH created new cross-disability communities where members increasingly recognized their individual experiences of discrimination, which often spurred frustrated ambitions, poverty, and a lack of choices, as collective experiences that transcended individual struggles. Many feared that the advances of war would erode in the postwar era and that people with disabilities would remain on the economic margins. Disability activists fought for broader services, with more funding and better administration, and for the right to help devise those services. They sought to build unity around the experience of disability and through the AFPH and coalitions with other organizations that sought to broaden the vision of American citizenship. But wartime disability policy had also launched another transformation—the medicalization of disability policy. As disability activists fought for a greater role in crafting the policy that would shape their lives, a growing body of experts would also stake a claim for controlling the future of American disability policy. The medical claim over disability drew on the war moment and the many tremendous demonstrations of the power of medicine and science.

Postwar Anxiety, Postwar Agenda

Anxiety about the postwar economy and a sense that contributing to victory should entitle people with disabilities to full access to the benefits of citizenship framed the development of the AFPH during the immediate postwar years. Like most of the American public, disabled people hoped for the end of the war but feared that it might bring a return to the economic depression of the 1930s. In a tight economy, people with disabilities were especially vulnerable to discrimination, being among the last hired and first fired. In 1945 AFPH member Melvin E. Schoonover expressed both a sense of relief and anxiety about the end of the war. "The war, thank God, is over," he wrote. "Shut-ins, like everyone else, are thinking about the future," but the future, in his estimation, was questionable. Homebound disabled people, he argued, did not "want to return to 'good old days'"—a time that "was not too good to them." Schoonover asserted that people with disabilities, like other Americans, had worked to win the war. "Not being able to fight on the battlefronts," he maintained, "they did vitally important work on the home front." Even when homebound, disabled people sold war bonds, telephoned war workers to get them to work on time, and took in work sorting and cleaning metal, rags, and paper.[13]

During the war, the federal government inundated Americans with images and slogans that linked everything from salvaging scrap metal, punctuality, safety, and job performance to the success of the military campaign, even the survival of individual soldiers. Americans had been told that what they did and said each day at work and at home mattered. Their work, propaganda emphasized, enabled soldiers to keep up the fight to protect the nation. For AFPH members, people with disabilities had answered the nation's wartime call for labor, and they demanded recognition of this service. In 1945, J. Cooke Howard, AFPH member and Director of the Division of the Deaf and Deafened in the Michigan Department of Labor, touted the war work of people with disabilities and warned AFPH members about what the future might have in store for them. The nation, he argued, had needed people with disabilities to fill vital positions in industry during the war, but he cautioned that they should not celebrate too soon because their similar World War I service had been quickly forgotten. Howard maintained that the federal government had a responsibility to them in the postwar era. "A nation enlisting everyone for war," he claimed, "assumes a responsibility to provide work for its people in peace."[14] Howard later asserted, "While we unstintingly honor the sons of Mars who faced the horrors of war, we must not forget the sons of Vulcan who forged the implements of war, and did their full part in the glorious victory."[15]

For many AFPH members and people with disabilities, Howard's warning quickly became their new reality as wartime employment opportunities disappeared in the postwar period. Pittsburgh member George Booth reported being pressured to give up his wartime job for a returning veteran. He had taken that job over another position because none of the garage's workers were serving in the armed forces, a situation, he hoped, that would improve his chances of long-term employment. Once the war ended, however, Booth was told that a young veteran had held the job before him.[16] The end of the war also brought a return of difficult times for AFPH member Acie Johnson, who held a job with Chrysler Corporation in Detroit during the war. When the war ended, he lost his job "like thousands of other physically handicapped people." Johnson, who was hard of hearing, wrote that it was "hard to understand why I haven't got a good job." He had been registered with the U.S. Employment Service for years and had "a fairly good education."[17]

Indeed, growing unemployment in the postwar period pushed AFPH members into action. A. E. Howell, president of his local AFPH chapter and placement specialist for the U.S. Employment Service in Colorado, wrote on behalf of "several hundred other handicapped persons in this area" to

Representative Kelley in May 1946, urging action to solve the growing unemployment among people with disabilities. Howell's work focused on placing disabled workers in jobs. He argued, however, that his job had grown increasingly difficult, with applications from disabled job seekers "increasing almost daily" and "the surplus of nonhandicapped now available."[18]

Unemployment, a temporary concern for most as the nation transitioned from a war to a peacetime economy, persisted for many people with disabilities. In 1948, Iride Valmassy, vice president of the Detroit Lodge of the AFPH, complained to the *Detroit Times*, "I worked during the war. I worked in one of the aircraft plants, but V-J Day came and that was the end of the job. If I was good enough then, why was it so hard to even get a chance after V-J?" In fact, it took Valmassy, an Italian immigrant and daughter of a factory worker, three years after the war to even get a "tryout" position as a typist. The postwar difficulties Valmassy confronted were compounded in that her status as both a disabled person and a woman contributed to her treatment as a temporary worker. Women and people with disabilities were particularly vulnerable to layoffs. Indeed, the number of women in the workforce declined sharply in the immediate postwar years with even greater declines in heavy industry where Valmassy had worked. In industries such as automobile, steel, and ship-building, women had held a quarter of the jobs during the war, but postwar layoffs dropped that figure down to 7.5 percent by 1946.[19]

As the war came to a close, the AFPH secured its second major victory with the enactment of National Employ the Physically Handicapped Week (NEPHW). The *A.F.P.H. Tribune* called the victory "the beginning of a movement that will benefit the Physically Handicapped," and indeed, through the week, the AFPH transitioned from presenting a critique and offering suggestions to shaping directly corrective policy.[20] The week, described as "a vast, national educational campaign," appeared in Paul Strachan's earliest outlines of the AFPH agenda. A week-long, national celebration focused on employment of disabled people, in Strachan's view, would both spark interest among the general public and energize disabled people themselves for a broader legislative campaign. He envisioned a grand event with official proclamations issued by everyone from the president to big city mayors; events organized by activists, advocates, women's groups, labor, industry, businesses, schools, and civic organizations; and support from all the biggest stars of the day. Ever mindful of the political clout of disabled veterans, he believed that the very public participation of veterans would ensure that Americans would understand the employment of disabled citizens as both a necessity and a patriotic service.[21]

In hearings on the NEPHW bill in the House of Representative in early May 1945, Mildred Scott, national secretary of the AFPH, argued that "the vast majority" of the twenty-five million disabled Americans had "been subjected to the most unfair discriminations"—discrimination in both industry and public employment, rooted in "ignorance and indifference." Rejecting charity, Scott contended that disabled Americans "want[ed] and demand[ed] opportunity and equality before the law, and the bar of public opinion." Changing public opinion was a vital step in securing employment gains, and employment, she maintained, would make disabled people "bulwarks and props of our democracy" instead of "tax-eaters" or "dependents upon an uncertain charity." Finally, she argued, "the welfare of the physically handicapped, both military and civilian, is the responsibility of the Congress."[22] The demand that Congress—the nation—address the needs of disabled citizens separated the AFPH from other civilian disability rights organizations that often focused efforts on state and local issues, and it countered political thinking of the day, in which disabled people were the responsibility of families, local charities and governments, and state programs.

It took three years for NEPHW to become law. Representative Jerry Voorhis (D-CA) first introduced a joint resolution to establish the week in June 1942, but it never came to a vote that year.[23] Less than a month after Germany surrendered, Voorhis explained the merits of setting aside a week each year to promote the employment of people with disabilities, emphasizing the needs of returning soldiers with disabilities. In May 1945, the Office of Surgeon General of the U.S. Army predicted that disabled veterans would "present a widespread problem of considerable magnitude." As early as June 1944, over 200,000 World War II veterans were already on the disability pension rolls, and in May and June of 1945 alone, the military shipped nearly 100,000 wounded soldiers and sailors to the United States for definitive care and rehabilitation. Faced with the prospect of reintegrating hundreds of thousands of disabled veterans, the House passed the resolution. The Senate followed suit just days before the United States dropped an atomic bomb on Hiroshima. On 11 August 1945, the day after the United States received Japan's surrender offer, President Truman signed the resolution, establishing the first week of October as NEPHW. The resolution called for ceremonies throughout the nation "to enlist public support for and interest in the employment of otherwise qualified but physically handicapped workers."[24] The week represented a perfect compromise between liberal plans to expand the national social insurance system, attack discrimination, and establish a machinery to make the promise of economic security a reality and conservatives who sought to roll back New Deal gains. At face value, it was a low-cost federal solution that hinged on the volunteer work of private citizens; however, the AFPH saw the week as something much bigger: an acknowledgement by the federal government of the discrimination disabled people faced, an opportunity to counter that discrimination, a chance to recruit members and promote the organization's agenda, and a justification for further federal coordination of disability services—an important AFPH aim.

Less than one month after V-J Day, AFPH members held a mass meeting in Washington, D.C.[25] Members adopted a resolution that outlined how the organization would respond to the new realities of the postwar world. It echoed concerns about the "uncertainties of employment" that had already begun and would certainly grow in the transition to peace and the emphasis on disabled people's contributions "to the War production effort" and the ultimate victory. Members agreed that the "acute" problems of disabled veterans and civilians "must be met by prompt, effective action." They demanded that reconversion plans "provide definitively for employment of otherwise qualified but physically handicapped workers" and immediate action "to afford equal opportunity for employment of Handicapped where they are capable of performing similar work to that of non-handicapped." With the war over and the AFPH's success with NEPHW, the organization narrowed in on its proposal for a federal agency, "properly financed and staffed," to provide disabled people rehabilitation, health services, assistive devices, education, training, and employment placement. Ultimately, members demanded that people with disabilities "be integrated into our social and economic life, as full partners in our way of living."[26] Unlike its first two successes—the investigation and the week that required limited federal resources and financial investment—any hope of gaining a new federal agency that would offer a wide range of new services and necessitate a significant expansion of the welfare state hinged on mobilizing members and recruiting a broad base of supporters.

Mobilizing Experience

In September 1944, Strachan told AFPH members, "No one can speak from the depths of the heart except those themselves handicapped. So, let your friends come in and help this organization. Get them to do so; make it greater,

Figure 4. This AFPH illustration depicts three disabled people, two men—both amputees—and one woman in a wheelchair, demanding that the gate of "employment" be opened "to home, happiness, [and] security." This image, featuring the slogan "Hire the Handicapped," appeared in the AFPH magazine *Valor* during October 1952. Courtesy of the Archives and Special Collections Division, City College of New York.

and give it the power to render more effective service to our own people."[27] Strachan's appeal to members served as a call to action, to organize, but it also suggested that people with disabilities had a unique service to offer the nation and other disabled Americans—their experience. AFPH leaders understood that the success of their agenda depended on the group's ability to organize people with disabilities. Implicit in the AFPH agenda and its efforts to recruit members was the idea that people with disabilities should have a role in creating and administering national disability policy and that members' personal experience of disability gave them expertise that should be brought to bear on these policies. Beyond seeking strength in numbers, the AFPH sought political power by encouraging members to vote and act in support of the organization's aims. The national organization promoted the growth of this political power and the organization itself by arguing that in supporting the organization members were fulfilling a responsibility to themselves and other people with disabilities and a duty to their nation.

AFPH leaders emphasized that people with disabilities could not rely on others to better their lot. In October 1945, Mildred Scott wrote about the importance of organization among people with disabilities. She claimed, "Unless we who are Physically Handicapped are willing to assume our share of the responsibility and to assist in creating a better understanding on the part of the public and business, in general, then we must continue to be content with a mere handout." For Scott, any hope for "better opportunities for education" and "a place to earn our living" would grow out of organization on the part of people with disabilities and the work of members to analyze the problems they faced, develop solutions, and gain cooperation to implement those solutions.[28] The language of responsibility—of citizenship—permeated leaders' guidance to members. In Scott's analysis, reliance on able-bodied individuals had produced the very circumstances that members struggled against. The response to disability had been "a mere handout"—charity. Only by assuming responsibility, by organizing, making demands as citizens, and working alongside other citizens to effect change could members expect to improve their circumstances.

Organized in a federated structure, the AFPH national headquarters and officers set the group's national political agenda, pushed for the enactment of that agenda, and produced two monthly publications, the *A.F.P.H. Tribune* in the mid- to late 1940s and *Valor* in the early 1950s. State departments pushed for local organization and addressed state-level concerns.[29] Local lodges provided a community and social space for members and also allowed them to address local issues. The AFPH offered "participating" membership to people with a broad range of disabilities and "associate" membership to interested able-bodied individuals to facilitate a broader political and financial base.[30] On the national level, the AFPH maintained a "non-segregated, non-discriminatory" policy. Still, the organization's southern chapters were racially segregated.[31]

AFPH membership expanded rapidly in the immediate postwar years—growth likely fueled by the promise of wartime employment, the sense that people with disabilities had contributed to the victory, anxieties about the postwar employment situation, and the AFPH's organizational efforts. Between May 1945 and May 1946, the organization expanded from sixty lodges to eighty-five.[32] By the fall of 1947, the organization's membership numbered 17,000, significant growth since May 1945 when the organization had around 2,000 members.[33] In the early postwar years, AFPH chapters spread across the country, with a heavy concentration in urban and industrial areas. Large cities often had multiple AFPH chapters. Members formed two lodges in Chicago, Indianapolis, Los Angeles, and Flint. Brooklyn alone was home to three lodges as was Washington, D.C. Additionally, the AFPH had lodges scattered throughout the Midwest, South, and West.[34] Without membership records and with the AFPH's practice of awarding associate memberships to donors and donor organizations, it is difficult to gauge the organization's growth from 1947 forward. In 1954, AFPH vice president J. Rosemond Cook told the African American newspaper the *Atlanta Daily World* that the organization had "some 16 million members." This exponential growth reflected the AFPH's growing success in securing financial support of its national efforts. By 1954, donors included private citizens and a host of unions, churches, and other organizations. It is certainly possible that some, if not many, of those associate members were unaware of their status. Still, these associate memberships allowed the AFPH to cement organizational ties between disability activists and a broad range of labor, civic, and religious organizations. These connections helped to lend weight to the AFPH agenda, expand the network of supporters and potential supporters, and encourage other organizations to back the AFPH by virtue of similar organizations' support—support demonstrated by financial contributions and associate memberships.[35]

AFPH leaders recognized that members gave the organization political legitimacy and power. A 1945 *A.F.P.H. Tribune* call for members suggested that uniting "in one powerful group" would allow the organization to "formulate a national policy that will compel attention." The advertisement counseled readers that unity through membership and organization offered people with disabilities the hope of change through "the collective effort and support of millions of people, instead of mere handfuls."[36] Strachan was more direct. In 1944, he told members, "To deal with Congress, effectively, we must have the power that only comes from association of large numbers of people united in a common cause." Tying together the themes of expertise through experience and the need for people with disabilities to speak for themselves, he argued, "We will not depend upon the nonhandicapped to tell our story for us."[37] In pushing for membership and unity, leaders suggested that AFPH members, by virtue of joining the organization and encouraging others to do so, gave the organization power. And by doing so, they would be better citizens in a nation more responsive to their needs.

Despite the organization's efforts, recruiting members continued to be a challenge. Reflecting on the difficulties of organizing a cross-disability movement, Strachan would later complain that if the AFPH asked ten disabled people to join the organization, only one would actually become a member. "Three," he claimed, "would say they do not need AFPH; they have a job, and they are not in need of money; they do not want any organization effort." He maintained, "Two would say they do not want it known that they have a handicap." The others, he declared, "would immediately start asking us for help beyond our means to give," demanding that the AFPH provide health care and jobs.[38]

Leaders called on members to unify around the organization's agenda, help develop and enact that agenda, and demonstrate that unity in the voting booth, through letters to elected officials, and with appearances before Congress. Thus, the AFPH called on its members to vote and to cast their ballots with issues of disability in mind. In 1946 the *A.F.P.H. Tribune* instructed readers to register to vote, imploring, "DO IT NOW!" Calling on readers to vote in primaries as well as general elections, the article went on to give advice about how to vote. "If the 25,000,000 Physically Handicapped make known their needs, and candidates for public office refuse to approve remedies," the *Tribune* explained, "then the Handicapped, in self-protection, should work and vote for those who pledge support to such programs."[39]

The AFPH's emphasis on voting called on many members to not only vote but also demand access to the polls to do so. AFPH member Nolan urged members to vote even if they had "to crawl to the polls."[40] His suggestion that some members might have physical difficulty voting drew on continuing conversations among members about access to the polls. Poverty restricted access to mobility aids like wheelchairs, and those who used wheelchairs still needed building access. Member Schoonover argued, "The truth is that the home-bound are, for all practical purposes, denied the use of the ballot."[41]

The organization sought to make clear to its members who their friends in Washington were. Nolan argued that AFPH members "should make it our business to know our own local and state and national office-holders. What do they do for us?" He also reminded members that congressmen like Voorhis, Kelley, and John J. Sparkman (D-AL), who had all supported the AFPH, needed members' votes.[42]

Beyond voting, AFPH leaders pushed members to use a range of tools to demonstrate their unity and support of the AFPH agenda. For example, Strachan claimed that the AFPH was "able to get about 20,000 letters to be sent to Congress" in support of establishing the House investigation. Whether

Congress actually received 20,000 letters or the AFPH could claim credit for all of them, AFPH leaders sought to encourage this type of engagement. Strachan told members, "But I shall expect more of 'you guys' next time. If you gave me 20,000 letters last time, I want 100,000 next time, and I do not want any alibis."[43]

Whether or not the AFPH always succeeded in motivating members to vote and speak out for the movement, Strachan used the potential of this alignment, and the even greater potential of the political alignment of all people with disabilities with the AFPH to leverage political action. He approached officials as the spokesperson of millions of disabled individuals, whether those individuals supported the AFPH agenda and voted on issues of disability or not. He rarely gave membership numbers, but often referenced the millions of disabled Americans. Perhaps this strategy and Strachan's doggedness forced consideration of his many requests. According to William Hassett, President Truman's correspondence secretary, Strachan was "one of the most persistent men with whom we deal." He declared, "There seems to be no limit to the requests which he makes of the President. As fast as one request is granted he comes back with two more."[44] Still, selling disabled individuals whose disabilities and experiences varied widely on the need to put political muscle behind these demands proved to be a more difficult task than Strachan had likely imagined.

The Drive for Unity and the Realities of Cross-Disability Organizing

The AFPH aimed to organize members across the spectrum of disabilities and regardless of members' gender, class, race, or home state, and it succeeded in bringing together a wide range of individuals with different disabilities and experiences. Indeed, one reporter, struck by the variety of disabilities among members attending an AFPH convention, wrote, "Nods of approval from those who could nod, the metallic clip of applause by those with metal pincers where others have hands, and floor thumping of legs manacled for mobility, greeted many of [Strachan's] words."[45] Still, the organization's emphasis on unity suggests that it had to be cultivated. Local communities would help to create a sense that individuals shared an identity as disabled people that transcended different categories of disability, different experiences of becoming disabled, and differences of race, class, gender, and region.

But this kind of organizing and unity was new and presented organizational challenges.

Dr. Ira D. Scott of the Veterans Administration (VA) told the AFPH's 1946 biennial convention that organizing people with different disabilities could be a difficult task. He spoke of the need "to avoid conflicts between the purposes of different groups having what so often seem to be almost identical interest." He commended Strachan's record on handling such conflicts, pointing to both his recognition that many of the lessons employers needed to learn about disability applied to all disabled individuals, regardless of the particular type or source of disability, and his acknowledgement that disabled veterans were in a different situation than disabled civilians.[46] Scott's speech indicates the difficulties the AFPH faced in creating a sense of unity. Even in arguing for a universal disabled identity, he suggested that disabled veterans stood apart.

The AFPH worked hard to recruit disabled veterans and draw on their political and cultural capital, but disabled veterans' own agenda, focused on securing and maintaining special benefits for disabled veterans, was often at odds with the AFPH's attempts to push for centralizing and expanding federal disability services for all.[47] In 1945, Millard W. Rice, national service director of the Disabled American Veterans (DAV), articulated the complications inherent in DAV-AFPH collaboration in a formal greeting he penned for the *A.F.P.H Tribune.* While acknowledging that the two organizations faced "similar" difficulties, he drew careful distinctions between veterans and civilians—distinctions that suggested that disabled veterans believed their needs should and would be met before those of civilians. Rice wrote that the DAV's legislative achievements could be "a stepping stone" to similar victories for disabled civilians. He acknowledged, however, the further complexity of the situation and the likely reason that disabled veterans and their organizations offered support of the AFPH—"the welfare of America's disabled defenders is inevitably linked up with the welfare of American citizens generally." Essentially, disabled veterans were also disabled citizens, and the VA alone could not address all of the difficulties they faced. With that reality in mind, Rice offered the AFPH "the hand of fraternal cooperation."[48]

Disabled veterans' activism had ensured that veteran and civilian rehabilitation programs operated separately with separate legislative mandates. The separateness of services and legislation meant that veterans' organizations tended to focus on the issues of veterans' rehabilitation, while the AFPH focused on civilian programs. This divided system meant that collaboration did not always make sense, but it also limited the degree to which activists recognized shared frustrations.

As with members of the AFPH, the experience of rehabilitation, and dissatisfaction with services—in this case services provided by the military and the VA—motivated disabled veterans' activism. The special circumstances of veterans' rehabilitation meant that veterans often received medical rehabilitation in specialized facilities, alongside numerous other disabled veterans with similar disabilities. Essentially, they experienced adjusting to a new disability and the rehabilitation process in groups, which facilitated disability activism and the growth of several new disability rights organizations by making apparent that personal disappoints were often collective grievances. For instance, blind soldiers at Old Farms, where the army rehabilitated soldiers who had been blinded in the war, founded the Blinded Veterans Association in March 1945 to ensure that blind veterans received adequate services from the VA. It quickly spread to the Philadelphia Naval Hospital, where blind sailors and marines received rehabilitation.[49] Likewise, veterans with spinal cord injuries founded the Paralyzed Veterans of America in 1946, which aimed to ensure access to benefits and health care, encourage research, promote accessibility, and push for greater job opportunities.[50]

The VA established Vocational Rehabilitation and Educational Divisions in all fifty-three regional VA offices. The advisement and guidance subdivision provided vocational counseling and developed training plans, while the education and training subdivision assisted veterans in finding an appropriate education or training institution, supervised veterans during training, and ensured job placement. The VA established guidance centers in partner colleges and universities across the country. The first center opened in 1944 at City College in New York. Centers spread rapidly with one in nearly every state. In 1946, the VA extended the program more directly into its medical facilities, assigning vocational advisers to eighty-six VA hospitals. Once a veteran was determined to be eligible for vocational rehabilitation services, the process began with extensive interviews and tests to determine aptitude, interests, skills, and deficits. Based on this data, medical information, and economic conditions in the area where the veteran lived, the vocational counselor developed occupational recommendations. Of the first 3,000 veterans who benefited from the program during World War II, around 1,000 pursued professional careers in field such as accounting, teaching, engineering, and law, another 1,000 followed skilled trades—by far the most common objective was to be a mechanic or repairman, and still others pursued careers as

Figure 5. The winners of a 1947 Veterans Administration sponsored bowling competition for paralyzed veterans pose with President Harry S. Truman. Truman's willingness to meet with these veterans demonstrates the keen awareness of disabled veterans in the postwar years. Photograph by International News Service. Courtesy of Corbis and the Harry S. Truman Library and Museum.

draftsmen or laboratory technicians, among other semi-professional occupations. Veterans enrolled in universities, colleges, trade or business schools, or on-the-job training programs with the supervision and guidance of a training officer. The training officer also supervised the veteran throughout the training program, assisting with special arrangements necessary because of the veteran's disability, such as transportation for blind veterans, and monitoring progress and performance.[51]

Many of the difficulties disabled veterans encountered in rehabilitation were unique to the veterans program. Because the vocational rehabilitation program assisted veterans with service-connected disabilities, the World War I program did not continue throughout the interwar years; thus, when Congress reestablished the veterans rehabilitation program in 1943, the VA faced the task of rebuilding the program and recruiting vocational counselors and training officers to serve disabled veterans who had already begun to return home. The urgent need for counselors necessitated a flexible approach to the educational and training requirements, and the immediate needs of disabled veterans afforded little time to develop a strong program from the start. The end result was that an underexperienced, undertrained staff would face an overwhelming influx of cases in a span of just a few years. Within three years, VA counselors confronted an influx of more than 50,000 new clients a month.[52]

Still, disabled veterans and civilians faced many shared challenges. Neither rehabilitation program had adequate staff to meet the needs of those who were eligible for services. Both disabled veterans and civilians faced professional supervision—VA vocational counselors and civilian rehabilitation counselors shaped training plans for clients and could challenge clients' own vocational aspirations. Able-bodied veterans receiving educational assistance through the G.I. Bill faced no such supervision. Disabled veterans could opt to receive G.I. Bill assistance instead of vocational rehabilitation, but doing so meant accepting smaller monthly payments during training.[53] Administered separately with separate legislative mandates, the veteran and civilian programs drew little combined activism. Indeed, the first edition of the *A.F.P.H. Tribune* veterans' column, "Uncle G.I. Joe Speaks," which appeared in October 1945, hinted at the linkages between these problems, arguing that the key to giving disabled veterans a "New Deal" instead of "a raw deal" was in solving the inefficiency and disorganization of rehabilitation nationally by establishing "one responsible agency with the proper authority to administer a national program for the physically handicapped from medical diagnosis and treatment to full employment." The column's author suggested that this centerpiece of the AFPH agenda would ensure that Americans could "look our returning disabled service man in the eye and say, 'Welcome home, my boy!' " But "Uncle G.I. Joe" stopped making these connections. Indeed, the November 1945 column focused on the need for better services and administration in the VA, even calling for new leadership of the agency.[54]

The distance between the programs contributed to other missed opportunities for coalition. Disabled veterans and civilians encountered similar difficulties gaining access to colleges and universities. In response to these difficulties, the American Legion and a group of disabled veterans, including Harold Scharper, who been one of the founders of the Paralyzed Veterans of America, fought first for access to the University of Illinois campus at

Galesburg in 1947 and then for access to the main campus when the Galesburg campus closed in 1949.[55] Because veterans sought access to college campuses as part of their vocational rehabilitation, veterans and veterans' organizations led the charge for greater access, and the issue appeared not to have captured the attention of the AFPH.

At the end of rehabilitation, civilians and veterans faced the same uncertain economy and employment discrimination. In August 1946, the Employment Service had a backlog of over 200,000 applications from disabled veterans alone. The Department of Labor estimated that it would take more than twenty months to find those applicants jobs.[56] These realities, unlike those connected to the process of rehabilitation, led to shared work on promoting National Employ the Physically Handicapped Week (NEPHW). Indeed, from the very beginning, Strachan argued that that veterans should "be given the spotlight" in celebrations of the week "to impress upon the public that its cooperation in the success of the program is not only an economic necessity but a patriotic duty as well."[57] Veterans' participation in NEPHW likely reflected the sense that employment discrimination was a key area where the fate of disabled veterans and civilians, as Rice put it, were "inevitably linked up."[58]

On the AFPH's side, the organization's recruitment of disabled veterans and veteran organizations demonstrated Strachan's keen awareness of their political capital during the war and postwar years. This understanding of the power of disabled veterans led the AFPH to honor veterans' insistence on the separateness of veteran and civilian rehabilitation programs and to recruit disabled veterans' participation in AFPH events and veteran organizations' approval of AFPH proposals, even if real collaboration was limited. For example, the AFPH recruited Rice to serve as a vice president of the AFPH in 1945.[59] A 1948 program featured disabled veteran and movie star Harold Russell.[60] At other events, AFPH leaders recruited participation from Veterans of Foreign Wars leadership and the DAV Honor Guard.[61] In addition to the DAV's pledge of "fraternal cooperation" in 1945, the AFPH secured a pledge of support from AMVETS (or American Veterans) leadership in 1948.[62]

Still, the AFPH had to navigate its relationship with veterans carefully. The DAV and other veterans' organizations understood disabled veterans and civilians as occupying very different positions. These organizations resisted congressional efforts at a unified disability policy during the war and would continue to police the boundary between veteran and civilian disability policy.[63] Yet the AFPH had much to gain in emphasizing the connections between service, duty, nation, and disability. In courting veterans' support, however, the AFPH always carefully acknowledged disabled veterans and veterans' services as exceptions. Thus, in seeking veterans' membership and assistance, and celebrating veterans' service as exceptional, the AFPH undermined its own claims about the universality of the disability experience and the need for the federal government to consider disabled people as a single group.

The AFPH's push for unity across different disabilities contributed to strained relationships with existing disability rights organizations. Strachan's 1941 falling out with National Association of the Deaf (NAD) leadership, discussed in Chapter 1, not only pushed Strachan to go all-in on the AFPH and cross-disability organization but also contributed to ongoing tensions between NAD and the AFPH and foreshadowed the AFPH's continual struggle to motivate people with different disabilities, needs, and experiences to find common ground in the shared disabled identity. In his dealings with the NAD, Strachan had been unwilling to compromise. He could be a difficult man to work with if one's views diverged from his own, and deaf leaders who had experienced this difficulty began to think Strachan was unreasonable.[64]

NAD leaders spoke out against the AFPH and many of its proposals, resisting, in particular, the notion that deaf Americans shared any commonality with other people with disabilities. For instance, Marcus L. Kenner, legislative representative of the NAD, argued in 1944, "we resent being dragged into this conglomeration and to be included in the generalizations made by the American Federation of the Physically Handicapped, especially the nearly 12,000,000 suffering from chronic diseases." Clearly equating people with visible disabilities and chronic diseases and a campaign for government assistance with begging, he told congressmen that the NAD had "warred against peddlers, beggars, and their ilk,"—individuals he viewed as immoral.[65]

Kenner claimed that AFPH "policies would undermine the individual initiative of the deaf and substitute Government largess for personal responsibility." He attempted to distance deaf Americans from the needs that many AFPH members described, arguing "the deaf are absolutely not living in 'misery, privation, and despair' as the American Federation of the Physically Handicapped would want you to believe."[66] Historian Robert Buchanan attributes the attitude of NAD leaders toward the AFPH to the reluctance of deaf Americans to be associated with other people with disabilities. Many deaf

Americans resented their association with disability and sought to obtain employment without assistance or what they viewed as government handouts. Pride in deaf community and culture motivated many to balk at government aid and the notion of themselves as members of a broader community of people with disabilities—a community often associated with poverty and dependence.[67]

For his part, Strachan warned against the "natural jealousies" between disability organizations, yet criticized organizations such as the NAD that resisted cross-disability organization. He argued that "some groups hold themselves aloof from other groups of unfortunates, as 'inferiors' and 'mendicants,' because certain of these groups avail themselves of benefits from Community Chests and other national, State, and private-aid means." Strachan claimed that the leaders of these groups had gained security and therefore had "no understanding of, and little sympathy for, the problems of those who are, or may be, in the uttermost depths of misery, suffering from lack of food, raiment, and shelter, and lacking opportunities for employment." He further compared these leaders to "fat aldermen, smacking their lips over 'soup for the poor.'"[68] Strachan's critique painted disability leaders who worked against the AFPH as a privileged lot who lacked the empathy, experience, vision, or desire to address the needs of people with disabilities, suggesting the class tensions that may well have informed divides in the disability rights community.

In spite of the NAD's opposition to the AFPH, many deaf Americans joined the AFPH, even former NAD leaders. AFPH member J. Cooke Howard, a former president of the NAD and the Gallaudet College Alumni Association, argued, "The deaf have, after forty years or more, been unable, through their national organization, to interest the Federal Government in their efforts to improve the status of the deaf." Howard told an AFPH mass meeting that the deaf "have now joined with other handicapped groups, through the American Federation of the Physically Handicapped, to secure such recognition."[69] Other deaf community leaders filled the AFPH Committee of the Deaf, including two past presidents of the California Association of the Deaf, a former president of the Dixie Association of the Deaf, deaf school teachers, and a leader in the Baltimore, Maryland, Division of the National Fraternal Society of the Deaf.[70] Deaf AFPH members responded to the NAD's harsh words about the AFPH by voting at a convention that the AFPH "was their sole representative." One deaf member wrote to the House Subcommittee on Aid to the Physically Handicapped asking them to "overlook the fact that a certain deaf organization purporting to represent all the deaf" testified against the AFPH, suggesting that the NAD had less than "300 active members."[71] The AFPH's response to the NAD's public statements about it certainly did not help to repair the rift between the organizations. Moreover, these responses gloss over the NAD and state-level organizations' success in combatting attacks on sign language and efforts to push deaf teachers out of deaf schools in favor of oral instruction and communication and hearing teachers.[72]

The AFPH also failed to build a coalition with the National Federation of the Blind (NFB), an organization that shared many of the AFPH's aims and that might have sharpened the AFPH's demands. Like the AFPH, the NFB offered a powerful critique of the authority of professionals and bureaucrats who sought to serve people with disabilities, and more specifically blind people. NFB activists criticized the administration of Aid to the Blind and the sheltered workshops with which the federal government contracted. The organization demanded that blind recipients of Aid to the Blind be allowed to earn additional money without having their aid reduced and that the aid be provided without state supervision. Further, the NFB attacked the conditions in sheltered workshops, which were run by state agencies and private charities and profited from the labor of blind workers while paying those workers less than the minimum wage. The group sought to organize those workers and demanded protection under the Fair Labor Standards Act.[73]

The NFB would express support of the AFPH's broad goals, while offering a critique of its proposals for pensions and support of sheltered workshops. The NFB's criticisms grew out of its constituents' experiences dealing with the Aid to the Blind bureaucracy and the poor working conditions blind people faced in many sheltered workshops.[74] NFB leaders' critiques of AFPH legislation in congressional hearings suggest that the AFPH either did not seek, did not receive, or disregarded the advice and support of the NFB in developing its proposals. That advice and support most certainly would have strengthened the AFPH's legislative initiatives. Because blind people had been drawn into the welfare state from the start, NFB leaders were in a unique position among people with disabilities to analyze how even inclusions could stigmatize.

As the AFPH's difficult relationships with other disability rights organizations demonstrate, the needs and interests of people with different disabilities were not always the same. The type and circumstances of a disability informed cultural perceptions, limitations, and access to resources. Race, class, and gender also shaped how people experienced disabilities and how society perceived those disabilities as well as the AFPH's successes and failures in organizing and creating unity.

The AFPH program had broad appeal across class lines as its emphasis on jobs was as much about achieving independence, be it financial or personal, as it was about directly improving the economic lot of disabled Americans. While members came from all walks of life, it is likely that most members came from working-class families. The vast majority of AFPH lodges were located in industrial areas, and many lodges affiliated with local unions. Most AFPH members needed employment as much as they wanted to lead productive lives. Certainly, there were exceptions, but the AFPH equated disability with poverty caused by discrimination and health care costs. While this analysis might not have held up for disabled citizens from very wealthy families, disability and inability to obtain employment undoubtedly caused financial strain for most members.

Still, the AFPH's zeal to demonstrate worthiness for citizenship and demands that members place disability and the interests of the organization above other facets of their identities made the AFPH vulnerable to the Red Scare. In 1950, Strachan urged members "to be alert to the danger of Communists and others who may try to 'worm their way' into AFPH." At that same convention, Senator Sparkman, who had by then been elected to fill a vacant seat in the Senate, argued that people with disabilities could and should play a significant role in meeting "the present challenge by a ruthless foe." Members voted that day to deny membership to anyone who would not take an oath of allegiance to the United States.[75] The anticommunist movement weakened organizations by purging radical voices and silencing many important debates. Communism had become the antithesis of American patriotism and loyalty, and in their quest to be viewed as proper and patriotic citizens, AFPH members reacted quickly to assert their loyalty to the nation while making radical members unwelcome.[76]

The complex entanglement of gender and disability discrimination created additional barriers to full citizenship for women with disabilities and consequently drew them to the AFPH in large numbers. Despite growing employment outside of the home and continued organization among women, women experienced discrimination in education and employment and a tightening of gender roles in the immediate postwar period. Women could expect to be paid less for equal work, and whether employed or not, they continued to hold full responsibility for the upkeep of the home and the care of the children.[77]

The situation was far more complex for women with disabilities. Parents often trained their disabled daughters to defy traditional roles, as women with disabilities, historians Paul K. Longmore and David Goldberger argue, "have often been stigmatized as unsuited for the traditional wife-and-mother role." Parents, instead, pushed disabled young women "to establish alternative valid identities through school and career." One disability activist in the 1930s reported that her mother encouraged her to earn a professional degree and to become self-supporting in preparation for the likelihood that she would never marry. "Defined as both unmarriageable and unemployable," Longmore and Goldberger find, women joined activist organizations to demand greater opportunities.[78] A similar dynamic was at work in postwar America. Disabled women faced employment and social discrimination. The AFPH offered women with disabilities a social space where they found acceptance, and some found marriage at a time when society questioned their capacity to fulfill the roles of wife and mother. That said, women, as much as men, took seriously the organization's mission to end employment and educational discrimination. Women in the AFPH fought alongside their male counterparts for antidiscrimination legislation and improvements in the administration of federal disability policy. One AFPH activist, Virginia A. Pearson, wrote, "I have no thought that I am indispensable to a better world, but to contribute my share and to be independent is a forceful urge within me."[79]

For women in the AFPH, this activist impulse placed them at odds with prevailing gender ideals. Still, as Longmore and Goldberger suggest, parents and community members had sent a clear message that disabled women could not expect to conform; instead, they should find ways to be self-supporting.[80] Through the AFPH, women did just that. They not only participated in local chapters but also held leadership roles within the national organization. Mildred Scott, the secretary of the organization for more than a decade and later the secretary-treasurer, worked tirelessly for people with disabilities. Iride Valmassy served not only as an officer in Detroit but also as a national vice president. Other women, like Margaret Nickerson Martin, Agnes Schnaus, Mary Krasnogor, and Florence Foerster, also served as national vice presidents.[81] These leaders echoed the needs of their fellow AFPH women when they demanded employment and even spoke out about the amplified discrimination they experienced as disabled women. In 1948, Valmassy told the *Detroit Times*, "It's still so much harder for a woman to get a chance. You can't even get in to see the employment managers."[82] Valmassy's struggle for employment, made difficult because of her disability and compounded because of her gender, reflected broader problems women with disabilities faced in postwar America.

African Americans with disabilities too experienced multiple and entangling layers of discrimination in the postwar period. Some responded to the call of the AFPH and joined local chapters. Yet the AFPH's federated structure tolerated segregation in southern chapters, tarnishing the legacy of the AFPH on issues of race. Moreover, the AFPH's relationship with the broader African American community was fraught with difficulty. Even as the AFPH sought to expand and improve federal services for people with disabilities, African Americans struggled to access those benefits. For example, Alice A. Dunnigan, a representative of the Associated Negro Press who was actively engaged in promoting NEPHW, told senators hearing testimony on the civilian rehabilitation program in 1950 that disabled African Americans faced a rehabilitation service that cared little about their welfare. She noted that while millions of African Americans had disabilities, they were not "being afforded the service they need, and assuredly, all-too-little of States' rehabilitation activities concerns itself with colored people."[83]

Initially, the AFPH's attempts to create broader employment opportunities for people with disabilities received little support from African American organizations that at times viewed the program with suspicion. Reporting on an AFPH-sponsored luncheon in celebration of NEPHW in 1951, Dunnigan wrote, "Only two or three Negroes, however, manifested enough interest in the employment of the Negro handicapped to participate," despite the fact that numerous invitations had been sent to organizations and individuals. Dunnigan admonished African Americans to pay more attention to issues of disability, reminding them that African Americans with disabilities had to "battle segregation, because of race and discrimination because of physical disability."[84]

Some African Americans viewed the efforts to educate the public about disabled workers as an active dismissal of racial discrimination. Whereas Dunnigan saw a campaign that could benefit African Americans with disabilities, others assumed that NEPHW represented an effort to elevate disabled white workers over able-bodied African American ones. The African American newspaper the *Pittsburgh Courier* printed a scathing review of the 1951 NEPHW campaign, arguing that prominent speakers had failed to highlight "the necessity for not discriminating against workers handicapped by color." The paper claimed, "We get rather weary of these pious patriotic pronouncements emanating from prominent leaders from time to time, failing, as they usually do, to touch upon the really pertinent issues of the day." While people with disabilities encountered increasing opportunities, the paper argued, African Americans continued to face discrimination on the basis of color. The article concluded that perhaps "a National Employ-the-Racially-Handicapped Week" was in order.[85] The *Pittsburgh Courier* highlighted the tensions between disability and African American activism. African Americans had yet to gain the full access to economic citizenship that people with disabilities demanded, and their response suggests that many African Americans viewed the campaign as a distraction to the pressing issues of racial discrimination.

The AFPH struggled to recruit African American support for the organization and its campaigns. However, the relationship changed significantly once J. Rosemond Cook, Jr., began a campaign to make African Americans aware of the AFPH and the AFPH's national leadership cognizant of the unique issues faced by disabled African Americans. A former Morehouse College football player, Cook had Buerger's disease, which led to the eventual loss of all his limbs. In 1952, he launched Atlanta Lodge 135 with thirty-one members, who were, according to *Valor*, "some of the most prominent leaders" of Atlanta's African American community. Cook hosted a weekly radio broadcast in Atlanta to discuss the "movement" and established the Colored Division of the Georgia Department of the AFPH. "Despite these handicaps," he told *Valor* readers, "I desire to live a normal life, and I want to devote my life to the promotion" of the AFPH.[86]

The AFPH condoned the South's Jim Crow system of separate and unequal treatment of African Americans by allowing segregation in its southern chapters. Cook then was compelled to organize separate chapters and state departments for African Americans with disabilities. Still, national AFPH publications covered his successes in Georgia with pride, and members elected Cook to serve as a national vice president, a role that gave him the opportunity to testify before a House committee about racial discrimination in Georgia's rehabilitation program. "J. Rosemond Cook ('Jim,' to the Convention)," *Valor* reported in October 1952, "talked, sang and acted his way into the hearts of the delegates, who elected him a Veep, after he pledged to devote the rest of his life to furthering AFPH work. Jim says he will organize the Colored people in the South, and elsewhere, and he has already made a splendid start in that direction."[87] *Valor*'s coverage of Cook's efforts hinted at the tensions that remained embedded in the organization around issues of race. The magazine used the term "Colored" when "Negro" was the preferred term, and its characterization of Cook as endearing himself to members by talking, singing, and acting suggested their acceptance of him was laden with racialized stereotypes of otherness. The national agenda of the AFPH never explicitly addressed the kind of double discrimination African Americans with disabilities faced, but still, the national organization welcomed Cook and his efforts to create state and local chapters. He used his power within the segregated chapters of Atlanta to force racial discrimination into the consciousness of national members and leaders.[88] In marginalizing African Americans, the Jim Crow system also created spaces for African American organizations and leadership; Cook exploited, as best he could, this space in the racist Jim Crow system to benefit African Americans with disabilities.[89] Yet, despite Cook's organizational work, the AFPH celebrated his successes without really rethinking the relationship between race and disability and addressing its own tolerance of segregation in the South.

The AFPH courted physically disabled members across the spectrum of disability and experiences of disability. Physical disability, dues, and eventually a loyalty pledge were the only requirements for full membership in the organization. Creating unity among such a diverse group of people proved to be a difficult task for the AFPH. People with different types of disabilities, disabled in different ways, with various financial means, and some facing multiple types of discrimination expressed different needs and desires. The federated structure of the AFPH would allow the organization to overcome some of these difficulties, giving groups a great deal of latitude to address issues of special concern to different lodges. In the end, the differences of class, gender, and race proved to be less of a sticking point for the organization than creating unity among people with different types of disabilities. The economic focus of the AFPH and its call to end educational and workforce discrimination appealed to members across class, gender, and race lines.

Local Communities

For those who joined and participated in the AFPH, the organization facilitated the growth of disability rights communities that contributed to the development of a collective identity and political critique. Members found commonality in shared experiences of discrimination and disappointment with state and federal services. They countered collective experiences of exclusion, isolation, discrimination, and dissatisfaction with rehabilitation with a new community formed around the experience of disability and the opportunity to create better circumstances. This is not to suggest that all AFPH members were unsuccessful and unemployed, but that most could easily remember a time when they felt excluded or treated unfairly.

The Shiawassee County, Michigan, chapter, a group of around twenty-five, created a community that allowed members to learn about others' disabilities, identify problems in the area, and take action as a group. Roger Arnett, who would eventually become a national vice president of the AFPH, organized the chapter. Arnett's wife LaVerna, who was also disabled, provided refreshments for the meetings. In doing so, she began to recognize the kinds of accommodations others might need. She noticed that one blind member refused food every time plates were passed. LaVerna responded by making him a sandwich, setting the plate of food on his lap, and describing to him what she had served him. The strategy worked. He had refused food because he did not know what was being served. LaVerna and other members continued to learn about creating an accessible environment. She realized that she should not refresh a blind person's coffee without telling the person or move furniture before a blind person visited. As members created an accessible AFPH community, they began to look to beyond the confines of the group toward the broader community. For example, the chapter worked with a local church group to build a ramp to make the church accessible.[90] Like AFPH groups across the country, the Shiawassee County AFPH chapter fostered a sense of community and shared interest, allowing members to recognize the broader social implications of a shared disability experience. Members created a more universal understanding of disability as the organization sensitized members to the challenges of disabilities beyond their own—an important step in uniting members around a national cross-disability agenda.

AFPH members organized political rallies and a host of social events. AFPH members in Detroit, New York City, and Washington, D.C., held mass meetings in support of AFPH legislation in 1946.[91] Later that year, one of several New York City chapters celebrated NEPHW with a ball.[92] Local chapters hosted card parties, banquets, dinners, picnics, and Valentine's Day, Halloween, and Christmas parties.[93] For example, in addition to political rallies, Detroit AFPH members held a "Grand Dance-Floor Show," sponsored a weekend retreat, and formed a baseball team, proudly reporting to the national organization that they had "licked" the Flint Association of the Deaf at a margin of 20-2 in 1945.[94] The frequency of these social events suggests the importance of the AFPH in members' social and recreational lives.

Local chapters also engaged in political activities by addressing local and state needs. For instance, Perry E. Seely, a national vice president of the AFPH, and members in the Los Angeles, California, area launched a "Jobs for the Handicapped" campaign in response to disabled workers "getting the 'axe'" in California plants in the fall of 1945.[95] Seely, along with other prominent deaf leaders in California, also led the charge to get a new state school for the deaf in southern California, arguing that population growth had left the state's facilities inadequate.[96] The campaign secured two million dollars for the new school.[97] Krasnogor, also a national vice president of the AFPH, pushed for legislation in her home state of Massachusetts mandating ramps in public and semipublic buildings.[98]

As the Cold War intensified, members sought new ways to demonstrate their patriotism and contribute to national defense. During World War II, members had supported the war effort in numerous ways, ranging from war employment to sorting scrap and calling workers, and then used their patriotism and wartime contributions to make arguments for disabled people's rights as citizens. During the Cold War era, members participated in civil defense. In 1952, Washington, D.C., Lodge 94 sponsored first-aid courses, where instructors trained individuals unable to perform mouth-to-mouth resuscitation to direct others in artificial respiration. In seeking this training, members continued their efforts to demonstrate both their patriotism and fitness as citizens.[99]

Like many AFPH chapters, Atlanta Lodge 135—the city's black chapter—played an important social role in the lives of disabled African Americans, hosting teas, gospel singing events, and a sweetheart ball, but unlike other chapters, Atlanta Lodge 135 provided important social services to African American community members often denied to them by existing local, state, and federal programs. In partnership with African American churches, chapter president Cook raised funds to provide scholarships, food, rent, coal, clothing, and assistive devices to disabled African Americans and their families. He referred individuals to the rehabilitation and state welfare programs and monitored the progress of those referrals. In 1955, he reported that in the previous fiscal year he had referred seventy-seven individuals "apparently eligible for rehabilitation and welfare benefits" to the proper agencies, but just twenty-two received help. Cook also arranged emergency transportation for disabled community members for physician and hospital visits, provided transportation to AFPH meetings, and referred disabled individuals to sympathetic employers.[100]

Participation in the AFPH community also sparked romance for many members. In 1952 *Valor*, the AFPH magazine, reported, "CUPID HAS JOINED AFPH! Proof is—from many Lodges we receive word that couples are pairing off, getting ready for the BIG LEAP YEAR. . . . [I]t seems that AFPH is turning into a sort of matrimonial bureau."[101] Engagements and marriages between members routinely filled the pages of *Valor*. For example, *Valor* reported that Mary Jane Fields of Indianapolis and John Weber of Detroit were "gonna get spliced." Fields, readers learned, had attended an AFPH meeting in Detroit after which Weber had "been keeping the roads hot, visiting her."[102] While often reported with light-hearted quips, marriage held increasing political weight in the postwar period, for all Americans. Marriage in the United States, historians have shown, has been intimately connected to civil rights. The institution served to define distinctions between citizens by legitimizing some families while stigmatizing others.[103] But, in the late 1940s and 1950s, Cold War anxieties and vilification of homosexuality added further political weight to the institution, as these tensions cemented links between marriage, reproduction, and citizenship.[104] In this context, few other experiences would have been as normative, and perhaps as meaningful, for AFPH members as marriage—an institution from which people with disabilities had often been excluded, socially and in some cases legally. Historically numerous states banned marriage for individuals deemed "idiots" or "insane," but many also included people with epilepsy among those banned from the institution.[105] Marriage offered AFPH members participation in an institution that stood at the center of American civic life.

The AFPH facilitated the development of vibrant communities of people with disabilities, which, in turn, cultivated a sense of commonality and a shared disability identity. In creating a separate space for disabled members to share in these activities, the AFPH community rejected cultural assumptions that physical disabilities equated social ones. In AFPH chapters, members' personal difficulties became collective and political as members came to understand these challenges as preventing their full participation in the economic and civic life of the nation. As members socialized, the experience of disability was both normalized and politicized. These social spaces fueled the national agenda and sustained the organization. The picnics, parties, and marriages that happened on the local level would shape activists' demands for inclusion and provide important opportunities for members to demonstrate their worthiness for the full citizenship they would demand on the national level.

Coalition

Alongside their drive for organization, AFPH leaders sought to develop coalitions to support the organization's efforts. Members' diverse identities and experiences of disability shaped their access to resources, the limitations they encountered, and the ways their disabilities were perceived. While these diverse experiences could challenge the unity the AFPH sought to foster, they also expanded the range of organizations with which the AFPH could engage. Members and leaders drew from their personal and individual experiences to access other movements to varying degrees of success. The interactions between the organization and other social movements shaped the AFPH ideology, its claims, demands, successes, and failures. But the AFPH and its members also influenced the organizations and movements that supported it as the AFPH worked to place disability on the agendas of allied organizations and frame it as a national concern.

In November 1945, Strachan told an AFPH mass meeting that he planned "to give labor, veterans, scientists, professors, and whatnot, the worst dose of 'gimme' they ever had in their lives."[106] The "dose of 'gimme'" Strachan intended to give organized labor and others would come in the form of specific assistance—money, personnel, support of specific legislative aims, and participation in AFPH events—as well as a broader ideological support. His assertion, however lighthearted the tone, signaled an important strategy for the AFPH—coalition building.

The disability rights movement was not a passive recipient of the knowledge and experience of other social movements. Instead, as scholar Susan Schweik argues, disability rights activism, particularly in the 1970s, happened within a matrix of movements. Many disability rights activists participated in the disability rights movement along with other social movements. Those activists facilitated alliances and coalition by making other social movement organizations conscious of disability. Operating within a matrix meant that activists participated in a reciprocal process, shaping and being shaped by multiple movements.[107]

The idea of a matrix of social movements is particularly powerful in the context of the AFPH and the "dose of 'gimme'" Strachan intended to administer. The differences that sometimes challenged unity within the AFPH also created opportunities for coalition, expanding the matrix of movements with which the organization could engage. The AFPH and its members used the ideologies, demands, and language of the organized labor movement, and to a lesser degree that of the African American civil rights movement and women's organizations, sought support and assistance from those movements, but also worked within those movements to highlight the ways that disability fit within the organizations' existing goals and to make disability a more central concern. Further, as the AFPH sought to build coalitions, its partner organizations participated in constructing the meaning assigned to the AFPH's demands, challenges, and successes.

The AFPH courted and won the support of organized labor, drawing on members' connections at the local level as well as Strachan's network from his days as a labor organizer. In November 1945, James B. Carey, secretary-treasurer of the CIO, told an AFPH mass meeting that he had been "advised, in a confidential way," not to attend the AFPH meeting and asked to dissuade the secretary of labor from attending. Carey did not reveal the source of this advice, but he suggested that he took the advice as "a credential for [the AFPH]" and a sign that the organization was "not in favor of the status quo." He drew a parallel between organized labor and the AFPH, arguing that both groups were "demanding that our nation give consideration to its human resources." Carey encouraged further organization among people with disabilities and emphasized that the AFPH, organized labor, and others were in the same fight, to "make democracy work" and ensure "that all people have the opportunity to secure dignity through employment."[108] Other union representatives spoke on unity between organized labor and disabled people as well, drawing parallels between economic handicaps and physical ones.[109]

Organized labor's interaction with the AFPH pushed labor leaders to think about disability's place within the labor movement's agenda. Labor leaders who spoke at the AFPH's mass meeting positioned the AFPH and organized labor in a similar fight, linking the AFPH agenda to labor's broader thinking about democracy, the postwar liberal agenda, and more specifically the drive for full employment.[110] The interactions between organized labor and disability activists influenced both movements. In many ways, disability had always been a labor issue, but in supporting the AFPH and disability rights, labor leaders began to understand disability in new ways. And the AFPH's calls for assistance pushed disability more firmly onto labor's postwar agenda. Likewise, labor leaders' advice, support, and ideological framing of disability issues helped to develop and shape the AFPH's own interpretative framework.[111]

Similarly, J. Rosemond Cook, Jr., reframed the AFPH agenda for African American members and allies by emphasizing racial discrimination in services and employment opportunities for African Americans with disabilities. While focused on Georgia, Cook and Atlanta Lodge 135 developed important connections with African American churches and civic organizations—different partnerships than northern whites developed. Cook and the Atlanta Lodge 135 helped to redefine African Americans' relationship with the AFPH. From its inception forward, the chapter cemented strong ties to African American churches and civic organizations. In its charter ceremony held at the Wheat Street Baptist Church, African American ministers from Atlanta's African Methodist Episcopal churches and several Baptist churches—many of the same churches that would play a central role in the African American civil rights movement—grounded the AFPH campaign in Christian doctrine, adding spiritual and moral backing to the organization's cause.[112] With the support of local churches, the *Atlanta Daily World*, and numerous other African American organizations, Cook reshaped the AFPH platform, at least locally, incorporating growing resistance against segregation and a Christian appeal to help less fortunate members of the community. On the national level, Cook's activities, as noted above, received much coverage in the pages of *Valor* and may have contributed to its national readership being more aware of the links between Jim Crow discrimination and the exclusion that people with disabilities frequently faced.

Men and women leaders of the AFPH marshaled gendered expectations and women's work to disrupt those expectations in an effort to gain the support of women's organizations. In May 1942, Strachan wrote, "Women, because of their natural sympathy for the unfortunate and because, also, as homemakers, they are particularly vulnerable and sensitive, when disaster strikes down the family support, should have a prominent place" in promoting NEPHW.[113] Strachan's analysis of women's role in the AFPH drew on traditional gender roles—women as homemakers and caregivers, more sensitive to the needs of "the unfortunate." In seeking the support of women's organizations and demanding expanded programs for people with disabilities, women in the AFPH drew on these gendered expectations while also suggesting that disability would make women's quest for greater opportunities difficult.

In 1949, Mildred Scott told Zonta Club members, a national service organization of professional women who sought to improve opportunities for women, that they, and women more broadly, should "concern themselves" with disability. Whereas Strachan had described women as "vulnerable" when the breadwinner experienced disability, Scott appealed to Zonta Club members as citizens, managers of finances, professionals, and women who might experience disability personally or through a family member. She noted that roughly one half of the estimated twenty-eight to fifty-five million Americans who had disabilities were women.[114]

Scott described how disability discrimination had negated her training and education and prevented her from becoming a teacher in Pennsylvania, where, like many other states, people with visible disabilities were barred from teaching. She encouraged members to develop a study group on disability to examine federal and state legislation and see for themselves the realities that people with disabilities encountered. Scott suggested that members imagine that they had "suffered a sudden, severe disability" that would prevent them from returning to their professions. She called on them to consider the costs and availability of services and challenged them to find out if the states they had grown up in were among the majority that exhausted rehabilitation appropriations long before new funds were available. Scott speculated that in those conditions many of the women would use up their savings rapidly and find the absence of services startling. Additionally, she asked the club to assist with NEPHW and write to Congress in support of AFPH legislation and individual members in their professional lives to consider giving qualified disabled applicants "a break."[115]

Still, family and gendered expectations figured into Scott's appeal to Zonta women. She portrayed disability as an economic problem that could threaten even secure American families. Scott claimed that women "are closer to disaster, when it strikes," and asked Zonta women to consider their role if a child or any other family member became disabled. Indeed, she described her own activism as an effort to ensure that "mothers, wives, daughters, sisters, and others who have assumed family responsibilities have things a bit easier than my own mother had." Essentially, AFPH women both spoke to the ways that disability could enhance the financial and legal hurdles women faced and drew on traditional family roles to appeal to other women and to justify their own activism—they were working to ease the difficulties their own and other families had or could experience.[116]

If difference represented an organizational challenge to the AFPH, it also presented opportunities for the organization to build coalitions and expand the matrix in which it operated. Through members' and leaders' diverse experiences, the organization gained access to potential coalition partners. Interactions with labor, African American civil rights, and women's organizations shaped the ways in which AFPH activists framed their demands and understood the problems they confronted. Further, these interactions helped to make other movement organizations, particularly the labor movement, more cognizant of issues of disability. As much as organized labor leaders came to understand AFPH demands for employment opportunities in line with their own efforts to secure postwar prosperity and greater opportunities and protections for workers, AFPH leaders worked to secure a place for disability in that agenda.

The Medicalization of Civilian Rehabilitation

While the AFPH recruited members and worked to create organizational unity and gain external support, the wartime Barden-La Follette Act continued to transform disability services in the early postwar years. As labor shortages and the pressure for quick results disappeared with the end of the war, the rehabilitation program focused on developing a bureaucracy to deliver the expanded services outlined in the act. With these wider services, policymakers and administrators set in motion a medicalization and professionalization of rehabilitation. As physicians, counselors, and a range of new experts redefined rehabilitation, people with disabilities increasingly became the subjects of expert scrutiny, marked as patients in need of care and correction, and serving as the means by which these professionals asserted their expertise and authority. Just as the war encouraged new expectations among people with disabilities, the medicalization of rehabilitation subverted those new expectations, as it marked Americans with disabilities as others and subjects. The state's efforts to make employment accessible to people with disabilities would come with supervision.

The implementation of the Barden-LaFollette Act necessarily meant that the separation between vocational and medical rehabilitation was disintegrating in the civilian rehabilitation bureaucracy as medicine now played an important role in both the rehabilitation bureaucracy and process. As the Federal Security Agency (FSA) began to fully realize the long-term potential of the Barden-LaFollette Act, the rehabilitation service reconceived disability and rehabilitation. Rehabilitation became less an educational and training program and more a program to provide medical treatment for people with disabilities. With new medical resources to call on, leaders in the rehabilitation program began to view disability increasingly in medical and psychological terms. In 1946, Dr. Albert W. Bryan, a medical administrative consultant to the Wisconsin Rehabilitation Division, argued that prior to the implementation of Barden-La Follette Act provisions for medical services, the rehabilitation program had been simply "training around" a person's disability by teaching the individual a new skill. It had been, according to him, a limited approach that served "to improve his vocational capacities rather than his vocational status." Now the federal-state rehabilitation program could provide medical care to remove or modify the disability as well as training.[117] The service now focused more explicitly on the disability and correcting the individual and less on the ways that education and training could prepare the disabled individual for an occupation.

Wartime medical advancements in the care of wounded soldiers made the marriage of the federal-state rehabilitation service and the medical profession an increasingly alluring proposition. Broadly, medical advances during the war had transformed physicians' capacity to save lives and treat disease. The introduction of sulfa drugs, penicillin, and the technology to more safely type, store, and transfuse blood and plasma on a wide scale led the Army Medical Department to declare in May 1945 that more than 60,000 soldiers had survived wounds that would have been fatal during World War I.[118] Physicians in the field of rehabilitation medicine had long sought legitimacy and professional status, and the needs of the war catapulted the marginal field of medicine into the limelight. Through their work with wounded soldiers and increasingly with the rehabilitation program, rehabilitation physicians achieved professional legitimacy and claimed dominance over a growing market—both people with disabilities in general and clients of the civilian rehabilitation program in particular.[119] Physicians and rehabilitation counselors claimed authority in the rehabilitation service because of their expertise in the field of disability, creating a hierarchy that weighted education and expertise of the practitioner over experience of disabled people.

The Barden-LaFollette Act radically altered the civilian rehabilitation program, both creating a space for rehabilitation medicine within the program and rapidly expanding the professional responsibilities of civilian rehabilitation workers. To "provide a comprehensive service" to people with disabilities in peacetime, the new Office of Vocational Rehabilitation (OVR) established several new layers of bureaucracy to manage the expansion of the rehabilitation program and police standards: two divisions, divisional sections, and eight regional offices. Additionally, it established two advisory committees—with representatives drawn from the fields of social welfare, education, and medicine as well as business, industry, and labor—"to bring outside professional advice in the matters of general policy," and more specifically to gain medical insight for the development and administration of the physical restoration program.[120]

State bureaucracies also grew dramatically, both in the number of people employed and in the diversity of positions held. In 1943, the states and territories employed 438 rehabilitation counselors. In 1945, the number had grown to 674.[121] In 1938, the U.S. Office of Education listed three state-level positions in the rehabilitation bureaucracy: state director, district director, and case worker or field agent.[122] By 1944, some states began to add new positions to their rehabilitation bureaucracies: medical administrative consultants, supervisors of physical restoration, and medical social work consultants. Moreover, states also appointed professional advisory committees to help shape new policies.[123] By 1945, the OVR reported fourteen different professional positions in the general state rehabilitation bureaucracies and an additional thirteen positions in states that maintained separate rehabilitation bureaucracies for blind people.[124]

The pressure to rapidly expand the size of state bureaucracies, provide workers for wartime manpower needs, and implement a new vision of rehabilitation at the same time slowed the codification of long-range policies. In 1944, the OVR sponsored sixteen regional conferences, and both state agencies and regional representatives of the OVR held numerous training sessions and workshops to educate employees about the possibilities of the new law.[125] Still, members of the rehabilitation bureaucracy struggled to define the contours of medicine's and physicians' role in rehabilitation. In 1946, Dr. Bryan sought to clarify OVR medical policies for *Journal of Rehabilitation* readers. He argued that the physical examination was the center of the new rehabilitation policy, making physicians central to the rehabilitation process. Eligibility for services centered on three criteria: age, disability, and the potential for rehabilitation to make the individual "employable or more advantageously employable." While the physical examination played an integral role in the determination of one's eligibility for rehabilitation, physicians' role in rehabilitation did not stop there.[126]

The state professional advisory committees, made up of physicians and specialists, advised state bureaucracies on a diverse set of issues, ranging from general policymaking to the specific workings of rehabilitation, including the "setting of standards" for everything from rates to services to prosthetic appliances. Beyond their role on the professional advisory committees, physicians who served as medical administrative consultants, like Bryan, provided advice on individual cases and the day-to-day execution of policies. They monitored standards, facilitated relationships with outside institutions and physicians, provided training to rehabilitation case workers, and evaluated cases and rehabilitation plans. In this new rehabilitation model, case workers worked alongside and under the supervision of physicians and the medical social work consultants. In Bryan's estimation, this bureaucracy placed medical and social concerns—"family problems, emotional attitudes, and economic resources of the individual"—at the center of the process, but it displaced the wartime priority of remunerative employment.[127]

Overall, medical treatment became an increasingly important part of the rehabilitation process. In 1944, the rehabilitation program provided physical restoration services to just 2 percent and prosthetic devices to 5 percent of the clients rehabilitated that year.[128] By 1953, the percentage of rehabilitants receiving medical care and prosthetic devices had grown dramatically. The civilian rehabilitation program provided surgical and medical treatments to 27.5 percent, hospital care for 20 percent, and prosthetic appliances to 24.9 percent of the disabled clients rehabilitated that year.[129]

In addition to physical restoration, the Barden-LaFollette Act opened the door to psychiatric services. In 1946, Dr. Milton Rosenbaum, psychiatrist and member of the Ohio Professional Advisory Committee, provided guidance on the use of psychiatric services in the rehabilitation process. To be considered eligible for these services, an individual had to be "more or less competent to handle his own affairs." Under the new law, a range of neuroses, depression, and schizophrenia qualified individuals for rehabilitation. But Rosenbaum also noted that people with physical disabilities might need psychiatric services if "emotional factors or mental attitudes" hindered the rehabilitation process. For people who qualified for psychiatric services, the program could offer hospitalization for up to ninety days and outpatient treatment.[130]

By making people with physical disabilities eligible for psychiatric services, the federal-state rehabilitation program reified the common association of physical disability with mental illness. This association informed not just psychiatry and psychology but also shaped medicine and rehabilitation more broadly. For example, a 1941 psychology textbook claimed that while people with disabilities used the same forms of adjustment as able-bodied people, disabled people were more likely than the able-bodied to use adjustment mechanisms that were not "of a socially desirable nature."[131] Moreover, nurse Alice B. Morrissey counseled *American Journal of Nursing* readers to accept the "new concept that the patient with a disability is truly a whole person, albeit one who has numerous problems" because "the problems of his mind" cannot be "separated from the ills of his body."[132] While this new focus on both the mind and body certainly might have benefited individuals who struggled to adapt to a disability, the underlying assumption that most people with disabilities would be "maladjusted" had the effect of placing all people with disabilities who sought rehabilitation services under a new layer of expert scrutiny accompanied by expectations of mental or emotional deviancy.

Though rehabilitation increasingly began to focus on the individual, medical social work consultants brought some attention to forces beyond the individual's control, in many ways providing an implicit challenge to physicians' and counselors' authority. Yet these new experts also brought their own claims to authority over disabled people's lives. For example, in 1946, Katharine F. Post, a medical social work consultant in Michigan, questioned if the rehabilitation program had been too quick to deny services to many people with disabilities, deeming some "not sufficiently cooperative" without analyzing the broader social context within which the individual operated. An individual's "resentment of imposed restrictions, or hurt over the disfigurement of a handicap," she wrote, "are often expressed in resentment against those who try to help." Post feared that counselors often met that resentment "with matching irritation," leading to a quick judgment of uncooperativeness. She also worried that physicians' insensitivity led many disabled people to decline rehabilitative help. Beyond the interactions between counselor and client, physician and patient, Post urged counselors to be aware of the ways that family relationships, past experiences in securing assistance, employer and community attitudes, and the location and hours of the rehabilitation office not only shaded a person's response to rehabilitation but also shaped its effectiveness and accessibility.[133]

Rehabilitation case workers—the people who handled the day-to-day business of rehabilitation, provided vocational guidance, developed training plans, and monitored individuals' progress—responded to the influx of new professionals in the field by asserting their own professional status, increasingly defining themselves as counselors and not case workers. This name change—case worker to counselor—reflected both a growing preoccupation with status and expertise and a desire to differentiate between the role of the counselor and the social worker—social workers had long been engaged in case work. In a series of editorials in the *Journal of Rehabilitation*, National Rehabilitation Association leadership focused much attention on the professional status of rehabilitation counselors, supervisors, and directors. While physicians claimed increased authority in rehabilitation because of their specific, professional knowledge of the body, the mind, and disease, rehabilitation counselors delineated their expertise as working knowledge in a broad array of fields. Harry D. Hicker, head of the California Bureau of Rehabilitation, declared that rehabilitation counselors and supervisors needed to have a special "vision" and understanding of "the world of occupations, the realms of the mind, the wonders of personality, the whys of behavior, the marvelous physical structure of man."[134]

As rehabilitation work became increasingly professionalized and medicalized, the disabled individual became the object of growing "expert" scrutiny. On the whole, the Barden-LaFollette Act led to the establishment of a multilayered bureaucracy that centered on correcting the individual through medicine, psychiatry, psychology, education, and training. Wartime labor needs and the time it took to develop a new bureaucracy had initially tempered this new medical focus. In the long term, as more attention was paid to medical interventions and psychological processes, the end goal of employment would increasingly get lost in the process.

The reconversion moment held considerable power, not just for disability activists but for a broad range of individuals whose lives had been transformed by the war. Reconversion's success or failure would determine whether wartime prosperity would continue or the dark days of the Depression would return. The process would sort out which wartime transformations were temporary dislocations and which were permanent gains. The AFPH sought to extend federal wartime efforts to bring disabled people into the workforce during the uncertain postwar period. People with disabilities translated Roosevelt's vision for a postwar world free from fear and want into demands that the state continue its wartime commitment to facilitate disabled people's access to the workforce, education, and health care. Still, the AFPH stood at a critical juncture. Having won a congressional investigation and the NEPHW in the context of the war, the organization forged ahead toward its goal of restructuring and reframing disability services and gaining federal support in ending employment discrimination—far broader goals that would provoke significant opposition—without the justification of the war emergency. Increasingly, AFPH leaders and policymakers would link the organization's agenda to the broader postwar liberal agenda, to Roosevelt's broad promises of economic security and Truman's developing Fair Deal. As AFPH activists prepared for the coming fight, they sought to foster unity around the experience of disability and cultivate allies among those who were at the fore of expanding the boundaries of citizenship and fighting to realize Roosevelt's vision for new freedoms and economic rights.

At the same time, however, civilian vocational rehabilitation was experiencing its own transformation—one that would shape the opposition that the AFPH would face. As the rehabilitation service expanded to incorporate physicians and social workers, the program adopted a greater emphasis on medicine, science, and professionalism. Physicians asserted authority over decisions about individuals' eligibility for the program, their occupational choices, and training plans. Their increasing involvement in rehabilitation marked people with disabilities as patients in need of care and medical correction, whose experiences mattered only in individual diagnoses. As physicians, counselors, and social workers struggled to define their position within the civilian rehabilitation program and against other professionals, people with disabilities increasingly became the subjects of multiple layers of expertise. More than just subjects of this expertise, people with disabilities also became the means through which these experts asserted their professional authority. The AFPH would challenge this new dynamic, but physicians and rehabilitation authorities would also draw on their expertise to resist AFPH efforts to remake rehabilitation in the postwar period.

Chapter 4

It's Good Business: Disability and Employment

As American Federation of the Physically Handicapped (AFPH) efforts to launch a public education campaign took shape and gained growing state support, American radio listeners might have heard about Frank and Catherine in October 1946. Frank was a large man who worked as a welder and whose boss thought of him "as a darned good investment." Catherine was an "attractive, good-humored and efficient" typist at the Veterans Administration (VA) where she was considered a team player and an "excellent" worker. In a calculated aside, listeners would have found out that Frank used a prosthetic arm and Catherine was blind. Throughout the month, but particularly during the week of 6–12 October, National Employ the Physically Handicapped Week (NEPHW), Americans learned the business and policy sense of hiring disabled employees. Sold as "loyal," "careful," and able to "match the output of unimpaired workers," disabled workers, Americans were told, made for "good business." More important, the fate of disabled citizens mattered to all Americans. According to information distributed widely by various federal agencies, unemployed disabled people represented "national liabilities," but jobs could transform those liabilities into "assets," productive and contributing members of communities.[1] The campaign and the message that unemployment among disabled citizens mattered to all Americans represented a critical step in the AFPH's broader agenda.

Understanding public education as vital to the success of the organization, AFPH leaders sought to achieve several goals through NEPHW. While the organization most certainly sought to counter employment discrimination and create more job opportunities, it also hoped the week would do more. In launching a national campaign that focused attention on disability and sought to show able-bodied Americans that they should care about disability issues, AFPH president Paul Strachan and other leaders hoped to cement support among disabled Americans for their organization and gain broad public support for the organization's agenda.

The week laid the foundation for the AFPH lobbying efforts to secure a federal coordinating body that would work for the employment of people with disabilities. That organization—the President's Committee on National Employ the Physically Handicapped Week—would become the longest lasting legacy of the AFPH. It was central to efforts to promote employment of people with disabilities in the 1940s and 1950s and accessibility legislation in the 1950s and 1960s. It provided a space where activists met across several decades, and the committee would eventually be led by disability activist Justin W. Dart, Jr., who played a central role in securing enactment of the Americans with Disabilities Act of 1990. But the fight to establish the President's Committee and control it laid bare the tensions between two competing ideas about disability. AFPH activists envisioned the President's Committee as a means to gain a voice in federal disability policy and as a wedge that would give the organization greater access to advocate for bigger and more meaningful changes. At the same time, physicians, rehabilitation counselors, and a broad range of professionals who claimed expertise in the field of disability were working to cement their own roles in shaping and controlling disability policy. Those claims to expertise marked people with disabilities as subjects, individuals in need of assistance and expert services. While often direct in their criticism of the growing range of professionals and bureaucrats in the field of disability, AFPH activists' demands for a right to shape disability policy stood as an implicit challenge to the authority of these professionals.

The idea that the economic struggles of people with disabilities held national significance, a claim that individuals on both sides of this debate made, melded easily into postwar liberal ideology. Inflation, housing shortages, layoffs, and labor unrest exacerbated the uncertainty of the postwar years and fears that the wartime boom would give way to a return of the hard times of the Great Depression. President Truman's postwar agenda focused on extending New Deal protections against economic uncertainty. He called on Congress to develop a policy and the apparatus to ensure the right to a job, regardless of race, religion, or color, as well as affordable housing and a higher wages. Most importantly, Truman's Fair Deal agenda sought to extend the security the state offered its citizens to a broad notion of "health security," with proposals for expanded social insurance coverage to include health and disability benefits, increased public health efforts, and federal support to construct health care facilities and facilitate medical and scientific research. Postwar liberals saw the economic marginalization of disabled Americans as a drain on the financial resources of family members, communities, the states, and the federal government as well as an impediment to continued economic growth.[2] As the 1946 report of the House of Representatives Subcommittee on Aid to the Physically Handicapped, discussed in Chapter 2, suggested, the Democrats, and even some Republicans, who supported at least part of this vision, would argue that disability—increased by the conduct of war and made more visible because of wartime necessities and activists' efforts—demanded these broader state protections, along with a host of new disability services, in the early postwar years.[3]

Both AFPH leaders and experts in the field of disability offered solutions to this problem. As a result, activists struggled to channel the growing sense that disability represented a problem of national significance into action on their agenda and on their terms. Even as the AFPH gained liberal allies and wedded their agenda to broader Fair Deal goals, their agenda exposed the distance between a consensus of purpose and federal action in the realm of disability policy. Thus, as the nation learned that hiring people with disabilities was "good business," conflicts emerged that would continue to thwart activist and liberal efforts to expand disability policy in the postwar era.

A National Campaign

The AFPH understood the enactment of NEPHW, signed into law in August 1945, as an early victory on a long road toward opportunity, justice, and equality. Central to this vision, the AFPH demanded a new federal agency to manage disability programs. The organization viewed the need to coordinate NEPHW events as an opportunity to begin centralizing federal authority in the field of disability. Almost as soon as NEPHW became law, Strachan began to lobby President Truman to establish a national committee to coordinate federal observances of NEPHW.[4] Strachan's calls for a coordinating agency initially went unheeded. Truman issued the first proclamation of NEPHW less than a month before the first observance was set to begin, too late to organize an elaborate federal program.[5] Still, NEPHW fostered impressive employment gains for people with disabilities in 1945. The U.S. Employment Service placed some 13,400 disabled Americans in the weeks surrounding

NEPHW, including some 8,100 disabled veterans. In the first twenty days of October, the Employment Service reported a 34 percent increase in the employment of disabled workers over the same time-span in September. NEPHW efforts reversed a thirteen-month decline in the employment of people with disabilities during the difficult transition to peace.[6]

The results of the 1945 campaign had been promising, but Strachan continued to push for a federal body to coordinate national NEPHW efforts, gaining leverage for his cause through his connections with the Department of Labor (DOL). Since Lewis B. Schwellenbach's appointment as secretary of labor in July 1945, Strachan cultivated a close relationship with the DOL, which eventually earned him the appointment of special consultant on disability for the department beginning in 1946.[7] In April 1946, Strachan appealed to the president through his press secretary Charles G. Ross, again asking that Truman establish a coordinating committee to prevent further lapses in organization. Playing to Truman's political instincts, Strachan emphasized that he had organized NEPHW to fall one month before national elections, arguing that people with disabilities "would be better convinced that this Administration has their interest at heart, if more emphasis is laid upon the employment-of-Handicapped angle." He pointed out that NEPHW could serve as a "powerful and potent means" of winning the "good will" of disabled citizens.[8]

While Strachan renewed his efforts to secure a federal NEPHW committee, the House Subcommittee on Aid to the Physically Handicapped held hearings on an AFPH bill that would have created the centralized disability agency the organization hoped for. The bill codified much of the AFPH's national agenda and thinking on disability policy. As first introduced in 1946 by Representative John J. Sparkman (D-AL), the federal commission bill represented the broad strokes of the AFPH's vision for making the promise of economic security accessible to people with disabilities. The bill would have established a federal commission on services for the physically handicapped in the DOL, transferred all federal offices and special units that dealt with problems of disability, including the Office of Vocational Rehabilitation (OVR), to the commission, and created a division for people with disabilities within the U.S. Civil Service Commission. Further, the bill called for a hiring quota system to ensure fair access to work for people with disabilities, a personal catastrophe loan system, a pension system for permanently and totally disabled people, disability prevention campaigns focused on safety and hygiene, and increased building access for people with disabilities.[9]

During those 1946 hearings on the federal commission bill, Secretary Schwellenbach argued that disability services—the medical and the work related—should no longer be administered separately. Instead, he proposed that the secretary of labor administer federal disability services in the DOL. "It seems to me," he argued, "that since the end objective is a matter involving the labor force, that the direction of the thing could better come from that side than it could from the purely physical side of rehabilitation."[10] Schwellenbach's testimony made plain that as secretary of labor he had larger designs for his department, designs that included managing the nation's disability policy.

Although Congress did not act on the AFPH's federal commission bill, the AFPH continued to push its agenda. The organization's policy designs increasingly became tied to the DOL. Moreover, to Strachan, and perhaps officials in the DOL, the drive to get the president to appoint a NEPHW committee also became intertwined with the AFPH's legislative agenda and activists' desire to have the DOL administer disability policy. In August 1946, Strachan persuaded Secretary Schwellenbach to write to President Truman in support of the proposed NEPHW committee.[11]

Still avoiding the committee issue, Truman nonetheless tasked the DOL, specifically the Retraining and Reemployment Administration (RRA), with coordinating the 1946 observance of NEPHW.[12] Headed by Major General G. B. Erskine, the RRA worked with some fifty-two federal agencies, coordinating federal, state, and local policy for unemployed war workers, survivors of servicemen killed in battle, and other Americans whose lives had been disrupted by the war. The agency's legislative mandate centered on retraining, reemployment, vocational education, and rehabilitation. With the goal of reducing overlap, Congress empowered the RRA to issue regulations, call conferences among agencies working on related issues, and define the responsibilities of various agencies involved.[13]

In October 1945, Truman appointed Erskine to head the RRA. Born in Louisiana in 1897, Erskine left Louisiana State University, abandoning his hopes of becoming a doctor, to join the marines during World War I. He was wounded in combat in France. In the interwar years, Erskine distinguished himself as an instructor for the marines. During World War II, he served as chief of staff to General Holland M. Smith and commanded a division at Iwo Jima. Erskine first demonstrated his interest in retraining and reemployment, when, after the Japanese surrender, he required his men to take a course on the G.I. Bill. He also created a voluntary divisional program to help his men prepare for peacetime. It is likely that his personal experience as a wounded soldier and his time as a military commander informed Erskine's advocacy for people with disabilities during and after his RRA tenure.[14]

Erskine established the Federal Interagency Committee on Employment of the Physically Handicapped in early July 1946 to combat growing employment problems among people with disabilities and to organize the 1946 observance of NEPHW.[15] From January through July 1946, three out of four disabled workers who applied for work with the Employment Service failed to find employment.[16] To reverse this trend, the Interagency Committee, which included representatives of the Employment Service, the Veterans Employment Service, the VA, the Federal Security Agency (FSA), the OVR, the Departments of Agriculture and Commerce, the Disabled American Veterans (DAV), and the AFPH, sponsored studies of the obstacles between people with disabilities and full employment. The committee then worked to mitigate those barriers.[17] It aggressively distributed information on the programs and opportunities available to disabled citizens, such as vocational rehabilitation. Most importantly, the committee promoted employment of people with disabilities by stressing success stories. To this end, it encouraged additional job performance evaluations of disabled workers, assuming that this information could be used to promote the value of disabled employees. Additionally, the committee pushed people with disabilities to sell their own worth as employees.[18]

Early in its planning, the Interagency Committee prepared and distributed information packets, featuring the slogan, "HIRE THE HANDICAPPED—IT'S GOOD BUSINESS."[19] The committee relied heavily on the Employment Service's connections at the state and local levels. Drawing on its existing networks of contacts in state and local branches of federal agencies, labor unions, civic organizations, and other groups, the Employment Service publicized the benefits of hiring disabled workers, making use of the committee's information packets and slogan. "This slogan," a DOL report announced, "appeared in shop windows, on street signs, in newspapers, magazines, trade journals, labor union publications, and civic organization publications in all sections of the country." Moreover, the Employment Service, in conjunction with the committee, spread the NEPHW message through hundreds of radio programs and motion picture shorts run by theaters throughout the country.[20]

The information packets stressed the wartime employment record of disabled workers and provided cooperating organizations with a wide variety of resources. The materials included suggestions for mayors' proclamations, a sample five-minute speech for local adaptation, various fact sheets, radio announcements scripts, and a statement of problems. In general, these marketing pieces relayed useful statistics and quotes, emphasizing various selling points. The materials targeted potential employers, explaining that people with disabilities had proven to be valuable employees during the war: they were less likely to leave a job, more likely to show up every day, and less likely than their able-bodied peers to have accidents. The campaign sought to humanize disabled workers, introducing Americans to successful workers with whom they could identify, who also happened to be disabled. Campaign materials outlined the need for action—the 85,000 disabled civilians and 228,000 disabled veterans who waited on Employment Service lists for jobs and some 1.5 million civilians who could be employed after some form of rehabilitation. Finally, campaign packets highlighted the fiscal sense of rehabilitation. Aid cost taxpayers three hundred to six hundred dollars per person per year, but for less than three hundred dollars, rehabilitation could turn that person into an employed taxpayer.[21]

The Interagency Committee's efforts produced results. Employment among people with disabilities climbed to the highest levels since May 1945. During the month of October 1946, Employment Service placements of disabled workers increased by 38 percent. Further, the campaign had achieved national results. Forty-six states showed gains in disabled worker placements.[22] In addition to workers hired with the help of the Employment Service, many disabled men and women found employment through private sources.[23]

Like Strachan, Erskine recognized that NEPHW represented only a small portion of the work that needed to be done to solve the employment problems people with disabilities faced. He also understood that the hopes and goals that informed NEPHW aligned perfectly with his own broader mandate to maintain the full employment of the war years. Disability figured prominently in five of the RRA's fifteen basic principles of employment. Broadly, the agency sought to produce economic growth and increase the number of skilled jobs. Erskine, however, demanded that employers and unions make a place for disabled workers in this postwar growth. To that end, the agency stressed that "sex, race, creed, color, or physical impairment should not be factors in the selection or retention of workers or in the amount of compensation paid." The RRA called on employers to evaluate the minimum physical requirements of each job to assist placement officers in finding work for people with disabilities that matched their physical abilities. Erskine further insisted that employers take the added step of installing equipment and offering training courses "to assist handicapped workers in adjusting and advancing in their jobs," and the RRA urged employers to take responsibility for finding jobs for workers injured on the job. Finally, Erskine called on unions to use their bargaining power to benefit disabled workers.[24]

After the conclusion of the 1946 celebration of NEPHW, Erskine continued his efforts to improve the employment prospects of people with disabilities, recommending a year-round effort to bring public attention to the value of disabled workers. He committed his own office to this agenda by making the Public Information Branch of RRA a repository for all releases on the subject of disability. In the wake of NEPHW, he collected copies of every pamphlet, news release, directive, regulation, and instructional letter related to disability, hoping his office would serve as a clearinghouse of information on disability policy, services, and statistics.[25]

Further, Erskine focused attention on failings with the civilian rehabilitation and workers' compensation programs. Recognizing that only a fraction of the people disabled each year received rehabilitation services, he urged program officials to pick up the pace and provide services to all people with disabilities who could benefit. To facilitate this goal, he recommended that the civilian rehabilitation program improve its contacts with physicians, private agencies, and workers' compensation personnel. Finally, he encouraged state legislatures to increase rehabilitation appropriations.[26]

Erskine considered most states' workers' compensation laws to be one of the most serious obstacles confronting the disabled worker. Insurance officials set employer compensation premiums according to the number of days missed per accident per employee. Accordingly, the severity of accidents, rather than frequency, actually determined the amount employers had to pay. Employers believed that disabled workers would take longer to recover from accidents and that they were at greater risk of becoming totally disabled and permanently unable to work, both of which would increase employers' compensation premiums. Erskine advocated legislation to establish a fund that paid for second injury claims. Through these funds, second injury claims would no longer affect employer premiums because such compensation would be paid through the fund rather than through normal channels. By removing the risk of higher premiums, he and others believed that people with disabilities would be hired more frequently. Erskine urged organizations, such as the DAV, to promote the passage of second injury fund legislation. His efforts to promote second injury funds gained traction. By 1968, all but four states had adopted some system for shifting all or part of second injury claims to a state fund.[27]

Despite Erskine's and the RRA's positive efforts to eliminate employment obstacles for people with disabilities, Congress never intended the RRA to be a permanent agency, providing a legislative mandate for the agency's work that expired in 1947. Given this reality, Erskine worked to build public backing and a support base for increasing opportunities for disabled workers. To this end, he formed the National Association for the Employment of the Handicapped (NAEH) in December 1946 to agitate for a NEPHW coordinating agency that would promote the employment of people with disabilities. Erskine recruited some 351 organizations to join the NAEH, including representatives of various labor, industry, and women's organizations. With this backing in place, he wrote to President Truman on behalf of the NAEH, recommending that he appoint the secretary of labor as coordinator of all the federal programs relating to the employment of people with disabilities. The job he envisioned for the secretary of labor extended well beyond NEPHW. Erskine wanted the secretary to have the authority to call federal conferences and coordinate federal policy as it related to the employment of people with disabilities.[28] Echoing the suggestions of Erskine, several members of the NAEH wrote to the secretary of labor, asserting their belief that focused efforts were needed and that the DOL should take the lead. The members offered their services in promoting NEPHW and suggested an annual appropriation of $122,200 to further the effectiveness of the program.[29] Dr. Meyer Wiener, also of the NAEH, wrote to John R. Steelman, special assistant to the president, requesting that his organization serve as an advisory body on NEPHW.[30] Erskine and many NAEH members conflated the issue of establishing a NEPHW coordinating body in the DOL with winning greater, even total, control over federal disability services for the department. Secretary Schwellenbach further muddied the waters when he joined the mounting campaign for DOL control of NEPHW.

In May 1947, Schwellenbach added his voice to the growing chorus. He asked President Truman to issue an executive order authorizing the DOL to promote NEPHW by forming a committee with representatives from public organizations, veterans' groups, industry, and organized labor. Schwellenbach's proposed executive order granted the DOL the authority "to coordinate the policies and activities of the Federal agencies, except those of the Veterans' Affairs, relating to the physically handicapped."[31]

Conflict Emerges

As the AFPH, the DOL, and Erskine, along with his supporters, fought for a coordinating agency for NEPHW, an interagency turf battle emerged, which threw into sharp relief the divisions between those who viewed disabled people as first and foremost in need of professional assistance and the activists who sought inclusion through employment along with their supporters who viewed discrimination as the key barrier to that goal. From outside the DOL, it appeared that the activists and the agency itself would use a NEPHW coordinating body to gain greater control over federal disability policy more generally. Indeed, Strachan had been clear that he intended to pursue both congressional and executive action to restructure disability services and achieve the AFPH's goals.[32] Increased DOL authority in the field would necessarily mean a loss of authority for the FSA. Thus, recognizing that Schwellenbach's policy designs extended beyond NEPHW, the FSA objected to the DOL's proposed executive order. FSA administrator Watson B. Miller supported launching a year-round educational campaign to benefit disabled people, but he argued that the DOL proposal was ill conceived. Miller maintained that the proposal "confuses the activities of a Committee of citizens . . . with the official administration" of disability policy in multiple federal agencies. Emphasizing the important role of his agency and its OVR in providing services to people with disabilities, ranging from medical care to vocational training, he argued that the FSA already did the work of coordinating federal disability policy that Schwellenbach proposed to do in the DOL. Moreover, Miller asserted that because his agency administered "the Federal side of more than 14 grant-in-aid programs" and because the DOL's state contacts ended with the state departments of labor, the FSA would be far better suited than the DOL to bring federal coordination to local and state activities. The DOL's proposal, Miller concluded, "would be in direct conflict with the functions of the Federal Security Agency."[33]

With the two agencies at a stalemate, Schwellenbach forged ahead without a clear executive order on the basis of a postscript from Truman. The president, in conjunction with his 1947 NEPHW proclamation, issued letters to the secretary of labor, the FSA administrator, and the VA administrator, urging each of them to take an active role in federal NEPHW efforts. The president, however, added a handwritten message to Schwellenbach's letter. He noted, "You may want to call upon officials and leading citizens outside the Federal government for all possible assistance in this program." On the basis of that message, Schwellenbach formed the President's Committee on NEPHW, and he appointed Vice Admiral Ross T. McIntire as chairperson.[34]

McIntire had held a variety of prestigious military, federal, and voluntary positions after receiving his medical degree from Willamette University in Oregon in 1912. He left his practice to join the navy during World War I. In 1935, President Roosevelt chose McIntire to serve as his personal physician, a position he held until Roosevelt's death in 1945. He also served as the navy surgeon general and chief of the Bureau of Medicine and Surgery of the navy. During his tenure as surgeon general, which began in 1938, McIntire oversaw a huge expansion of the navy's medical department as a result of World War II. Further, McIntire worked with the Red Cross to organize their blood drive program in 1947.[35]

Implementing the president's suggestion, the DOL invited representatives of industry, organized labor, women's and veterans' organizations, civic and professional organizations, the press and radio, and government agencies with responsibility in the field of disability policy, including representatives of the Interagency Committee that Erskine had formed, to join the President's Committee on NEPHW.[36] Creating an agenda for the new committee fell to Strachan and Merle E. Frampton, who headed the Planning Committee for the new organization. Since he first began advocating for a coordinating agency for NEPHW in 1945, Strachan had consistently suggested that Frampton head the agency.[37] Born in West Virginia in 1903, Frampton received a Ph.D. in sociology from Harvard University in 1934 and thereafter worked as a disability advocate. He served as the director of the New York Institute for the Education of the Blind from 1935 to 1971, he organized the first training program for special education at Columbia University's Teachers College in 1936, and he also launched a program to educate children with multiple disabilities. During World War II, Frampton joined the navy, where he served as the chief of rehabilitation services.[38]

While Strachan failed to get Frampton appointed as chairperson of the committee, as head of the Planning Committee, Frampton was positioned to shape its direction. As a result, Strachan played a significant role in creating the eight-point plan of action for the President's Committee. Frampton's Planning Committee recommended the development of "management-labor institutes" to encourage employers to hire people with disabilities and to educate employers and employees about the federal-state programs available to disabled people through the Employment Service and the civilian rehabilitation program. Additionally, the Planning Committee developed numerous publicity schemes, including essay contests for students, expositions in large cities where people with disabilities could demonstrate their working abilities to the public, and awards for individuals and organizations for furthering the employment of people with disabilities. Finally, the Planning Committee called for research on workers' compensation laws, community rehabilitation centers, and schools for people with disabilities.[39] Much of committee's plan of action drew on the AFPH agenda that had from the beginning emphasized the need for public education and research with the ultimate goal of opening more jobs to people with disabilities.

In its early months, the President's Committee on NEPHW realized consensus on a number of issues, despite broader disagreements between the DOL and FSA over federal disability policy. The Planning Committee's agenda gained general approval at the November 1947 meeting of the President's Committee. Members also voted to add a point to the committee's program, authorizing a committee to investigate employment possibilities for people with disabilities in federal, state, and local government agencies, a point very much in line with AFPH demands for greater consideration for people with disabilities in public employment. Finally, members of the President's Committee voted to make McIntire's temporary status as chair of the committee permanent.[40]

While the President's Committee reached agreement on a plan of action, discussions of the committee's name and purpose as well as the task of securing appropriations served as a catalyst for a clash that would threaten its survival. In his opening remarks to the committee, Schwellenbach emphasized the limitations of having a single week each year designated to promote the employment of disabled people. By 1947, it was clear that placements of disabled workers peaked during the month of October, only to begin declining in the following months. Schwellenbach said that addressing the problem of unemployment among people with disabilities would be "a week by week job." The job, he argued, came "naturally into the work of the Department of Labor" because the department housed the Employment Service, an agency tasked with finding work for the unemployed. Schwellenbach committed the DOL to providing the committee with staff as the budget allowed and expressed hope that Congress, in the up-coming session, would grant the DOL additional appropriations to fund the work of the committee. Perhaps anticipating what was to come, Schwellenbach told the committee, "I see no reason for the slightest degree of controversy."[41]

Following Schwellenbach's lead, members emphasized that the work of

Figure 6. Christened "Opportunity" by Secretary of Labor Maurice J. Tobin, this American Legion sponsored stunt plane carried the "Hire the Handicapped" slogan throughout the Washington, D.C., area during the 1948 observance of National Employ the Physically Handicapped Week. Photograph by Acme. Courtesy of Corbis.

the President's Committee had to extend beyond a single week a year, a point that sparked discussions about the committee's name, President's Committee on NEPHW. In turn, that discussion generated debates about the degree to which the DOL should manage disability policy. Robert Ramspeck, executive vice president of the Air Transport Association of America and former member of the House of Representatives, who would later be appointed vice-chairperson of the committee, echoed Schwellenbach's concern about the inadequacy of focusing the committee's efforts on a single week in the year. Other members agreed, expressing concern over the committee's "unfortunate" and "clumsy" name. One member argued that emphasizing the word "week" in the name of the committee misrepresented the purpose of the

Figure 7. "Opportunity Wanted," drawn by Mort Greene, earned a prize in 1953 from the Illinois Governor's Committee for Employment of the Physically Handicapped, the state's counterpart to the national President's Committee. It appeared on the cover of *Performance: The Story of the Handicapped*, a publication of the President's Committee, in January 1954. Courtesy of the National Archives, College Park, Maryland.

committee, which should work for the continued employment of disabled workers. Ultimately, members agreed to have the Planning Committee study the political implications of changing the committee's name, directing the committee to consider alternate names, with suggestions ranging from the President's Committee for the Employment of the Handicapped to the President's Advisory Committee for the Employment of the Handicapped, and to change the organization's name if such a change would not damage the committee's ability to secure appropriations.[42]

Eager to secure financial resources for the President's Committee, Millard Rice of the DAV proposed that the Planning Committee endorse appropriation plans that would enable the DOL to maintain "a separate section" devoted to disability services and coordinating the activities of the President's Committee. Schwellenbach, however, asked Rice to amend his motion and to delete the reference to a new division, arguing that appropriations for the committee would no doubt be obtained through the Employment Service. Rice's amended motion passed. However, the issues of appropriations, a separate division in the DOL, and the purpose of the committee would push many members, who viewed discussions of a separate DOL division and a year-round campaign as a challenge to the authority of the FSA and the OVR in the field of disability policy, to resign and fight against appropriations.[43]

The Planning Committee, as instructed, drafted a budget for the President's Committee for 1948. Whereas the November meeting had set in motion the beginnings of controversy, the Planning Committee's proposed budget enflamed committee members who had begun to question the motives of the DOL and the President's Committee. The budget hinged on the executive order Schwellenbach had proposed in May, an executive order Truman had yet to issue. To implement the executive order, the budget called on the DOL to create a Division of Services for Handicapped and a Federal Inter-Agency Committee on Services to Handicapped. Through the President's Committee, the proposed Inter-Agency Committee, and the Division of Services for Handicapped, the DOL would "take all steps necessary, through promotion and coordination, to achieve a maximum of economic security and gainful employment for the handicapped and to eliminate overlapping functions and efforts of Federal agencies in these fields." The budget proposed that the secretary of labor possess coordinating authority over other federal agencies in the field of disability policy, the power to review other programs, and the authority to issue regulations to accomplish a coordinated federal program on disability. Further, the budget vested the chairperson of the President's Committee with the power to work with private and state agencies to effectuate a coordinated policy on all levels.[44] These proposals encroached on the authority of several agencies and were bound to generate opposition, particularly in the FSA and among rehabilitation officials.

In the early months of 1948, the National Rehabilitation Association launched a campaign to block appropriations for the President's Committee, reacting to what they viewed as the thinly veiled efforts of the DOL to control disability policy. National Rehabilitation Association members, their allies in other disability-focused professional organizations, and many representatives of blind advocacy organizations sent a flurry of protest letters and telegrams to the president, members of Congress, and the secretary of labor. They supplemented their correspondence with personal visits to members of congress, Bureau of the Budget officials, and the secretary of labor.[45] For example, H. Earle Correvont, president of the National Rehabilitation Association, wrote to President Truman in February 1948, tendering his organization's resignation from the President's Committee. He claimed that much of the November 1947 meeting focused on the establishment of a permanent division for people with disabilities in the DOL and securing appropriations to that end. He wrote that his organization believed that the existing federal-state program of vocational rehabilitation, administered by the FSA, should be improved rather than replaced by a new division in the DOL with broad powers in the field.[46] Through its president, C. F. Feike, the States' Vocational Rehabilitation Council also objected to the establishment of a permanent program in the DOL. Feike, like Correvont, argued that the existing program of vocational rehabilitation should be strengthened instead of creating a new agency. In view of its objections, the organization also withdrew from the President's Committee.[47]

National Rehabilitation Association officials also accused the President's Committee of trying to quash private efforts on behalf of people with disabilities.[48] This accusation no doubt contributed to great unease among blind advocates about the President's Committee and the DOL. Numerous blind advocacy groups objected to the DOL's proposed executive order and the Planning Committee's proposed budget. For example, Peter J. Salmon, executive director of the Industrial Home for the Blind in Brooklyn, New York, feared that the proposed executive order would mean that the OVR would be transferred to the DOL, a move that he insisted would prove harmful to people with disabilities. Salmon maintained that the committee's original purpose was useful but that the proposed executive order exceeded its authority.[49] Barney Mamet of the Associated Blind, Inc., New York, argued that blind people needed special consideration in planning improved conditions for people with disabilities, consideration he thought would be lacking in the DOL. Mamet hoped that a plan for coordinating disability services could be devised within the FSA and administered through the OVR.[50] The Greater New York Council of Agencies for the Blind and the American Association for the Blind expressed similar concerns.[51]

The conflict between the President's Committee and the National Rehabilitation Association and a range of professional and advocacy organizations mirrored a growing struggle between the National Federation of the Blind (NFB) and state and federal bureaucrats and advocacy organizations for the blind. That fight would culminate in the NFB's "right to organize" campaign in the late 1950s, which sought federal protection of blind people's right to join activist organizations free from harassment or threats of losing benefits and the right to have a voice in shaping the policies that aimed to help them.[52] Both the controversy over the Planning Committee's proposed budget and the NFB's "right to organize" campaign suggest that many professionals, bureaucrats, and advocates perceived disability activism as a threat to their authority. In the case of the Planning Committee's proposed budget, and the DOL's growing interest in disability policy, the threat moved beyond activist claims for a right to participate in the development of disability policy.

The Roots of Conflict

The DOL's fight for greater authority in disability services, prompted by the AFPH, polarized activists, advocates, professionals, and policymakers, all of whom hoped to expand federal disability services but had differing ideas about what expanded programs should do. The disputes surrounding the committee exposed two very different understandings of disability and the purpose of disability policy. The AFPH and the DOL advocated a work-centered disability policy that focused on eliminating employment discrimination, while the FSA, rehabilitation officials, and medical professionals pushed for an expert-centered policy that sought to "fix" individuals with disabilities.

Forced to answer growing opposition to the President's Committee, Schwellenbach admitted that "quite a number of purely Labor Department functions were established in, or transferred to, other agencies" prior to his tenure as secretary of labor. He confessed to launching a number of studies of other agencies, including the OVR, because, he wrote, it was "natural" to want to expand the department's "field of activity." While Schwellenbach purported to have "struck" the OVR from his "list" early in 1947, few in the FSA and the civilian rehabilitation program likely believed such a claim in light of Schwellenbach's proposed executive order and the Planning Committee's proposed budget.[53]

The DOL and FSA had clashed over control of programs and ideology since Roosevelt established the FSA in 1939. Control of the Employment Service proved to be a sticking point in the agencies' rivalry. Established in the DOL in 1933, the Employment Service was transferred to the FSA upon the latter's founding, moved to the War Manpower Commission in 1942, and returned to the DOL in 1945. The Employment Service's postwar place in the DOL provided, in large measure, Schwellenbach's justification for managing disability services in the Labor Department. The agency served unemployed Americans, and Schwellenbach viewed employment as disabled people's greatest need, echoing the AFPH's assertions.[54] The bureaucratic fate of the Employment Service was by no means certain, however. In 1947, Truman sought to make the DOL's hold on the Employment Service permanent with his reorganization plan. Truman and the DOL, however, faced a Republican-controlled Congress that was hostile to both organized labor and the legislative legacies of the New Deal. In 1947, Congress worked to curtail the power of organized labor, culminating in the passage of the Taft-Hartley Act, which placed severe restrictions on organized labor. In this context, Congress rejected the notion that the Employment Service belonged in the DOL, arguing that the Bureau of Employment Security, which was under the control of the FSA, and the Employment Service should be administered by the same agency. Truman responded in 1948 by issuing a new reorganization plan, which would have given the DOL permanent authority over both the Employment Service and the Bureau of Employment Security. Congress not only rejected this new reorganization plan but also secured the transfer of the Employment Service to the FSA through a supplemental appropriations bill, passed over Truman's veto.[55] Congress's growing antagonism toward the DOL and conflict over the proper administrative home of the Employment Service fed the mounting tensions between the DOL and the FSA.

Beyond bureaucratic rivalry and partisan politics, ideology played a key role in the emerging disagreement between disability activists and rehabilitation officials and the ongoing one between the DOL and FSA. These disagreements mirrored earlier tensions both between the state administrators of workers' compensation and the rehabilitation program and the DOL and the U.S. Public Health Service. Though vocational rehabilitation had been designed to operate in tandem with workers' compensation programs, the programs never functioned well together. The bureaucracy of worker's compensation typically worked within or closely with the state departments of labor. Meanwhile, administration of vocational rehabilitation generally fell to the states' educational bureaucracies.[56]

This separation exemplified more than bureaucratic duplication and administrative inconvenience. It embodied the ideological divide between the two services meant to aid injured workers. On the one hand, legislators had designed workers' compensation to serve any person injured at work, regardless of the severity of the injury. The rehabilitation program, on the other hand, understood its mandate as one of achieving the greatest returns by serving only those disabled people with the best chances of returning to employment.[57]

Likewise, the issue of workplace safety generated conflict between the DOL and the Public Health Service. The agencies disagreed about the fundamental purpose of such programs. Whereas the DOL viewed its role in occupational safety as one of protecting workers, the Public Health Service viewed its work in terms of improving health more generally and not in protecting a specific group of people. Scholars David Rosner and Gerald Markowitz argue that "the Public Health Service also deeply believed that at its most fundamental level occupational safety and health was a health issue, not a labor issue."[58] Many of these same questions about who qualified for services and the proper role of the federal government in administering protective and corrective public policies would shape continuing debates about vocational rehabilitation.

During the 1946 hearings on the federal commission bills, Schwellenbach argued that federal disability policy should not stop at finding jobs for people with disabilities. Disability policy should work toward removing disabled workers from "a segregated category" of employment by teaching employers to treat disabled workers like any other employee, "matching the capacities and aptitudes" of the person to the available jobs.[59] In this testimony, Schwellenbach expressed the widespread view among officials in the DOL and activists in the AFPH that federal disability policy must address employment discrimination against people with disabilities if disabled people were to achieve economic security.

In contrast, rehabilitation workers, medical professionals, and officials in the FSA increasingly viewed rehabilitation as a medical and educational process to be handled by expert physicians, counselors, psychologists, and social workers. In this view, if medicine, counseling, and training could make the disabled individual conform more closely to the ideal of the physically fit employee, employers would readily accept them. As physicians and rehabilitation officials responded to the AFPH's federal commission bill and the bureaucratic maneuvering of the DOL, they began to outline a philosophy on federal disability policy that emphasized the growing importance of medicine in correcting disabilities. Dr. Raymond Hussey, dean of the School of Occupational Health of Wayne University in Detroit, Michigan, member of the Professional Advisory Committee of the OVR, and representative of the American Medical Association (AMA), argued that the federal commission bill emphasized the end goal of employment over all other phases of rehabilitation. "True," he maintained, "employment is the last stage, but only the last stage." Hussey contended that rehabilitation presented "a medical problem" and vocational training "an educational problem." He viewed job placement for people with disabilities as a separate problem for the Employment Service and the DOL and saw no need for "a new group with no experience in this field" to address the medical and educational "problems" of people with disabilities. On the one hand, Hussey argued that the bill would place medical programs in the wrong hands, but on the other hand, he criticized the AFPH bill for not placing enough restrictions on the medical care available to people with disabilities.[60] Although he was careful to defend the medical nature of rehabilitation, as a representative of the AMA, an organization that invested incredible resources in blocking national health and disability insurance, he rejected the proposition that the federal government should provide people with disabilities unfettered access to medical treatment. In essence, Hussey claimed medical authority over disability and people with disabilities while upholding the fee-for-service model of medical care.[61]

Dr. Henry Kessler, representing both the AMA and the National Rehabilitation Association, rejected the notion that the DOL had any place in the field of disability policy. "Retraining," he argued, "belongs in expert hands, under expert advice and expert guidance." He held that the same was true with educating people with disabilities and finding them employment. Placing a disabled person in a job, he maintained, required careful assessment of the individual's physical abilities. It was "a job for the physician, for a medically trained individual, who has the medical and physiological knowledge to evaluate an individual's capacity for work." Kessler admitted that American society continued to view "the handicapped individual, the deformed individual as in league with the devil, with malignancy, and sin, evil spirit," Yet, he argued, legislation could not remedy the problem of prejudice, only "education and time" could "correct that attitude." It was the job of the rehabilitation program, in his eyes, to provide education and employment, but the "dominant" service should be "physical restoration . . . because we are dealing with physically handicapped individuals."[62] The testimony of Hussey and Kessler demonstrated that physicians and representatives of civilian rehabilitation sought to protect the rehabilitation program from the influence of outsiders in the DOL. This protective impulse grew out of both the celebration of medical expertise and the assertion of the professional and technical knowledge and skills of the rehabilitation service. Both that celebration and assertion of knowledge had the effect of reinforcing disabled people's othered status.

When celebrating their own expertise, rehabilitation officials presented disabled people as objects to be "fixed" by those with the technical knowledge to do so, which served to reduce disabled people to case studies and erase their ability to articulate their own experiences or even direct them. In 1950, J. Hank Smith, president of the States Vocational Rehabilitation Council, presented a series of rehabilitation cases to a Senate subcommittee. Smith told the committee about a woman who "had a very bad harelip and a cleft palate with considerable disfiguration." Denied work at a local factory because of her looks, the woman chopped cotton to support herself. Her rehabilitation counselor arranged for her to receive plastic surgery. Smith commented that he was moved by what had been done for the woman's children, who now had "a lot prettier mother to look at." In the same session, Smith presented the case of a young man who had been badly burned as a child and could not find work because of his appearance. As in the woman's case, the rehabilitation office arranged for plastic surgery. Smith showed the committee a photograph of the young man, remarking, "Look at the smile on that face. He knows he is not the horrible looking individual that he was a few years ago."[63] Employers rejected these individuals because of their appearance, not their inability to work. Smith's case histories and his disparaging remarks about the physical appearance of people with disabilities demonstrate the tendency of rehabilitation professionals to view disability as a condition to be corrected through bodily interventions, not as people to be accepted.

Such attitudes caused AFPH members to grow increasingly hostile to the federal-state rehabilitation program. Because of the attitudes of state rehabilitation counselors and doctors, who sought to "correct" people with disabilities, and indeed only those few they deemed feasible and sufficiently cooperative, AFPH activists believed that rehabilitation officials approached the problems of people with disabilities with condescension as a kind of charity work. The means-tested nature of many of the new benefits of rehabilitation, including medical treatment, prosthetic devices, and financial support for vocational or university education, reified by an approach that smacked of charity, further highlighted the feeling that disability services were a kind of benevolent aid, far from a dignified right of citizens. For many activists, rehabilitation, as administered by the FSA, represented another form of dependency, the opposite of real economic security. These activists aimed chiefly for economic security through employment, an aim that they believed the DOL would address more effectively. They also, no doubt, hoped to alter the widespread stereotype of disabled people as charity cases through association with the DOL, an agency that served the needs of workers.

In 1948, Strachan argued, "the so-called 'Rehabilitation Experts' prefer the 'professional' (?) status they presumably have, in FSA, as opposed to being in, or under, an agency, which, (Oh, horrors!) deals with guys who have dirt under their finger-nails."[64] In contrast to the DOL, which the public associated with workers and the working class, the FSA distinguished itself as an organization of university-trained health, education, and community professionals. E. B. Whitten, executive director of the National Rehabilitation Association, later testified that the state departments of labor "do not have the same position of strength and prestige that the State departments of education have in the States." He argued that the "attitude" of DOL officials grew out of a "lack of knowledge and experience in the field of education, public welfare, medical programs, and so forth."[65] Ultimately, the National Rehabilitation Association feared that DOL control of rehabilitation would alter its basic fabric, pushing the focus of rehabilitation from medical care, education, and experts to jobs and workers.

Forging Ahead

Mired in controversy, the President's Committee forged ahead, still hopeful that Congress would grant the new organization appropriations in 1948. In January 1948, Representative and disabled World War I veteran William Jennings Miller (R-CT) appealed to his congressional colleagues to offer the

President's Committee "stronger support." Drawing on NEPHW rhetoric that emphasized the fiscal sense of ensuring the employment of people with disabilities, he argued, "Its purpose is not only to restore unfortunate, suffering people to usefulness and happiness but to render them productive citizens who can and will take up their share of our tax load."[66] In the same month, representatives Miller and Augustine B. Kelley (D-PA) and senators George D. Aiken (R-VT) and Sparkman (D-AL) introduced resolutions to secure appropriations for the President's Committee, but the legislation never saw the floor of the House or Senate.[67]

Committee leaders hoped to quash the controversy by addressing it directly. In February, Frampton penned a letter to all members of the President's Committee. He accused "a small group of self-seeking state rehabilitation men headed by H. Earle Correvont of Michigan" of spreading "sheer falsification" and of being "determined to destroy the effectiveness of the Committee's work." In response to charges that the President's Committee sought the transfer of the OVR from the FSA to the DOL, Frampton included a telegram from the secretary of labor to Kessler of the National Council on Rehabilitation, denying the accusation. Frampton also complained that Correvont and others had accused the committee of attempting to "destroy all private agencies in the field" and some of the leadership of the committee of "seeking Federal jobs." While Frampton argued that both charges were outrageous, the National Rehabilitation Association campaign against the President's Committee no doubt played an important role in the committee's continued inability to secure appropriations.[68]

In March, Admiral McIntire, Frampton, and Ramspeck met with President Truman to learn whether or not he wanted the committee to continue a year-round campaign "to keep the problem of the handicapped before the public." By then, the three men understood that the committee would need the president's aid to secure appropriations and continue its work.[69] They received a two-part answer. On 7 June, the president requested $72,500 in additional appropriations for the DOL to "supplement and strengthen" the Employment Service program for disabled workers by fostering promotional work. When Truman issued this request, he also wrote to Schwellenbach, warning, "You recognize how important it is that the activities of the Committee be conducted in a manner which will assure that there is no infringement upon statutory functions of the Federal Security Agency."[70] With the warning, Truman no doubt sought to keep administrators of both the DOL and the FSA happy.

The death of Schwellenbach on 10 June 1948 added to the uncertainty the President's Committee faced. Days later Congress stripped the DOL of the Employment Service, and the President's Committee found itself on even shakier ground. The DOL's justification for launching the committee and securing appropriations had rested on the argument that it was expanding the scope of the Employment Service. Committees in both the House and the Senate rejected the appropriation, and on 19 June, Senator Sparkman failed to have the appropriation added as an amendment on the Senate floor. In response to Sparkman's amendment, Senator Joseph Hurst Ball (R-Minn.) argued, "Frankly, the committee felt that there was no justification whatever for adding employees at the Federal level to deal with this question, since the only employment of handicapped people that can possibly take place is managed at the State level."[71] Senator Ball's response to the Sparkman amendment mirrored conservative concerns about the wartime expansion of the civilian rehabilitation program. While nearly all conservatives considered aiding disabled civilians a laudable goal, most believed it was a problem for the state governments. The states' rights philosophy defined midcentury conservative thinking on many issues, disability included.

Without appropriations, the fate of the President's Committee seemed uncertain at best. Frampton resigned from his post as vice chairperson. With the tone of a farewell letter, William P. McCahill, executive secretary of the President's Committee, wrote to acting secretary of labor John Gibson on 17 June, thanking him for being "a real fighter for what may very well be a lost cause."[72] By the end of June, however, the White House agreed to provide a stenographer and help with staffing issues if the DOL could not find the $7,500 Admiral McIntire estimated the committee would need to survive until the end of October.[73]

While the committee survived into the spring of 1949, it still had not secured permanent funding. In March, Vice Chair Ramspeck of the President's Committee complained to President Truman that he had not made good on his promises to sustain the committee. He blamed the president's inaction and indecisiveness for both the committee's lack of funding and the FSA's attempts to place the President's Committee under its administration. Ramspeck pleaded, "If the work of the Committee for 1949 is to be done effectively it is imperative that this matter be settled. We should be moving forward; but we are standing still."[74]

Following his reelection and the seating of a Democratic-controlled Congress, President Truman finally secured appropriations for the President's

Committee and settled the question of where it would be administered. On 11 July 1949, Truman signed H. J. Resolution 228, which authorized an appropriation for the President's Committee. In a letter to the new secretary of labor, Maurice J. Tobin, the president expressed his desire that the committee remain in his department.[75]

Even as Strachan had first envisioned NEPHW, he imagined something much bigger—a coordinating agency that would begin a year-round process of chipping away at disability discrimination and expanding the range of employment options open to people with disabilities. He envisioned a group that could examine existing laws, employment patterns, and vocational instructions and push for better legislation. He saw the week as not only a platform from which disability activists could influence policy but also as a vehicle to generate support for broader reforms. He hoped that NEPHW, and the President's Committee, would lend official weight to the organization's claim that facilitating the employment—and by extension, citizenship—of people with disabilities would serve the welfare of the nation. The AFPH emphasis on employment and claims that unemployed disabled individuals represented a drain on the nation, however effective in generating support, had its dangers. In painting unemployed disabled people in this way, the organization contributed to the stigmatization of individuals who could not work. One week a year set aside to consider disability, and a voluntary committee, also certainly had its limitations. But as the controversy the President's Committee provoked suggests, the week and the committee held the potential for something beyond those limits.

President Truman settled the conflict over the bureaucratic location of the committee, but the ideological disagreements that had bubbled to the surface during the controversy would boil over in the years to come. The bureaucratic and ideological clashes that plagued the President's Committee during its first two years would spill into legislative debates as the AFPH launched yet another legislative campaign for its federal commission bill. Moreover, while the president had made it clear that the President's Committee would remain in the DOL, what agency, if any, would control disability services as a whole remained an unanswered question.

Chapter 5

Work or Welfare: The Limits of the Body Politic

In 1947, George Meany, then secretary-treasurer of the American Federation of Labor (AFL), wrote that local unions had a responsibility to themselves and to people with disabilities to demand and enforce contracts that gave hiring preference to people whose disabilities would not hinder their ability to work at a particular job. Additionally, he argued that union contracts should protect injured and disabled union members from being fired by employers if they could perform other work for the company. Meany instructed members to ask themselves whether their right to work would be protected by their contracts if they suffered a major injury.[1]

In making a case that the AFL had a broad social responsibility to people with disabilities, Meany reminded members how little separated them from a work-related disability. During the workday, he pointed out, a worker suffered some type of injury every five seconds. Each two-minute interval brought an accident so severe that the worker would have some type of permanent disability. Members of the AFL could expect that one of their brothers or sisters would become permanently disabled every twelve minutes during the workday. Meany maintained that the labor movement had a responsibility to aid veterans and civilians with disabilities, whether union members or not. "Will these men and women," he asked, "graduate from the hospital only to rot on park benches . . . ?" The AFL, he argued, was "determined that the handicapped shall be reemployed in respectable jobs—union jobs."[2]

In linking disability, the workplace, and unions to the plight of all disabled citizens, Meany articulated a growing awareness of disability among organized labor leaders in the postwar period. This awareness grew out of the carefully cultivated relationship between disability activists in the American Federation of the Physically Handicapped (AFPH) and leaders in the labor movement. This partnership drew on a shared desire to expand the securities the state provided its citizens. The New Deal had created mechanisms to protect workers against unemployment and provide financial support to retirees and needy blind citizens. These protections offered little help to those workers disabled on the job and unable to work to retirement age and even less for people with disabilities who had never worked. State workers' compensation laws offered some financial relief to workers disabled on the job, but by and large, most people with disabilities remained outside the national safety net in 1947. Until Congress extended aid provisions for the "permanently and totally disabled" in 1950, public assistance to disabled people was limited to blind Americans, and Social Security Disability Insurance would not become law until 1956.

As the AFPH sought to make state promises of opportunity and security accessible to disabled people, disability activists gained the support of organized labor. After President Truman moved to settle conflict over the President's Committee on National Employ the Physically Handicapped Week (NEPHW) in 1949, AFPH activists focused their energies on Congress. The organization's legislative campaign operated as a magnifying glass in the immediate postwar years, exposing the ways that the state privileged able bodies, the failures of federal disability policy, tensions between the civilian rehabilitation program and many of its constituents, and starkly different notions of disability and visions for disability policy. The AFPH's drive to improve rehabilitation melded with organized labor's broad vision of health and economic security for the nation, creating a powerful critique of the state and civilian rehabilitation that had failed to help workers.[3]

The AFPH and the Federal Commission Bill

In 1948, the AFPH plunged forward with a new strategy for expanding federal services for people with disabilities and wresting control of disability services from the Federal Security Agency (FSA) and the Office of Vocational Rehabilitation (OVR). The AFPH's efforts in 1946 to secure a federal commission on disability services and the organization's work in the President's Committee on NEPHW had focused on giving the Department of Labor (DOL) administrative control over federal disability services. In 1947, Congress passed the Taft-Hartley Act over President Truman's veto, placing harsh restrictions on closed shops and striking power, opening the door to state legislation that banned union shops altogether, and giving employers greater power at the bargaining table and to express their views on unionization. Further, in 1947 and 1948, Congress blocked Truman's efforts to place the U.S. Employment Service permanently in the DOL.[4]

Congress's growing hostility to organized labor and the DOL encouraged the AFPH to try a new tactic. In June 1948, the AFPH asked John J. Sparkman (D-AL) to introduce a new version of the federal commission bill, which called for the establishment of a new federal agency to administer disability policy, independent of the DOL.[5] Paul Strachan conceded that the move had been based on the political climate, fuming that with a Republican "anti-Congress" in power "NO proposition, favoring the Department of Labor, WOULD HAVE A CHANCE!"[6]

In this renewed campaign for a federal commission on disability services, the AFPH made further concessions to the changing political environment. The organization dropped the quota system that would have required businesses to employ a certain percentage of disabled workers. In 1946, the AFPH hoped to convert ten federal war plants into training centers for people with disabilities and disability professionals. By the time the AFPH launched its second campaign for a federal commission on disability services in 1948, however, the issue of surplus properties was moot. Further, the AFPH included provisions for people with mental disabilities, a change from the 1946 bill that had generated criticism from the FSA for focusing solely on physically disabled individuals when the Barden-La Follette Act had extended rehabilitation services to people with mental illness and intellectual disabilities.[7] The AFPH's decision to alter its most radical demand for a quota system and push for an independent agency led to broader congressional support. In February 1949, Sparkman introduced the federal commission bill yet again (S. 1066), this time with a diverse group of senators, ranging from Democrats such as Claude Pepper (FL) and Lister Hill (AL) to Republicans such as Wayne Morse (OR) and Ralph Brewster (ME).[8] In March, Representative Augustine Kelley (D-PA) introduced an identical federal commission bill in the House (H.R. 3095).[9]

The federal commission bills, as introduced in 1949, represented the AFPH's response to postwar changes in rehabilitation and conflicts over the President's Committee on NEPHW. The bills proposed transferring the civilian rehabilitation program and all its funding from the FSA to a new independent agency, the Federal Commission on Services for the Physically Handicapped, eliminating the OVR altogether.[10]

While OVR relied on expert-driven advisory councils, the AFPH called for an advisory council that weighted experience over expertise, with members from disabled people's organizations, industry, organized labor, and the public. Likewise, the bills would create a committee of federal officials, whose agencies managed disability policies, allowing the administrator of the proposed federal commission to coordinate policies and programs. Because the President's Committee had yet to receive clear executive or legislative authorization, AFPH leaders included in their bill a legislative mandate for a National Commission on Employment of the Handicapped. This commission would operate much like the President's Committee, facilitating voluntary participation of individuals and organizations outside the federal government to promote the employment of disabled people. The 1949 bills introduced a revolving loan fund for states that had exhausted rehabilitation funds to address the lapses in services caused by states continually draining their appropriations long before they were due to receive additional funds.[11]

The AFPH made some effort to address the concerns of National Federation of the Blind (NFB) activists, who had expressed worry that the AFPH's federal commission legislation "would repeal the whole vast accumulation of aid-to-the-blind legislation which has been so carefully built up for the last 10 years on the Federal level," and appease the professionals who served blind people and had opposed DOL control of disability policy.[12] The bills clearly outlined that all previously established agencies and benefits for blind citizens would be continued but that those entitlements would not prevent blind people from receiving additional benefits from the new federal commission.[13]

AFPH demands for economic security and full participation in civic life framed the legislation. As in the 1946 bill, three provisions of the 1949 bills sought to improve services for people with severe disabilities by authorizing loans to finance work projects or sheltered workshops, grants to nonprofit organizations to support education for disabled people unable to leave their homes or beds, and a pension system for people with severe disabilities who would not benefit from rehabilitation. Additionally, the 1949 bills, like the 1946 bill, called for increased safety and accessibility in public buildings "to facilitate the free and safe movement" of people with disabilities and a division for people with disabilities within the Civil Service Commission.[14]

Because many AFPH members saw pensions as the least desirable means to financial security and had little faith in the civilian rehabilitation program, the 1949 bills outlined a much more detailed program for financial assistance for individuals rejected from rehabilitation that included a system of protections designed to ensure greater access to rehabilitation and pensions if rehabilitation remained unfeasible. Whereas the 1946 bill called for thirty-dollar monthly payments to be made by the Bureau of Public Assistance of the Social Security Board to all people with disabilities who were rejected for rehabilitation, the 1949 bills mandated grants to the states and placed the onus of administering and distributing pensions on the states.[15]

Under the program, states would be required to designate an administrative agency to manage the program, issue sixty-dollar monthly payments to people deemed unfeasible for rehabilitation, and protect the privacy of recipients and applicants. The desire to cultivate the opportunity to work remained central even in this pension program. AFPH legislation mandated that pension recipients could receive annual medical examinations to reassess their eligibility for rehabilitation. Further, the experience of being rejected from rehabilitation had taught activists the necessity of an appeal mechanism for people denied pensions under the program. The bills placed the entire financial burden of the program on the federal government but left space for states to supplement federal benefits.[16]

In hearings in 1946 and 1949, the NFB criticized how the bills would administer aid. Extending the language of the Social Security Act's Aid to the Blind provision, the bills targeted "needy individuals who are physically or mentally handicapped." In an effort to link the aid program to rehabilitation, eligibility was further constrained to permanently disabled individuals, deemed unfeasible for rehabilitation, and "without means of livelihood and support." While the NFB supported the idea of aid for people with disabilities, its executive director A. L. Archibald argued that blind people's experience with Aid to the Blind had taught them that means-tested aid punished individuals who "gain[ed] even a slender toehold on the economic ladder, $1 is deducted from his aid for every dollar which he earns. This is the exact equivalent of a 100 percent income tax." The NFB maintained that disability pensions "should be given on the basis of compensation for loss of earning power due to blindness or other handicapped," or that "the means test be modified to exclude from consideration generous amounts of income in order to encourage recipients of the pension to do all within their power to lead as nearly as possible a normal life."[17]

Further, the NFB called attention to the AFPH's support of sheltered workshops. Archibald asserted, "The blind have had a rather long experience with sheltered employment, and in the main in a good many parts of the country, it has not been a happy one." He criticized the low wages and "poor working conditions" that often characterized sheltered employment and called for protections of sheltered employees under the Fair Labor Standards Act.[18] The NFB's stance on AFPH legislation drew on the organization's ongoing efforts to promote mainstream employment for blind people and gain protections for blind workers in sheltered shops as well as its critique of Aid to the Blind that focused on the miserly benefits coupled with state supervision.[19]

The NFB's criticism pointed out contradictions in the AFPH agenda. Like the welfare state more broadly, the AFPH bills promised work and a range of benefits to those who could be fitted for work and aid to those who could not. While the bills would have created an elaborate system to keep the window of opportunity open to those deemed unfeasible for rehabilitation, the system proposed by the AFPH privileged work and workers. AFPH members and leaders attacked rehabilitation bureaucrats and experts, chafing at being the objects of what they perceived as condescension and the subjects of new levels of expert scrutiny and supervision. Yet the AFPH's focus on work would have established a system that replaced the exclusions and supervision that they were challenging with new types of exclusions and supervision. At the core, the organization sought to make the promises of the New Deal accessible to people with disabilities. AFPH leaders sought legislation that would make possible their participation in the existing order.[20]

In seeking integration, the AFPH's agenda, as articulated in the bills it developed, reproduced some of the exclusions of the broader economic order and the welfare state. For example, the 1946 federal commission bill had called for the establishment of a personal catastrophe loan system, which would allow individuals to borrow money to purchase assistive devices that would help them return to work. The bill specified that the federal commission could "make such investigations as may be necessary, and shall certify that the applicant is worthy and of good character, and that he appears likely, with the help of a loan, to be restored to useful and gainful employment, and that he has not the instant means of independent action." That language most certainly would have made people with disabilities the objects of scrutiny, but that language had a greater context—a context in which immigration restriction had been tied to disability and disability to a propensity for "becoming a public charge" and in which disabled people's economic and civic marginalization grew out of a notion that they could not or should not work.[21]

In defining eligibility in this way, the AFPH challenged assumptions that people with disabilities could not be "worthy applicants." Indeed, AFPH vice president Margaret Nickerson Martin defended the loan system: "The implication that handicapped people should never be asked to repay a loan is just another facet of the attitude maintained by certain groups who feel that handicapped people are charity cases just because they are handicapped. They imply that all handicapped are indigent because of their handicap rather than because of their individual status." Thus, in countering the notion that people with disabilities would inevitably be "charity cases," AFPH members and leaders at times undermined their broader vision that disability discrimination, not individual fault, locked people with disabilities in a cycle of poverty. While reproducing some exclusionary mechanisms, the bills simultaneously cast those exclusions in a new light. It is important to note, however, that the AFPH imagined a federal commission administering these policies staffed largely by people with disabilities, and that distinction might have mitigated the indignities of the system.[22]

The AFPH's demand for research represented another contradiction in the group's agenda. The organization challenged the medicalization of the rehabilitation bureaucracy and demanded a greater role for people with disabilities in shaping federal disability policy, yet the AFPH also advocated research on the prevention and treatment of disability. Indeed, the organization sponsored legislation to foster research on cerebral palsy, epilepsy, and leprosy, or Hansen's Disease.[23] Both the cerebral palsy and epilepsy bills called for national research institutes. The AFPH also sponsored conferences, special sessions during conventions, and other events that focused on specific diseases and drew on the expertise of professionals and researchers. For example, the AFPH's Second National Conference on Placement of the Severely Handicapped in 1952 accommodated some two hundred delegates, three days of meetings, and panels on epilepsy, multiple sclerosis, poliomyelitis, and muscular dystrophy.[24] The hearings on the AFPH research-focused bills revealed the tension between the hope for better treatment and the uncomfortable othering that accompanied being the subject of research. Strachan told the Senate committee considering the leprosy bill, "since I belong to that great fraternity, the physically handicapped, and since we are in a sense, if my friends will forgive me, guinea pigs for doctors and administrators to use, our viewpoint may not be necessarily important." He went on to condemn research conducted without a practical aim in mind and the tendency to "hoard" findings. He argued, "I don't want to stop with the doctors. I don't want to stop with research." Strachan, instead, asked the committee to "take into consideration the necessity of doing something for the patients themselves as well as making adequate provision for research."[25]

In referring to himself and other people with disabilities as "guinea pigs" whose opinions might not matter, Strachan highlighted the unease in the relationship, yet by demanding research with a practical outcome, members sought to participate in shaping the process. Ironically, the AFPH's drive for research, tempered as it was, generated results. The campaign coincided with Truman's efforts to increase medical research as part of his Fair Deal and the growth of lay lobbying efforts in support of medical research, and the AFPH bills were drawn into a much larger bill that greatly expanded the size and scope of the National Institutes of Health.[26]

Despite these contradictions in the AFPH agenda, the organization, through the federal commission bills of 1946 and 1949, expressed an implicit critique of the FSA's administration of vocational rehabilitation. The economic impetus of the AFPH agenda dovetailed with organized labor's views on disability and its belief that the federal government should safeguard Americans against the economic and health uncertainties of work and life. Moreover, the AFPH's critique of the civilian rehabilitation program resonated with organized labor leaders who were frustrated by the program's failure to work with organized labor and for workers.

Organized Labor Enters the Fray

In 1946, with the House Committee on Labor scheduled to hold hearings on the federal commission bill, AFPH chief Strachan contacted AFL president William Green for assistance. Strachan's own ties to organized labor generally, and the AFL specifically, helped him to build his case. He conjured Green's personal knowledge of "affliction, in the shape of Physical Disability," arguing that this "affliction" plagued workers more so than others. Strachan's appeal and the AFPH's broader agenda must have resonated with Green, who had spent twenty years in the coal mines, witnessing the horrors mine work inflicted on workers.[27] The terrible conditions in the mines, Green remembered, left miners "abnormally susceptible to tuberculosis, rheumatism and other diseases." Poor health was "almost inevitable" for miners.[28] Green assured Strachan of AFL support, and he assigned AFL legislative representative Lewis G. Hines, former Pennsylvania secretary of labor, to handle the matter.[29] While Strachan continued to cultivate this special relationship with the AFL, he also successfully appealed to the Congress of Industrial Organizations (CIO), United Mine Workers of America (UMWA), International

Association of Machinists (IAM), and many other unions for financial and legislative support.

While disability and safety concerns had long fueled unionization campaigns, the AFPH agenda provided a practical link for union leaders between traditional concerns about safety and their new focus on securing health care and expanding the protections of the welfare state.[30] As labor leaders confronted the towering wartime casualties of the battlefield and the factory floor, they advocated for more than workplace safety and access to health care. Their activism on behalf of the AFPH and their financial support for the organization reified their conviction that earning a living was a right that the federal government should protect, and they worked to extend this right to people with disabilities.

Labor leaders were keenly aware of the abysmal health care their members often received. With the notable exception of the UMWA, comprehensive care did not yet exist for union members, and few Americans could afford private insurance. By the 1950s, only 3.5 million Americans had health insurance. Union leaders were also aware that 25 percent of all small loans were made to cover medical bills, and war bonds were more likely to be cashed to meet medical expenses than for any other cause.[31] In this context, unions increasingly took up the drive to win health insurance benefits either at the bargaining table or through congressional action. Organized labor supported the Truman administration's efforts to win national health insurance funded by Social Security taxes—legislation that met fierce opposition from the American Medical Association (AMA) and the growing conservative coalition of Republicans, who were largely hostile to Truman's liberal Fair Deal plans, and southern Democrats, who feared the emphasis on equal access in Truman's health agenda would undermine the Jim Crow system of racial segregation.[32] Improving federal disability policy dovetailed with labor leaders' new health agenda. While historians of the postwar labor movement have argued that workplace safety and class rhetoric played little role in organized labor's campaign for national health care, the dangers of the workplace and employers' disregard of worker safety provided a natural connection between organized labor and disability.[33]

Concern for safety haunted the pages of AFL publications. For instance, in 1952 in the wake of a mining disaster in West Frankfort, Illinois, the *AFL Weekly News Service* slammed legislators who blocked safety legislation in the name of states' rights and employers for their indifference to the safety of working people and to the pleas of their unions. The article explained that

Figure 8. The International Association of Machinists produced this tri-fold pamphlet on "Organized Labor's Program for the Physically Handicapped," for the President's Committee on National Employ the Physically Handicapped Week. It called for health services, education, equal opportunity and pay, union protection, and full employment more broadly. Courtesy of the International Association of Machinists and Aerospace Workers and the George Meany Memorial Archive, University of Maryland Libraries. Pamphlet image © AFL-CIO, used with permission.

weak safety regulations resulted in dead workers. In West Frankfort, federal mine inspectors had recommended that coal operators take measures to seal off or ventilate unused shafts, but the operators ignored inspectors' recommendations. One hundred and nineteen coal miners died in a preventable explosion in West Frankfort. The article concluded, "Hooray for 'state's rights'"[34]

Postwar industrial workers faced a frightening combination of health and safety issues: accidents and occupational illnesses, both exacerbated by management and medical neglect. In many ways, the coal mines represented the most extreme example of unsafe working conditions and employer abuses. Disasters in the mines were not uncommon, and the massive loss of life from a single accident struck a horrifying chord. Conditions in the coal mines made miners susceptible to a wide range of occupational diseases, such as miner's asthma, or black lung. Coal operators were notorious for their lack of concern for miners' health and safety. Judging by the Centralia, Illinois, mining disaster where coal operators received the maximum punishment, a one thousand dollar fine, for willful neglect in the deaths of 111 miners, operators could easily cut costs by paying nominal fines rather than maintaining safe mines.[35] Coal operators were also known for employing company doctors who ignored the health and well-being of miners. One UMWA official told the story of a miner who "had gotten a pick stuck through his foot." A company-chosen physician ordered the man to return to work, despite the fact that the miner's foot was so swollen that he was unable to wear a shoe.[36] While the coal mines presented the ultimate example of unsafe conditions and physician and employer neglect, miners were not alone in their concern for health and safety.

During the World War II congressional investigation on disability policy and in the several hearings on the AFPH's federal commission bills, organized labor leaders articulated a class-informed understanding of disability and offered a pointed critique of the civilian rehabilitation program's failure to aid workers. Much as Strachan's 1946 appeal to Green had emphasized that working people were more likely to become disabled than others, labor leaders agreed with this assessment when they argued that disability was a problem of the working class. The dangers of the workplace and employers' disregard of worker safety provided a natural connection between organized labor and disability.

Union testimony emphasized the link between industrial accidents and disability. For example, CIO representative William J. Pachler pointed out that each year, from 1930 to 1948, about two million workers suffered injuries at work, and about 100,000 of these injuries resulted in permanent disabilities.[37] Hines, a national legislative representative of the AFL, reminded committee members that more workers were injured on the home front than soldiers on the battlefield during World War II. Increasing rates of industrial accidents, he claimed, represented "a real menace to the economic security" of the nation.[38] Thomas Kennedy, vice president of the UMWA, argued that his union's interest in disability grew out of experience. Shocking accident rates meant that in a span of six years every miner could expect to be injured, or killed, on the job.[39] Similarly, George R. Nelson of the IAM asserted that high accident rates among their members had brought IAM leaders "face to face with the real problems confronting the handicapped."[40] In the postwar period, accident rates had declined from the wartime high in 1943, when accidents caused 2.28 million temporary disabilities and killed or permanently disabled 128,000 Americans.[41] Still, the Bureau of Labor Statistics (BLS) placed them in the millions. In 1949, accidents caused 1.87 million temporary disabilities and killed or permanently disabled some 96,000 Americans.[42]

Union leaders not only pointed to industrial accidents but also argued that the vast majority of disabled people were workers. Hines argued "that a great many of these folks are members of our organizations."[43] Hartman Barber of the Brotherhood of Railway and Steamship Clerks, Freight Handlers, Express and Station Employees maintained "that most of the 28,000,000 physically handicapped are workers, or potential workers."[44] Harry Read of the CIO agreed that "it is the working people who become disabled and handicapped in the overwhelming majority of instances."[45] Pachler contended that of those who desperately needed a satisfactory federal disability program, "the greatest numbers . . . [would] be wage earners."[46]

Given labor leaders' arguments that the vast majority of disabled people were wage workers, it should be no surprise that organized labor had always been a major supporter of vocational rehabilitation. AFL president Samuel Gompers assisted Progressive reformers in transforming the veteran pension system to emphasize rehabilitation for disabled soldiers during World War I, and Arthur J. Holder, a one-time national vice president of the IAM, had, in conjunction with the AFL, worked for civilian rehabilitation.[47] Despite labor's role in securing rehabilitation, members of the federal-state civilian rehabilitation program did little to build a working relationship with organized labor. Tensions grew in the 1940s and 1950s as labor leaders complained about program officials' condescending attitudes and their lack of concern for disabled workers in general and disabled union members specifically. These problems seemed to many union leaders to stem from antiunion sentiment on the part of some state rehabilitation officials and the medical focus of the rehabilitation program—a focus made possible by wartime changes in rehabilitation policy.

In 1944, Secretary-Treasurer David J. McDonald of the United Steel Workers of America called the administration of rehabilitation in Pennsylvania "regrettable—if not scandalous." In particular, he pointed to the

Pittsburgh office, where, he charged, the backlog of applicants approached the thousands. Officials there, he said, did little more than train people for "the watchmaking industry." Because of this lack of vision, McDonald argued, administrators failed people with disabilities when it came to placement.[48]

In 1946, Lewis Hines recognized that organized labor needed information about the rehabilitation program. He bristled, however, at the idea of "having some social worker come around and address your union meeting, talking over their heads for 10 or 15 minutes and walking out and having them forget all about it." Hines argued that the job should fall to someone who knew about organized labor and knew the people in the area. Hines pointed to the work of his own union, the Metal Polishers, Buffers, Platers, and Helpers International Union, in rehabilitating veterans and industrial workers with single leg amputations and training them for metal polishing work. His union gave its business agents the responsibility of convincing employers to hire these disabled workers. "With the pressure of the union behind that," he maintained, the program would certainly produce results. In Hines's view, organized labor needed to play a central role in the rehabilitation process, and the civilian rehabilitation program needed to both educate union members about the service and work with union leaders to make the program effective.[49]

In 1950, representing the CIO, Read complained about the attitude of the medical and technical members of the rehabilitation program. He argued that they had "the tendency to make laboratory items of people," much as Strachan argued that disabled people became "guinea pigs" in the medical-rehabilitation system. To rehabilitation officials, Read contended, "The worker becomes a case number." He believed that the DOL could "change their outlook and their attitude."[50] Moreover, he, like many other labor leaders, argued that employment should be "the key objective" of rehabilitation, a job at which the rehabilitation program seemed to be failing.[51] Likewise, Nelson of the IAM asserted that his union wanted disabled people to be "put to work. . . . so they can take their place along with the rest of us."[52]

Labor leaders' testimony during congressional hearings on AFPH initiatives indicated growing dissatisfaction with the efficiency and attitude of members of the civilian rehabilitation program. While labor's increasing advocacy for people with disabilities and engagement with rehabilitation pushed the program to be more responsive to labor, rehabilitation officials' first attempts to build ties with organized labor demonstrated only the lack of knowledge about organized labor and union policies and politics among state rehabilitation leaders and workers, the program's inability to provide adequate services to people with severe disabilities, and its underfunding and understaffing at the state level.

Shortly after Meany published his 1947 article on labor's responsibility to people with disabilities, OVR Information Service head W. Oliver Kincannon, a former reporter and member of the Social Security Administration's information service, notified state directors about the article and suggested that state offices make "prompt contacts" with the AFL to build on the organization's commitment to aid people with disabilities. Kincannon's memorandum also served as a primer for state directors on making connections with the AFL and other unions. Emphasizing the top-down, bureaucratic nature of unions, he pointed out that building relationships first with state federation presidents, then district officials, and then local officials would make working with unions at the regional and local levels easier. Kincannon suggested that state directors and counselors at the local level seek opportunities to speak at union meetings and educate union members about rehabilitation services, while warning that "union members are quick to spot 'talking down' and resent it." Implicit in the memorandum was the OVR's recognition that many of its state officials had built few connections with organized labor and conversely that unions needed and wanted information about the vocational rehabilitation program.[53] The memorandum had little immediate effect, as more than two years later the OVR would still be confronting the problem of establishing a working relationship with organized labor.

One union, the UMWA, however, went to great lengths in the late 1940s and early 1950s to force the civilian rehabilitation program to respond to the needs of its members. Much as coal miners faced extraordinarily unsafe conditions, their union took extreme measures to provide members with disability benefits. In wage negotiations for the bituminous coal fields in 1946 and 1947, UMWA president John L. Lewis secured a union-led and employer-funded health care and pension system for miners. Coal operators paid royalties on each ton of coal mined to the UMWA Welfare and Retirement Fund.[54] Recognizing the financial weight of providing continued care for disabled miners, leaders of the fund looked to the OVR and the rehabilitation program as a way to supplement union services. In January 1948, the fund secured a cooperative agreement with the OVR. The fund would refer beneficiaries with disabilities who might benefit from the rehabilitation program's services, sending referrals and medical reports to the federal OVR. The OVR would then transmit the referrals to the appropriate state agency that would determine the eligibility of individual miners for service and provide the fund with either justification for an applicant's rejection or the successful applicant's rehabilitation plan. Fund officials made it clear that the union would not pay for services that UMWA members were entitled to through the federal-state rehabilitation program, but the fund agreed to pay for any services not provided by the rehabilitation program that would make an individual's rehabilitation more successful. The OVR agreed to instruct state rehabilitation officials to work closely with the fund, sharing information about the progress of fund beneficiaries and any needed supplementary services.[55]

The fund tested the limits of state rehabilitation programs when it launched a major campaign to locate and provide medical treatment and rehabilitation services for miners who had been disabled in the mines prior to its establishment. The fund formed relationships with major hospitals and rehabilitation clinics across the country, and fund and union officials scoured union records and contacted local officials to find miners in need of rehabilitation. Fund physicians transported bed-bound miners from remote mining communities, sometimes carrying men by stretcher for miles to the nearest paved road to begin their journey to a hospital that might be on the other side of the nation.[56]

As officials of the fund worked to provide medical care for these "distress benefit cases," they also pressured the federal-state rehabilitation program to provide vocational guidance and training while these men received medical treatments. In the late 1940s, the fund referred thousands of miners, taxing state programs with the sheer volume of cases. When, in April 1948, the fund completed the referral process for "distress benefit cases" in Alabama, it had already referred 226 cases in that state alone. Local UMWA representatives estimated under normal circumstances the fund would refer five new cases a week in Alabama. Officials in Alabama quickly rejected 167 of those early referrals and struggled to process the other cases. Between 1949 and 1954, the fund referred more than 12,000 beneficiaries to the federal-state rehabilitation program, which accepted only 47 percent of the referrals.[57]

While the fund cemented a close working relationship with the OVR and numerous state agencies, the relationship also revealed the inadequacies of the civilian rehabilitation program, some of which grew out of a lack of staff and funding—slow processing and poor service—and others that were connected to the program's administration—a high rejection rate and negative attitudes about working-class people and unions. The fund invested a great deal of time and resources into policing the program and alerting the OVR when states failed to consider UMWA members in a timely fashion or when services seemed inadequate. For example, in November 1950, T. Russell Esken, assistant to the area medical administrator for the UMWA Welfare and Retirement Fund, wrote to Kenneth E. Pohlmann, director of rehabilitation for the fund, complaining about the Ohio Bureau for Vocational Rehabilitation. Of 169 referrals, no action had been taken by the Ohio rehabilitation bureau on 102 of the cases. Ohio rehabilitation officials had rejected twenty-two of the fund's referrals. According to Esken, "Counseling and guidance was supposedly given" to eight miners who had returned to the mines or were "doing odd jobs." Of the cases that had received rehabilitation in Ohio, Esken concluded that "all services provided by the Ohio State Bureau for Vocational Rehabilitation could have been purchased for a minimal sum in the open market, and the Fund could have dispensed with the necessity for these referrals with a great saving in money spent for clerical time, stationery, etc."[58] Pohlmann forwarded Esken's complaints to the OVR, adding that the fund was "not happy" about the situation. Further, Pohlmann noted that it appeared that "the Ohio Bureau is not too much concerned about the problem." He requested that M. B. Perrin, director of rehabilitation in Ohio, and the regional representative of the OVR investigate the situation, and he asked permission to arrange a meeting between Ohio rehabilitation officials and the fund.[59]

For his part, Perrin expressed considerable resentment toward the fund and its accusations. "Just because our horn has not been tooted from the housetop," he wrote, "does not mean that we in any way attempted to shirk our responsibility to the disabled miner." Perrin argued that fund representatives had failed, despite repeated invitations, to accompany counselors on trips to miners' homes. Moreover, he faulted the disabled miners and their unwillingness to cooperate for the situation. Harkening back to Gilded Age ideas that charity could be a corrupting force in the lives of individuals, Perrin posited, "Welfare funds, compensation funds, and the willingness on the part of other members of the family to sacrifice in the interest of the disabled miner has caused him to set a pattern of satisfaction from which he cannot be shaken." He also pointed out that information supplied by the fund as to the status of fund referrals in Ohio was out of date and did not reflect numerous cases that were being or had been rehabilitated by Ohio's rehabilitation bureau. He further claimed that "some one in Mr. Esken's office went off the deep end" when gathering information about the Ohio rehabilitation bureau.[60]

After local fund and Ohio rehabilitation officials held a conference, the fund softened its critique of the Ohio program, arguing that the problem did not grow out of "a lack of willingness or ability" but from the inadequate number of counselors in Ohio. In February 1951, shortly after fund officials had conferred with Ohio officials, Pohlmann again brought the Ohio situation to the attention of the OVR. This time, however, he reminded OVR officials of their "responsibility to see that the State provides better services." He pointed out that deficiencies in the Ohio program resulted from too few counselors to handle the caseload. He asked the OVR to investigate the situation in Ohio and suggested that through a conference between OVR representatives, Ohio rehabilitation officials, and representatives of the fund and the UMWA a plan might be worked out "to bring services in that state up to par with those of West Virginia."[61]

While the OVR responded quickly to fund complaints, the fund took extraordinary measures to ensure that its beneficiaries received the government benefits to which they were entitled, referring beneficiaries, monitoring referrals, assessing rejections, and policing standards, efficiency, and attitudes. Despite the fund's efforts, about half of all of the miners they referred were deemed unfeasible for rehabilitation. While the fund's relationship with the OVR no doubt improved rehabilitation services for injured miners and in the region more generally, it also demonstrated that the civilian rehabilitation program failed to help thousands of workers, even when those workers benefited from the strong advocacy of the fund.

The OVR's failure to address the needs of even a majority of working class men and women who needed rehabilitation and to build strong ties to organized labor, outside the UMWA, led many unions, including the UMWA, to question the leadership of the FSA and to support disability activists' calls for rehabilitation reform. This growing dissatisfaction among labor leaders and disability activists' constant, public critique pushed the FSA into action.

A Countermeasure and Failed Compromise

While the AFPH courted increasing support from organized labor, the FSA responded to the mounting dissatisfaction among labor leaders and disability activists with the rehabilitation program. The FSA drafted a bill to expand rehabilitation services and bolster the OVR shortly before the 1949 House hearings on the federal commission bill and launched a campaign to win over the AFL. The FSA's bill undermined AFPH activists' plans for the 1949 hearings as the FSA pressured AFPH's supporters, including the AFL, to examine the FSA bill before they testified in support of the federal commission bill. Additionally, the FSA, as the agency that housed the rehabilitation program, initially secured support from the Bureau of the Budget and the Truman administration, placing government officials who supported the AFPH bill in an increasingly awkward position. For example, secretary of labor Maurice J. Tobin had intended to testify at the 1949 hearing on behalf of the AFPH, but in light of the administration's support of the FSA bill, he chose not to testify and "embarrass the Administration," thus seemingly withdrawing support from the AFPH.[62]

In response, the AFPH launched a campaign to reverse the White House's position on the bills. The White House received some 242 petitions, letters, and telegrams in support of the AFPH's bill from disability activists and their supporters. Sixty-nine percent of this correspondence came from individuals or groups of people who specifically identified themselves as disabled and, of those, 63 percent mentioned their affiliation with the AFPH. Nine percent of the mail the White House received in support of the federal commission bills came from organized labor, including telegrams from CIO secretary-treasurer James Carey, IAM president A. J. Hayes, and Glass Bottle Blowers Association president Lee W. Minton as well as letters and telegrams from union locals across the country. Many AFPH chapters sent letters on behalf of the chapter with numerous signatures, and even some independent letter writers obtained the signatures of family and friends. A great majority of the correspondence came from the AFPH strongholds of New York, Indiana, Pennsylvania, and Michigan, but letters came from all over the country.[63]

Typical of this letter writing campaign, one AFPH member wrote, "only those who are sick and Handicapped can know what a terrible problem it is, we don't mind the afflictions that we have to bear it's the financial problem that is the real burden." The writer condemned Washington bureaucrats and rehabilitation officials who were blocking the AFPH's bill, arguing, "The men who have the Rehabilitation jobs are working and doing every thing they possibly can to help throw this bill out, ARE YOU GOING TO ALLOW THIS TO HAPPEN?"[64]

As the pile of letters and telegrams grew, a White House memorandum analyzing the campaign explained that the FSA worked from the "assumption" that employment was only one of many goals of rehabilitation. People with disabilities, however, had made it very clear that the administration's efforts needed to focus on employment and not on "charity and welfare." The memo suggested, "It may well be that a thorough housecleaning is needed at the State level, a housecleaning that can come only with a different top agency responsible for operations." Further, it noted, "In clearing the FSA bills, the Bureau [of the Budget] may be giving its implied approval to existing conditions which are far from desirable."[65]

Secretary Tobin also intervened, pushing the White House to reverse its approval of the FSA bills and to adopt a more neutral position. President Truman assigned D. H. Stowe, one of his administrative assistants, to work out a compromise between the FSA, the DOL, and the AFPH. When Stowe's efforts failed, the DOL drafted a "compromise" bill of its own. Basically an amended version of the AFPH bill, the DOL bill focused on improving employment opportunities for people with disabilities, provided for a less controversial funding system than the heavily federal AFPH bill, and offered no provisions for pensions. The DOL's bill did little to satisfy the FSA because it placed administrative control of disability services in the DOL, resurrecting the old turf battle.[66]

Ultimately, the Truman administration withheld approval from all of the bills, allowing the FSA, DOL, and AFPH bills a hearing before a subcommittee of the Senate Labor and Public Welfare Committee in May 1950. As one *Washington Post* reporter wrote, "An undercover battle between Secretary of Labor Maurice J. Tobin and Federal Security Administrator Oscar R. Ewing for control of Federal aid to the physically handicapped will be aired in public this week."[67] In pushing for its federal commission bill, the AFPH again stirred the bureaucratic and ideological conflict that had surfaced over the President's Committee on NEPHW.

In the 1950 Senate hearing, Ewing of the FSA and Tobin of the DOL squared off, presenting the clearest statements of the ideological differences that divided the agencies. Tobin, echoing the analysis offered by disability activists, argued that the main thrust of the rehabilitation program should be employment. "We would," he maintained, "not have a really effective program for the physically handicapped if it is not made certain that the end result is a job."[68] He pointed to employer discrimination against people with disabilities and emphasized the benefits to the national economy that would come from ending such discrimination.[69] Tobin also understood that failing to find jobs for people with disabilities meant that they would be cut off from a wide range of public and private benefits, including old-age pensions, survivor's benefits, workers' compensation, and unemployment benefits—what historian Alice Kessler-Harris has termed economic citizenship. "The handicapped individual," he declared, "has a right to participate as fully as anyone else in our system of social and economic security."[70]

Tobin argued for placing services for disabled people within the DOL because the department already had responsibilities in industrial safety and accident prevention. The DOL, he noted, was also charged with implementing fair labor standards, which were all too relevant given the widespread employment discrimination against people with disabilities. He pointed out that the BLS had already collected valuable information on disabled workers and that the bureau's ongoing services would be vital in building a sound program for them. If the rehabilitation program was to end in a job, he asserted, the Employment Service, which had been transferred back to the DOL in 1949, would be the critical component. Finally, he concluded, "As the Department most closely connected with the problems of the labor force, not only through the activities of the Employment Services, but of its other bureaus, the DOL is the logical one to administer this program."[71]

Ewing, however, viewed rehabilitation as a process to be handled by experts in the fields of medicine and counseling. He attacked both the AFPH and DOL bills, telling the Senate subcommittee that the DOL's emphasis on jobs was "misplaced."[72] FSA officials also argued that rehabilitation was intertwined with the "health, education, and social security services" that the agency provided. Moreover, they insisted that their personnel had "the experience and special knowledge" to make rehabilitation successful.[73] These officials emphasized that the OVR had the support of the National Rehabilitation Association, the American Public Welfare Association, and the AMA—all organizations that served people with disabilities or advocated for them, but did not represent them.[74]

Despite the fact that vocational rehabilitation was designed to put people with disabilities into the workforce, the program had no formal employment policies or agencies. As FSA officials attempted to counter DOL arguments about the significance of the end goal of employment, they downplayed the importance of the Employment Service, emphasized the importance of the rehabilitation counselor in the employment process, and inadvertently exposed the haphazard way that rehabilitants actually secured employment. Because the rehabilitation counselor was out and about in the community, he would often stumble upon jobs for his clients, noted G. Lyle Belsley, commissioner for special services for the FSA, who had previously worked for the War Production Board and earned a Ph.D. in economics and public administration from the Robert Brookings Graduate School of Economics and Government.[75] Ewing reported that a 1949 study of five state vocational rehabilitation programs and their relationship to Employment Service showed that just 30 percent of rehabilitation clients received placements through either the rehabilitation office or Employment Service. Seventy percent had found employment on their own, through employer initiatives, or with the aid of other organizations or agencies. Ewing argued, "I do not think the key word is welfare, nor do I think that it is employment, I think the key word is rehabilitation, which encompasses the whole program. . . . Our job is to carry [the disabled individual] to the point where he is both self-confident and self-supporting."[76] Thus, these professionals did not define the security that rehabilitation provided in terms of work. Rather, it was the outcome of medical, psychological, and educational interventions that changed the disabled individual and made him employable. Organized labor, disability activists, and the DOL argued that jobs, not just medical intervention, should be the heart of rehabilitation.

Rather than creating a space for compromise, the hearing renewed disagreements about disability policy. The AFPH's compromise to fight for an independent agency instead of pushing for DOL control of disability services generated broader congressional support and initially met with support from organized labor. By 1950, however, many labor leaders renewed their commitment to DOL control of rehabilitation, arguing that the program should be handled by the DOL not only because they wanted to strengthen the department but also because they believed its employees had a better understanding of the job market and would be more apt to provide services to workers disabled on the job. Such an approach, Read of the CIO argued, would "secure a closer liaison between the administrators of the program and their clients who are primarily wage and salary earners."[77] Barber of the Brotherhood of Railway and Steamship Clerks, Freight Handlers, Express and Station Employees contended that most disabled people were workers and "activities of government affecting them should be included in the workers' department—the Department of Labor."[78] With labor insisting on DOL authority over disability services, at the 1950 Senate hearings the AFPH backpedaled on its independent agency idea, and Senator Sparkman presented a revised version of the federal commission bill that placed administrative responsibility for federal disability policy in the DOL.[79]

Just as AFPH leadership recognized the importance of organized labor's support, administrators of the FSA and OVR began to realize that they were losing a powerful potential ally in organized labor to the AFPH. In the months leading up to the House hearings on the federal commission bill, the OVR made a concerted effort to contact national labor leaders about the activities of the federal-state rehabilitation program. In March and April 1949, Kincannon and OVR Labor Information Specialist Herbert Borchardt held conferences with union leaders and members of unions' national education and research departments, including the AFL, CIO, IAM, United Steelworkers of America, and the National Railway Labor Executives Association. Kincannon and Borchardt tried to provide union officials with information about the rehabilitation services available to injured workers, and they emphasized that the DOL represented a "department *of* Labor," but the FSA, they argued, was the "Department *for* Labor."[80]

In July 1949, just one day before hearings were set to begin in the House on the federal commission bill, W. C. Hushing, AFL legislative director, received word that an administration bill had been drafted by FSA administrator Ewing. Hushing asked Green to give Ewing a chance to explain the benefits of his agency's bill. Much as Tobin initially had been forced to walk a fine line in public with the administration backing the FSA's bill, the AFL decided to withhold direct support from both the AFPH and FSA bills, taking a more careful approach to avoid conflict with both President Truman and Ewing, a key supporter of expanding social insurance in the Truman administration, particularly national health insurance. The AFL referred the bills to a subcommittee for a hearing of their own. At the 1949 House hearings, the union emphasized the need for expanded and better services for people with disabilities without taking a stand on the individual bills.[81] While waiting until the AFL subcommittee had made a decision, Green continued to offer AFL support to the AFPH, writing to Strachan, assuring him that he had instructed Hines and Walter J. Mason, both members of the AFL Legislative Department, "to work with you, serve with you and help and assist you."[82]

When the AFL subcommittee convened in June 1950, it heard testimony from officials of the FSA and DOL as well as Strachan and Mildred Scott of the AFPH. The subcommittee reported to Green that the FSA provided statistical evidence that only 5 percent of the cases referred for rehabilitation services had disabilities related to industry, while 88 percent of referrals and applications fielded by the program involved disabilities that resulted from chronic disease. "The implication of these data," the committee report read, "was that the problem of rehabilitation was not a 'labor problem' which should be administered by the Department of Labor."[83]

The subcommittee, however, argued that the FSA's "statistical picture did not square with the facts of the existing situation." In essence, the subcommittee viewed the lack of disabled workers served as evidence of the FSA's failure to reach them and not as proof that disability most often happened outside the workplace. In fact, it reported that under questioning FSA officials "admitted that little had been done to adequately place before either wage earners or their employers the nature or purpose of the rehabilitation program." The subcommittee wrote that FSA administration of the program had pushed the rehabilitation program far from the original objectives of aiding workers and placing disabled people in jobs. "Medical attention," the committee argued, "has been emphasized to the point where re-training and job placement have become secondary." In the end, the subcommittee unanimously voted to support the DOL bill, but it also offered support to the federal commission bill, except for the provision for pensions, which the subcommittee believed would "jeopardize" the legislation given the "economy-minded Congress." While subcommittee members did not wish to "disparage" the contribution of medicine to rehabilitation, they ultimately concluded that these contributions should not dictate the process—a process they believed should be about work.[84]

In the wake of the AFL subcommittee's decision that the DOL should head federal disability services, rehabilitation officials began to take careful stock of their relationship with organized labor. For example, in June 1950, J. Hank Smith, director of rehabilitation in Tennessee, issued a memorandum to all of his district supervisors and counselors, designating the period from 21 August to 22 September a time to build strong ties with organized labor. Smith wrote, "By misusing the President's Committee in particular, Paul Strachan has been able to sell the representatives of organized labor . . . on the proposition that Rehabilitation has accomplished nothing and has done nothing for the working man in particular." Smith charged that rehabilitation officials all over the nation "made themselves vulnerable by ignoring local labor unions." He maintained that rehabilitation officials had spent considerable time showing films and giving talks for women's, school, and civic groups, but the same could not be said to be true for organized labor. "Had we discharged this obligation," he argued, "Strachan would never have been in a position to have attacked us so successfully."[85]

At the federal level, Kincannon of the OVR admitted that the state programs had focused considerable efforts on work with the medical community and organizations in related fields, but had done little to court the support of organized labor outside the OVR's relationship with the UMWA. OVR officials had repeatedly instructed the states to build working relationships with local union officials, but did not monitor states' progress on the labor front. Kincannon also admitted that he saw truth in union accusations that state rehabilitation officials were "anti-labor." He believed that this anti-union attitude grew out of "a combination of scholastic background and a complete unfamiliarity with Labor" on the part of state rehabilitation officials. Kincannon thought that the OVR had achieved positive results when the federal office undertook concerted efforts to educate state officials and push them to work with organized labor. He concluded, "It is natural that all Labor will vote consistently for improvement of the Department of Labor," but he hoped through continued work the OVR could push organized labor to a point where "that opposition to retention of OVR in FSA will be philosophical, rather than active."[86]

In August 1950, the OVR instructed regional representatives of the rehabilitation program to report to the national office all of the activities that their regions had undertaken to improve relations with organized labor. The reports revealed that many states had done very little to build an effective, two-way relationship with representatives of labor. For example, the director of rehabilitation in Nevada reported that while the state program "had no regular meetings with Labor Groups," officials contacted state labor leaders for legislative aid. The Oregon Commission for the Blind made it a regular policy to contact organized labor when they wanted to place a rehabilitation client in a union job. Officials in Oregon reported that they found this "individual labor unions on individual problems" policy effective because labor representatives were "people of a more practical term of mind," who needed "something definite and specific to sink their teeth into." One counselor in Oregon told the state director of rehabilitation that the relationship with organized labor could be greatly improved if rehabilitation workers went "to the unions offering our services rather than asking for a favor (as we usually do)." C. F. Feike, director of rehabilitation in Oregon, argued that changing the attitude of local labor leaders seemed an impossible task "when there is a continuous flow of propaganda coming from a national source," and he wished that the AFL and CIO on the national level "would adopt an attitude of non-criticism and allow the individual states to form their own opinions."

Feike also expressed dissatisfaction with the idea that rehabilitation officials should "stress their services for any particular disability group." After all, organized labor, he rationalized, did not represent the whole of the working class. The OVR concluded that this survey revealed "the great need" for states agencies to "adopt a more positive approach in developing understanding and support of the vocational rehabilitation program among Labor organizations."[87]

While the OVR worked to win the support of organized labor, senators in the Subcommittee on Vocational Rehabilitation of the Physically Handicapped of the Senate Committee on Labor and Public Welfare sought compromise where the administration had failed. During the 1950 Senate hearings, chairperson Paul H. Douglas (D-IL) gave both the DOL and FSA "an admonitory tap on the wrist" for trespassing too far into the legislative functions of government. He, nevertheless, welcomed their advice on disability policy "with the understanding that they are to be on tap but not on top." Douglas also warned the Bureau of the Budget not to play administrative favorites, arguing that the agency "is presumably neutral" and "presumably tries to keep above the competition of all the power struggles of the greedy and hungry public agencies."[88]

After hearing eight days of testimony, Douglas, along with subcommittee members, Herbert H. Lehman (D-NY) and George D. Aiken (R-VT), drafted an expansive compromise measure that they believed would both improve civilian rehabilitation and address many of the critiques of organized labor and disability activists in the AFPH. The Douglas bill, sponsored by a coalition of Democrats and a few liberal Republicans, built on the Barden-La Follette Act of 1943, the Randolph-Shepard Act of 1936, and the FSA, DOL, and AFPH bills.[89]

The bill proposed retaining administration of rehabilitation in the FSA and the federal-state sharing of rehabilitation costs, but it expanded the scope of the existing program. It sought to introduce a number of new services as well as administrative and financial changes. AFPH activists consistently criticized the rehabilitation program for its failure to address the needs of people with severe disabilities. As a result, the Douglas bill encouraged states, through the lure of federal grants, to develop workshops, home-employment programs, and business initiatives for people with severe disabilities. Additionally, the bill attempted to force the rehabilitation program to concentrate its efforts on people with severe disabilities by making disabled citizens who needed only job counseling or placement assistance ineligible for rehabilitation services. To help these individuals, the Douglas bill provided the Employment Service greater authority in assisting disabled people to find employment. The bill addressed the AFPH's call for increased employment opportunities within the federal government by establishing a division for people with disabilities in the Civil Service Commission. In addition, the bill adopted the AFPH's proposal of a revolving loan program for states and extended the idea to provide loans to assist in the establishment and maintenance of workshops for people with severe disabilities. In response to the AFPH's calls for the federal government to collect more information about disability, the Douglas bill charged the Bureau of Employment Security with the responsibility of gathering information about employer policies and practices relating to disabled workers. Finally, the Douglas bill called for the establishment of federal and state advisory councils on rehabilitation and mandated that people with disabilities be represented on these councils, ensuring that "the suggestions and criticisms" of people with disabilities would "be brought to bear on the operation and improvement of the program."[90]

The Douglas bill also addressed deficiencies in the rehabilitation program that were mutually recognized by rehabilitation officials, AFPH activists, the FSA, the DOL, and labor leaders. All sides agreed that inadequate funds presented a major problem, and the Douglas measure sought to encourage increased state participation in supporting rehabilitation through numerous federal grant programs. The bill also provided variable grants to the states based on per capita income, offering additional federal support (up to 75 percent) for states with lower per capita incomes and less federal aid (as low as 40 percent) for states with higher incomes. Committee members also believed that the new funding structure would encourage states to offer medical services. In the previous funding model, the federal government had covered all administrative costs, including the costs for vocational guidance and counseling. The Douglas bill would have awarded all federal funding on the variable grant model, removing incentives to focus only on counseling. All sides had also pushed for rehabilitation centers, where services could be offered at a central location. The Douglas bill encouraged the development of these centers through a new grant program and coordination with the Hospital Survey and Construction Act of 1946, which provided federal funds for hospital construction. Finally, the bill provided for grants for research and training in the field of rehabilitation, addressing the shared concern of the need for more qualified personnel and better techniques.[91]

Beyond retaining the program in the FSA, the bill drew on several suggestions proposed by leaders in rehabilitation. Much as the FSA had proposed additional services for blind citizens, the Douglas bill provided for federal grants-in-aid to bolster services for blind Americans, including providing federal funds to support the Randolph-Shepard Act, which gave blind people the right to operate vending stands in federal buildings, and to encourage states to develop and provide services for people adjusting to blindness. Additionally, the Douglas bill sought to enhance the status of the OVR by making it a full-fledged bureau.[92]

In deciding to keep the rehabilitation program in the FSA, Douglas argued that rehabilitation should be a medical and educational process. He did not discount the need for job placement services. However, by making people who needed only employment assistance ineligible for rehabilitation, he both privileged the medical and educational aspects of rehabilitation and emphasized the need to serve people with disabilities who were not ready for jobs. Douglas also maintained that transferring rehabilitation to the DOL would certainly cause at least a temporary "loss of efficiency which accompanies major administrative changes in a long-time program." He argued, "The shortcomings in the present program cannot be remedied by a mere transfer to another agency." Further, the Douglas committee seemed far more impressed than the AFL by FSA figures that disability in the United States was a product of disease and not work. Where AFL leaders questioned whether rehabilitation officials had attempted to reach out to disabled workers, the Douglas committee believed the FSA's statistics that roughly half of all of their referrals came from health, education, and welfare agencies and not from workers' compensation administrators as evidence that disability was not a class problem but a far-reaching medical issue.[93]

Douglas's own opinions about the process of rehabilitation might have influenced the committee's decision in the FSA's favor. Douglas, an economist who taught at a number of universities prior to his election to the Senate but primarily the University of Chicago, had written an article in 1918 on the War Risk Insurance Act that would mandate a system of rehabilitation for World War I soldiers. He praised the law for recognizing "the necessity of medical care" and including provisions for reeducation. "The disabled person needs, not only a money grant," he wrote, "but also training, so that his disability will be the slightest possible hindrance to his re-entering industry."[94] Douglas's 1918 assessment of the value of medical care and the importance of reducing the disability fit well with FSA officials' position that rehabilitation needed to alter the individual to fit within the broader economy.

Moreover, AFPH demands that policymakers focus attention on the broad workings of social and economic discrimination came at precisely the time when policymakers began to discount society's role in creating social evils. In the Cold War context, policy increasingly focused on correcting faults within the individual who needed aid. Rehabilitation officials, physicians, and other professionals drew on the authority they had built during the war and postwar years and offered an answer to the problem of disability that focused on the disabled individual, instead of systemic issues in the American system. Moreover, as they envisioned rehabilitation, the process demonstrated the medical and technological power of the United States and harnessed this power to "fix" those who did not live up to the American ideal. Disability activists and their organized labor allies, however, pointed over and over again to the carnage wrought by American industry. They offered both a critique of industrial capitalism and exclusions embedded in the American system. As the Cold War turned hot, a medical and professional rehabilitation that focused on individuals promised to solve these problems without altering the system.[95]

Between May 1950, when Senate subcommittee hearings were held, and August, when the Senate Committee on Labor and Public Welfare approved the Douglas bill, Communist North Korea had invaded South Korea, and President Truman committed U.S. forces to hold back the Communist threat. This new military conflict, according to the committee report, brought "to mind the grim lessons of World War II." Ultimately, the committee report stated that even before the escalation of hostility in Korea the need for a better rehabilitation program was clear, but with this new military engagement, the need had become more pressing. "Before the national situation becomes more critical," the report read, "the committee recommends that Congress lay the groundwork for an intensive program so that we shall be ready for an all-out effort and be able to build soundly for the future."[96]

Even in the midst of renewed military operations, the Douglas compromise bill ultimately failed. Where World War II labor shortages and battlefield casualties pushed Congress into action and encouraged compromises, disability legislation stalled during the Korean War. With many of the World War II mechanisms to bring people with disabilities into the workforce still functioning, the urgency that informed earlier compromises was missing. Without any additional legislation, the Employment Service placed 277,000 disabled people into jobs in 1951, nearly matching World War II records.[97] AFPH president Strachan's reaction to the Douglas bill likely muddied the waters further. In a letter to the organized labor legislative representatives who worked closely with the AFPH, Strachan railed against the bill, arguing that Douglas was "off the reservation" and claiming that the Douglas bill "COMPLETELY IGNORED RECOMMENDATIONS OF LABOR as well as AFPH." While Strachan fired off letters to every member of the Senate, he urged his labor supporters to contact the members of the Senate Labor and Public Welfare Committee. Strachan, unwilling to accept compromise, used all his connections to block the bill.[98] His efforts were no doubt aided by the fact that Truman's domestic agenda and liberal legislation more generally faced considerable opposition from Republicans and southern Democrats.

While the Douglas bill passed the Senate on 13 September 1950, the measure never made it to the House floor.[99] Douglas introduced the bill again in 1951, but the AFPH again worked to block the measure. The organization had its own bill introduced into the House fifteen separate times before the end of July 1951.[100] Ultimately, neither measure passed either house. Without the urgency that had made legislation necessary during World War II, the divides about how to approach rehabilitation prevented action.

In 1950, Congress did, however, reach an important compromise that would expand public assistance for disabled people—one that grew much more out of organized labor's efforts than the AFPH's. While labor made little progress on Social Security in the 1940s, circumstances had changed by 1950. Securing protections for disabled members at the bargaining table meant that unions had to make concessions on other priorities; thus, expanding social insurance to disabled workers would free unions to focus negotiations on wages and other benefits. Even as support for old age pensions grew, organized labor faced opposition from the AMA and conservative resistance to expanding Social Security to include disability. In 1950, organized labor pushed to include disability in the amendments that would expand coverage and benefits. The move failed, but a compromise extended public assistance to needy disabled individuals through the Aid to the Permanently and Totally Disabled program, similar to the Aid to the Blind provision.[101]

Both the success of the Douglas bill in the Senate in 1950 and the ultimate failure of the bill in 1951 hinted at the trouble the AFPH would face in the coming years. With the Douglas bill, Senate liberals attempted to create a middle ground, arguing that people with disabilities needed access to medical care, educational support, and jobs. The measure addressed many of the AFPH's major concerns about federal disability policy and would have

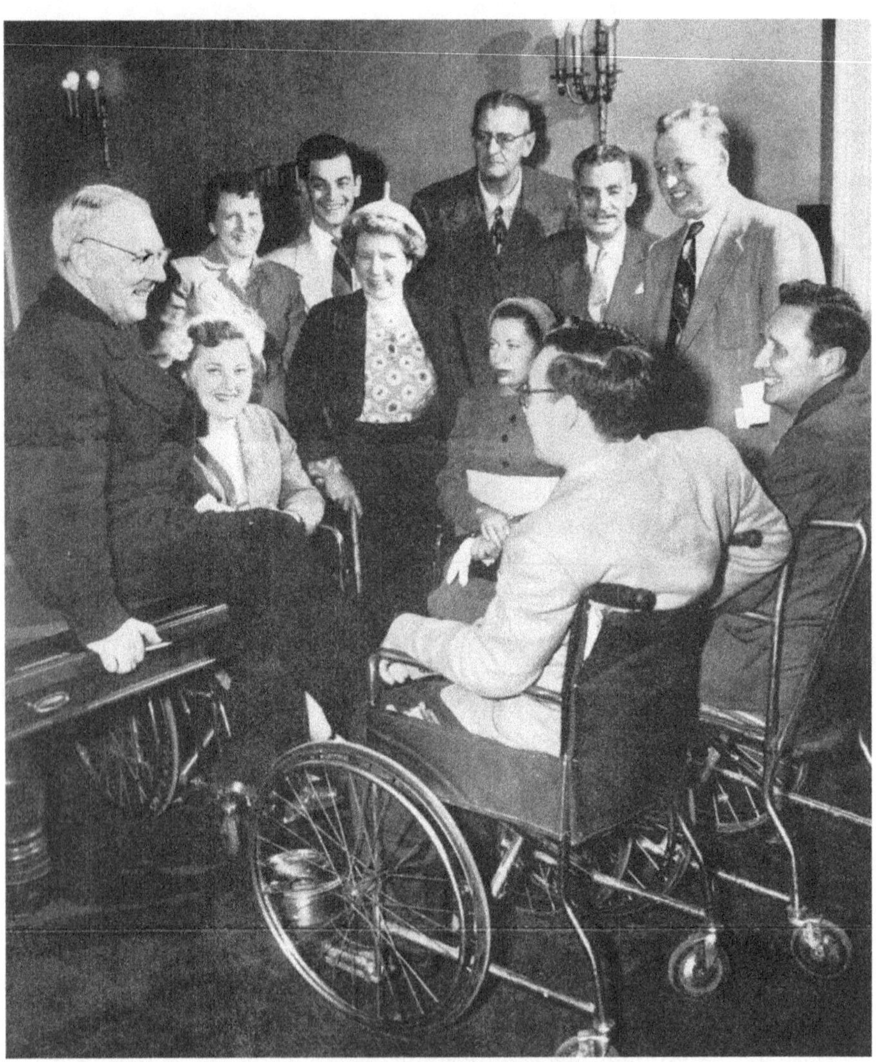

Figure 9. A committee of ten AFPH leaders met with Representative Graham A. Barden (D-NC), who chaired the House Committee on Education and Labor, in March 1952 to urge hearings on the organization's bill that sought to establish a federal agency to serve people with disabilities. Mildred Scott is shown wearing a hat and standing in the center of the group; Paul Strachan stands behind her. Courtesy of the George Meany Memorial Archive, University of Maryland Libraries. Image © AFL-CIO, used with permission.

created several programs to help people with both severe and minor disabilities find employment. Still, Strachan actively blocked the Douglas bill, experience and hard feelings making him unwilling to trust rehabilitation policy to the FSA and OVR.

It is impossible to know if the Douglas bill would have passed in the House without Strachan's strident efforts to block the measure. It is clear, however, that the sense of crisis that had spurred considerable attention to issues of disability was beginning to wane. As Truman and liberal legislators faced considerable hostility to Fair Deal aims, liberals in Congress began to search for common ground. However, years of fighting had magnified philosophical differences and stirred resentment among disability activists and labor leaders for decades of denied services and the air of professional authority that rehabilitation counselors had purposefully cultivated.

AFPH leaders believed that legislative success hinged on their ability to convince the American public that disability mattered to every American, that disability policy could save tax dollars and increase national wealth, whereas a lack of effective policy could drain federal and state coffers. These efforts inadvertently lent additional weight and authority to rehabilitation bureaucrats and medical experts in the field—the people who could claim expertise and experience in addressing the problem AFPH leaders had worked to convince Americans they had.

Chapter 6

Götterdämmerung: Rehabilitating Rights in the 1950s

In December 1950, the American Federation of the Physically Handicapped (AFPH) declared that the "Gotterdammerung of the Rehab Gods" was at hand. Referencing Richard Wagner's operatic telling of the demise of the German gods, writers for *Valor*, the mouthpiece of the AFPH, predicted that after decades of exercising nearly "unlimited powers" over people with disabilities, leaders of the federal-state civilian rehabilitation program, like the gods in Wagner's famous opera, would be defeated. Until these leaders recognized "that they are SERVANTS, NOT MASTERS of the Handicapped," the article contended, the AFPH would "continue its relentless battle to redress the balance of power . . . swung so far against the Handicapped."[1]

Citing changes within the administration of the Federal Security Agency (FSA) and the Office of Vocational Rehabilitation (OVR), *Valor* argued that the signs pointed to an eventual victory for the AFPH. The article reported that FSA official G. Lyle Belsley was "looking for another $15,000 a year sinecure," since his position as commissioner of special services had been eliminated in the administrative reworking of the rehabilitation service. Michael J. Shortley, who had headed the OVR since it was established in 1943, had been transferred to a new post as a regional director for the FSA, while Mary E. Switzer, who had been a special assistant to FSA chief Oscar Ewing, had been promoted to director of the OVR. Switzer, *Valor* writers assessed, "has had little practical experience, other than charity," which they argued was "very definitely" the wrong approach. Indeed, upon the announcement of her promotion, Ewing told the press that Switzer had a "well-earned reputation as a leader in the health and welfare programs of the Federal Government."

During World War II, Switzer had worked closely with physicians, nurses, public health experts, veterinarians, and dentists on the Procurement and Assignment Service, which matched these professionals to military needs. Moreover, as the AFPH had noted, Switzer had strong ties to important disability-focused charities. She served on the professional advisory committee for the International Society for the Welfare of Cripples and on the professional education and publications committees for the National Foundation for Infantile Paralysis.[2]

These administrative changes, *Valor* hypothesized, represented a weak, last-ditch effort on the part of Ewing to prevent further attacks on the OVR. According to the article, however, Ewing's "innocuous and unimportant changes" did not "alter the past and present policies and failures of Ewing and OVR to do a real job for the physically handicapped." While *Valor* writers were displeased with Ewing's efforts to revitalize the OVR, they believed that the AFPH's campaign to expose the failures of civilian rehabilitation had finally forced the FSA into action. It would, *Valor* writers argued, be only a matter of time before the AFPH would score greater gains in securing rights and better services for people with disabilities.[3]

Despite the predictions of *Valor* writers, in December 1950 it was not rehabilitation leaders who were headed for twilight, but the AFPH. As the organization entered the 1950s, the window of opportunity created by World War II was rapidly closing. A shifting political landscape, changes within the organized labor movement, and the growing prestige and power of medicine played significant roles in the downfall of the AFPH.[4] Equally as important, persistent financial strain and leadership choices would isolate the group from its former allies and further tax its inadequate resources.

A Crisis in Leadership

The AFPH never found sure financial footing even as the group received considerable organizational and financial support from organized labor. AFPH leaders worked closely with legislative representatives of the American Federation of Labor (AFL), the Congress of Industrial Organizations (CIO), the United Mine Workers of America (UMWA), the International Association of Machinists (IAM), and the Railroad Brotherhoods. These representatives formed the AFPH's Labor Associates Committee and held monthly luncheons from 1952 to 1954 to discuss disability legislation proposed by the

AFPH. Labor leaders such as Walter Reuther and Emil Mazey of the United Automobile Workers (UAW); William Green, George Meany, and Walter J. Mason of the AFL; David Dubinsky of the International Ladies Garment Workers Union; Albert J. Hayes of the IAM; and Hugo Ernst of the Hotel, Restaurant Employees and Bartenders International Union of America, to name only a few, lent their names to the AFPH's national council.[5]

Organized labor also provided a majority of the AFPH's funds. In 1952, Paul Strachan noted that the organization required at least sixty thousand dollars a year to function, but that the poverty disabled individuals so often experienced meant that its members paid dues irregularly. On average membership dues accounted for just $5,000 a year. That same year, the AFPH reported that it had received nearly its entire operating budget from "supporting organizations"—$40,041 in 1951 and $32,735 in 1952. Twenty-nine AFL affiliates donated money to the AFPH in 1952 with combined contributions exceeding $15,000. Large and regular AFL contributors included the Ladies Garment Workers, the Carpenters, and the Machinists. The UMWA gave the

Figure 10. Congress of Industrial Organizations regional director Sam Sponseller organized this new Cleveland, Ohio, AFPH chapter in 1952, demonstrating the wide-ranging support organized labor offered the AFPH. Here, he presents the chapter president and eleven other members of the chapter with the group's official charter from the AFPH. The photograph originally appeared in *Valor*'s October 1952 issue. Courtesy of the Archives and Special Collections Division, City College of New York.

AFPH $10,000 that year, and CIO unions contributed more than $7,000. In 1953, some thirty-one affiliates of the AFL had in total contributed more than $14,000. Contributions of the CIO and its member unions exceeded $20,000 that year.[6] While organized labor provided virtually the sole financial support for the AFPH by the 1950s, the organization never raised enough money to fully fund all of its legislative efforts.

Strachan pushed to expand the organization's agenda with his plans for an AFPH Institute of Human Engineering even as the group struggled to finance its legislative campaign. He estimated that the project would require more than $5.6 million to launch and see it through its first two years. Strachan envisioned a sprawling complex of numerous buildings, including health and medical research centers, with a fifty-bed hospital and facilities for outpatient care; a selective placement, diagnostic and referral clinic; college of vocational education, fine arts, agricultural and mechanical arts, and human engineering research; an administrative center; and a complex of dormitories, motels, and a trailer court for residents, faculty, staff, physicians, and students. He proposed to build this massive institute on the west coast of Florida because of "the great therapeutic and healing values of sun, air, and water," the amount of available acreage, and the location's proximity to rail and highway. In Strachan's view, the institute would be the only place in the world where people with disabilities could receive full medical treatment, education, training, vocational guidance, and placement into employment.[7]

Strachan aimed to make the institute "the foremost training center in the U.S.A., and probably, the entire world, for those who work with Handicapped," not only in vocational guidance but also in medicine through special courses for physicians. Strachan's plans for the institute upended the authority-client relationship. AFPH members had been challenging the authority of professionals in the field of rehabilitation for a decade, and by proposing to make a center developed and run by disabled people the "the foremost training center" for able-bodied professionals who worked with people with disabilities, Strachan sought to reframe disabled people's relationship with providers. Moreover, as the organization's proposals to reframe rehabilitation repeatedly failed in Congress, perhaps Strachan came to view training service providers as the most effective way to implement long-term change.[8]

On the one hand, the institute promised greater autonomy for disabled people in the medical and rehabilitation system and recognition of the value of disabled people's experience and opinions, at least on a limited scale. On the other hand, the proposal seemed to be moving away from the drive for inclusion. At the national and local levels, members and leaders had pushed for equal employment access and greater opportunities for civic and social participation in the national and local communities. In calling for a single, massive institute for people with disabilities, Strachan seemed to be moving toward a policy of separation. Moreover, organized labor's support for the AFPH had grown out of the organization's drive to expand national disability services—something the institute would have done only indirectly.

Beyond the tension in goals, Strachan's decision to divide the AFPH's meager resources between waging a national legislative campaign to overhaul federal disability policy and building the institute forced him to boost fundraising goals. Strachan's aggressive campaign for funds, especially for the institute, which seemed to offer few practical benefits to organized labor, no doubt sowed the seeds of the eventual break between organized labor and the AFPH. Moreover, the institute departed from the AFPH's goal of nurturing unity by cultivating members' political engagement and empowerment.

Preoccupied with the institute, Strachan closed doors to action through the executive branch by breaking ties with the President's Committee on National Employ the Physically Handicapped Week (NEPHW). In March 1952, Strachan wrote a frustrated and angry letter to President Truman and resigned from the President's Committee. Through his committee work, Strachan had attempted to secure through executive action what the AFPH had not secured through legislation: Department of Labor (DOL) control of federal disability services. Although the DOL had gained jurisdiction over NEPHW and the President's Committee, Strachan's broader goal, to gain more leverage over disability policy by moving disability services to the DOL from the FSA, had failed.[9]

Furthermore, the growing influence of the rehabilitation establishment within the President's Committee disturbed Strachan, who railed, "I soon found that the Staff of that Committee, backed by the Chairman, was filling up the Committee with a lot of 'do-gooders, social welfare workers, and the like', most of whom, we, the Handicapped, know, from bitter experience, 'WILL DO ANYTHING IN THE WORLD FOR THE HANDICAPPED, EXCEPT, <u>GET OFF OUR BACKS</u>'!"[10] Strachan argued that privilege had clouded the vision of these social welfare workers, rendering them unable, and perhaps unwilling, to address the problems of people with disabilities who needed and wanted employment. "In short, Mr. President," he wrote, "these gentry have had this Program in charge for nearly 200 years and they signally failed to develop, or apply, any real remedy for the problems of the Handicapped they profess to serve."[11]

His resignation was unduly harsh. He charged that the staff of the President's Committee "lacks vision and is not competent," that it had "departed entirely" from its mission, that leaders of the committee "do not want, nor welcome, civilian handicapped as members," that it offered people with disabilities only "hot air," and finally that the committee dealt in "delusion and deception." Much of Strachan's critique misrepresented the truth, while also demonstrating his increasingly abrasive tone, which served only to alienate former allies. Mildred Scott, secretary-treasurer of the AFPH, had not been welcomed as a member of the executive committee, but five members of the executive committee, including Strachan, were disabled people. The President's Committee had, even under extreme financial pressures, continued to forge ahead on an agenda almost fully shaped by Strachan, and his efforts to use the committee to secure control of federal disability services for the DOL had never been an open goal shared by the entire committee. The hostility and bitterness of Strachan's resignation no doubt caused him and the AFPH to lose allies. Moreover, he abandoned the opportunity to continue to influence the work of the committee and to force further executive action on the AFPH agenda.[12] Through his drive to launch the institute and his resignation from the President's Committee, Strachan began to alienate his allies, which would in turn limit his organization's possibilities.

A Changing Political Landscape

As Strachan's leadership began to close doors to the AFPH, external events closed other doors. Strachan heralded the election of 1952 as having great potential to improve opportunities for people with disabilities. Regardless of the outcome of the election, he predicted, Ewing would no longer head the FSA. "Then, perhaps," Strachan declared, "we may well see a beginning on a real program for our 30,000,000 Handicapped citizens."[13]

In November 1952, Dwight D. Eisenhower soundly defeated Democratic candidate Adlai Stevenson, ushering in nearly a decade of Republican control of the White House. Along with Republican majorities in both Houses, the Eisenhower administration brought numerous changes not necessarily favorable to Strachan and the AFPH. President Eisenhower moved quickly to promote the FSA to a cabinet-level department. While Truman had called for a similar reorganization, Congress, hostile to his Fair Deal plans, rejected the proposal. Under Eisenhower's leadership, however, Congress fast-tracked the reorganization plan, and Eisenhower signed legislation creating the Department of Health, Education, and Welfare (HEW) on 1 April 1953.[14] The agency's new standing provided the OVR and the rehabilitation service greater protection against activist demands that disability services be moved to DOL.

While Strachan believed that any new administration, Republican or Democrat, would bring greater opportunities for the AFPH, he apparently had not considered that in addition to losing an opponent, Ewing, he would undoubtedly lose allies as well. During the Truman years, Strachan had cultivated close ties with the DOL and secretaries of labor Lewis Schwellenbach and Maurice Tobin. While Schwellenbach and Tobin had both believed that the DOL should control federal disability services, Eisenhower's secretary of labor, James P. Mitchell, had little interest in expanding the DOL into the realm of disability policy. Strachan and a group of union officials from the AFL, CIO, the Railway Brotherhoods, and the UMWA met with Mitchell in the spring of 1954 to urge his support for AFPH legislation. Mitchell, however, refused to testify on behalf of the AFPH's rehabilitation program. Strachan reported that Mitchell told him that "he did not want to become controversial (Oh, my God!) with Mrs. [Oveta Culp] Hobby," chief of the new HEW. Within the DOL, a department that had once been full of some of Strachan's strongest supporters, officials now sought to "forestall the day when another question is asked by Strachan." For his part, Strachan argued that Mitchell was "incompetent, pusillanimous, and anti-Labor in his thoughts and actions, as well as anti-Handicapped."[15]

Beyond changes in the political climate and in the executive branch, 1952 also brought dramatic changes in the organized labor movement. Shortly after the national election, Philip Murray, head of the CIO, died. His death was followed quickly by the passing of AFL president William Green, and leadership of the organized labor movement fell to a new generation of labor leaders. The CIO, under the leadership of Walter Reuther, faced a continuing internal power struggle between its left-leaning and more centrist unions. As liberals in the federal government charted a more moderate course, Reuther hoped to gain stability for the CIO's industrial unions and strength in numbers for a broader reform agenda by uniting the CIO and the AFL. In December 1952, Reuther approached Meany about merging the two unions, a project that absorbed considerable time and energy for three years. The merger became official in December 1955 and left Meany in charge of the new AFL-CIO.[16]

The merger ultimately might have spelled increased support for the AFPH, but Meany, while negotiating the merger occupied his time, paid disability little attention. Green had been a miner with first-hand knowledge of the results of industrial accidents and occupational illnesses. While Green, throughout his tenure as president, never altered the AFL's policy of non-partisanship in politics, he had offered the AFPH a great deal of support.[17] Green's death was a blow to the AFPH, since Meany never offered Strachan the same attention Green had. Unlike Green, Meany proved unwilling to meet with Strachan to discuss the AFPH platform. In 1954, Strachan complained, "Gompers talked with me a great deal; Green, a lot, and why not you, also? I ain't got Rocky Mountain Spotted Fever, George."[18] Even by 1959, Meany had never found time to hold a conference with Strachan on disability policy.[19] It is unclear if Meany's reluctance to aid the AFPH came from the pressures of the merger, or if Meany was simply not as interested in the issue of disability. It is clear, however, that the new executive landscape and changes in the leadership of organized labor made the road to legislative victory increasingly rocky for disability activists.

A Final Victory, an Ultimate Defeat

In many ways, the import of Strachan and the AFPH could be measured in the responses that AFPH initiatives elicited from officials in the federal-state rehabilitation program. The Senate's 1950 and 1951 decisions to side with the FSA and the agency's new status as a cabinet-level department seemed to give the rehabilitation program a greater sense of security in the face of the AFPH's continued attack. In 1953, the House Committee on Education and Labor created a special subcommittee to investigate the need for further legislation in the fields of rehabilitation and disability policy. Whereas earlier AFPH initiatives had triggered a hailstorm of critiques and counter-plans from the rehabilitation officials, during the 1953 House hearings, the only AFPH testimony that seemed to worry them was that of J. Rosemond Cook, who described the racial discrimination that he and other African Americans in Georgia had experienced in their dealings with the state's rehabilitation program.

Cook charged, “The administration of the facilities of the Federal program for the handicapped is wholly inadequate and inequitably administered for the benefit of Negroes in the South.” He told the story of an African American woman in Georgia who had polio and was enrolled in college to become a teacher. The young woman had received some assistance to attend college from the rehabilitation program, but it had never covered her full expenses. After two years of attending school and working a part-time job to pay the deficit, she found that she no longer had the physical strength to hold a job and do well in school. Cook worked with her to get additional support from the rehabilitation program, but he could report little success. Cook, a quadruple amputee, had also had a negative experience with the program in Georgia. He applied for prosthetic devices to allow him to walk, but even after passing a medical examination, he had not received assistance or word of a decision. Even after calling the office every day for three months, he still did not get a response.[20]

Following Cook’s testimony, the OVR launched an investigation of these charges of racial discrimination. Throughout the investigation, national, regional, and Georgia rehabilitation officials continually attacked Cook’s character and personality. One OVR memorandum reported that the Georgia rehabilitation program had worked well with Cook for a time, but eventually officials in Georgia found they “simply could not take the time for 10 or 15 telephone calls every day, most of them on extremely obscure subjects and involving long-winded dissertations.”[21]

Paul S. Barrett, director of rehabilitation in Georgia, reported that Cook had first received assistance in Georgia in 1945, when he was provided artificial limbs and placement with the Bell Aircraft Corporation. Barrett quoted Cook’s follow-up paperwork in which Cook had written that the aid he had received from the rehabilitation service had “been invaluable” as it made him “self-supporting.” Barrett further reported that Cook had moved to Pittsburgh, Pennsylvania, in 1948, where he received additional aid from the rehabilitation program. Upon his return to Atlanta in 1952, he began to contact Georgia rehabilitation officials regularly. Barrett claimed that Cook “evidently does not follow the physician’s instructions for self care,” an assumption he based on the fact that Cook had needed forty-eight operations since 1943. Moreover, Barrett added that Cook’s Atlanta counselor noted, “This is a very pathetic case.” The counselor reported that he had “made every effort to find some vocation for which this quadruple amputee would be suited,” but that Cook’s work with African Americans with disabilities was “about as good a vocation as he could follow," as he would not be "feasible for any (other) work."[22]

Barrett firmly denied Cook's charges of racism. He reported that 28.8 percent of the people his agency had served in the previous ten years had been African Americans—a figure, he noted, that closely mirrored the total percentage of African Americans who lived in Georgia. Barrett also appealed to a former AFPH member and client of the Georgia rehabilitation service, Robert L. Thornton, for support. Thornton, who had served as president of the white Atlanta chapter, responded that he had discontinued his affiliation with the AFPH and that Cook's criticisms were unfounded. "I wish to assure you," he wrote, "that I do not appreciate nor uphold action of this sort. I do know and could cite numerous cases of handicapped Negroes who have been given special training and every consideration within your limitations through the State Vocational Rehabilitation Division." Thornton's resignation from the AFPH and support of the rehabilitation program in Georgia suggests that he, and perhaps others, viewed the national organization's approval of Cook as a threat to Jim Crow. Moreover, it demonstrates the limits of disability unity when confronted with challenges to the existing racial order.[23]

Despite Thornton's charges, Cook spoke for a broad community of African Americans in Atlanta. In the weeks leading up to Cook's testimony, the African American newspaper the *Atlanta Daily World* called Cook's plans to testify in support of rehabilitation reform and expansion "a most worthy project," describing the "abject poverty" that many disabled African Americans experienced. A group of African American ministers and "prominent citizens" formed a committee, chaired by Reverend Thomas G. Blue, to raise funds to pay for Cook's travel to Washington. On 12 July, African American churches throughout Atlanta held collections to help pay for the trip. Some twenty-three ministers had donated to the cause, along with a handful of other citizens. Given the community support for Cook's travel to Washington, D.C., it is likely that others in the African American community shared his view that African Americans received unequal treatment from the rehabilitation program. It certainly indicates broad support for better services for African Americans with disabilities.[24]

Rehabilitation officials' reaction to Cook's charges of racism, their efforts to undermine him as a representative of the disabled African American community, and the poor treatment he and others had received when seeking additional services reflected not only the separate and unequal realities of the Jim Crow South but also officials' response to the increasing momentum for

African American rights. Growing pressure from civil rights leaders had pushed the Truman administration to advocate for a number of civil rights measures, ranging from banning the poll tax to providing federal protection against lynching. While the measures died in Congress and were met with outrage by nearly every southern Democrat in Congress, they demonstrated the rising tide for civil rights. Cook's charges of racism and the bitter and dismissive response from Georgia officials mirrored broader efforts for civil rights and southern whites' responses.[25]

Cook's experiences, his testimony, and the response it engendered from rehabilitation officials also reflected ongoing conflicts between disability service providers and disability activists. The National Federation of the Blind (NFB) would wage a campaign later in the decade for legislation guaranteeing their "right to organize." The legislation sought to both ensure that officials seek guidance from blind people in developing and administering policies meant to aid them and prevent officials from using access to services to prevent disability activism. That blind activists sought legal protection from officials using their authority to prevent activist work suggests the level of power rehabilitation workers wielded.[26] Counselors had wide latitude in determining eligibility for services, as they were instructed to consider factors ranging from age and physical condition to attitude.[27] While AFPH members did not claim that they had been denied services because of their work with the organization, it is possible that rehabilitation counselors, alongside issues of race, contributed to Robert L. Thornton's decision to leave the group and that an activist bent led some individuals to be judged too uncooperative.

Numerous representatives of organized labor also testified at the 1953 House hearings, but the OVR no longer seemed to find labor's critique of the rehabilitation bureaucracy as troubling as it once did. Harry Read, secretary of the CIO Occupational Safety and Health Committee; Thomas Kennedy, vice president of the UMWA; James Brindle, acting director of the Social Security Department of the UAW; Walter J. Mason, member of the AFL Legislative Committee; and George Nelson, legislative representative of the IAM, all attacked the rehabilitation program's failure to address the growing needs of people with disabilities. Additionally, all of these union representatives argued that rehabilitation and disability services belonged in the DOL.[28] Given Secretary Mitchell's position on disability policy, labor's drive to move disability services to the DOL no longer seemed as alarming to the OVR. Moreover, President Eisenhower had plans for civilian rehabilitation that had nothing to do with the DOL or the AFPH's designs for the program—plans that would ultimately reinforce professional authority, reduce federal oversight, and further contribute to the medicalization of rehabilitation.

In his 1954 State of the Union address, President Eisenhower provided the rough outline of a four-part plan for improving the national health care system. While "flatly opposed to the socialization of medicine," Eisenhower asserted that the federal government still had a role to play in securing the health of the nation. Aiding people with disabilities cut across all four parts of his proposal. First, Eisenhower called on Congress to gradually expand the rehabilitation program, arguing that "far more disabled people can be saved each year from idleness and dependence." Second, he held that the federal government had a responsibility to stimulate medical research. Third, he maintained that the Hill-Burton Hospital Survey and Construction Act of 1946, which provided federal funds for hospital construction, needed to be broadened to encourage growth of rehabilitation facilities, nursing care and diagnostic centers, and institutions to aid people with chronic illnesses. Fourth, Eisenhower contended that private insurance plans were "soundly based on the experience and initiative of the people in their various communities," but the federal government should offer a "reinsurance service" to allow private companies to expand coverage to "more of the many families which want and should have" the protection of insurance.[29] With reinsurance, a scheme developed by a Blue Cross administrator in Philadelphia, private companies would continue to provide insurance, but the federal government would secure insurance companies against "catastrophic costs." Reinsurance, the Eisenhower administration maintained, would encourage private companies to provide coverage for sick and elderly people. The vast majority of insurance companies rejected reinsurance, and the American Medical Association lobbied against the program as a move toward socialized medicine.[30] While Eisenhower's reinsurance plan failed, both the Senate Committee on Labor and Public Welfare and the House Committee on Education and Labor immediately began to work on Eisenhower's plans for expanding rehabilitation.

Shortly after his State of the Union address, Eisenhower provided Congress with a more detailed outline of his health plan. He set a five-year goal to increase the number of people served by the rehabilitation program from roughly 60,000 per year to 200,000 per year by 1959. The president proposed that the nation could meet this goal primarily through increased spending at the state level, but even under Barden-La Follette provisions, in which the federal government covered 100 percent of states' administrative costs and 50 percent of the costs for all other rehabilitation services, states consistently struggled to finance their existing programs. Additionally, the president called for $1.5 million to be set aside for research and training grants to ensure that there were enough qualified professionals to support the growth of the program. Finally, the president requested an additional ten million dollars to fund an expansion of the Hill-Burton Act to cover new rehabilitation facilities.[31]

Eisenhower's proposals were modest. HEW officials estimated that the backlog for civilian rehabilitation services was over two million, and the list of individuals in need and waiting for the service grew each year. Estimates placed the number of new cases of disability, eligible for rehabilitation services and not receiving private assistance, at 250,000 each year, whereas the program had served around 60,000 of those individuals. Eisenhower's aim to rehabilitate 200,000 a year would mean that the list of those waiting would continue to grow. By contrast, the 1950 Douglas bill had not set a definitive appropriation, but the Senate Committee on Labor and Public Welfare report noted that with sufficient funding leaders in the FSA believed they could be serving 250,000 disabled individuals a year by the mid-1960s. Lack of funding and trained professionals in the field continually constrained efforts to grow the program, and Eisenhower's proposal for $1.5 million in training grants represented a mere drop in the bucket given the scope of the problem. In 1954, the federal-state rehabilitation program employed around 1,200 counselors, and HEW expected that number would need to grow to at least 3,000 to meet the goals the president had outlined. Beyond counselors, the program would require additional medical support and more physicians trained to work in field.[32]

On 19 January 1954, only one day after Eisenhower sent his extended health plan to Congress, H. Alexander Smith (R-NJ) and a group of mainly Republican senators introduced two bills: one to strengthen the federal-state rehabilitation program, and one to expand the Hill-Burton Act.[33] The Health Subcommittee of the Senate Committee on Labor and Public Welfare, chaired by William Purtell (R-CT), held extensive hearings on the two measures in March and April. In June, the Committee on Labor and Public Welfare reported favorably on an amended version of Smith's rehabilitation bill. The Republican-controlled committee cast rehabilitation as a program that could allow them to contract the welfare state through its potential to reduce dependency and the need for public assistance programs. The committee's report emphasized that the federal, state, and local governments spent hundreds of millions of dollars each year providing financial support to dependent people with disabilities, who could instead, through investment in the rehabilitation program, be made into tax payers. The Republican position on rehabilitation mirrored one of the central messages of the AFPH's public education efforts—that disability drained community and government resources, but rehabilitation could reverse the flow of funds. In contrast, however, the committee had very different views about the federal-state balance of power in the rehabilitation program than the AFPH and congressional liberals.[34]

As amended by the Health Subcommittee, the Senate rehabilitation bill sought to reduce federal oversight of state rehabilitation programs. In 1943, the FSA had established the OVR to set standards and monitor state rehabilitation programs, but the bill sought to roll back some of this federal control. It eliminated provisions that required federal approval of fee schedules and made state programs, instead of the OVR, responsible for establishing minimum standards. Basically, the measure allowed the states "to develop, adopt and carry out standards of their own determination" in the field of rehabilitation. The bill envisioned the HEW and the OVR as providing a "consultative service" instead of the earlier regulatory role these agencies played. If the HEW secretary deemed a state plan not in compliance with the law, the bill provided that funds could not be withheld without a hearing and also established an appeal mechanism. By contrast, the Committee on Labor and Public Welfare's 1950 report had highlighted criticisms of the state bureaucracies and called for "a greater degree of leadership" at the federal level.[35]

Like the Douglas bill, Senate Republicans sought to alter rehabilitation funding. State programs would be guaranteed at least the same appropriation received in 1954, but appropriations made over the 1954 base allotment would be gradually reduced over a five-year period until appropriations were made on a modified Hill-Burton formula. The Hill-Burton formula based the size of federal appropriations on state per capita income, with poorer states receiving greater federal aid. Under the Senate rehabilitation bill, after 1959, the federal government would pay up to 65 percent and as little as 45 percent of state costs, depending on state income. The Douglas bill had proposed a higher maximum of 75 percent and lower minimum of 40 percent. Thus, the Senate rehabilitation bill sought to place more of the burden for funding rehabilitation on the states, at least states with higher per capita income, while also providing state programs with greater control and flexibility, and less federal oversight.[36]

Expansions to existing services were few. The bill maintained all of the services provided under the World War II expansion of the rehabilitation program, but made explicit the earlier implicit provision that states provide "physical restoration" services. It also eliminated the ninety-day limitation on hospitalization, a change the Douglas bill had also proposed. The 1954 Senate measure allotted meager funds for federal grants for research and training and also set aside federal funds for grants to build workshops and purchase vending stands for people with severe disabilities. In addition, the bill required state plans to make provisions for increased cooperation with other federal, state, and local agencies, like the public assistance programs. In requiring greater cooperation with public assistance programs, Senate Republicans hoped to use rehabilitation to take disabled people off welfare rolls and put them into jobs, reducing welfare spending. Finally, the bill made provisions for an advisory council, staffed by twelve experts in the field of rehabilitation, contrary to the AFPH's demands for representation.[37]

The Republican-controlled House Committee on Education and Labor, under the chairmanship of Samuel K. McConnell, Jr. (R-PA), prepared a very similar rehabilitation bill. Much like the Senate, House Republicans sought to redefine the role of the federal government in the rehabilitation program. House Republicans argued that the HEW and the OVR should offer the states "technical advice and assistance," aid the states in meeting personnel shortages, and support the states "through research and dissemination of information on improved rehabilitation methods and procedures." The House committee took a more liberal approach to funding the rehabilitation program in general, proposing higher maximum and minimum federal grants (ranging from 72 percent to the poorest states to 52 percent to the richest states) while also guaranteeing that federal appropriations for individual state programs would never fall below 1954-levels. Still, the committee placed more restrictions on granting federal funds to train new rehabilitation professionals than did the Senate. These restrictions included limiting the availability of training grants to the first two years of the act's operation and preventing individuals from receiving training assistance for more than six months.[38]

For disability activists, these administration bills fell short in several key ways beyond reducing federal oversight of a program that was at best unevenly administered by the states. They did not adequately address the educational needs of home-bound disabled people or the fact that numerous states exhausted rehabilitation appropriations long before state legislatures could replenish the funds. The bills did not address accessibility, the need for better services for people with disabilities in the U.S. Employment Service, or the need for federal legislation to push states to amend their workers' compensation laws to better support disabled people's employment. Finally, these bills provided no mandate for the representation of people with disabilities in policymaking decisions.

With both the Senate Committee on Labor and Public Welfare and the House Committee on Education and Labor working toward the same goal, the AFPH rallied its supporters to make a final play to implement its own plan for rehabilitation. Since 1950, the AFPH had yet again expanded the scope of its federal commission bill. Now seeking an independent federal agency for people with disabilities, housed in the DOL for "housekeeping purposes," the AFPH bill called for federal disability services, including the HEW's rehabilitation program and the DOL's President's Committee on NEPHW, to be directed by the "Federal Agency for Handicapped" and its administrator. Like earlier incarnations of the measure, the federal agency bill would have abolished the OVR and established a pension system. While Congress had already established Aid to the Permanently and Totally Disabled, which provided public assistance to unemployed and low-income disabled people, the AFPH continued to call for a pension system linked to rehabilitation. Essentially, the AFPH envisioned a system in which individuals would receive pensions if the rehabilitation program determined they were unfeasible for rehabilitation because their disabilities were too severe. Likewise, in the 1954 bill, AFPH activists continued to call for increased efforts to make public buildings accessible to people with disabilities and the creation of a division for people with disabilities in the U.S. Civil Service Commission as well as a revolving loan fund to ensure that states could continue their rehabilitation efforts even when appropriations had been exhausted. Moreover, provisions for loans to support work projects and business enterprises for people with disabilities and grants to encourage educational initiatives for homebound people with disabilities continued to be a large part of the AFPH platform.[39]

In its 1954 bill, the AFPH proposed several new programs and expansions. Mirroring the Douglas bill and the Eisenhower administration health plan, the AFPH proposed to make federal funds available to assist in the construction of rehabilitation centers, such as the AFPH Institute of Human Engineering. The 1954 AFPH bill provided additional federal grants to the states to develop programs for people with severe disabilities. In addition, the AFPH bill called on the Employment Service to institute plans "for the promotion and development of employment opportunities" for people with disabilities and required that every state and federal employment office designate at least one person to carry out the Employment Service's new functions in disability policy. In early drafts of the bill, funding had been heavily weighted on the federal side, but in 1954, the AFPH also adopted the variable grant system proposed in the Douglas bill, with federal support ranging from 75 to 40 percent based on the per capita income of the state, a higher maximum and lower minimum than proposed by Republicans in the House and Senate. Finally, the 1954 bill proposed to create a federal "second injury fund."[40]

Since G. B. Erskine had directed the 1946 celebration of NEPHW, many activists and advocates had called for second injury funds on the state level. Employers, they argued, balked at hiring people with disabilities for fear that a second injury might leave disabled workers permanently unable to work, sending their compensation costs and insurance premiums skyrocketing. Second injury funds eliminated this risk by establishing a fund to pay compensation costs for second injuries that resulted in total disabilities. Second injury funds gained traction in the states in the postwar years, but coverage varied significantly across states. The 1954 AFPH bill proposed to place a 0.1 percent tax on the total wages employers paid each year to establish a federal second injury fund. The AFPH bill would have required states to revise their workers' compensation laws to work in conjunction with the fund.[41]

Throughout June 1954, AFPH activists and their labor supporters scrambled to make a dent against the widely supported administration rehabilitation bills in a Republican-controlled Congress. For their part, Democrats on the Senate Committee on Labor and Public Welfare clashed with the conservative leadership of the committee. Minority members Herbert Lehman (NY), James Murray (MT), Lister Hill (AL), Matthew Neely (WV), and Paul Douglas (IL) issued a pointed critique of the Senate administration bill in a supplement to the committee's otherwise glowing report. They argued that "the Senate should be fully aware of the fact that the enactment of this bill and the fullest utilization of its provisions during the next few years will not deal adequately with the massive human and economic problems of the physically handicapped." They maintained that they had voted to report the bill "because even the small progress projected by this legislation . . . is desirable." The group criticized the bill because it set a five-year goal to rehabilitate only 200,000 people a year in the face of the overwhelming backlog of over two million people who needed rehabilitation services and the reality that more than 250,000 additional people would need rehabilitation each year. Moreover, they argued that the proposed $1.5–2 million appropriations for traineeships and research fellowships for rehabilitation professionals were woefully inadequate. The Democrats pointed out that their amendment to provide $5 million for grants to pay for individual training and to build training programs had been rejected by the committee. On the Senate floor, Lehman was even more critical of the measure, slamming it as a "piddling little program."[42]

Given their critiques of the administration bill, it is not surprising the Democratic members of both the Senate Committee on Labor and Public Welfare and the Health Subcommittee supported AFPH initiatives to block and alter the administration bill. Within the Health Subcommittee, Lehman offered a motion to substitute the AFPH bill for the administration bill. While Hill supported Lehman's motion, the three Republicans on the subcommittee outweighed the Democrats and defeated the motion. Murray offered a similar motion to the full committee, which was also voted down by the Republican-controlled committee.[43]

As the AFPH worked to change the bill, the organization focused on eight key points. Strachan hoped to have the AFPH's definition of disability added to the administration bill and to alter the terminology of the bill, replacing "disabled" and "disabled person" with "physically handicapped." He asserted that people with disabilities abhorred the term "disabled," as employers associated the term with " 'incapacity,' and a lot of other unpleasant things." Additionally, Strachan fought to have AFPH provisions for grants to support educational programs for homebound people with disabilities and for a revolving loan fund for state rehabilitation programs added to the administration bill. He also hoped to win amendments that would push the Employment Service to take a more active role in finding employment for people with disabilities, establish federal loans for work projects and cooperative enterprises for people with disabilities, launch a federal second injury fund, and create a federal interagency committee to coordinate federal activities relating to rehabilitation and employment of people with disabilities. Finally, he sought to replace the Senate bill's provisions for an advisory council with similar provisions from the AFPH bill. Where the Senate administration bill envisioned an advisory council of professionals and technical experts, the AFPH amendment provided for an advisory council with representation of people with disabilities and organized labor.[44]

With votes rapidly approaching in both houses, Strachan launched a campaign to appeal to his supporters in Congress. Murray had agreed to offer the AFPH bill as a substitute for the administration bill on the Senate floor, but prepared for the failure of Murray's motion, Strachan sent a flurry of letters to Capitol Hill, appealing to Democrats and a few Republican allies to offer various provisions of the AFPH bill as amendments to the administration bills. He also asked Harley Kilgore (D-WV) to offer a series of provisions from the AFPH bill as amendments en bloc.[45] Strachan implored Senators Edwin Johnson (D-CO), Guy Gillette (D-IA), Warren Magnuson (D-WA), Estes Kefauver (D-TN), George Smathers (D-FL), Wayne Morse (R-OR), Richard Russell (D-GA), and John J. Sparkman (D-AL) to offer AFPH provisions as single amendments if the substitution failed and if the amendments were defeated en bloc.[46]

Strachan's efforts to block or alter the administration bill in the House seemed less coordinated than his efforts in the Senate. When Strachan issued his appeals to various representatives, he had no one nailed down to offer the AFPH bill as a substitute, but he still asked for support of such a motion. Strachan called on Representatives Franklin D. Roosevelt, Jr. (D-NY), Clyde Doyle (D-CA), Homer Angell (R-OR), John Dingell (D-MI), Emanuel Celler (D-NY), John McCormack (D-MA), George Rhodes (D-PA), and John Fogarty (D-RI) to offer the same individual amendments he hoped to win in the Senate.[47] Moreover, Strachan appealed to members of the AFPH-Labor Associates to pressure Augustine Kelley (D-PA), Roy Wier (D-MN), Charles Howell (D-NJ), or Carl Elliott (D-AL) to offer the AFPH bill as a substitute for the administration bill. Strachan complained that, besides Wier, the sponsors of the AFPH bill who also served on the House Committee on Education and Labor had not "made any real effort to fight" for the AFPH bill and that "they simply 'went along for the ride.'" Even with the odds stacked against the AFPH, Strachan told the AFPH-Labor Associates, "if we put a little extra zip on the ball, we may well drag something out of this, that really means something, yet."[48]

When the administration bill made it to the Senate floor, Lehman led the charge to alter the bill. "We have," he argued, "a situation in this country where millions of persons are literally crying out for aid so that they may join their fellow citizens in the ordinary pursuits of life and labor." Even in the midst of the great need to expand the program, the administration, he maintained, was "merely crawling along." Failing to expand the rehabilitation service sufficiently, Lehman argued, was "both inhumane and economically stupid." He again offered his amendment to authorize a $5 million annual appropriation to fund traineeships, research fellowships, and grants to expand training facilities. The Senate, as the Committee on Labor and Public Welfare had, rejected Lehman's amendment.[49]

Murray followed Lehman's lead, attacking the administration bill for being "limited in scope and in vision." In Murray's assessment, the administration bill could not "be regarded as anything like an adequate program." As promised, he offered the AFPH bill as a substitute. The substitute failed, but other senators offered additional AFPH amendments.[50] Senator Johnson of Colorado pushed for the AFPH amendment to define disability and alter the wording of the administration bill to replace "disabled" with "physically handicapped." Johnson's amendment also failed.[51] Hubert Humphrey (D-MN), who would serve as vice president under President Lyndon B. Johnson and be the Democratic nominee for president in 1968, sought to add AFPH provisions that would have directed the Employment Service to provide greater services to people with disabilities. Humphrey, however, withdrew the amendment when Purtell assured him that a similar amendment had been accepted by the House and that the Senate would not object to the amendment in conference with the House.[52]

Senator Sparkman, who had sponsored numerous AFPH bills and was running mate to Adlai Stevenson in his unsuccessful bid for the presidency in 1952, presented two amendments: one, a modified version of an AFPH amendment, to require that at least three members of the advisory council proposed by the administration bill be disabled people, and the other, an amendment of his own, to increase the annual appropriation for the President's Committee on NEPHW from $75,000 to $250,000. While the Senate voted down increased appropriations for the President's Committee, the amendment to secure representation for people with disabilities on the advisory council passed.[53] Morse did not offer an AFPH amendment; however, he did present an amendment of his own that authorized the secretary of HEW to assist in establishing a "pilot demonstration rehabilitation center" in Washington. The amendment provided annual appropriations of $1 million to aid construction and maintenance of such a center. After considerable debate, the amendment passed by a narrow margin of 44 to 41.[54] The Senate unanimously passed the amended administration bill.[55]

Despite the fact that Strachan's campaign in the House was less organized, Democrats in the House proved to be much more successful at amending the House's administration bill. AFPH supporters in the Senate faced the stout opposition of Purtell, the Republican chair of the Health Subcommittee, but

Republican leaders in the House seemed less vehement in their opposition to altering the House bill. Moreover, Strachan had appealed to the AFPH Labor Associates to take up the fight in the House. While it is unclear what actions the Labor Associates took, it is clear that the AFPH agenda fared far better in the House than in the Senate. While Rhodes of Arizona did not offer an AFPH amendment, he succeeded in softening restrictions on training grants, expanding the maximum period of support from six months to a full year.[56] Representative Kelley, who had headed the World War II House investigation of disability policy, pushed through the AFPH amendment to establish grants for educational programs for home-bound people with disabilities. The amendment provided for a $5 million appropriation for the first year and $2 million annually thereafter. He also secured an amendment to increase appropriations for the President's Committee on NEPHW to $250,000.[57] Harry Sheppard (D-CA), who had sponsored the legislation that established NEPHW, pushed the AFPH Employment Service amendment through the House.[58] The House, however, rejected an AFPH amendment offered by Charles Bennett (D-FL) to establish a revolving loan fund for state rehabilitation programs.[59] On the following day, the House voted unanimously in favor of the amended measure and also voted to substitute the House rehabilitation bill for the bill passed in the Senate on the previous day.[60]

In conference, representatives of the House and Senate ironed out differences on amendments as well as provisions for funding the rehabilitation program and administering training grants. They agreed to guarantee that federal rehabilitation grants to states would not fall below the levels appropriated for 1954 and to fund rehabilitation through variable grants, with a federal maximum of 70 percent and minimum of 50 percent. The conference committee settled on the Senate's more liberal provisions for training grants, except that the conference bill limited individual training assistance to a period of two years. The amendments to provide additional appropriations for the President's Committee, to mandate representation of people with disabilities on the National Advisory Council, and to require the Employment Service to promote the employment of people with disabilities and devote at least one staff member at every federal and state employment office to addressing the employment needs of people with disabilities all made it through the conference unscathed. The amendment to provide funds for a pilot rehabilitation center survived the conference, but funding for the initiative was reduced dramatically. The conference committee dropped the amendment to establish grants to improve educational opportunities for home-bound people with disabilities. Provisions, however, were made to require the Secretary of HEW to study homebound disabled people's needs and opportunities open to them, especially in rural areas, within six months of the enactment of the law. On 3 August, Eisenhower signed the Vocational Rehabilitation Amendments of 1954 into law.[61]

In a letter to AFPH national and lodge officers, Strachan put a positive spin on the amendments. While far from characterizing the legislation as a full victory, Strachan wrote that the act represented "the first steps towards Congressional enactment of our own program." He encouraged AFPH lodges to develop programs to promote rehabilitation and employment of people with disabilities and to apply for grants through the new law.[62] Strachan's willingness to work for amendments instead of investing all of his resources into blocking the legislation as he had with the Douglas bill and his optimistic outlook on the new law begs the question of what might have been accomplished if Strachan had played ball sooner. Eisenhower's plan to be rehabilitating 200,000 Americans a year by the end of the decade hinged in large measure on states increasing funding for the program. Moreover, under the new law, rehabilitation would have considerably less federal direction than contemplated by the Douglas bill and certainly less than most of the AFPH's heavily federal proposals.

In addition to the rehabilitation amendments, the Eisenhower administration succeeded in extending the Hill-Burton Act to cover the construction of new facilities for people with disabilities, including rehabilitation centers, treatment facilities, and centers to provide nursing care. On 12 July, Eisenhower signed the bill that provided $60 million in federal funds annually for three years to be matched by local and state funds to assist in the construction of new facilities. The administration estimated that these new medical centers would provide rehabilitative care for 12,000 patients a year and spaces for 2,200 new patients in nursing facilities and 2,700 chronically ill patients in specialized treatment centers.[63]

Taken together, the new rehabilitation law and the Hill-Burton extension further medicalized federal disability policy. The AFPH had fought for greater access to medical care and new and better treatments, including funding for rehabilitation centers, but AFPH members had always placed employment opportunities and the economic security that jobs would bring first. Moreover, they demanded a role in shaping and administering federal policy. While the AFPH succeeded in gaining some representation for disabled people in the administration of civilian rehabilitation, these new laws emphasized the medical, professional, and technical aspects of rehabilitation over the need to stimulate employment opportunities or include disabled people in the decisions that affected them. Strachan offered a brave face to the world, but the new rehabilitation legislation represented a blow to the AFPH program as much as it was a final victory. Moreover, it remained to be seen whether the federal-state rehabilitation would achieve its goal of rehabilitating 200,000 disabled people a year by the end of the decade.

Things Fall Apart

Even as the AFPH struggled to win modest gains in Congress, financial troubles continued to plague the organization. In both 1954 and 1955, the AFPH closed the financial year more than $10,000 in the red. Including unpaid salaries and debt, the organization had close to $100,000 in liabilities.[64] Troubling as the organization's financial condition was, Strachan exacerbated the situation by making claims to some $66,000 in unpaid salary. He asked that the AFPH Executive Council and Convention agree to pay him $5,000 on his retirement and $5,200 a year thereafter until his back-salary had been paid in full.[65] Patrick Gorman, secretary-treasurer of the Amalgamated Meat Cutters and Butcher Workmen of America who also served as a national vice-president of the AFPH, objected to Strachan's proposal. Copying his response to Meany, Gorman argued that a man in Strachan's position could not, "at this late date, make any claims for back salary," especially such a large sum. Gorman resigned his position as a vice president of the AFPH in disapproval. While Strachan wrote to Meany claiming that Gorman was "nuts," Gorman's critique of his leadership and Strachan's response no doubt sullied the reputation of both Strachan and the AFPH among labor leaders who received a copy of the correspondence.[66]

Beyond financial difficulties, Strachan grew increasingly dissatisfied with the AFL's position on potential Social Security payments to disabled people. The AFPH had continually called for a pension system for people with disabilities to be administered alongside the rehabilitation program, tying pensions to decisions about an individual's feasibility for rehabilitation. While both the AFL and the CIO supported pensions for people with disabilities, they advocated establishing such a system as an expansion of Social Security. Strachan appealed to long-time AFL vice president Matthew Woll in an attempt to change the AFL's policy. Strachan, however, was rebuffed. Walter

Mason, who had served as the point man in AFL relations with the AFPH since 1946, wrote to Strachan that he was "rather confused and somewhat disturbed about the views expressed in the letter to Vice President Woll," because Mason and Strachan had already discussed the subject. Mason asserted, "I thought I made our policy very clear."[67] Strachan's frustrations with the AFL must have grown when Meany resigned his post as a national vice president of the AFPH after the 1955 AFL-CIO merger.[68]

The newly united AFL-CIO focused considerable attention on winning disability protections through social insurance. The AFL-CIO Social Security Committee, under the leadership of Nelson Cruikshank, made Social Security Disability Insurance its first priority and pushed hard for the program. A compromise, limiting benefits to people with disabilities over the age of fifty and giving states the power to determine an individual's eligibility, helped to eliminate the opposition of the insurance industry and gain the support of southern Democrats. With the slimmest of margins, the measure that had passed in the House barely squeaked through the Senate. The campaign came to a successful close when Eisenhower signed Social Security Disability Insurance into law on 1 August 1956. While the bill fell far short of the AFL-CIO expectations, the measure, at least, provided additional assistance to some people with disabilities.[69]

Despite Strachan's growing bitterness and displeasure with the AFL-CIO, Meany made one last effort to place the AFPH on sure financial footing. In May 1956, Meany issued a letter to all AFL-CIO affiliates, urging the unions to make contributions to the AFPH.[70] Even the AFL-CIO's financial assistance, however, could no longer hold the organization together. Strachan's health took a turn for the worse in 1956, forcing him to leave his leadership post for three months. When he returned to work in November, he found that the AFPH's funds were completely exhausted. He pleaded to the AFL-CIO and its affiliates for additional assistance, writing that the organization would need at least $25,000 to make it to the new year.[71]

Seeing the writing on the wall, Mildred Scott, long-time secretary and treasurer of the AFPH, resigned from the organization in early 1957. In 1959, she wrote to John Carmody, a labor arbitrator at the time and long-time friend of the AFPH, lamenting the group's demise. Recognizing that "labor was the backbone, insofar as finances were concerned," she felt that Strachan had taken on too much with the institute, and his drive to raise the needed funds for the project had alienated his labor allies.[72]

By July, Strachan had also decided that 1957 would be his final year with the AFPH.[73] Before he left his post, however, he issued a scathing report, attacking organized labor. Addressed to "all actual members," the report accused various AFL-CIO officials of being "hell-bent to MAKE AFPH over." He contended that the AFL-CIO had tried to force the AFPH to give up its fight to improve the rehabilitation program and to increase employment opportunities for people with disabilities and to accept Social Security instead. Moreover, he charged that many labor leaders who were also national vice presidents of the AFPH had not aided the AFPH and their promises of financial support very often failed to materialize. Finally, Strachan begged AFPH members to send contributions to keep the national office open. While he sent the report to only a few labor representatives, most of the AFPH's biggest supporters quickly learned of its contents.[74] The report's tone and accusations no doubt destroyed any chance of continued support among labor leaders. Shortly after issuing his invective, he shut down the AFPH's national office and moved to Florida.[75]

In the spring of 1958, rehabilitation officials hoped that Clarence Averill would be elected the new president of the AFPH at the organization's upcoming convention in Grand Rapids, Michigan. Ralf Peckham, state director of the rehabilitation program in Michigan, believed that Averill's leadership "would certainly usher in a completely different atmosphere" as he was "certainly not the 'evangelist' type."[76] Ultimately, new leadership could not solve the organization's mounting problems. According to Mildred Scott, the AFPH "folded" under the financial and organizational pressure of attempting to campaign for an expansive national legislative agenda, raise funds, and launch the massive institute. Supporters and members, it seemed to Scott, believed that building the institute would necessitate "a never-ending drive for funds." While some members of the AFPH, including Averill, founded a new organization, the National Association of the Physically Handicapped (NAPH), Strachan remained wedded to the AFPH institute and endeavored to make the institute a reality by continuing his fundraising efforts. For Scott's part, she wrote that she never joined the NAPH because, like the organization she had worked tirelessly for, she "too was weary." Strachan, she complained, "was quite bitter and critical of many."[77]

Neither Strachan nor the AFPH went quietly into the good night. Even after the national organization had folded, Strachan continued to campaign for the AFPH institute well into the late 1960s. Though battling cancer and removed to Florida, he inundated HEW and rehabilitation officials with letter after letter requesting information about grant programs administered by the rehabilitation program. Apparently disregarding the application materials that officials had sent to him, Strachan requested a $3 million grant for the institute in a postscript to a 1967 letter. Moreover, he offered his services as a consultant to Switzer, then chief of the expanded Vocational Rehabilitation Administration (VRA). In June 1967, when Strachan realized that the VRA had hired someone else to fill the position, he wrote to Switzer that he was beginning to understand that "you and the VRA DON'T WANT ME AROUND TO BOTHER YOU." He confessed, "I would probably worry you a lot, at that." Strachan wished Switzer well and told her to " 'take up the torch' and go for broke." Shortly after, Strachan faded from the national scene.[78] He passed away in September 1972 in George Washington University Hospital.[79]

Strachan's leadership had galvanized a national movement of people with disabilities demanding greater opportunities and better services, but his choices in those final years also contributed to the downfall of the organization. As Strachan's health began to fade and as doors began to close to the AFPH, the persistence that had earlier made Strachan an effective leader turned into obsession. He became increasingly bitter and critical of his allies, alienating a new generation of labor leaders who were already not as interested in the AFPH agenda as previous leaders had been. The AFPH crumbled under the weight of Strachan's attacks on the organization's supporters and the combined financial pressures of its legislative campaign and the drive for the institute.

Ultimately, the 1954 rehabilitation amendments did not yield the growth Eisenhower had demanded. The number of individuals rehabilitated dipped from 66,193 in 1951 to 57,981 in 1955. By 1960, just under 90,000 a year received rehabilitation, well below Eisenhower's goal of 200,000 and further still from meeting the needs of the estimated 250,000 new individuals each year who would need rehabilitation. Federal investment in the program climbed steadily throughout the Eisenhower years but not at a pace that would meet national needs. Moreover, the rising cost of rehabilitation—it jumped from an average of $625 per person to $1,144—meant that the funding did not go as far.[80]

World War II had been both a moment of promise and consequence for people with disabilities. The (dis)ability binary helped to define inclusion and exclusion because it defined notions of fitness for work, service, motherhood, and fatherhood. Wartime labor shortages and returning veterans with disabilities challenged these assumptions. As the federal government pushed employers to hire disabled workers and launched and expanded programs designed to support their entry into the workforce, the promise of the New Deal, which had largely excluded people with disabilities, took on new meaning. The state's wartime efforts to draw disabled people into the nation's workplaces demonstrated that the state could make opportunity, employment, and security accessible to people with disabilities.

More broadly, the war represented a civil rights moment. People with disabilities, alongside women, African Americans, and other people of color, were drawn into the war effort, whether through military service, work, volunteer efforts, or the daily sacrifices every American made. The wartime climate infused work, already cast as both an obligation and promise of citizenship, with deeper meaning. Propaganda linked work on the home front to victory, imbuing it with a sense of service to the nation. The sense of contributing to the war—one fought in defense of a nation that would distinguish itself from its enemies by emphasizing Americans' individual rights—and the new expectations that wartime necessities helped to generate led many Americans to demand that the nation make the American promise a reality for a broader range of people.

On the one hand, World War II civilian rehabilitation policy represented the clearest articulation of the state's promise of inclusion. The federal and state governments now provided a wider range of services to an increasing number of disabled Americans to support their entry into the workforce. On the other hand, in opening the door to medical and psychiatric services, World War II policy contributed to the othering of people with disabilities. Under the Barden-La Follette Act the rehabilitation bureaucracy grew, but so too did the idea that disabled people needed medical interventions and expert guidance to transform them from dependents to workers. A growing body of experts would increasingly shape the terms of disabled people's inclusion in the workforce and full citizenship. World War II rehabilitation policy created new mechanisms for inclusion, but in so doing it reinforced the fundamental otherness of people with disabilities.

The war also made disability more visible. The nation required soldiers and workers. In the drive to fill that need, policymakers began to discover the extent of disability. Staggering accident rates in the nation's factories and the assurance that war itself would disable thousands of soldiers made the discovery much more dire. Indeed, the pressures that infused work with new meaning during the war inscribed the problem of disability with new and greater significance.

In this moment of promise and consequence—central to many of the American social movements of the twentieth century—the AFPH was born. AFPH members and leaders identified and articulated the myriad ways that being on the other side of belonging limited what was possible for them. But the organization did more than catalogue these limits; it facilitated a collective dream of inclusion. AFPH leaders and members imagined a state that made full citizenship accessible to people with physical disabilities. While the organization certainly sought inclusion in the New Deal era and wartime promises of opportunity, economic security, and work, it also demanded that the state facilitate that inclusion through a range of policies that would support disabled people's access to the workplace, better educational opportunities, health care, and improved medical treatments as well as their physical access to public spaces. Beyond federal support of their right to employment, activists called on the federal government to participate in a campaign to educate the public and work toward the undoing of disability discrimination. Further, disability activists demanded that people with disabilities define and shape these policies. In this context, the AFPH campaign represented both an implicit and explicit challenge to the growing authority of a range of experts in the rehabilitation bureaucracy. AFPH organizing efforts hinged on the notion that having experienced disability members offered a unique service to the nation and that experience was necessary to form effective and just policy. More than just demanding that their experiences and opinions be taken into account, the AFPH imagined a disability bureaucracy staffed as much as possible by people with disabilities themselves.

Through the personal connections of AFPH president Paul Strachan and members' networks at the local level, the AFPH gained the support of organized labor. The labor movement helped to finance the AFPH, but equally as important, the labor leaders offered the AFPH legislative and organizational support, testifying in support of AFPH aims and lending weight to the organization's objectives. Through their interactions with the AFPH, labor leaders helped to frame the AFPH's agenda, both as a movement about workers, in support of greater protections for them, and as a movement in line with labor's broader vision of democracy and for the state. At the same time, these interactions bridged older concerns about health and safety, particularly in the context of the workplace, and labor's newer drive to expand the securities the state offered workers and citizens. As labor leaders participated in the AFPH's campaign for opportunity and security for people with disabilities, they offered a critique of the rehabilitation bureaucracy's failure to serve working people. Labor leaders' support of the AFPH highlighted workers' vulnerability to accidents and disease and the need for greater protection of workers against the uncertainties of disability. In so doing, interactions with the AFPH helped to make disability a more central part of labor's postwar agenda.

Even as the AFPH gained the support of organized labor and imagined a more inclusive state, that vision was constrained by, as much as it challenged, (dis)ability, gender, race, and sexuality privileges and exclusions. AFPH activists sought inclusion in a system built on exclusions, and the organization and their proposals embodied that contradiction. AFPH members positioned themselves as members of a broader group of excluded Americans, linking disability to gender and race, but they did not challenge the notion that exclusion had its place in the social order. Indeed, some of those same members claimed citizenship rights for people with *physical* disabilities by emphasizing their abilities as compared to people with cognitive and mental disabilities. Further, like the broader welfare state to which they sought access, the AFPH envisioned a model of entitlement and aid—a series of programs to make work accessible to people with disabilities and aid for those who could not work. That model would have made people with disabilities who needed aid subject to the same indignities and restrictions that NFB leaders and other "welfare" recipients did and would continue to critique. Even as the AFPH fought to remake rehabilitation, demanding greater sensitivity to the needs, experiences, and aspirations of people with disabilities, the organization's campaign highlighted an essential otherness—people with disabilities needed state support in a system and a society defined by disability exclusions to gain inclusion. Still, the AFPH imagined that model in new ways. In seeking to link decisions about rehabilitation to pensions, they imagined a state that would have financial incentive to include. Further, they imagined a system where people with disabilities would be the arbiters of benefits and help to dictate the terms of inclusion.

In the end, the AFPH's efforts to gain national attention to issues of disability by rooting their campaign in the horrors of war, a time when the loss of manpower both on the battlefield and the factory floor had grave consequences, and portraying disability as a problem that mattered to Americans whether able or disabled also benefited rehabilitation bureaucrats and experts. AFPH members and leaders posed a problem, but others joined in offering solutions. Rehabilitation bureaucrats and other professionals in the field of disability had worked to build authority over disability issues and policy. Those claims of expertise before the New Left and feminist challenges of the 1960s and 1970s would have been particularly powerful as physicians and a range of experts held tremendous power in the postwar years.[81] In that climate, the AFPH's campaign for an accessible and inclusive state pitted individuals who represented a national problem against a range of professionals who were viewed as having specialized knowledge, the kind of knowledge postwar society esteemed. The answers these experts offered were in many ways easier to fit into the Cold War context. Unlike the AFPH, which pointed to broad social problems, they sought to correct the individual. Further, the AFPH's critique of experts and professionals in the field of rehabilitation coincided with a surge in the power and effectiveness of medicine. Increasingly, the rehabilitation program had the power to correct, or at least dramatically alter, many disabilities. From that position of power, rehabilitation bureaucrats and a range of experts also claimed to have an answer to the problem of disability—an answer both rooted in and supportive of disability as a defining otherness. Still, the AFPH had gained important ground for the disability rights movement, winning greater room for people with disabilities in shaping the state.

Epilogue

In 1952, American Federation of the Physically Handicapped (AFPH) vice president J. Rosemond Cook, Jr., wrote that the AFPH had been "born of the needs, aspirations, and dreams of the millions of handicapped men and women."[1] Those aspirations and dreams led thousands of disabled Americans to demand that the state make economic security and citizenship accessible. The AFPH provided an important forum for disabled people to be heard. Members demanded "justice, equal rights, and opportunity."[2] Their critique of federal policy put a human face on the failures of disability policy that robbed people with disabilities of equal opportunity to make their aspirations and dreams a reality. AFPH members fought to shape the policies that would in turn shape their lives. By connecting faces, stories, and hopes to policy, AFPH members challenged assumptions about aid and entitlement, arguing that bringing people with disabilities more fully into the economic life of the nation was both a moral and economic imperative.

At the heart of the AFPH legislative campaign was the idea that the federal government had a responsibility to move disabled citizens from the economic and civic margins to the center of the welfare state. To a degree, but certainly not on the terms the AFPH had set, disability did become central to the welfare state in the 1940s and 1950s. The terms of that inclusion would serve to animate the longer disability rights movement in the decades to come. In 1943, Congress expanded the nature and availability of rehabilitation. Over the course of the following two years, a subcommittee of the House of Representatives Committee on Labor investigated the problem of disability, collecting thousands of pages of testimony about the conditions people with disabilities faced and the federal, state, and local programs designed to help them. Further, in 1945, Congress set aside the first week in October as National Employ the Physically Handicapped Week (NEPHW), launching a national campaign to encourage employers to hire people with disabilities. The week in 1947 led to the creation of the Department of Labor-based President's Committee on NEPHW, a coordinating agency for the federal government's efforts to increase employment among people with disabilities. In 1950, Congress expanded public assistance to people with disabilities through the Aid to the Permanently and Totally Disabled program. Policymakers again expanded vocational rehabilitation services in 1954, and the long fight for Social Security Disability Insurance achieved a landmark victory in 1956.

After that first expansion of rehabilitation in 1943, the AFPH played a role in shaping those changes, even when those changes did not necessarily align with the AFPH agenda. The organization applied constant pressure on the executive and legislative branches to address the problem of disability. Indeed, the organization's public education campaign centered in part on convincing the public that disability was a national problem that demanded a solution. The AFPH tempered even the Vocational Rehabilitation Amendments of 1954. While those amendments would serve to further medicalize disability, AFPH activists and their supporters attempted to soften that effect by securing representation of people with disabilities on the National Advisory Council and additional employment support for people with disabilities through the U.S. Employment Service. For organized labor, Social Security Disability Insurance represented an incomplete victory, as states had the power to determine eligibility and benefits were limited to people with disabilities over the age of fifty, a restriction that was lifted four years later. Just a year after Social Security Disability Insurance passed, Paul Strachan would break ties with organized labor over their commitment to the program. He viewed the campaign for Social Security Disability Insurance as a sign that labor leaders believed that disabled people should accept assistance instead of demanding employment. But through Aid to the Permanently and Totally Disabled and Social Security Disability Insurance, disability had become part of both the aid and entitlement sides of the welfare state. An expanded vision of rehabilitation bridged those programs, offering the promise of converting individuals dependent on aid to workers who would be entitled to state-sponsored protections. In the end, those inclusions reified the (dis)ability binary as both Aid to the Permanently and Totally Disabled and Social Security Disability Insurance drew on the assumption that disability would take an individual out of the workforce.

Still, the AFPH left a permanent imprint on the national dialogue about disability. AFPH prodding created a renewed interest in federal disability policy among organized labor leaders. Together, disability activists and union representatives challenged the authority and sensitivities of experts and physicians in the field of disability policy. While this challenge did not end in victory for the AFPH, it did force the rehabilitation bureaucracy to be increasingly aware of the widespread social and economic discrimination that shaped the opportunities available to people with disabilities. Moreover, the critique forced the rehabilitation bureaucracy to examine its policies and the attitudes and assumptions that informed those policies.

To untangle meaning and significance from the AFPH, and its ultimate collapse, requires a broad view, considering the longer history of the disability rights movement. The organization's demands and claims did not vanish from the memories of lawmakers, and the disability communities the AFPH fostered continued to grow. Numerous obituaries of former AFPH members, ranging from the late 1980s to the early 2000s, mention their continued participation in the National Association of the Physically Handicapped (NAPH), the organization that emerged to take the place of the AFPH. Members continued to participate in the local community that the AFPH had facilitated, and not all of these activists retired from the national, political arena. Indeed, the NAPH continued to participate in the President's Committee and worked alongside other disability rights organization to gain national disability rights legislation.[3] Perhaps more important in the longer narrative of the disability rights movement, the institutional spaces the AFPH created also persisted and grew. Its institutional legacy was central to accessibility campaigns in the 1950s and 1960s and helped to foster a new generation of activists in the 1970s. But these young disabled activists had been robbed of knowledge of their past and deprived of the opportunity to understand their activism and ideas in the context of those who had come before them.

By the 1970s, the President's Committee on Employment of the Handicapped had become hostile ground to conquer instead of a legacy to reclaim. In 1973, disability activists Ralf Hotchkiss and Judy Heumann castigated the President's Committee on Employment of the Handicapped, calling the committee "an Uncle Tom to five administrations which have done little to correct the basic forms of discrimination against the handicapped." They argued that the committee's slogan—"Hire the Handicapped, It's Good Business"—was "as inappropriate in the drive for civil rights of the disabled as a slogan 'Hire the Blacks—They Work Like Slaves' would be in the racial struggle." In their minds, the slogan emphasized the "obedience records" of disabled workers as the most significant reason to hire them—an obedience that grew out of disabled people's recognition that discrimination forced them to "cling tenaciously to any job, regardless how menial." Hotchkiss and Heumann went on to claim that the slogan had "been rightfully—but quietly—opposed since its inception by the bulk of the disabled community."[4] Missing from this harsh critique, however, was the fact that the President's Committee and its slogan grew out of the efforts of disability activists in the AFPH three decades earlier.

Given that critique, and the fact that disability activists of the 1970s failed to see themselves as part of a longer movement, it might be easy to think of the disability movement of the 1940s and 1950s as a kind of disjointed prologue to the later disability rights movement. But the legacies of the AFPH helped to shape the continuing struggle for disability rights. From 1942 to 1958, the AFPH fought to implement a bold agenda that centered on winning opportunity, work, and security for people with disabilities and was premised on the idea that people with disabilities had a right to earn a living and a right to economic security. The President's Committee and NEPHW, which had served as the impetus for creating such a committee, represented two of the AFPH's most successful campaigns. Though Strachan and other disability activists had hoped to use the President's Committee as a springboard to win much of their legislative agenda—a wish that did not materialize—the President's Committee proved to be a powerful force in pushing for the employment of people with disabilities. From 1947 to 1952, over 1.1 million disabled Americans received job placements through the Employment Service, and more than 300,000 were rehabilitated and then placed in jobs through state vocational rehabilitation agencies.[5] By 1957, estimates placed the number of disabled citizens who had been employed since the committee began its activities at well over 2.6 million.[6] Apparently, numerous businesses took the refrain, "Hire the Handicapped, It's Good Business," to heart.

By the 1970s, young disability activists viewed the committee with considerable skepticism, judging it to be a conservative force within the disability rights community. While many of these activists were not aware of the past efforts of disability activists to alter the political landscape, this generation of activists benefited from the hard-won gains of the AFPH. While Strachan had resigned from the committee in frustration, it continued to push at the barriers that prevented people with disabilities from achieving full equality. In 1959, the committee worked with the National Society for Crippled Children and Adults (NSCCA) and the American Standards Association to codify standards of accessibility. These standards provided the foundation for numerous state accessibility laws, beginning in South Carolina in 1963, as well as the federal Architectural Barriers Act of 1968 that required that all new federal buildings be made accessible to people with disabilities. Moreover, the President's Committee, working alongside the NSCCA, helped to galvanize and facilitate local- and state-level campaigns for accessibility, which prodded federal lawmakers to take action. The organizations encouraged surveys of local buildings and drew on the strategies that had been central to the AFPH and the President's Committee from the start—public education and coalition efforts. The President's Committee and the NSCCA provided local and state activists with tools to succeed, hosting workshops and providing guidelines for local surveys, information about successful campaigns and accessibility standards, and support from national partner organizations.[7]

While these first accessibility laws were admittedly limited, the committee's slow and steady progress within the federal bureaucracy provided a foundation for future activism and legislation and also led to the employment of millions of disabled workers. Perhaps as important as the gains the committee managed to win for people with disabilities, the institutional space of the committee provided a place for activists to meet, and it worked as a springboard for a new wave of activism. For example, many of the activists who would become leaders in the disability rights movement in the 1970s participated in the President's Committee. Disability rights activist Fred Fay led an accessibility campaign on the campus of the University of Illinois that grew out of the work of the President's Committee and the NSCCA. Ed Roberts, another national leader in the disability rights movement in the 1970s and a central figure in the Independent Living Movement, and other disabled students at the University of California, Berkeley, formed a Disabled Students Program on campus and secured funding to attend President's Committee meetings in Washington, D.C.[8] In 1972 and 1973, led by Heumann, president of the New York-based Disabled in Action, protesters filed out of President's Committee meetings and led demonstrations in Washington. These activists protested educational, employment, housing, transportation, and architectural discrimination as well as President Richard M. Nixon's repeated veto of the rehabilitation bill, which would become the Rehabilitation Act of 1973. Section 504 of the bill banned discrimination against people with disabilities in all federal programs and in organizations that received federal funds.[9]

Sustained disability rights activism in the 1960s and 1970s, as historian

Lindsey Patterson demonstrates, prompted the bill's antidiscrimination provisions. Some of this activism grew out of the AFPH and its institutional and organizational legacies. Patterson also points to the legislative synergy among disability, broader civil rights, and rights-based disability legislation, noting that a number of senators including Charles Percy (R-IL), Alan Cranston (D-CA), Hubert Humphrey (D-MN), Jennings Randolph (D-WV), and Robert Dole (R-KS) "took leading roles in disability rights or broader civil rights initiatives in the mid-1960s and early 1970s."[10] These synergies can be traced further back. Humphrey had been a co-sponsor of the Douglas bill and pushed for an AFPH amendment to the Vocational Rehabilitation Amendments of 1954. Randolph had served on the House Subcommittee to Investigate Aid to the Physically Handicapped that heard repeatedly from AFPH activists.

The President's Committee—by then named the President's Committee on Employment of People with Disabilities—and the disability rights movement came full circle when president George H. W. Bush appointed Justin W. Dart, Jr., as chair of the committee in 1989. Prior to his appointment, Dart, a wealthy and well-connected polio survivor and wheelchair user, had served as head of the Rehabilitation Services Administration during the Ronald Reagan administration, a position he sought to use to ensure people with disabilities played a role in all aspects of federal disability policy—something AFPH members had demanded forty years earlier. In the wake of Dart's very public critique of the agency—he told Congress that it was "a vast, inflexible federal system which, like the society it represents, still contains a significant portion of individuals who have not yet overcome obsolete, paternalistic attitudes about disability"—he was asked to resign in 1987, less than a year after he accepted the position. Still, President Reagan appointed him to serve on the National Council on Disability, which drafted civil rights legislation that would in 1990 become the Americans with Disabilities Act (ADA). Dart also chaired the Congressional Taskforce on the Rights and Empowerment of Americans with Disabilities. He served as chair of the President's Committee during the final push for the ADA, which provided disabled people equal access to employment and public accommodations by requiring employer accommodations and public accessibility. During his tenure with the President's Committee, he continued his work to make the ADA a reality and then met with business leaders around the country to push for compliance. Indeed, in his role as chair of the President's Committee, he addressed a group of disability protestors gathered at the Capitol Steps, demanding passage of the bill that would become the ADA. "Two centuries," he said, "is long enough for people with disabilities to wait before the constitutional promise of justice is kept."[11]

The campaigns to secure the ADA and the Rehabilitation Act of 1973 and ensure the implementation of Section 504 generated much momentum within the disability rights community. Disability activists marshaled new tactics, strategies, and coalitions in these campaigns, but 1973 was not the beginning of the disability rights movement. It was a new chapter in a movement of many social movements with a much longer history—a history that neither began nor ended with the AFPH, but was transformed by it nonetheless. Just as the New Deal and the horrors of World War II informed the AFPH, the organization helped to shape the activism that would follow and that moved the nation closer to AFPH members' dreams of an accessible state and inclusive citizenship.

Notes

Introduction

1. Congress, House, Representative Kelley of Pennsylvania paying tribute to Mildred Scott, 81st Cong., 1st sess., *Congressional Record* 95, pt. 16 (11 October 1949): A6220–22; Congress, House, Committee on Labor, Subcommittee to Investigate Aid to the Physically Handicapped, *Hearings, Part 8, Aid to Victims of Orthopedic Impairments, To Disabled Seamen, etc.*, 78th Cong., 2nd sess. (Washington, D.C.: GPO, 1945), 1098; Maxine Cheshire, "Her Decisions Can Affect 28 Millions," *Washington Post*, 11 March 1955, 64; 1940 U.S. census, Dallas County, Texas, population schedule, Dallas City, JP #1, Block 57, p. 3B, line 70, household 99, Mildred Scott; digital image, Ancestry.com, accessed 8 July 2015; 1930 U.S. census, Washington County, Pennsylvania, population schedule, Cecil Township, p. 6A, line 7–14, dwelling 95, Elijah F., Minnie, Mildred, Charles, Floyd, Clair, Dorothy, and John Scott; digital image, Ancestry.com, accessed 8 July 2015; 1920 U.S. census, Washington County, Pennsylvania, population schedule, Cecil, p. 2A, line 29–36, dwelling 28, Elijah F., Minnie B, Velma J., Mary M., Charles, George F., Clair F., and Dorothy B. Scott, digital image, Ancestry.com, accessed 8 July 2015.

2. Ibid.

3. House, Subcommittee to Investigate Aid to the Physically Handicapped, *Hearings, Part 8*, 1095.

4. Congress, House, Kelley paying tribute to Scott; Cheshire, "Her Decisions Can Affect 28 Millions," 64.

5. "Strachan, Paul A(mbrose)," *Current Biography Yearbook*, "1952," (New York: H.W. Wilson, 1952), 562–63; Paul Strachan to Walter Mason, 9 April 1953, #23/20, Record Group 21-001, Legislation Department, Legislative Reference Files, George Meany Memorial Archives, National Labor College, Silver Spring, Md. (hereafter Meany Archives); Mrs. William Strachan to Audra Jennings, 11 March 2003, letter in possession of the author; Thomas L. Stokes, "Help for the Handicapped," *Lincoln Evening Journal*, 19 August 1946, 4; Fred J. Zusy, "Helps Handicapped: Deaf Man Leads Drive," *Abilene Reporter-News*, 5 October 1947, 14; Robert S. Allen, "The Washington Merry-Go-Round: Handicapped Aid Plan Lauded," *Washington Post*, 13 August 1949, B11; Sam Stavisky, "A Self-Described Cynic Leads the Battle for Decent Jobs for Nation's Handicapped," *Washington Post*, 4 October 1948, 2; "One Dead, One Hurt in Auto-Train Accident," *Atlanta Constitution*, 16 November 1929, 25A; and Paul Strachan to Marcus Kenner, 3 October 1941, Box 2, Folder 17, Papers of Thomas L. Anderson, Gallaudet University Archives, Washington, D.C.; Jean R. Halley, "Paul A. Strachan, 83, Fought For Physically Handicapped," *Washington Post*, 19 September 1972, C4.

6. Congress, House, Kelley paying tribute to Scott.

7. Rosemarie Garland-Thomson, "Integrating Disability, Transforming Feminist Theory," *NWSA Journal* 14 (Fall 2002): 5. See also Kim E. Nielsen, *A Disability History of the United States* (Boston: Beacon Press, 2012): xi–xxi; Kim E. Nielsen, "Historical Thinking and Disability," *Disability Studies Quarterly* 28 (Summer 2008); Catherine J. Kudlick, "Disability History: Why We Need Another 'Other'," *American Historical Review* 108 (June 2003): 763–93; and Douglas C. Baynton, "Disability and the Justification of Inequality in American History," in *The New Disability History: American Perspectives*, ed. Paul K. Longmore and Lauri Umansky (New York: New York University Press, 2001), 33–57.

8. Historian Robin D. G. Kelley argues that social movements develop "new knowledge, new theories, new questions" and facilitate a reimagining of society. Robin D. G. Kelley, *Freedom Dreams: The Black Radical Imagination* (Boston: Beacon, 2002), 8–9.

9. Numerous disability activist organizations had been active long before the AFPH. The National Association of the Deaf (NAD), founded in 1880, and the National Fraternal Society of the Deaf, founded in 1901, represented deaf Americans. Disabled American Veterans (DAV), founded in 1920, represented the interests of disabled veterans. The National Federation of the Blind (NFB), founded in 1940, worked to create increased opportunities for blind people. Pan-disability activism was also not new. Scholars Paul K. Longmore and David Goldberger have shown that New Yorkers with a wide-range of disabilities organized to protest their exclusion from Works Progress Administration (WPA) jobs during the Great Depression. The AFPH was unique in its national scope and cross-disability membership. See, Fred Pelka, *The ABC-Clio Companion to the Disability Rights Movement* (Santa Barbara, Calif.: ABC-Clio, 1997); and Paul K. Longmore and David Goldberger, "The League of the Physically Handicapped and the Great Depression: A Case Study in the New Disability History," *Journal of American History* 87 (December 2000): 888–922.

10. Labor's active role in the AFPH highlights the continued importance of disability to workers and their unions. For histories that focus on disabled workers, see Audra Jennings, "'The Greatest Numbers . . . Will Be Wage Earners': Organized Labor and Disability Activism, 1945–1953," *Labor: Studies in Working-Class History of the Americas* 4 (November 2007): 55–82; Sarah F. Rose, "'Crippled' Hands: Disability in Labor and Working-Class History," *Labor* 2 (Spring 2005): 27–54; and John Williams-Searle, "Cold Charity: Manhood, Brotherhood, and the Transformation of Disability, 1870–1900," in *The New Disability History*, ed. Longmore and Umansky, 157–86.

11. Baynton, "Disability and the Justification of Inequality in American History," 33–57.

12. Barbara Young Welke, *Law and the Borders of Belonging in the Long Nineteenth Century United States* (Cambridge: Cambridge University Press, 2010), 1–2, 8.

13. Welke, *Law and the Borders of Belonging*; Margot Canaday, *The Straight State: Sexuality and Citizenship in Twentieth-Century America* (Princeton, N.J.: Princeton University Press, 2009), 3. See also Cybelle Fox, *Three Worlds of Relief: Race, Immigration, and the American Welfare State from the Progressive Era to the New Deal* (Princeton, N.J.: Princeton University Press, 2012); Carolyn Herbst Lewis, *Prescription for Heterosexuality: Sexual Citizenship in the Cold War Era* (Chapel Hill: University of North Carolina Press, 2010); Robyn Muncy, "Coal-Fired Reforms: Social Citizenship, Dissident Miners, and the Great Society," *Journal of American History* 96 (June 2009): 72–98; Ira Katznelson, *When Affirmative Action Was White: An Untold History of Racial Inequality in Twentieth-Century America* (New York: Norton, 2005); Alice Kessler-Harris, *In Pursuit of Equity: Women, Men, and the Quest for Economic Citizenship in*

20th-Century America (Oxford: Oxford University Press, 2001); Michael Willrich, "Home Slackers: Men, the State, and Welfare in Modern America," *Journal of American History* 87 (September 2000): 460–89; Suzanne Mettler, *Dividing Citizens: Gender and Federalism in New Deal Public Policy* (Ithaca, N.Y.: Cornell University Press, 1998); Nancy Fraser and Linda Gordon, "A Genealogy of Dependency: Tracing a Keyword of the U.S. Welfare State," *Signs* 19 (Winter 1994): 309–36; Linda Gordon, *Pitied But Not Entitled: Single Mothers and the History of Welfare, 1890–1935* (New York: Free Press, 1994); and Linda Gordon, ed., *Women, the State, and Welfare* (Madison: University of Wisconsin Press, 1990).

14. For histories of disability policy, see Beth Linker, *War's Waste: Rehabilitation in World War I America* (Chicago: University of Chicago Press, 2011); Ruth O'Brien, *Crippled Justice: The History of Modern Disability Policy in the Workplace* (Chicago: University of Chicago Press, 2001); Richard K. Scotch, "American Disability Policy in the Twentieth Century," in *The New Disabilities History*, ed. Longmore and Umansky, 375–92; Richard K. Scotch, *From Good Will to Civil Rights: Transforming Federal Disability Policy*, 2nd ed. (Philadelphia: Temple University Press, 2001); Edward D. Berkowitz, *Disabled Policy: America's Programs for the Handicapped* (Cambridge: Cambridge University Press, 1987); Edward D. Berkowitz, *Rehabilitation: The Federal Government's Response to Disability, 1935–1954* (New York: Arno Press, 1980); Edward D. Berkowitz, "Strachan and the Limits of the Federal Government," *International Review of History and Political Science* 17 (February 1980): 65–81; and Edward D. Berkowitz, "Growth of the U.S. Social Welfare System in the Post-World II Era: The UMW, Rehabilitation, and the Federal Government," *Research in Economic History* 5 (1980): 233–47.

15. John Fabian Witt, *The Accidental Republic: Crippled Workingmen, Destitute Widows, and the Remaking of American Law* (Cambridge, Mass.: Harvard University Press, 2004), 2.

16. Gerald Markowitz and David Rosner, "Death and Disease in the House of Labor," *Labor History* 30, 1 (1989), 115–16; David Rosner and Gerald Markowitz, "Safety and Health on the Job as a Class Issue: The Workers' Health Bureau of America in the 1920s," *Science & Society* 48 (Winter1984/1985): 466.

17. Witt, *The Accidental Republic*, 2–5, 10–12, 126–28. See also Anthony Bale, "America's First Compensation Crisis: Conflict over the Value and Meaning of Workplace Injuries Under the Employers' Liability System," in *Dying for Work: Workers' Safety and Health in Twentieth-Century America*, ed. David Rosner and Gerald Markowitz (Bloomington: Indiana University Press, 1987), 34–52; and Berkowitz, *Disabled Policy*, especially chapter 1.

18. Welke, *Law and the Borders of Belonging*, 56–60, 118–19; Douglas C. Baynton, "Defectives in the Land: Disability and American Immigration Policy, 1882–1924," *Journal of American Ethnic History* 24 (Spring 2005): 31–44; Michael B. Katz, *In the Shadow of the Poorhouse: A Social History of Welfare in America* (New York: Basic, 1986), 58–84; and Susan Schweik, "Begging the Question: Disability, Mendicancy, Speech and the Law," *Narrative* 15 (January 2007): 58–59. See also Susan Schweik, *The Ugly Laws: Disability in Public* (New York: New York University Press, 2009). On intellectual disabilities, see Allison C. Carey, *On the Margins of Citizenship: Intellectual Disability and Civil Rights in Twentieth-Century America* (Philadelphia: Temple University Press, 2009); and James W. Trent, Jr., *Inventing the Feeble Mind: A History of Mental Retardation in the United States* (Berkeley: University of California Press, 1994). For information about the eugenics movement, see Christine Rosen, *Preaching Eugenics: Religious Leaders and the American Eugenics Movement* (Oxford: Oxford University Press, 2004); Nancy Ordover, *American Eugenics: Race, Queer Anatomy, and the Science of Nationalism* (Minneapolis: University of Minnesota Press, 2003); and Martin S. Pernick, *The Black Stork: Eugenics and the Death of*

"Defective" Babies in American Medicine and Motion Pictures Since 1915 (New York: Oxford University Press, 1996). See also Susan Burch and Hannah Joyner, *Unspeakable: The Story of Junius Wilson* (Chapel Hill: University of North Carolina Press, 2007).

19. See Linker, *War's Waste*, 1–34; and K. Walter Hickel, "Medicine, Bureaucracy, and Social Welfare: The Politics of Disability Compensation for American Veterans of World War I," in *The New Disabilities History*, ed. Longmore and Umansky, 236–67.

20. For histories of rehabilitation, see Linker, *War's Waste*; Berkowitz, *Disabled Policy*; Glenn Gritzer and Arnold Arluke, *The Making of Rehabilitation: A Political Economy of Medical Specialization, 1890–1980* (Berkeley: University of California Press, 1985); Berkowitz, *Rehabilitation*; Berkowitz, "Growth of the U.S. Social Welfare System in the Post-World II Era"; C. Esco Obermann, *A History of Vocational Rehabilitation in America* (Minneapolis: Denison, 1965); Committee on Veterans' Affairs, *The Provision of Federal Benefits for Veterans: An Historical Analysis of Major Veterans' Legislation, 1862–1954* (Washington, D.C.: GPO, 1955); and U.S. Office of Education, *Vocational Rehabilitation of the Physically Handicapped: The Evolution, Scope, Organization, and Administration of the Program of Vocational Rehabilitation of the Physically Handicapped in the United States* (Washington, D.C.: GPO, 1936).

21. O'Brien, *Crippled Justice*, 64–66; Scotch, "American Disability Policy in the Twentieth Century," 381; Berkowitz, *Rehabilitation*, 84–87; and U.S. Office of Education, *Administration of Vocational Rehabilitation* (Washington, D.C.: GPO, 1938), 11.

22. Fraser and Gordon, "A Genealogy of Dependency," 320–21; and Brad Byrom, "A Pupil and a Patient: Hospital-Schools in Progressive America," 133–56, in *The New Disability History*, ed. Longmore and Umansky, 135. See also Willrich, "Home Slackers."

23. J. Rosemond Cook, Jr., "The Work of the Federation of the Physically Handicapped," *Atlanta Daily World*, 18 November 1952, 3.

24. Franklin D. Roosevelt, Annual Address to Congress, 6 January 1941, Franklin D. Roosevelt Presidential Library and Museum; http://www.fdrlibrary.marist.edu/od4frees.html (accessed 12 April 2008). See Edwin Amenta, *Bold Relief: Institution Politics and the Origins of Modern American Social Policy* (Princeton, N.J.: Princeton University Press, 1998). For a general history of the New Deal see David M. Kennedy, *Freedom from Fear: The American People in Depression and War, 1929–1945* (New York: Oxford University Press, 1999).

25. Barbara J. Nelson, "The Origins of the Two-Channel Welfare State: Workmen's Compensation and Mothers' Aid," in *Women, the State, and Welfare*, ed. Gordon, 123–51.

26. Kessler-Harris, *In Pursuit of Equity*, 11.

27. Fraser and Gordon, "A Genealogy of Dependency," 321–22. Notions of dependency would continue to shift in the postwar era. See also Jennifer Mittelstadt, "'Dependency as a Problem to Be Solved': Rehabilitation and the American Liberal Consensus on Welfare in the 1950s," *Social Politics* 8 (Summer 2001): 228–57; and Jennifer Mittelstadt, *From Welfare to Workfare: The Unintended Consequences of Liberal Reform, 1945–1965* (Chapel Hill: University of North Carolina Press, 2005).

28. See generally, Fox, *Three Worlds of Relief*; Felicia Kornbluh, "Queer Legal History: A Field Grows Up and Comes Out," *Law and Social Inquiry* 36 (Spring 2011): 537–59; Lewis, *Prescription for Heterosexuality*; Muncy, "Coal-Fired Reforms: Social Citizenship, Dissident Miners, and the Great Society"; Katznelson, *When Affirmative Action Was White*; Kessler-Harris, *In Pursuit of Equity*; Willrich, "Home Slackers"; Mettler, *Dividing Citizens*; Fraser and Gordon, "A Genealogy of Dependency"; Gordon, *Pitied But Not Entitled*; Felicia Kornbluh, "Welfare

Mothers," *Women's Review of Books* 12 (November 1994): 16–17; and Gordon, ed., *Women, the State, and Welfare.*

29. G. B. Erskine, "Hire the Handicapped," *Fortune* 34 (November 1946): 22. For more on how the wartime economy challenged racial and gendered ideas about work and contributed to demands for rights, see Maggie Rivas-Rodriguez, ed., *Mexican Americans and World War II* (Austin: University of Texas Press, 2005); Megan Taylor Shockley, *"We, Too, Are Americans": African American Women in Detroit and Richmond, 1940–54* (Urbana: University of Illinois Press, 2004); Martha Biondi, *To Stand and Fight: The Struggle for Civil Rights in Postwar New York City* (Cambridge, Mass.: Harvard University Press, 2003); Ronald Takaki, *Double Victory: A Multicultural History of America in World War II* (Boston: Little, Brown, 2000); Kenneth William Townsend, *World War II and the American Indian* (Albuquerque: University of New Mexico Press, 2000); Susan M. Hartmann, *The Home Front and Beyond: American Women in the 1940s* (Boston: Twayne, 1982); Alice Kessler-Harris, *Out to Work: A History of Wage-Earning Women in the United States* (Oxford: Oxford University Press, 1982); and Karen Anderson, *Wartime Women: Sex Roles, Family Relations, and the Status of Women during World War II* (Westport, Conn.: Greenwood, 1981).

30. Congress, House, Committee on Interstate and Foreign Commerce, Subcommittee, *Hearings, H.R. 1980, Health of School Children*, 80th Cong., 1st sess. (Washington, D.C.: GPO, 1947), 26–28.

31. Chief of the Bureau of Statistics, Treasury Department, *Statistical Abstract of the United States* (Washington, D.C.: GPO, 1947), 216.

32. Congress, House, H.J. Res. 23, 79th Cong., 1st sess., *Congressional Record* 91, pt. 4 (4 June 1945): 5508.

33. Paul A. Strachan, "Helping Disabled Is Good Business," *Washington Post*, 29 July 1951, B2.

34. Felicia Kornbluh, "Disability, Antiprofessionalism, and Civil Rights: The National Federation of the Blind and the 'Right to Organize' in the 1950s," *Journal of American History* 97 (March 2011): 1025. For other histories of the disability rights movement that emphasize developments before the 1970s, see Audra Jennings, "'An Emblem of Distinction': The Politics of Disability Entitlement, 1940–1950," in *Veterans' Policies, Veterans' Politics: New Perspectives on Veterans in the Modern United States*, ed. Stephen R. Ortiz (Gainesville: University Press of Florida, 2012), 94–116; Nielsen, *A Disability History of the United States*; Lindsey Patterson, "Points of Access: Rehabilitation Centers, Summer Camps, and Student Life in the Making of Disability Activism, 1960–1973," *Journal of Social History* 46, 2 (2012): 473–99; Sarah F. Rose, "The Right to a College Education?: The G.I. Bill, Public Law 16, and Disabled Veterans," *Journal of Policy History* 24, 1 (2012): 26–52; Naomi Rogers, "Polio Chronicles: Warm Springs and Disability Politics in the 1930s," *Asclepio* 61, 1 (2009): 143–74; Jennings, "'The Greatest Numbers . . . Will Be Wage Earners'"; Paul K. Longmore, *Why I Burned My Book and Other Essays on Disability* (Philadelphia: Temple University Press, 2003); Susan Burch, *Signs of Resistance: American Deaf Cultural History, 1900 to World War II* (New York: New York University Press, 2002); Longmore and Umansky, eds., *The New Disability History*; Longmore and Goldberger, "The League of the Physically Handicapped and the Great Depression"; and Robert M. Buchanan, *Illusions of Equality: Deaf Americans in School and Factory, 1850–1950* (Washington, D.C.: Gallaudet University Press, 1999). For histories of the disability rights movement that focus on disability rights activism from the 1970s forward, see Fred Pelka, *What We Have Done: An Oral History of*

the Disability Rights Movement (Amherst: University of Massachusetts Press, 2012); and Susan Schweik, "Lomax's Matrix: Disability, Solidarity, and the Black Power of 504," *Disability Studies Quarterly* 31, 1 (2011). Many histories of the disability rights movement position the movement as a development of the 1960s and 1970s. See for example, Sharon Barnartt and Richard Scotch, *Disability Protests: Contentious Politics, 1970–1999* (Washington, D.C.: Gallaudet University Press, 2001); Doris Zames Fleischer and Frieda Zames, *The Disability Rights Movement: From Charity to Confrontation* (Philadelphia: Temple University Press, 2001); Scotch, *From Good Will to Civil Rights*; and Joseph P. Shapiro, *No Pity: People with Disabilities Forging a New Civil Rights Movement* (New York: Random House, 1993).

35. Jacquelyn Dowd Hall, "The Long Civil Rights Movement and the Political Uses of the Past," *Journal of American History* 91 (March 2005): 1233–63.

36. This study draws on and extends the recent work that has analyzed organized labor's role in establishing and facilitating expansions of the welfare state. See Tracy Roof, *American Labor, Congress, and the Welfare State, 1935–2010* (Baltimore: Johns Hopkins University Press, 2011); Muncy, "Coal-Fired Reforms"; Jill Quadagno, *One Nation Uninsured: Why the U.S. Has No National Health Insurance* (New York: Oxford University Press, 2005); Dorothy Sue Cobble, *The Other Women's Movement: Workplace Justice and Social Rights in Modern America* (Princeton, N.J.: Princeton University Press, 2004); Jennifer Klein, *For All These Rights: Business, Labor, and the Shaping of America's Public-Private Welfare State* (Princeton, N.J.: Princeton University Press, 2003); and Kevin Boyle, *The UAW and the Heyday of American Liberalism, 1945–1968* (Ithaca, N.Y.: Cornell University Press, 1995). For work that explores the significance of disability and health and safety in context of labor politics, see Michael J. Broadway and Donald D. Stull, "'I'll Do Whatever you Want, But It Hurts': Worker Safety and Community Health in Modern Meatpacking," *Labor: Studies in Working-Class History of the Americas* 5 (Summer 2008): 27–37; Roger Horowitz, "'That Was a Dirty Job!' Technology and Workplace Hazards in Meatpacking over the Long Twentieth Century," *Labor: Studies in Working-Class History of the Americas* 5 (Summer 2008): 13–25; Rose, "'Crippled' Hands"; Daniel E. Bender, *Sweated Work, Weak Bodies: Anti-Sweatshop Campaigns and Languages of Labor* (New Brunswick, N.J.: Rutgers University Press, 2004); Witt, *The Accidental Republic*; Williams-Searle, "Cold Charity"; Richard P. Mulcahy, *A Social Contract for the Coal Fields: The Rise and Fall of the United Mine Workers of America Welfare and Retirement Fund* (Knoxville: University of Tennessee Press, 2000); Alan Derickson, *Black Lung: Anatomy of a Public Health Disaster* (Ithaca, N.Y.: Cornell University Press, 1998); Claudia Clark, *Radium Girls: Women and Industrial Health Reform, 1910–1935* (Chapel Hill: University of North Carolina Press, 1997); David Rosner and Gerald Markowitz, "Hospitals, Insurance, and the American Labor Movement: The Case of New York in the Postwar Decades," *Journal of Policy History* 9, 1 (1997): 74–95; Alan Derickson, "Health Security for All? Social Unionism and Universal Health Insurance, 1935–1958," *Journal of American History* 80 (March 1994): 1333–56; David Rosner and Gerald Markowitz, *Deadly Dust: Silicosis and the Politics of Occupational Disease in Twentieth-Century America* (Princeton, N.J.: Princeton University Press, 1991); Gerald Markowitz and David Rosner, "'The Streets of Walking Death': Silicosis, Health, and Labor in the Tri-State Region, 1900–1950," *Journal of American History* 77 (September 1990): 525–52; Markowitz and Rosner, "Death and Disease in the House of Labor"; Alan Derickson, *Workers' Health, Workers' Democracy: The Western Miners' Struggle, 1891–1925* (Ithaca, N.Y.: Cornell University Press, 1988); Rosner and Markowitz, eds., *Dying for Work*; Barbara Ellen Smith, *Digging Our Own Graves: Coal Miners and the Struggle over Black Lung Disease* (Philadelphia: Temple University Press, 1987); Bennett M. Judkins, *We Offer Ourselves as*

Evidence: Toward Workers' Control of Occupational Health (Westport, Conn.: Greenwood, 1986); Rosner and Markowitz, "Safety and Health on the Job as a Class Issue"; and Berkowitz, "Growth of the U.S. Social Welfare System in the Post-World War II Era."

37. President Harry S. Truman, Special Message to the Congress Presenting a 21-Point Program for the Reconversion Period, 6 September 1945, Public Papers of the Presidents, Harry S. Truman, 1945–1953; http://trumanlibrary.org/publicpapers/index.php?pid=136&st=&st1=, accessed 29 May 2015; President Harry S. Truman, Special Message to the Congress Recommending a Comprehensive Health Program, 19 November 1945, Public Papers of the Presidents, Harry S. Truman, 1945–1953. See also Quadagno, *One Nation Uninsured*; James T. Patterson, *Grand Expectations: The United States, 1945–1974* (New York: Oxford University Press, 1996); Alonzo L. Hamby, *Man of the People: A Life of Harry S. Truman* (New York: Oxford University Press, 1995); and Susan M. Hartmann, *Truman and the 80th Congress* (Columbia: University of Missouri Press, 1971).

38. Congress, House, Committee on Labor, Subcommittee to Investigate Aid to the Physically Handicapped/Subcommittee on Aid to the Physically Handicapped, *Hearings, Parts 1–25*, 78th–79th Congresses (Washington, D.C.: GPO, 1945–46).

Chapter 1. Salvaging People: Disability in a Nation at War

1. "New York's 100 Neediest Cases," *New York Times*, 6 December 1942, D1.

2. Ibid.

3. David M. Kennedy, *Freedom from Fear: The American People in Depression and War, 1929–1945* (New York: Oxford University Press, 1999), 626–27, 644–46; Susan M. Hartmann, *The Home Front and Beyond: American Women in the 1940s* (Boston: Twayne, 1982), 1–12; John Morton Blum, *V Was for Victory: Politics and American Culture During World War II* (San Diego: Harcourt Brace, 1976), 90–105.

4. Ibid.

5. Katherine B. Oettinger, "Title V of the Social Security Act: What It Has Meant to the Children," *Social Security Bulletin* 23 (August 1960): 43.

6. Kim E. Nielsen, *A Disability History of the United States* (Boston: Beacon, 2012), 146–47.

7. Congress, Senate, Proposal to Establish a Rehabilitation Service, 77th Cong., 2nd sess., *Congressional Record* 88, pt. 6 (9 October 1942): 7977–78.

8. "Strachan, Paul A(mbrose)," *Current Biography Yearbook*, "1952" (New York: H.W. Wilson, 1952), 563.

9. See Felicia Kornbluh, "Disability, Antiprofessionalism, and Civil Rights: The National Federation of the Blind and the 'Right to Organize' in the 1950s," *Journal of American History* 97 (March 2011): 1023–47.

10. On veteran politics, see Stephen R. Ortiz, ed., *Veterans' Policies, Veterans' Politics: New Perspectives on Veterans in the Modern United States* (Gainesville: University Press of Florida, 2012); Sarah F. Rose, "The Right to a College Education?: The G.I. Bill, Public Law 16, and Disabled Veterans," *Journal of Policy History* 24, 1 (2012): 26–52; Stephen R. Ortiz, *Beyond the Bonus March and GI Bill: How Veteran Politics Shaped the New Deal Era* (New York: New York University Press, 2010); Margot Canaday, *The Straight State: Sexuality and Citizenship in Twentieth-Century America* (Princeton, N.J.: Princeton University Press, 2009); Suzanne Mettler, *Soldiers to Citizens: The G.I. Bill and the Making of the Greatest Generation* (Oxford: Oxford University Press, 2005); Margot Canaday, "Building a Straight State: Sexuality and Social

Citizenship under the 1944 G.I. Bill," *Journal of American History* 90 (December 2003): 935–57; Robert F. Jefferson, "'Enabled Courage': Race, Disability, and Black World War II Veterans in Postwar America," *Historian* 65 (September 2003): 1102–24; David A. Gerber, ed., *Disabled Veterans in History* (Ann Arbor: University of Michigan Press, 2000); Michael J. Bennett, *When Dreams Came True: The G.I. Bill and the Making of Modern America* (Washington, D.C.: Potomac Books, 1996); Hartmann, *The Home Front and Beyond*; and Susan M. Hartmann, "Prescriptions for Penelope: Literature on Women's Obligations to Returning World War II Veterans," *Women's Studies* 5 (1978): 223–39.

11. Kennedy, *Freedom from Fear*, 516–64, 605, 637–38; and Hartmann, *The Home Front and Beyond*, 1–12.

12. Kennedy, *Freedom from Fear*, 760–76; and Hartmann, *The Home Front and Beyond*, 5–6.

13. Many historians have examined how the booming wartime economy and labor shortages of World War II created opportunities for women and people of color to move into higher-paying jobs. Historians have also addressed how these changes in the wartime economy, service to the country on the battlefield or factory floor, and the democratic ideals of the war changed expectations of many women and people of color. See Maggie Rivas-Rodriguez, ed., *Mexican Americans and World War II* (Austin: University of Texas Press, 2005); Megan Taylor Shockley, *"We, Too, Are Americans": African American Women in Detroit and Richmond, 1940–54* (Urbana: University of Illinois Press, 2004); Martha Biondi, *To Stand and Fight: The Struggle for Civil Rights in Postwar New York City* (Cambridge, Mass.: Harvard University Press, 2003); Ronald Takaki, *Double Victory: A Multicultural History of America in World War II* (Boston: Little, Brown, 2000); Kenneth William Townsend, *World War II and the American Indian* (Albuquerque: University of New Mexico Press, 2000); Hartmann, *The Home Front and Beyond*; Alice Kessler-Harris, *Out to Work: A History of Wage-Earning Women in the United States* (Oxford: Oxford University Press, 1982); and Karen Anderson, *Wartime Women: Sex Roles, Family Relations, and the Status of Women During World War II* (Westport, Conn.: Greenwood, 1981).

14. Congress, House, Extension of Remarks of Representative Harry R. Sheppard of California, 77th Cong., 2nd sess., *Congressional Record* 88, pt. 9 (13 May 1942): A1752.

15. "U.S. Told to Let Handicapped Aid War Effort," *Washington Post*, 20 August 1942, 28.

16. Congress, House, Extension of Remarks of Sheppard (29 April 1942), A1599–1600; (12 May 1942), A1729–30; and (13 May 1942), A1751–52.

17. Congress, House, Extension of Remarks of Sheppard (12 May 1942), A1729–30; (13 May 1942), A1751–52.

18. Mary E. MacDonald, "Vocational Rehabilitation in the Postwar Period," *Journal of Rehabilitation* 12 (March 1946): 13.

19. Office of Vocational Rehabilitation, *Objectives of Counseling the Disabled for Job Readiness: A Supplement to the Proceedings of the Fourth Annual Workshop of Guidance, Training and Placement Supervisors* (Washington, D.C.: Federal Security Agency, 1952), 2; Mary E. MacDonald, *Federal Grants for Vocational Rehabilitation* (Chicago: University of Chicago Press, 1944), 182; Federal Security Agency, *Annual Report of the Federal Security Agency: Office of Vocational Rehabilitation, 1951* (Washington, D.C.: GPO, 1952), 17.

20. U.S. Office of Education, *Administration of Vocational Rehabilitation* (Washington, D.C.: GPO, 1938), 1–2, 53–58.

21. U.S. Office of Education, *Administration of Vocational Rehabilitation*, 1–3.

22. Ibid., 10–13, 20–24.

23. Ibid., 1–3, 15–16; Glenn Gritzer and Arnold Arluke, *The Making of Rehabilitation: A*

Political Economy of Medical Specialization, 1890–1980 (Berkeley: University of California Press, 1985), 38–60; Frank J. Bertalan and Frederick B. Arner, *The Provision of Federal Benefits for Veterans: An Historical Analysis of Major Veterans' Legislation, 1862–1954* (Washington, D.C.: GPO, 1955), 190–99; and C. Esco Obermann, *A History of Vocational Rehabilitation in America* (Minneapolis: Denison, 1965), 164–74.

24. U.S. Office of Education, *Administration of Vocational Rehabilitation*, 1–3, 15–16.

25. Ibid., 19–20.

26. Congress, House, Extension of Remarks of Sheppard (13 May 1942), A1752.

27. Congress, House, Extension of Remarks of Sheppard (12 May 1942), A1729–30; and Congress, House, Message from the President, 76th Cong., 1st sess., *Congressional Record* 84, pt. 4 (13 April 1939): 4234–35.

28. Congress, House, Extension of Remarks of Sheppard (13 May 1942), A1751–52.

29. Congress, House, Extension of Remarks of Sheppard (12 May 1942), A1730.

30. Congress, House, Extension of Remarks of Sheppard 7 (13 May 1942), A1751.

31. Ibid., A1751–52.

32. Ibid., A1751.

33. Congress, House, Extension of Remarks of Sheppard (12 May 1942), A1729–30.

34. Ibid., A1729.

35. Tracy Roof, *American Labor, Congress, and the Welfare State, 1935–2010* (Baltimore: Johns Hopkins University Press, 2011), 34–35.

36. William A. Irvin, "Killed, Not in Action: 102,000," *New York Times*, 28 June 1942, SM13.

37. Prince M. Carlisle, "Drive Begun to Cut Plant Accidents," *New York Times*, 12 April 1942, F1.

38. Chief of the Bureau of Statistics, Treasury Department, *Statistical Abstract of the United States* (Washington, D.C.: GPO, 1946), 217.

39. Louis F. Buckley, "The Effect of the War upon Labor in the United States," *Social Science* 17 (July 1942), 280.

40. Mrs. William Strachan to Audra Jennings, 11 March 2003, letter in possession of the author; Fred J. Zusy, "Helps Handicapped: Deaf Man Leads Drive," *Abilene Reporter-News*, 5 October 1947, 14; Sam Stavisky, "A Self-Described Cynic Leads the Battle for Decent Jobs for Nation's Handicapped," *Washington Post*, 4 October 1948, 2; "One Dead, One Hurt in Auto-Train Accident," *Atlanta Constitution*, 16 November 1929, 25A; and Paul Strachan to Marcus Kenner, 3 October 1941, Box 2, Folder 17, Papers of Thomas L. Anderson, Gallaudet University Archives, Washington, D.C. (hereafter Anderson Papers).

41. Robert S. Allen, "The Washington Merry-Go-Round: Handicapped Aid Plan Lauded," *Washington Post*, 13 August 1949, B11.

42. Paul Strachan, "Thoughts on the Holiday Season," American Federation of the Physically Handicapped Christmas mailing, December 1948, Box 1289, Official File 443, The Physically Handicapped (1945–47), Harry S. Truman Papers, Harry S. Truman Library, Independence, Mo. (hereafter Truman Papers).

43. Allen, "The Washington Merry-Go-Round," B11; "Strachan, Paul A(mbrose)," 562; 1910 U.S. census, Fulton County, Georgia, population schedule, Atlanta Ward 2, p. 3B, dwelling 41, family 56, James A. Lula M., and Paul A. Strachan; digital image, Ancestry.com, accessed 12 April 2015.

44. "Strachan, Paul A(mbrose)," 562–63; Paul Strachan to Walter Mason, 9 April 1953, #23/20, Record Group 21-001, Legislation Department, Legislative Reference Files, Meany

Archives; Allen, "The Washington Merry-Go-Round," B11; Jean R. Halley, "Paul A. Strachan, 83, Fought For Physically Handicapped," *Washington Post*, 19 September 1972, C4; Stavisky, "A Self-Described Cynic Leads the Battle for Decent Jobs for Nation's Handicapped," 2; and K. Walter Hickel, "War, Region, and Social Welfare: Federal Aid to Servicemen's Dependents in the South, 1917–1921," *Journal of American History* 87 (March 2001): 1362.

45. Allen, "The Washington Merry-Go-Round," B11; "Strachan, Paul A(mbrose)," 562; Stavisky, "A Self-Described Cynic Leads the Battle for Decent Jobs for Nation's Handicapped," 2; *Atlanta, Georgia, City Directory, 1924*, 1024; digital image, Ancestry.com, accessed 17 April 2015; *Atlanta, Georgia, City Directory, 1926*, 1239; digital image, Ancestry.com, accessed 17 April 2015.

46. Mrs. William Strachan to Audra Jennings, 11 March 2003.

47. Ibid.; and "Strachan, Paul A(mbrose)," 562–63.

48. Paul Strachan to Irving Fusfeld, 18 August 1941, Box 2, Folder 17, Anderson Papers.

49. Ibid.

50. "Strachan, Paul A(mbrose)," 562–63; Paul Strachan to Tom Anderson, 15 September 1941, Box 2, Folder 17, Anderson Papers.

51. Paul Strachan to Tom Anderson, 11 September 1941, Box 2, Folder 17, Anderson Papers; Susan Burch, *Signs of Resistance: American Deaf Cultural History, 1900 to World War II* (New York: New York University Press, 2002), 88, 124–26; and Robert M. Buchanan, *Illusions of Equality: Deaf Americans in School and Factory, 1850–1950* (Washington, D.C.: Gallaudet University Press, 1999), 104–26.

52. Tom Anderson to Paul Strachan, 13 September 1941, Box 2, Folder 17, Anderson Papers; Paul Strachan, 15 September 1941, Box 2, Folder 17, Anderson Papers; and Paul Strachan to Tom Anderson, 18 September 1941, Box 2, Folder 17, Anderson Papers.

53. See, for example, Paul Strachan to Tom Anderson and Marcus Kenner, 22 September 1941, Box 2, Folder 17, Anderson Papers.

54. Report, and Recommendations of, Paul A. Strachan, Part One and Part Two, no date, Box 2, Folder 17, Anderson Papers.

55. Tom Anderson to Paul Strachan, 9 November 1941, Box 2, Folder 17, Anderson Papers.

56. Paul Strachan to Tom Anderson, 10 November 1941, Box 2, Folder 17, Anderson Papers; Tom Anderson to Paul Strachan, 16 November 1941, Box 2, Folder 17, Anderson Papers; and Paul Strachan to Tom Anderson, 10 December 1941, Box 2, Folder 17, Anderson Papers.

57. Congress, House, Extension of Remarks of Sheppard (29 April 1942), A1599–1600.

58. DAV, *Wars and Scars: The Story of Compassion & Service for Our Nation's Disabled Veterans* (Disabled American Veterans, no date), 4–6, http://www.dav.org/learn-more/about-dav/history/, accessed 8 May 2015.

59. Congress, Senate, Committee on Education and Labor, Subcommittee, *Hearings, Vocational Rehabilitation of War-Disabled Individuals*, 77th Cong., 2nd sess. (Washington, D.C.: GPO, 1942), 61–62.

60. See Kornbluh, "Disability, Antiprofessionalism, and Civil Rights"; and Thomas A. Krainz, "Transforming the Progressive Era Welfare State: Activists for the Blind and Blind Benefits," *Journal of Policy History* 15, 2 (2003): 223–64.

61. "Says War Work Needs 10,500,000 More in '42: Federal Employment Director Describes Mobilizing Task," *New York Times*, 12 March 1942, 16.

62. Ibid.; Lee Kennett, *G.I.: The American Soldier in World War II* (Norman: University of

Oklahoma Press, 1987), 9, 19–22; Kennedy, *Freedom from Fear*, 632–37; Hartmann, *The Home Front and Beyond*, 47; Wayne Coy to the President, 24 May 1940, Official File 504, Advisory Committee on Vocational Education, 1941–1945, Box 2, Franklin D. Roosevelt Papers, Franklin D. Roosevelt Library, Hyde Park, N.Y. (hereafter Roosevelt Papers).

63. Lewis B. Hershey to Mrs. Franklin D. Roosevelt, 25 September 1941, Official File 1413, Selective Service Legislation, Box 1, Folder Apr.–Dec. 1941, Roosevelt Papers.

64. Paul McNutt to the President, undated, Official File 504, Advisory Committee on Vocational Education, 1941–1945, Box 2, Roosevelt Papers.

65. Ibid.

66. Ibid.

67. Ibid.

68. Ibid.

69. Ibid.

70. "Policy on the Employment of the Physically Handicapped in War Industries," National Labor Supply Committee, Office of Production Management, 2 January 1942, Official File 504, Advisory Committee on Vocational Education, 1941–1945, Box 2, Roosevelt Papers.

71. Ibid.

72. Ibid.; Kennedy, *Freedom from Fear*, 620.

73. Paul McNutt to the President, undated, Official File 504.

74. Memo for the Director of the Budget, 12 March 1942, Official File 504, Advisory Committee on Vocational Education, 1941–1945, Box 2, Roosevelt Papers; Paul McNutt to the President, 30 March 1942, Official File 836, Physically Handicapped Persons, 1941–1943, Box 2, Roosevelt Papers; Memo, 8 April 1942, Official File 504, Advisory Committee on Vocational Education, 1941–1945, Box 2, Roosevelt Papers; Memo for the President from Harold Smith, 22 April 1942, Official File 504, Advisory Committee on Vocational Education, 1941–1945, Box 2, Roosevelt Papers.

75. Memo for the President from Wayne Coy, 17 July 1942, Official File 504, Advisory Committee on Vocational Education, 1941–1945, Box 2, Roosevelt Papers; Committee on Veterans' Affairs, *The Provision of Federal Benefits for Veterans: An Historical Analysis of Major Veterans' Legislation, 1862–1954* (Washington, D.C.: GPO, 1955), 198–99.

76. Memo for the President from Wayne Coy, 17 July 1942, Official File 504, Advisory Committee on Vocational Education, 1941–1945, Box 2, Roosevelt Papers.

77. For example, in January 1941, Senator William Barbour (R-NJ) introduced a bill to prevent employment discrimination against people with disabilities (S. 479), Representative Harold Knutson (R-MN) introduced a bill to extend Social Security to provide aid to needy people with disabilities (H.R. 2818). Senators Barbour and William Smathers (D-NJ) sponsored a bill to use vocational rehabilitation appropriations for both vocational and "physical" rehabilitation (S. 818) in February. The following month, Representative George O'Brien (D-MI) introduced a bill to create new rehabilitation services for "handicapped employables" (H.R. 4793). In June, Senator Robert Reynolds (D-NC) sponsored a bill to provide rehabilitation services through the civilian program to some people disabled in military service (S. 1711). Representative John Hunter (D-OH), in July, introduced a resolution to launch an investigation of the ways the U.S. government might use the labor of older and disabled people in defense work. In May the following year, Representative Barden (D-NC) and Senator La Follette (PRG-WI) sponsored joint resolutions to appropriate an additional million dollars for the rehabilitation program (H.J. Res. 312 and S.J. Res. 149). At the behest of leaders of the DAV, Senator Homer Bone (D-WA)

and Representative Clinton Anderson (D-NM) introduced joint resolutions to direct and authorize the chairman of the WMC to speed the "utilization" of people with disabilities in wartime employment in July 1942. Congress, Senate, Senator Barbour of New Jersey introducing S. 479, 77th Cong., 1st sess. *Congressional Record* 87, pt. 1 (23 January 1941): 256; Congress, House, Representative Knutson of Minnesota introducing H.R. 2818, 77th Cong., 1st sess., *Congressional Record* 87, pt. 1 (29 January 1941): 386; Congress, Senate, Barbour introducing S. 818, 77th Cong., 1st sess., *Congressional Record* 87, pt. 1 (10 February 1941): 821; Congress, House, Representative O'Brien of Michigan introducing H.R. 4793, 77th Cong. 1st sess., *Congressional Record* 87, pt. 4 (19 May 1941): 4234; Congress, Senate, Senator Reynolds of North Carolina introducing S. 1711, 77th Cong., 1st sess., *Congressional Record* 87, pt. 5 (30 June 1941): 5756; Congress, House, Representative Hunter of Ohio introducing H.Res. 267, 77th Cong. 1st sess., *Congressional Record* 87, pt. 6 (9 July 1941): 5916; Congress, House, Representative Barden of North Carolina introducing H.J. Res. 312, 77th Cong. 2nd sess., *Congressional Record* 88, pt. 3 (11 May 1942): 4080; Congress, Senate, Senator La Follette of Wisconsin introducing S.J. Res. 149, 77th Cong., 2nd sess., *Congressional Record* 88, pt. 3 (14 May 1942), 4169; Congress, Senate, Senator Bone of Washington introducing S.J. Res. 155, 77th Cong., 2nd sess., *Congressional Record* 88, pt. 5 (13 July 1942): 6077; Congress, House, Representative Anderson of New Mexico introducing H.J. Res. 334, 77th Cong. 2nd sess., *Congressional Record* 88, pt. 5 (13 July 1942): 6112; and Congress, House, Extension of Representative Sweeney's Remarks on Disabled American Veterans, 77th Cong., 2nd sess., *Congressional Record* 88, pt. 9 (15 July 1942): A2771.

78. Workers in the civil rehabilitation program organized the National Civilian Rehabilitation Conference in 1923, which became the National Rehabilitation Association in 1927. Obermann, *A History of Vocational Rehabilitation in America*, 241, 276–86, 358, 368–69.

79. "Vocational Rehabilitation for Veterans," *Social Service Review* 17 (June 1943): 219; Congress, Senate, La Follette introducing S. 2714, 77th Cong., 2nd sess., *Congressional Record* 88, pt. 5 (13 August 1942): 6819–20; Congress, House, Barden introducing H.R.7484, 77th Cong., 2nd sess., *Congressional Record* 88, pt. 5 (13 August 1942): 6853; Congress, House, Barden introducing H.J. Res. 312, 77th Cong. 2nd sess., *Congressional Record* 88, pt. 3 (11 May 1942): 4080; and Congress, Senate, La Follette introducing S.J. Res. 149, 77th Cong., 2nd sess., *Congressional Record* 88, pt. 3 (14 May 1942): 4169.

80. Congress, Senate, Committee on Education and Labor, Subcommittee, *Hearings, Vocational Rehabilitation of War-Disabled Individuals*, 77th Cong., 2nd sess. (Washington, D.C.: GPO, 1942), 25–27; and Congress, House, Committee on Education, *Hearings, Vocational Rehabilitation Education and Training*, 78th Cong. 1st sess. (Washington, D.C.: GPO, 1943), 42, 96–102.

81. Congress, Senate, Committee on Education and Labor, Subcommittee, *Hearings, Vocational Rehabilitation of War-Disabled Individuals*, 77th Cong., 2nd sess. (Washington, D.C.: GPO, 1942), 58–71.

82. Ibid., 11–12, 16.

83. Ibid., 12–13.

84. Ibid., 25, 27.

85. Franklin Delano Roosevelt, "The President Reports on the Home Front," Fireside Chat, 12 October 1942, in the *Public Papers and Addresses of Franklin D. Roosevelt*, vol. 11, compiled by Samuel I. Rosenman (New York: Random House, 1950), 416–26.

86. Congress, House, Committee on Education, *Hearings, Vocational Rehabilitation Education and Training*, 32–33.

87. Congress, Senate, Committee on Education and Labor, Subcommittee, *Hearings, Vocational Rehabilitation of War-Disabled Individuals*, 75–76.

88. Ibid., 78–80.

89. Ibid.

90. Frederick A. Ogg, "Personal and Miscellaneous," *American Political Science Review* 36 (October 1942): 947; and Congress, House, Committee on Education, *Hearings, Vocational Rehabilitation Education and Training*, 96–102.

91. Congress, House, Barden introducing H.R. 699, 78th Cong., 1st sess., *Congressional Record* 89, pt. 1 (6 January 1943): 24; Congress, Senate, La Follette introducing S. 180, 78th Cong., 1st sess., *Congressional Record* 89, pt. 1 (7 January 1943): 36; Congress, House, Committee on Education, *Hearings, Vocational Rehabilitation Education and Training*, 7.

92. Congress, Senate, Debate over S. 180, 78th Cong., 1st sess., *Congressional Record* 89, pt. 2 (5 March 1943): 1609.

93. Congress, House, Barden introducing H.R. 699, 78th Cong., 1st sess., *Congressional Record* 89, pt. 1 (6 January 1943): 24; Congress, Senate, La Follette introducing S. 180, 78th Cong., 1st sess., *Congressional Record* 89, pt. 1 (7 January 1943): 36; Congress, Senate, Remarks of Senator Wheeler of Montana on Vocational Rehabilitation, 78th Cong., 1st sess., *Congressional Record* 89, pt. 2 (5 March 1943): 1568–69; Congress, Senate, Debate over S. 180 and S. 786, 78th Cong., 1st sess., *Congressional Record* 89, pt. 2 (5 March 1943): 1580–95, 1605–12; Congress, House, Debate over S. 786, 78th Cong., 1st sess., *Congressional Record* 89, pt. 2 (15 March 1943): 1986–88; Congress, Senate, Message from the President, 78th Cong., 1st sess., *Congressional Record* 89, pt. 2 (25 March 1943): 2447–48; Congress, House, Debate over H.R. 2536, 78th Cong., 1st sess., *Congressional Record* 89, pt. 4 (10 June 1943): 5654–79; Congress, Senate, Debate over H.R. 2536, 78th Cong., 1st sess., *Congressional Record* 89, pt. 5 (22 June 1943): 6253–64; Congress, Senate, Amendment of Vocational Rehabilitation Act—Conference Report, 78th Cong., 1st sess., *Congressional Record* 89, pt. 5 (29 June 1943): 6726; Congress, House, Vocational Rehabilitation Act Amendments, 1943, 78th Cong., 1st sess., *Congressional Record* 89, pt. 5 (29 June 1943): 6750–56; and Congress, House, Message from the President, 78th Cong., 1st sess., *Congressional Record* 89, pt. 6 (14 September 1943): 7550. For an extended discussion of disabled veterans' efforts to separate veteran and civilian disability policy, see Audra Jennings, "'An Emblem of Distinction': The Politics of Disability Entitlement, 1940–1950," in *Veterans' Policies, Veterans' Politics*, ed. Ortiz, 94–116.

94. Congress, House, Debate over H.R. 2536, 78th Cong., 1st sess., *Congressional Record* 89, pt. 4 (10 June 1943): 5654–79.

95. Ibid., 5656–61.

96. Ibid., 5657–58.

97. Ibid., 5676–77; Congress, Senate, Debate over H.R. 2536, 78th Cong., 1st sess., *Congressional Record* 89, pt. 5 (22 June 1943): 6253–64; Congress, Senate, Amendment of Vocational Rehabilitation Act—Conference Report, 78th Cong., 1st sess., *Congressional Record* 89, pt. 5 (29 June 1943): 6726; Congress, House, Vocational Rehabilitation Act Amendments, 1943, 78th Cong., 1st sess., *Congressional Record* 89, pt. 5 (29 June 1943): 6750–56; and Congress, House, Message from the President, 78th Cong., 1st sess., 7550.

98. Congress, House, Committee on Labor, Subcommittee to Investigate Aid to the Physically Handicapped, *Hearings, Part 1, Aid to the Blind*, 78th Cong., 2nd sess. (Washington, D.C.: GPO, 1945), 153–59.

99. Memo on the Basic Provisions of the Vocational Rehabilitation Program of the Veterans

Administration, Approved 24 March 1943, Official File 4675k, World War II—Miscellaneous, Box 27, Roosevelt Papers.

100. Michael J. Shortley, "Rehabilitation of the Civilian Disabled," *Annals of the American Academy of Political and Social Science* 239 (May 1945): 101–8.

101. Ibid., 103–4.

102. Ibid., 105–6.

103. Ibid., 106.

104. Ibid., 104.

Chapter 2. From the Depths of Personal Experience: Disability Activists Demand a Hearing

1. Congress, House, Committee on Labor, Subcommittee on Aid to the Physically Handicapped, *Hearings, Part 23, H.R. 5206*, 79th Cong., 2nd sess. (Washington, D.C.: GPO, 1946), 2340, 2342.

2. Congress, House, Extension of Remarks of Representative Jennings Randolph of West Virginia, 78th Cong., 2nd sess., *Congressional Record* 90, pt. 10 (1 September 1944): A3840.

3. Congress, House, Extension of Remarks of Representative Augustine B. Kelley of Pennsylvania, 78th Cong., 2nd sess., *Congressional Record* 90, pt. 11 (12 September 1944): A3980; and "Lauds American Federation of Handicapped," *Del Rio News Herald* (Del Rio, Texas), 22 August 1944, 4.

4. Congress, House, Committee on Labor, Subcommittee to Investigate Aid to the Physically Handicapped/Subcommittee on Aid to the Physically Handicapped, *Hearings, Parts 1–25*, 78th–79th Congresses (Washington, D.C.: GPO, 1945–46).

5. House, Subcommittee on Aid to the Physically Handicapped, *Hearings, Part 23, H.R. 5206*, 2340, 2342.

6. Ibid., 2340–41.

7. President Franklin D. Roosevelt, State of the Union Message to Congress, 11 January 1944, The American Presidency Project, http://www.presidency.ucsb.edu/ws/?pid=16518, accessed 30 May 2015.

8. Scholars have focused considerable attention to the ways that gender, class, race, and sexuality informed and shaped the state. See Cybelle Fox, *Three Worlds of Relief: Race, Immigration, and the American Welfare State from the Progressive Era to the New Deal* (Princeton, N.J.: Princeton University Press, 2012); Carolyn Herbst Lewis, *Prescription for Heterosexuality: Sexual Citizenship in the Cold War Era* (Chapel Hill: University of North Carolina Press, 2010); Barbara Young Welke, *Law and the Borders of Belonging in the Long Nineteenth Century United States* (Cambridge: Cambridge University Press, 2010); Margot Canaday, *The Straight State: Sexuality and Citizenship in Twentieth-Century America* (Princeton, N.J.: Princeton University Press, 2009); Robyn Muncy, "Coal-Fired Reforms: Social Citizenship, Dissident Miners, and the Great Society," *Journal of American History* 96 (June 2009): 72–98; Ira Katznelson, *When Affirmative Action Was White: An Untold History of Racial Inequality in Twentieth-Century America* (New York: Norton, 2005); Alice Kessler-Harris, *In Pursuit of Equity: Women, Men, and the Quest for Economic Citizenship in 20th-Century America* (Oxford: Oxford University Press, 2001); Michael Willrich, "Home Slackers: Men, the State, and Welfare in Modern America," *Journal of American History* 87 (September 2000): 460–89; Suzanne Mettler, *Dividing Citizens: Gender and Federalism in New Deal Public Policy* (Ithaca, N.Y.: Cornell University Press, 1998); Nancy Fraser and Linda Gordon, "A Genealogy of Dependency: Tracing a Keyword of the U.S.

Welfare State," *Signs* 19 (Winter 1994): 320–21; Linda Gordon, *Pitied But Not Entitled: Single Mothers and the History of Welfare, 1890–1935* (New York: Free Press, 1994); and Linda Gordon, ed., *Women, the State, and Welfare* (Madison: University of Wisconsin Press, 1990).

9. See Kessler-Harris, *In Pursuit of Equity*.

10. Congress, House, Subcommittee of the Committee on the Judiciary, Unpublished Hearings, *H. J. Res. 23, To establish the first week in October of each year as National Employ the Physically Handicapped Week*, 79th Cong., 1st sess., 4 May 1945, 12–13.

11. Douglas C. Baynton, "Disability and the Justification of Inequality in American History," in *The New Disability History: American Perspectives*, ed. Paul K. Longmore and Lauri Umansky (New York: New York University Press, 2001), 33.

12. Congress, House, Extension of Remarks of Representative Augustine B. Kelley, 78th Cong., 2nd sess., *Congressional Record* 90, pt. 11 (12 September 1944): A3979.

13. "Y.W.C.A. Organizes Club to Help City's Physically Handicapped Residents," *Harrisburg Telegraph*, 15 April 1941, 19; "Club to Join Federation," *Harrisburg Telegraph*, 6 May 1943, 21; and Nobe Frank, "Harrisburgesque," *Harrisburg Telegraph*, 12 June 1944, 13.

14. Congress, House, Extension of Remarks of Representative Joseph Mruk of New York, 78th Cong., 2nd sess., *Congressional Record* 90, pt. 9 (24 May 1944): A2583–85.

15. Ibid.

16. Ibid.

17. Congress, House, Representative Voorhis of California introduces H. J. Res. 325, 77th Cong., 2nd sess., *Congressional Record* 88, pt. 4 (9 June 1942): 5087.

18. Congress, House, Extension of Remarks of Representative Jerry Voorhis of California, 77th Cong., 2nd sess., *Congressional Record* 88, pt. 10 (14 December 1942): A4301–2.

19. Congress, House, Extension of Remarks of Representative Joseph Mruk, A2584.

20. Congress, House, Debate over H.R. 230, 78th Cong., 2nd sess., *Congressional Record* 90, pt. 5 (20 June 1944): 6324–28.

21. Ibid.

22. Ibid.

23. House, Subcommittee to Investigate Aid to the Physically Handicapped/Subcommittee on Aid to the Physically Handicapped, *Hearings, Parts 1–25*.

24. House, Committee on Labor, Subcommittee to Investigate Aid to the Physically Handicapped, *Hearings, Part 4, New York City*, 78th Cong., 2nd sess. (Washington, D.C.: GPO, 1945), 578–84.

25. House, Subcommittee on Aid to the Physically Handicapped, *Hearings, Part 23, H.R. 5206*, 2327.

26. Ibid., 2540.

27. House, Subcommittee to Investigate Aid to the Physically Handicapped, *Hearings, Part 4, New York City*, 578–84.

28. House, Subcommittee on Aid to the Physically Handicapped, *Hearings, Part 23, H.R. 5206*, 2340, 2546–47.

29. Chief of the Bureau of Statistics, Treasury Department, *Statistical Abstract of the United States* (Washington, D.C.: GPO, 1922-1948); Federal Security Agency, *Annual Report of the Office of Vocational Rehabilitation, 1944–1952* (Washington, D.C.: GPO, 1944–1952).

30. House, Subcommittee on Aid to the Physically Handicapped, *Hearings, Part 23, H.R. 5206*, 2540–62.

31. Ibid., 2569–70.

32. Ibid., 2540–41.

33. Ibid., 2581–82.

34. Ibid., 2539. For more information on county institutions for the poor, which had historically housed the indigent, the elderly, and people with disabilities, but between 1850 and 1930 increasingly served the needs of the elderly, see Michael B. Katz, *In the Shadow of the Poorhouse: A Social History of Welfare in America* (New York: Basic, 1986).

35. Congress, House, Committee on Labor, Subcommittee to Investigate Aid to the Physically Handicapped, *Hearings, Part 5, Pittsburgh, PA.*, 78th Cong., 2nd sess. (Washington, D.C.: GPO, 1945), 766–68.

36. House, Subcommittee on Aid to the Physically Handicapped, *Hearings, Part 23, H.R. 5206*, 2548–49.

37. Congress, House, Committee on Labor, Subcommittee on Aid to the Physically Handicapped, *Hearings, Part 20, Spastics*, 79th Cong., 1st sess. (Washington, D.C.: GPO, 1945), 2060–61.

38. Congress, House, Committee on Labor, Subcommittee to Investigate Aid to the Physically Handicapped, *Hearings, Part 3, Aid to the Deaf and Hard of Hearing*, 78th Cong., 2nd sess. (Washington, D.C.: GPO, 1945), 296–98.

39. Ibid., 241–44.

40. Congress, House, Committee on Labor, Subcommittee to Investigate Aid to the Physically Handicapped, *Hearings, Part 8, Aid to Victims of Orthopedic Impairments, To Disabled Seamen, etc.*, 78th Cong., 2nd sess. (Washington, D.C.: GPO, 1945), 1100.

41. See Fred Pelka, *The ABC-Clio Companion to the Disability Rights Movement* (Santa Barbara, Calif.: ABC-Clio, 1997), 111–13.

42. William J. Ellis, "The Handicapped Child," *Annuals of the American Academy of Political and Social Science* 212 (November 1940): 143.

43. Melvin E. Schoonover, "What the Shut-In Wants and Needs," *A.F.P.H. Tribune* (October 1945): 18.

44. James A. Scott, "Educational Facilities Available for Physically Handicapped Negro Children," *Journal of Negro Education* 6 (July 1937): 455–67. For more information on the history of the African American experience of deafness, see Mary Herring Wright, *Sounds Like Home: Growing Up Black and Deaf in the South* (Washington, D.C.: Gallaudet University Press, 1999); and Susan Burch and Hannah Joyner, *Unspeakable: The Story of Junius Wilson* (Chapel Hill: University of North Carolina Press, 2007).

45. House, Subcommittee on Aid to the Physically Handicapped, *Hearings, Part 20, Spastics*, 2060–61.

46. For a discussion of the Galesburg program and university accessibility more generally in the 1940s and 1950s, see Sarah F. Rose, "The Right to a College Education?: The G.I. Bill, Public Law 16, and Disabled Veterans," *Journal of Policy History* 24, 1 (2012): 26–52.

47. Audra Jennings, "'An Emblem of Distinction': The Politics of Disability Entitlement, 1940–1950," in *Veterans' Policies, Veterans' Politics: New Perspectives on Veterans in the Modern United States*, ed. Stephen R. Ortiz (Gainesville: University Press of Florida, 2012), 94–116.

48. Congress, House, Committee on Labor, Subcommittee on Aid to the Physically Handicapped, *Hearings, Part 15, Amputees*, 79th Cong., 1st sess. (Washington, D.C.: GPO, 1945), 1654–58.

49. Ibid., 1709–15.

50. Ibid.

51. Ibid.

52. Ibid, 1703–7.

53. Ibid., 1612.

54. House, Subcommittee to Investigate Aid to the Physically Handicapped, *Hearings, Part 8, Aid to Victims of Orthopedic Impairments, To Disabled Seamen, etc.*, 1097–98.

55. House, Subcommittee on Aid to the Physically Handicapped, *Hearings, Part 15, Amputees*, 1791.

56. Ibid., 1791–92.

57. Ibid., 1685.

58. Federal Security Agency, *Annual Report of the Office of Vocational Rehabilitation, 1944* (Washington, D.C.: GPO, 1944), 7.

59. House, Subcommittee to Investigate Aid to the Physically Handicapped, *Hearings, Part 5, Pittsburgh, PA.*, 766–68.

60. House, Subcommittee on Aid to the Physically Handicapped, *Hearings, Part 23, H.R. 5206*, 2342–43.

61. For example, see John Rogers's letter in Congress, Senate, Subcommittee of the Committee on Labor and Public Welfare, *Hearings, Vocational Rehabilitation of the Physically Handicapped*, 81st Cong., 2nd sess. (Washington, D.C.: GPO, 1950), 439.

62. In 1963, South Carolina was the first state to mandate that public buildings be accessible to people with disabilities. The first federal accessibility law, the Architectural Barriers Act of 1968, was limited in scope because it applied only to new federal buildings. Curb-cuts have a longer history than state or federal protection of accessibility. Warm Springs, Georgia, installed curb-cuts in the 1920s because of the polio rehabilitation clinic there. Disabled veterans pushed the University of Illinois at Urbana-Champaign to institute curb-cuts in the 1940s, but by and large, they were not widely implemented by cities until after the late 1960s. Pelka, *The ABC-Clio Companion to the Disability Rights Movement*, 25–27, 82–83.

63. Arthur Hakenen and Stanley Corneliuson, "Cox and Wickert: A Unique Partnership," *Journal of Rehabilitation* 13 (December 1947): 17.

64. House, Subcommittee to Investigate Aid to the Physically Handicapped, *Hearings, Part 8, Aid to Victims of Orthopedic Impairments, To Disabled Seamen, etc.*, 1098, 1100.

65. Ibid., 1108.

66. House, Subcommittee to Investigate Aid to the Physically Handicapped, *Hearings, Part 5, Pittsburgh, PA.*, 769–770.

67. Congress, House, Extension of Remarks of Representative Augustine B. Kelley, 78th Cong., 2nd sess., *Congressional Record* 90, pt. 11 (12 September 1944): A3979.

68. For more on social anxieties connected to the demobilization of war veterans, see David A. Gerber, "Heroes and Misfits: The Troubled Social Reintegration of Disabled Veterans in *The Best Years of Our Lives*," in *Disabled Veterans in History*, ed. David A. Gerber (Ann Arbor: University of Michigan Press), 70–95, esp. 71; Susan M. Hartmann, "Prescriptions for Penelope: Literature on Women's Obligations to Returning World War II Veterans," *Women's Studies* 5 (1978): 223–39.

69. N. S. Haseltine, "13,250 D. C. Disabled Have an Inning," *Washington Post*, 3 October 1948, B6. For more on The Best Years of Our Lives, see Gerber, "Heroes and Misfits."

70. House, Subcommittee to Investigate Aid to the Physically Handicapped, *Hearings, Part 4, New York City*, 362–67.

71. Ibid., 362–67.

72. Congress, House, Committee on Labor, Subcommittee on Aid to the Physically Handicapped, *Hearings, Part 19, Employment of the Physically Handicapped*, 79th Cong., 1st sess. (Washington, D.C.: GPO, 1945), 1947–48.

73. Ibid., 1948–52.

74. Congress, House, Committee on Labor, Subcommittee to Investigate Aid to the Physically Handicapped, *Hearings, Part 6, Detroit, Mich.*, 78th Cong., 2nd sess. (Washington, D.C.: GPO, 1945), 958–65.

75. Ibid., 933–34.

76. Margaret Stedman, "There Are No Cripples in Wartime," *Hygeia* 22 (October 1944): 750–53, 774–75.

77. Edsel Ford, "Why We Employ Aged and Handicapped Workers," *Saturday Evening Post*, 6 February 1943, 16–17.

78. Enid Griffis, "The Blind Do It Better," *Harper's Magazine* 186 (April 1943): 522–24.

79. "Lower Handicap," *Business Week*, 20 February 1943, 92.

80. "War Jobs for the Handicapped," *Science Digest* 13 (March 1943): 57–58.

81. Stedman, "There Are No Cripples in Wartime," 753.

82. "War Jobs for the Handicapped," 58.

83. Ford, "Why We Employ Aged and Handicapped Workers," 17.

84. T. Otto Nall, "War Workers in Wheel Chairs." *Survey Midmonthly* 80 (July 1944): 200.

85. Marcia Dane, "The Handicapped are Employable," *Survey Midmonthly* 81 (September 1945): 226.

86. Clarence A. Trump and Frances J. Montgomery, "Impaired Workers in Industry," *Monthly Labor Review* 59 (October 1944): 677–79, 683.

87. Vera Lundquist, "Building Lives and Weapons," *Nation's Business* 31 (December 1943): 46, 48.

88. "The Able Disabled," *Time*, 21 June 1943, 36.

89. Frances J. Montgomery and Sylvia E. Lurie, "Use of Handicapped Workers in War Industry," *Monthly Labor Review* 57 (September 1943): 435; "Placement of Handicapped Workers in 1944," *Monthly Labor Review* 60 (May 1945): 1008–9; and "Meeting of Committee on Employ the Handicapped Week, 1950," *Monthly Labor Review* 71 (October 1951): 490–91.

90. G. B. Erskine, "Hire the Handicapped," *Fortune* 34 (November 1946): 22.

91. House, Committee on Labor, Subcommittee on Aid to the Physically Handicapped, *Report: Aid to the Physically Handicapped*, 79th Cong., 2nd sess. (Washington, D.C.: GPO, 1946), 1, 14.

92. President Harry S. Truman, Special Message to the Congress Presenting a 21-Point Program for the Reconversion Period, 6 September 1945, Public Papers of the Presidents, Harry S. Truman, 1945–1953, http://tru,anlibrary.org/publicpapers/index.php?pid=136&st=&st1=, accessed 29 May 2015; President Harry S. Truman, Special Message to the Congress Recommending a Comprehensive Health Program, 19 November 1945, Public Papers of the Presidents, Harry S. Truman, 1945–1953, accessed 29 May 2015. See also Jill Quadagno, *One Nation Uninsured: Why the U.S. Has No National Health Insurance* (New York: Oxford University Press, 2005); James T. Patterson, *Grand Expectations: The United States, 1945–1974* (New York: Oxford University Press, 1996); Alonzo L. Hamby, *Man of the People: A Life of Harry S. Truman* (New York: Oxford University Press, 1995); Paul Starr, *The Social Transformation of American Medicine: The Rise of a Sovereign Profession and the Making of a Vast Industry* (New York: Basic,

1982); and Susan M. Hartmann, *Truman and the 80th Congress* (Columbia: University of Missouri Press, 1971).

93. Hartmann, *Truman and the 80th Congress*, 15, 41–43, 138–41, 156–57.

94. Subcommittee on Aid to the Physically Handicapped, *Report: Aid to the Physically Handicapped*, 1–2.

95. Ibid., 2–3.

96. Ibid., 4–6, 20.

97. Ibid., 5–7, 15–16.

98. Ibid., 7–8, 17.

99. Ibid., 5, 9–10.

100. Ibid., 10.

101. House, Subcommittee on Aid to the Physically Handicapped, *Hearings, Part 23, H.R. 5206*, 2424.

102. Subcommittee on Aid to the Physically Handicapped, *Report: Aid to the Physically Handicapped*, 5–6, 10. For more on the Hill-Burton Act, see Quadagno, *One Nation Ininsured*, and Starr, *The Social Transformation of American Medicine.*

103. Subcommittee on Aid to the Physically Handicapped, *Report: Aid to the Physically Handicapped*, 10–12.

104. Ibid., 11–13, 16–18.

105. Ibid., 12.

106. Ibid., 5, 10, 20.

107. Ibid., 16–17.

108. Congress, House, Committee on Labor, Subcommittee on Aid to the Physically Handicapped, *Hearings, Part 15a, Supplement to Part 15, Hearings on Amputations*, 79th Cong., 1st sess. (Washington, D.C.: GPO, 1945), 1–7.

109. Ibid.

110. "Artificial Limb Price-Fixing Charged to 45 Firms by Federal Indictment," *The New York Times*, 15 November 1945, 8; "Limb Firms Indicted for Price Fixing," *Washington Post*, 15 November 1945, 1; "Court Reverses Convictions of Artificial Limb Makers," *Washington Post*, 28 January 1947, 3.

111. House, Subcommittee on Aid to the Physically Handicapped, *Hearings, Part 15a, Supplement to Part 15, Hearings on Amputations*, 9–24; Congress, House, Message from the President, 80th Cong., 2nd sess., *Congressional Record* 94, pt. 8 (26 July 1948): 9365–66; Charles Hurd, "Veterans to Pass on Artificial Limbs," *New York Times*, 3 November 1945, 4; Charles Hurd, "Engineer, Who Lost Leg, Named Chief of Prosthetics for 'Vets,'" *New York Times*, 14 November 1945, 8; "$1,000,000 For Help To War Disabled," *New York Times*, 27 October 1945, 13. For a more in-depth account of veterans' activism and national prosthetics programs see, Jennings, "'An Emblem of Distinction,'" 94–116.

112. Subcommittee on Aid to the Physically Handicapped, *Report: Aid to the Physically Handicapped*, 11–12, 14.

113. Ibid., 14–15; Gerald Markowitz and David Rosner, "More Than Economism: The Politics of Workers' Safety and Health, 1932–1947." *Milbank Quarterly* 64, 3 (1986): 346.

114. Subcommittee on Aid to the Physically Handicapped, *Report: Aid to the Physically Handicapped*, 5, 12–13, 15, 19.

115. Ibid., 20.

116. Congress, House, Committee on Labor, Subcommittee to Investigate Aid to the Physically Handicapped, *Hearings, Part 1, Aid to the Blind*, 78th Cong., 2nd sess. (Washington, D.C.: GPO, 1945), 84–95.

Chapter 3. Toward a New Freedom from Fear: Disability and Postwar Uncertainty

1. Congress, House, Committee on Labor, Subcommittee on Aid to the Physically Handicapped, *Hearings, Part 23, H.R. 5206*, 79th Cong., 2nd sess. (Washington, D.C.: GPO, 1946), 2563; Congress, House, Committee on Education and Labor, *Hearings: Federal Commission for Physically Handicapped*, 81st Cong., 1st sess. (Washington, D.C.: GPO, 1949), 183–85; and Congress, Senate, Subcommittee of the Committee on Labor and Public Welfare, *Hearings, Vocational Rehabilitation of the Physically Handicapped*, 81st Cong., 2nd sess. (Washington, D.C.: GPO, 1950), 461–62.

2. Franklin D. Roosevelt, Annual Address to Congress, 6 January 1941, Franklin D. Roosevelt Presidential Library and Museum, http://www.fdrlibrary.marist.edu/fourfreedoms, accessed 16 June 2015.

3. House, Subcommittee on Aid to the Physically Handicapped, *Hearings, Part 23, H.R. 5206*, 2563.

4. James T. Patterson, *Grand Expectations: The United States, 1945–1974* (New York: Oxford University Press, 1996), 3–9.

5. Ibid.; Susan M. Hartmann, *The Home Front and Beyond: American Women in the 1940s* (Boston: Twayne, 1982), 7, 24.

6. Patterson, *Grand Expectations*, 10–12.

7. Ibid., 8; Hartmann, *The Home Front and Beyond*, 7–8.

8. Ibid., 7–8.

9. Ibid., 8–11.

10. Patterson, *Grand Expectations*, 39–55.

11. Ibid., 19–25; Hartmann, *The Home Front and Beyond*, 5.

12. Hartmann, *The Home Front and Beyond*, 24, 144–52.

13. Melvin E. Schoonover, "What the Shut-In Wants and Needs," *A.F.P.H. Tribune* (October 1945): 17–18.

14. "Address by J. Cooke Howard at A.F.P.H. Mass Meeting," *A.F.P.H. Tribune* (October 1945): 15.

15. J. Cooke Howard, "Military Casualties Less Than Those on the Home Front," *A.F.P.H. Tribune* (November 1945): 5.

16. House, Subcommittee on Aid to the Physically Handicapped, *Hearings, Part 23, H.R. 5206*, 2540–41.

17. Ibid., 2545.

18. Ibid., 2537.

19. "Susan Peters Cooks Up Plot with Crippled Detroit Girl," article from *Detroit Times* appearing in AFPH Newsletter, December 1948, Box 1289, Official File 443, The Physically Handicapped (1945–47), Truman Papers; 1930 United State Census (Free Schedule), Precinct 38, Wayne County, Michigan; p. 3243, sheet 6B, family 61, dwelling 55, lines 74–80; 5 April 1930, accessed 21 December 2015 from http://www.ancestry.com; Hartmann, *The Home Front and Beyond*, 24.

20. "'National Employ the Physically Handicapped Week' Is October 7th through 13th, 1945,'" *A.F.P.H Tribune* (October 1945): 3.

21. Congress, House, Extension of Remarks of Representative Harry R. Sheppard of California, 77th Cong., 2nd sess., *Congressional Record* 88, pt. 9 (12 May 1942): A1729–30.

22. Congress, House, Subcommittee of the Committee on the Judiciary, Unpublished Hearings, *H. J. Res. 23, To establish the first week in October of each year as National Employ the Physically Handicapped Week*, 79th Cong., 1st sess., 4 May 1945, 9–19.

23. Congress, House, Representative Voorhis of California introduces H.J. Res. 325, 77th Cong., 2nd sess., *Congressional Record* 88, pt. 4 (9 June 1942): 5087.

24. Congress, House, H.J. Res. 23, 79th Cong., 1st sess., *Congressional Record* 91, pt. 4 (4 June 1945): 5508; Congress, Senate, H.J. Res. 23, 79th Cong., 1st sess., *Congressional Record* 91, pt. 6 (1 August 1945): 8274; and Congress, House, H.J. Res. 23, 79th Cong., 1st sess., *Congressional Record* 91, pt. 6 (5 September 1945): 8322; Technical Information Division, Office of the Surgeon General, U.S. Army, "The Physically Disabled," *Annals of the American Academy of Political and Social Science* 239 (May 1945): 10; Albert E. Cowdrey, *Fighting for Life: American Military Medicine in World War II* (New York: Free Press, 1994), 371.

25. Advertisement, "Mass Meeting of the American Federation of the Physically Handicapped," *Washington Post*, 30 August 1945, 7.

26. "Resolution Unanimously Adopted at A.F.P.H. Mass Meeting August 30, 1945," *A.F.P.H. Tribune* (October 1945): 23.

27. Congress, House, Extension of Remarks of Representative Augustine B. Kelley, 78th Cong., 2nd sess., *Congressional Record* 90, pt. 11 (12 September 1944): A3979.

28. Mildred Scott, "Why the Handicapped Should Organize," *A.F.P.H. Tribune* (October 1945): 11.

29. Publication of the *A.F.P.H. Tribune* and *Valor* depended on the organization's finances, and particularly in the 1950s, the regular publication of *Valor* was spotty at best.

30. "Send in Your Memberships Now!," *A.F.P.H. Tribune* (August 1946): 17.

31. Dawn Watson, "AFPH Chooses Negro Amputee as a National Vice President," *Pittsburgh Courier*, 23 August 1952, 2.

32. Congress, House, Subcommittee of the Committee on the Judiciary, Unpublished Hearings, *H. J. Res. 23, To establish the first week in October of each year as National Employ the Physically Handicapped Week*, 79th Cong., 1st sess., 4 May 1945, 12–13; House, Subcommittee on Aid to the Physically Handicapped, *Hearings, Part 23, H.R. 5206*, 2316.

33. Fred J. Zusy, "Fights for Jobs for Physically Handicapped," *Marion Star* (Marion, Ohio), 26 September 1947, 6; Subcommittee of the Committee on the Judiciary, Unpublished Hearings, *H. J. Res. 23, To establish the first week in October of each year as National Employ the Physically Handicapped Week*, 12–13.

34. "Lodge Notes," *A.F.P.H. Tribune* (October 1945): 18, 20–21; "Lodge Notes," *A.F.P.H. Tribune* (November 1945): 12–13; Sam Brownstein, "An Appeal to Reason," *A.F.P.H. Tribune* (March 1946): 14; "Lodge Notes," *A.F.P.H. Tribune* (March 1946): 15–16, 20; "Clifton Hicks Authors 'The Little Lion,'" *A.F.P.H. Tribune* (June 1946): 8; "Joseph A. Strohmeyer Elected National Vice-President," *A.F.P.H. Tribune* (June 1946): 10; "Lodge Notes." *A.F.P.H. Tribune* (June 1946): 16–17; "Patients at Carville, La. U.S. Marine Hospital Form Lodge 86," *A.F.P.H. Tribune* (June 1946): 23; "Lodge Notes," *A.F.P.H. Tribune* (August 1946): 18–19; "Handicapped Group Plans Yule Party," *Washington Post*, 6 December 1949, 9; "Who's Who and How Come , IN AFPH," *Valor* (December 1950): 19; and "Handicapped to Hold Valentine Party," *Washington Post*, 13 February 1952, 17.

35. Edward Peeks, "Local AFPH Strives to Find Employment for Handicapped," *Atlanta Daily World*, 7 January 1954, 1, 4; "Group Memberships Added Physically Handicapped,"

Atlanta Daily World, 7 February 1954, 2; and "AFPH Fiscal Report for Year 1954–1955," *Atlanta Daily World*, 26 July 1955, 2. The spelling of Cook's last name varied throughout numerous sources, sometimes appearing as "Cook" or "Cooke." Early articles in the *Atlanta Daily World* use "Cook." For clarity, I use "Cook" throughout.

36. "Why You Should Join A.F.P.H.," *A.F.P.H. Tribune* (November 1945): 15.

37. Congress, House, Extension of Remarks of Kelley, A3980.

38. Proceedings of the AFPH Council Meeting, 24 March 1952, folder 7, box 8, UAW Veterans Collection, Archives of Labor and Urban Affairs, Wayne State University, Detroit, MI.

39. "Register and Vote!," *A.F.P.H. Tribune* (June 1946): 18.

40. "We Who Are About to Vote," *A.F.P.H. Tribune* (September 1946): 12.

41. Schoonover, "What the Shut-In Wants and Needs," 18.

42. "We Who Are About to Vote," 12.

43. Congress, House, Extension of Remarks of Kelley, A3980.

44. William Hassett to Truman, Memorandum, 4 September 1946, Box 558, President's Personal File 2779, American Federation of the Physically Handicapped, Truman Papers.

45. N. S. Haseltine, "Convention of Handicapped Asks U.S. Aid Human Salvage," *Washington Post*, 21 August 1948, B2.

46. "Third Biennial Convention, AFPH," *A.F.P.H. Tribune* (September 1946): 2.

47. For an extended discussion of disabled veterans' wartime and postwar activism, see Audra Jennings, "'An Emblem of Distinction': The Politics of Disability Entitlement, 1940–1950," in *Veterans' Policies, Veterans' Politics: New Perspectives on Veterans in the Modern United States*, ed. Stephen R. Ortiz (Gainesville: University Press of Florida, 2012), 94–116.

48. "Greetings from Millard W. Rice," *A.F.P.H. Tribune* (October 1945): 21.

49. For more on the Blinded Veterans Association see David A. Gerber, "Blind and Enlightened: The Contested Origins of the Egalitarian Politics of the Blinded Veterans Association," in *The New Disability History*, ed. Paul K. Longmore and Lauri Umansky (New York: New York University Press, 2001), 313–34.

50. Doris Zames Fleischer and Frieda Zames, *From Charity to Confrontation: The Disability Rights Movement*, updated ed. (Philadelphia: Temple University Press, 2011), 173–74.

51. Frank T. Hines, "Vocational Rehabilitation Program of the Veterans Administration," *Annals of the American Academy of Political and Social Science* 239 (May 1945): 93–100; C. Harold McCully, "Developments of a Decade of VA Counseling," *Personnel and Guidance Journal* 36 (September 1957): 21–27.

52. McCully, "Developments of a Decade of VA Counseling," 21–27.

53. Ibid.; Hines, "Vocational Rehabilitation Program of the Veterans Administration," 93–100; and Sarah F. Rose, "The Right to a College Education?: The G.I. Bill, Public Law 16, and Disabled Veterans," *Journal of Policy History* 24, 1 (2012): 28.

54. "Uncle G. I. Joe Speaks—The Veteran Problem," *A.F.P.H. Tribune* (October 1945): 22. See also "Uncle GI Joe Speaks," *A.F.P.H. Tribune* (November 1945): 1–2; and "Uncle G. I. Joe Speaks," *A.F.P.H. Tribune* (March 1946): 11.

55. See Rose, "The Right to a College Education?"

56. Max D. Kossoris and Henry S. Hammond, "The Physically Impaired in Industry," *Monthly Labor Review* 63 (December 1946): 918–23.

57. Congress, House, Extension of Remarks of Sheppard of California, A1730.

58. "Greetings from Millard W. Rice," 21.

59. "Lodge Notes," *A.F.P.H. Tribune* (November 1945): 12.

60. N.S. Haseltine, "13,250 D. C. Disabled Have an Inning," *Washington Post*, 3 October 1948, B6.

61. "Neely to Speak: Handicapped Unit to Hold Mass Meeting," *Washington Post*, 26 February 1950, M10.

62. "Greetings from Millard W. Rice," 21; "D. C. Department Holds Mass Meeting," AFPH Newsletter, December 1948, Box 1289, Official File 443, The Physically Handicapped (1945–47), Truman Papers.

63. See Jennings, "'An Emblem of Distinction.'"

64. See Robert M. Buchanan, *Illusions of Equality: Deaf Americans in School and Factory, 1850–1950* (Washington, D.C.: Gallaudet University Press, 1999), 10426; and Susan Burch, *Signs of Resistance: American Deaf Cultural History, 1900 to World War II* (New York: New York University Press, 2002), 124–27.

65. Congress, House, Committee on Labor, Subcommittee to Investigate Aid to the Physically Handicapped, *Hearings, Part 4, New York City*, 78th Cong., 2nd sess. (Washington, D.C.: GPO, 1945), 604.

66. Ibid.

67. Buchanan, *Illusions of Equality*, 116–17.

68. Congress, House, Extension of Remarks of Sheppard of California, A1600.

69. "Address by J. Cooke Howard at A.F.P.H. Mass Meeting," 15.

70. August P. Herdtfelder, who had been a teacher at the West Virginia State School for the Deaf and a leader in the Baltimore, Maryland, Division of the National Fraternal Society of the Deaf; Alan B. Crammatte, a Gallaudet graduate and a teacher for many years at deaf schools; Alice T. Terry, who was twice president of the California Association of the Deaf; Ernest C. Herron, who had served as president of the Dixie Association of the Deaf; and Perry E. Seely, who had been active in the NAD and also served as president of the California Association of the Deaf, all served on the committee. Congress, House, Committee on Labor, Subcommittee to Investigate Aid to the Physically Handicapped, *Hearings, Part 3, Aid to the Deaf and Hard of Hearing*, 78th Cong., 2nd sess. (Washington, D.C.: GPO, 1945), 239–41.

71. House, Subcommittee on Aid to the Physically Handicapped, *Hearings, Part 23, H.R. 5206*, 2583.

72. See Burch, *Signs of Resistance*; and Susan Burch, "Reading Between the Signs: Defending Deaf Culture in Early Twentieth-Century America," in *The New Disability*, ed. Longmore and Umansky, 214–35.

73. Felicia Kornbluh, "Disability, Antiprofessionalism, and Civil Rights: The National Federation of the Blind and the 'Right to Organize' in the 1950s," *Journal of American History* 97 (March 2011): 1028–33.

74. See for example, House, Subcommittee on Aid to the Physically Handicapped, *Hearings, Part 23, H.R. 5206*, 2421–25.

75. "Sen. Sparkman Lauds Work of Handicapped," *Washington Post*, 29 August 1950, B2.

76. For more on anti-communism and its impact on American culture see Ellen Schrecker, *Many Are the Crimes: McCarthyism in America* (Boston: Little, Brown, 1998); and Patterson, *Grand Expectations*, especially chapter 7.

77. Women's historians have demonstrated that the postwar era represented an important era for women's activism and feminist action, but the period was still marked by considerable discrimination and a tightening of gender roles compared to the war years. See Dorothy Sue Cobble, *The Other Women's Movement: Workplace Justice and Social Rights in Modern America*

(Princeton, N.J.: Princeton University Press, 2004); Alice Kessler-Harris, *In Pursuit of Equity: Women, Men, and the Quest for Economic Citizenship in 20th-Century America* (Oxford: Oxford University Press, 2001); Susan M. Hartmann, *The Other Feminists: Activists in the Liberal Establishment* (New Haven, Conn.: Yale University Press, 1998); Joanne Meyerowitz, ed., *Not June Cleaver: Women and Gender in Postwar America, 1945–1960* (Philadelphia: Temple University Press, 1994); Dorothy Sue Cobble, *Dishing It Out: Waitresses and Their Unions in the Twentieth Century* (Urbana: University of Illinois Press, 1991); Elaine Tyler May, *Homeward Bound: American Families in the Cold War Era* (New York: Basic, 1988, 1999); Hartmann, *The Home Front and Beyond*; and Alice Kessler-Harris, *Out to Work: A History of Wage-Earning Women in the United States* (Oxford: Oxford University Press, 1982).

78. Paul K. Longmore and David Goldberger, "The League of the Physically Handicapped and the Great Depression: A Case Study in the New Disability History," *Journal of American History* 87 (December 2000): 915.

79. Virginia A. Pearson, "Mind Over Matter," *Valor* 3 (July 1952): 6, 19, 21.

80. Longmore and Goldberger, "The League of the Physically Handicapped and the Great Depression," 915.

81. For more on gender, disability, and activism, see "Engendering and Regendering Disability: Gender and Disability Activism in Postwar America," in *Disability Histories*, ed. Susan Burch and Michael Rembis (Urbana: University of Illinois Press, 2014), 345-63.

82. "Susan Peters Cooks Up Plot with Crippled Detroit Girl."

83. Senate, Subcommittee of the Committee on Labor and Public Welfare, *Hearings, Vocational Rehabilitation of the Physically Handicapped*, 447–50. For more information about racial discrimination in the administration of federal programs in the South, see, Ira Katznelson, *When Affirmative Action Was White: An Untold History of Racial Inequality in Twentieth-Century America* (New York: Norton, 2005).

84. Alice A. Dunnigan, "Only Few Negroes at Employ the Handicapped Dinner," *Atlanta Daily World*, 17 October 1951, 8.

85. "Hiring the Physically Handicapped," *Pittsburgh Courier*, 20 October 1951, 22.

86. "Who's Who and How Come, in AFPH," *Valor* (July 1952), 22.

87. "Who's Who and How Come, in AFPH," *Valor* (October 1952): 16.

88. Recent scholarship has sought to emphasize the agency of African Americans within the racist system of segregation. See for example, Darlene Clark Hine, "Black Professionals and Race Consciousness: Origins of the Civil Rights Movement, 1890–1950," *Journal of American History* 89 (March 2003): 1279–94. Historian Dorothy Sue Cobble has also demonstrated the ways that union women used sex segregation to propel themselves into national leadership roles. See Cobble, *Dishing It Out*.

89. See, Hine, "Black Professionals and Race Consciousness," 1279–94.

90. Dorothy Clarke Wilson, *Handicap Race: The Inspiring Story of Roger Arnett* (New York: McGraw-Hill, 1967), 140–41.

91. "Lodge Notes," *A.F.P.H. Tribune* (March 1946): 20.

92. "Deaf, Blind Attend Ball," *New York Times*, 13 October 1946, 9.

93. See for example, "Who's Who and How Come, IN AFPH," *Valor* (December 1950): 19; "Handicapped Group Plans Yule Party," *Washington Post*, 6 December 1949, 9; "Who's Who and How Come, IN AFPH," *Valor* (December 1950): 19; "Handicapped to Hold Valentine Party," *Washington Post*, 13 February 1952, 17; and "Who's Who and How Come, IN AFPH," *Valor* (August 1951): 19.

94. "Lodge Notes," *A.F.P.H. Tribune* (October 1945): 20; "Lodge Notes," *A.F.P.H. Tribune* (June 1946): 17; and "Who's Who and How Come, IN AFPH," *Valor* (August 1951): 19.

95. "Lodge Notes," *A.F.P.H. Tribune* (October 1945): 21.

96. "A.F.P.H. Vice-President Seely Leads Movement for New State School for Deaf in Southern California." *A.F.P.H. Tribune* (March 1946): 11.

97. "Lodge Notes." *A.F.P.H. Tribune* (June 1946): 16.

98. "Who's Who and How Come, IN AFPH," *Valor* (July 1953): 12.

99. "AFPH Lodge 94 Sponsors First-Aid Class," *Valor* 3 (July 1952): 8. For more about civil defense, see Laura McEnaney, *Civil Defense Begins at Home: Militarization Meets Everyday Life in the Fifies* (Princeton, N.J.: Princeton University Press, 2000); and Paul Boyer, *By the Bomb's Early Light: American Thought and Culture at the Dawn of the Atomic Age* (New York: Pantheon, 1985).

100. See for example, "AFPH Silver Tea to Draw Matrons," *Atlanta Daily World*, 11 October 1953, 3; "'Greatest Singing Jubilee of '53,'" Display Ad, *Atlanta Daily World*, 8 March 1953, 5; "Delta Rett Club to Give Musicale to Benefit AFPH," *Atlanta Daily World*, 27 October 1953, 3; Edward Peeks, "Local AFPH Strives to Find Employment for Handicapped," *Atlanta Daily World*, 7 January 1954, 1; and "AFPH-Fiscal Report for Year 1954–1955," *Atlanta Daily World*, 26 July 1955, 2.

101. "Who's Who and How Come, IN AFPH." *Valor* 3 (July 1952) 6, 19, 21.

102. "Who's Who and How Come, IN AFPH." *Valor* 2 (February 1951): 17.

103. See especially Nancy F. Cott, *Public Vows: A History of Marriage and the Nation* (Cambridge, Mass.: Harvard University Press, 2000).

104. Margot Canaday, *The Straight State: Sexuality and Citizenship in Twentieth-Century America* (Princeton, N.J.: Princeton University Press, 2009); Carolyn Herbst Lewis, *Prescriptions for Heterosexuality: Sexual Citizenship in the Cold War Era* (Chapel Hill: University of North Carolina Press, 2010). See also, Rickie Solinger, *Wake Up Little Susie: Single Pregnancy and Race Before Roe v. Wade* (New York: Routledge, 2000); and May, *Homeward Bound.*

105. Scholar Barbara Young Welke argues, "Even for categories of disability where law did not formally bar marriage, disabled individuals were often generally understood to be unmarriageable, in the case of a man incapacitated from providing for a family and in the case of a woman incapacitated from caring for children and a household." Barbara Young Welke, *Law and the Borders of Belonging in the Long Nineteenth Century United States* (Cambridge: Cambridge University Press, 2010), 67.

106. "Address by N. P. Alifas at A.F.P.H. Mass Meeting," *A.F.P.H. Tribune* (November 1945): 10.

107. Susan Schweik, "Lomax Matrix: Disability, Solidarity, and the Black Power of 504," *Disability Studies Quarterly* 31, 1 (2011); and Kornbluh, "Disability, Antiprofessionalism, and Civil Rights," 1026.

108. "Address by James B. Carey at A.F.P.H. Mass Meeting," *A.F.P.H. Tribune* (November 1945): 11, 13.

109. "Address by N. P. Alifas at A.F.P.H. Mass Meeting," *A.F.P.H. Tribune* (November 1945): 7, 10.

110. For more about full employment and labor's postwar agenda, see Tracy Roof, *American Labor, Congress, and the Welfare State, 1935–2010* (Baltimore: Johns Hopkins University Press, 2011); and Kevin Boyle, *The UAW and the Heyday of American Liberalism, 1945–1968* (Ithaca, N.Y.: Cornell University Press, 1995).

111. For more about organized labor's relationship with disability activism, see Audra Jennings, "'The Greatest Numbers . . . Will Be Wage Earners': Organized Labor and Disability Activism, 1945–1953," *Labor: Studies in Working-Class History of the Americas* 44 (November 2007): 55–82.

112. Ozeil Fryer Woolcock, "AFPH Local Will Receive Charter at Program Today," *Atlanta Daily World*, 3 August 1952, 8.

113. Congress, House, Extension of Remarks of Sheppard of California, A1730.

114. Congress, House, Representative Kelley of Pennsylvania paying tribute to Mildred Scott, 81st Cong., 1st sess., *Congressional Record* 95, pt. 16 (11 October 1949): A6220–22. For an extended discussion of gender and disability in the AFPH, see, Audra Jennings, "Engendering and Regendering Disability: Gender and Disability Activism in Postwar America," in *Disability Histories*, ed. Susan Burch and Michael Rembis (Urbana: University of Illinois Press, 2014), 345–63.

115. Ibid.

116. Ibid.

117. Albert W. Bryan, "The Medical Administrative Consultant in the State Program of Vocational Rehabilitation," *Journal of Rehabilitation* 12 (June 1946): 32.

118. Technical Information Division, "The Physically Disabled," 10. See also Cowdrey, *Fighting for Life.*

119. For a history of rehabilitation medicine, see Glenn Gritzer and Arnold Arluke, *The Making of Rehabilitation: A Political Economy of Medical Specialization, 1890–1980* (Berkeley: University of California Press, 1985).

120. FSA, *Annual Report of the Office of Vocational Rehabilitation, 1944* (Washington, D.C.: GPO, 1944), 1–7.

121. David Amato, "The Time Factor in Rehabilitation," *Journal of Rehabilitation* 12 (October 1946): 17.

122. U.S. Office of Education, *Administration of Vocational Rehabilitation* (Washington, D.C.: GPO, 1938), 11–12.

123. FSA, *Annual Report of the Office of Vocational Rehabilitation, 1944*, 3–5.

124. FSA, *Annual Report of the Office of Vocational Rehabilitation, 1945* (Washington, D.C.: GPO, 1945), 11.

125. FSA, *Annual Report of the Office of Vocational Rehabilitation, 1944*, 2, 4.

126. Bryan, "The Medical Administrative Consultant in the State Program of Vocational Rehabilitation," 32.

127. Ibid., 32–35.

128. FSA, *Annual Report of the Office of Vocational Rehabilitation, 1944*, 5.

129. U.S. Department of Health, Education, and Welfare, *Facts and Figures on Vocational Rehabilitation, 1953* (Washington, D.C.: U.S. Department of Health, Education, and Welfare, 1954), 36.

130. Milton Rosenbaum, "The Psychiatric Aspects of the Vocational Rehabilitation Program," *Journal of Rehabilitation* 12 (March 1946): 24–27.

131. Rudolf Pinter, Jon Eisenson, and Mildred Stanton, *The Psychology of the Physically Handicapped* (New York: F.S. Crofts, 1941), 17.

132. Alice B. Morrissey, "Psychosocial and Spiritual Factors in Rehabilitation," *Journal of American Nursing* 50 (December 1950): 763.

133. Katharine F. Post, "Problems of the Individual in Making Use of Available Resources," *Journal of Rehabilitation* 12 (December 1946): 3–8, 32.

134. Harry D. Hicker, "Professional Growth in Rehabilitation Service," *Journal of Rehabilitation* 12 (August 1946): 2.

Chapter 4. It's Good Business: Disability and Employment

1. "National Employ the Physically Handicapped Week, October 6–12, 1946," Fact Sheet, Interagency Committee on the Employment of the Physically Handicapped, RRA, DOL, no date, Folder National Employ the Handicapped Comm, Erskine, Box 3, Graves B. Erskine Papers, Truman Library, Independence, Mo. (hereafter Erskine Papers); Packet of Radio Spot Announcements, Interagency Committee on the Employment of the Physically Handicapped, RRA, DOL, no date, Folder National Employ the Handicapped Comm Erskine, Box 3, Erskine Papers; "National Employ-the-Physically-Handicapped Week," U.S. Employment Service, Reports and Analysis Division, 15 November 1946, Folder Information File Employ the Phy. Handicapped Week Oct. 6–12, 46 Erskine, Box 4, Erskine Papers.

2. President Harry S. Truman, Special Message to the Congress Presenting a 21-Point Program for the Reconversion Period, 6 September 1945, Public Papers of the Presidents, Harry S. Truman, 1945–1953; accessed 29 May 2015; President Harry S. Truman, Special Message to the Congress Recommending a Comprehensive Health Program, 19 November 1945, Public Papers of the Presidents, Harry S. Truman, 1945–1953; accessed 29 May 2015. See also Jill Quadagno, *One Nation Uninsured: Why the U.S. Has No National Health Insurance* (New York: Oxford University Press, 2005); James T. Patterson, *Grand Expectations: The United States, 1945–1974* (New York: Oxford University Press, 1996); Alonzo L. Hamby, *Man of the People: A Life of Harry S. Truman* (New York: Oxford University Press, 1995); John Patrick Diggins, *The Proud Decades: America in War and Peace, 1941–1960* (New York: Norton, 1988); Paul Starr, *The Social Transformation of American Medicine: The Rise of a Sovereign Profession and the Making of a Vast Industry* (New York: Basic, 1982); and Susan M. Hartmann, *Truman and the 80th Congress* (Columbia: University of Missouri Press, 1971).

3. House, Committee on Labor, Subcommittee on Aid to the Physically Handicapped, *Report: Aid to the Physically Handicapped*, 79th Cong., 2nd sess. (Washington, D.C.: GPO, 1946).

4. Paul Strachan to Harry S. Truman, 31 August 1945, Box 1290, Official File 443-A, NEPHW (1945–47), Truman Papers.

5. Harry S. Truman, Presidential Proclamation, 22 September 1945, Box 1289, Official File 443, The Physically Handicapped (1945–47), Truman Papers.

6. Congress, House, Representative Ramspeck of Georgia Extends Remarks on NEPHW, 79th Cong., 1st sess., *Congressional Record* 91, pt. 8 (5 November 1945): 10402-3; Merle E. Frampton, Randal J. Hicks, Millard W. Rice, W. E. Ditmars, and Jay C. Hormel to Lewis B. Schwellenbach, 28 February 1947, Box 1290, Official File 443-A, NEPHW (1945–47), Truman Papers.

7. Paul Strachan to Harry S. Truman, 28 March 1952, Box 1291, Official File 443-B, President's Committee on Employment of the Physically Handicapped 1952–1953, Truman Papers. It is difficult to pinpoint when the DOL hired Strachan as a special consultant, but correspondence between Strachan, Schwellenbach, and John Gibson, assistant secretary of labor, suggests that Strachan regularly corresponded, spoke, and met with Schwellenbach and Gibson throughout 1946, and his status as a special consultant to the DOL was being solidified in the late summer and fall of 1946. See Strachan to Gibson, 31 August 1946; Gibson to Strachan, 6 September 1946; Strachan to Gibson, 7 September 1946; Strachan to Gibson, 8 September 1946; Strachan to Gibson, 3 September 1948; Gibson to Strachan, 9 September 1948, Folder Labor Physically

Handicapped, Box 8, John Gibson Papers, Harry S. Truman Library, Independence, Missouri (hereafter, Gibson Papers).

8. Paul Strachan to Charles G. Ross, 17 April 1946, Box 558, President's Personal File 2779, American Federation of the Physically Handicapped, Truman Papers.

9. Congress, House, Committee on Labor, Subcommittee on Aid to the Physically Handicapped, *Hearings, Part 23, H.R. 5206*, 79th Cong., 2nd sess. (Washington, D.C.: GPO, 1946).

10. Ibid., 2297–2306.

11. Memo Secretary of Labor to President, 13 August 1946, Box 558, President's Personal File 2779, American Federation of the Physically Handicapped, Truman Papers.

12. Graves B. Erskine, Speech before Army Air Forces Conference, Mitchel Field, NY, 5 December 1945, Folder Whole Blood Broadcast, MBC; 12 Nov. 1945, Erskine, Box 1, Erskine Papers.

13. Ibid.; Graves B. Erskine, News Program, 23 August 1946, Folder News Broadcast-Mr. Eid, WRC 23 Aug. 1946, Erskine, Box 1, Erskine Papers.

14. "Erskine, G(raves) B(lanchard)," *Current Biography Yearbook*, "1946" (New York: H.W. Wilson, 1946), 182–85.

15. "Order No. 9," Retraining and Reemployment Administration, Department of Labor, 3 July 1946, Folder National Employ the Handicapped Comm, Erskine, Box 3, Erskine Papers.

16. Graves B. Erskine, Speech before the Annual National Convention of the Disabled American Veterans, Portland, Ore., 2 September 1946, Folder Dis. Am Vet Conv, Portland, Ore.; 2 Sep. 1946, Erskine, Box 1, Erskine Papers.

17. "National Employ-the-Physically-Handicapped Week, October 6–12, 1946," Reports and Analysis Division, United States Employment Service, Department of Labor, 15 November 1946, Folder Information File Employ the Phy. Handicapped Week 6–12 Oct. 1946, Erskine, Box 4, Erskine Papers.

18. "A Statement of Objectives and Policies," Interagency Committee on the Employment of the Physically Handicapped, Retraining and Reemployment Administration, Department of Labor, 15 August 1946, Folder National Employ the Handicapped Comm, Erskine, Box 3, Erskine Papers.

19. Information packet, Interagency Committee for Employment of the Physically Handicapped, Retraining and Reemployment Administration, Department of Labor, no date, Folder National Employ the Handicapped Comm, Erskine, Box 3, Erskine Papers.

20. "National Employ-the-Physically-Handicapped Week, October 6–12, 1946."

21. "Hire the Handicapped," 5-minute Speech for Local Adaptation, Interagency Committee on the Employment of the Physically Handicapped, RRA, DOL, no date; "Mayor's Proclamation," Interagency Committee on the Employment of the Physically Handicapped, RRA, DOL, no date; "Jobs for the Handicapped, " Fact Sheet, Interagency Committee on the Employment of the Physically Handicapped, RRA, DOL, no date; "National Employ the Physically Handicapped Week, October 6–12, 1946," Fact Sheet, Interagency Committee on the Employment of the Physically Handicapped, RRA, DOL, no date; "A Statement of the Problem for Publicity Purposes," Interagency Committee on the Employment of the Physically Handicapped, RRA, DOL, 15 September 1946; Packet of Radio Spot Announcements, Interagency Committee on the Employment of the Physically Handicapped, RRA, DOL, no date, Folder National Employ the Handicapped Comm, Erskine, Box 3, Erskine Papers.

22. "National Employ-the-Physically-Handicapped Week, October 6–12, 1946."

23. Graves B. Erskine, Speech before the Southern Governors' Conference, Miami, 6

December 1946, Folder Southern Gov. Conf., Miami, FL; 6 Dec. 1946, Erskine, Box 2, Erskine Papers.

24. Graves B. Erskine, Speech before the 65th Annual Convention of the AFL, Chicago, 11 October 1946, Folder A.F. of L, 65th ann. Conv, Chicago, 1946, Erskine, Box 1, Erskine Papers.

25. Graves B. Erskine, Speech before the Cooperating Committee, Washington, D.C., 9 December 1946, Folder Statement before the Coop. Com. on Emp. of Phy. Hand. Washington, 9 Dec. 1946, Erskine, Box 2, Erskine Papers.

26. Graves B. Erskine, Speech before the Southern Governors' Conference; Graves B. Erskine, Speech before Meeting of State Directors of Vocational Rehabilitation, St. Louis, 1 December 1946, Folder St. Dir. Of Voc. Reh. Meeting, St. Louis, Missouri, 1 Dec. 1946 Erskine, Box 2, Erskine Papers.

27. Graves B. Erskine, Speech before the Annual National Convention of the Disabled American Veterans; Official Report of Proceedings of the Department of Labor, Meeting of President's Committee on NEPHW, Washington, D.C., 4 November 1947, Box 1291, Official File 443-B, President's Committee on Employment of the Physically Handicapped 1952–1953, Truman Papers; "Workmen's Compensation: Encouraging Employment of the Handicapped in Michigan: A Proposal for Revision of the Michigan Second Injury Fund," *Michigan Law Review* 67 (December 1968): 393; Arthur Williams, Jr., "Workmen's Compensation and the Handicapped," *American Risk and Insurance* 26 (Summer 1959): 17.

28. Graves B. Erskine to Harry S. Truman, 18 April 1947, Box 1289, Official File 443, Physically Handicapped (1945–47), Truman Papers; Meyer Wiener to John R. Steelman, 17 April 1947, Box 1291, Official File 443-B, President's Committee on Employment of the Physically Handicapped 1952–1953, Truman Papers.

29. Merle E. Frampton, Randal J. Hicks, Millard W. Rice, W. E. Ditmars, and Jay C. Hormel to Lewis B. Schwellenbach, 28 February 1947.

30. Meyer Wiener to John R. Steelman, 17 April 1947, Box 1291, Official File 443-B, President's Committee on Employment of the Physically Handicapped 1952–1953, Truman Papers.

31. Lewis B. Schwellenbach to President, 13 May 1947, Box 1290, Official File 443-A, NEPHW (1945–47), Truman Papers.

32. Congress, House, Extension of Remarks of Representative Harry R. Sheppard of California, 77th Cong., 2nd sess., *Congressional Record* 88, pt. 9 (12 May 1942): A1729–30.

33. Watson B. Miller to F. J. Bailey, 5 June 1947, Box 1290, Official File 443-A, NEPHW (1945–47), Truman Papers.

34. Ruth-Ellen Ross, *The President's Committee on Employment of People with Disabilities: 50 Years of Progress* (Washington, D.C.: President's Committee on Employment of People with Disabilities, 1997); Press Release, 27 August 1947, Box 558, President's Personal File 2779, American Federation of the Physically Handicapped, Truman Papers.

35. "Admiral McIntire: Dead in Chicago," *New York Times*, 9 December 1959, 45.

36. Official Report of Proceedings of the Department of Labor, Meeting of President's Committee on NEPHW, Washington, D.C., 4 November 1947, Box 1291, Official File 443-B, President's Committee on Employment of the Physically Handicapped 1952–1953, Truman Papers.

37. Paul Strachan to Harry S. Truman, 31 August 1945, Box 1290, Official File 443-A, NEPHW (1945–47), Truman Papers; Paul Strachan to Charles G. Ross, 17 April 1946, Box 558, President's Personal File 2779, American Federation of the Physically Handicapped, Truman Papers.

38. "Merle E. Frampton, 95, Advocate for the Blind," *New York Times*, 4 January 1999, A 17; "Frampton, Merle E(lbert) 1903–1998," *Contemporary Authors*, vol. 172 (Detroit: Gale Group, 1999).

39. Official Report of Proceedings of the Department of Labor, Meeting of President's Committee on NEPHW, Washington, D.C., 4 November 1947, Box 1291, Official File 443-B, President's Committee on Employment of the Physically Handicapped 1952–1953, Truman Papers.

40. Ibid.

41. Ibid.

42. Ibid.

43. Ibid.

44. Proposed Budget, Folder PC BUDGET FISCAL YEAR 1948, Box 40, Record Group 220, Records of Temporary Committees, Commissions, and Boards, President's Commission on Employment of the Handicapped, 1946–1972 (hereafter Record Group 220 PCEH), National Archives, College Park, MD (hereafter National Archives II).

45. Memo for Dr. Frampton, 18 February 1948, Folder PRESIDENT'S COMMITTEE-1947-51, Box 19, Record Group 220 PCEH, National Archives II; Frampton to All members of the President's Committee on NEPHW, 27 February 1948, Folder PRESIDENT'S COMMITTEE-1947-51, Box 19, Record Group 220 PCEH, National Archives II.

46. H. Earle Correvont to Harry S. Truman, 13 February 1948, Box 1291, Official File 443-B, President's Committee on Employment of the Physically Handicapped 1952–1953, Truman Papers.

47. C. F. Feike to Harry S. Truman, 1 March 1948, Box 1291, Official File 443-B, President's Committee on Employment of the Physically Handicapped 1952–1953, Truman Papers.

48. Frampton to All members of the President's Committee on NEPHW, 27 February 1948.

49. Peter J. Salmon to Harry S. Truman, 29 January 1948, Box 1291, Official File 443-B, President's Committee on Employment of the Physically Handicapped 1952–1953, Truman Papers.

50. Barney Mamet to Harry S. Truman, 29 January 1948, Box 1291, Official File 443-B, President's Committee on Employment of the Physically Handicapped 1952–1953, Truman Papers.

51. Berthold Lowenfeld to Lewis Schwellenbach, 4 February 1948; American Association of Workers for the Blind, 23 January 1948, Folder EMPLOYMENT SERVICE–PHYSICALLY HANDICAPPED, Box 32, Record Group 174, General Records of the Department of Labor, Office of the Secretary, Secretary Lewis B. Schwellenbach, 1945–48 (hereafter Record Group 174 Schwellenbach), National Archives II.

52. See Felicia Kornbluh, "Disability, Antiprofessionalism, and Civil Rights: The National Federation of the Blind and the 'Right to Organize' in the 1950s," *Journal of American History* 97 (March 2011): 1023–47.

53. Schwellenbach to H. Earle Correvont, 7 February 1948, Folder EMPLOYMENT SERVICE—PHYSICALLY HANDICAPPED, Box 32, Record Group 174 Schwellenbach, National Archives II.

54. Congress, House, Message from the President, 80th Cong., 2nd sess., *Congressional Record* 94, pt. 1 (19 January 1948): 303.

55. Hartmann, *Truman and the 80th Congress*, 141–43.

56. Edward D. Berkowitz, *Disabled Policy: America's Programs for the Handicapped* (Cambridge: Cambridge University Press), 155–59.

57. Berkowitz, *Disabled Policy*, 155–59. On the DOL-FSA conflict, see also Edward D. Berkowitz, *Rehabilitation: The Federal Government's Response to Disability, 1935–1954* (New York: Arno, 1980).

58. David Rosner and Gerald Markowitz, "Research or Advocacy: Federal Occupational Safety and Health Policies During the New Deal," in *Dying for Work: Workers' Safety and Health in Twentieth-Century America*, ed. David Rosner and Gerald Markowitz (Bloomington: Indiana University Press, 1987), 85, 91.

59. House, Subcommittee on Aid to the Physically Handicapped, *Hearings, Part 23, H.R. 5206*, 2297–2306.

60. Ibid., 2364–65.

61. See Quadagno, *One Nation Uninsured*; and Colin Gordon, *Dead on Arrival: The Politics of Health Care in Twentieth-Century America* (Princeton, N.J.: Princeton University Press, 2003).

62. House, Subcommittee on Aid to the Physically Handicapped, *Hearings, Part 23, H.R. 5206*, 2367–75.

63. Congress, Senate, Subcommittee of the Committee on Labor and Public Welfare, *Hearings, Vocational Rehabilitation of the Physically Handicapped*, 81st Cong., 2nd sess. (Washington, D.C.: GPO, 1950), 423–26.

64. Paul A. Strachan to John W. Gibson, 29 December 1948, Box 1289, Official File 443, Physically Handicapped (1945–47), Truman Papers.

65. Senate, Subcommittee of the Committee on Labor and Public Welfare, *Hearings, Vocational Rehabilitation of the Physically Handicapped*, 373.

66. Congress, House, Representative Miller of Connecticut speaking on the President's Committee on NEPHW, 80th Cong., 2nd sess., *Congressional Record* 94, pt. 1 (13 January 1948): 140; "Miller, William Jennings," *Biographical Directory of the United States Congress, 1774–Present*; http://bioguide.congress.gov/scripts/biodisplay.pl?index=M000764, assessed 21 July 2007.

67. Congress, House, H.J. Res. 302, 80th Cong., 2nd sess., *Congressional Record* 94, pt. 1 (21 January 1948): 372; Congress, House, H.J. Res. 303, 80th Cong., 2nd sess., *Congressional Record* 94, pt. 1 (21 January 1948): 372; Congress, Senate, S.J. Res. 176, 80th Cong., 2nd sess., *Congressional Record* 94, pt. 1 (21 January 1948): 377.

68. Frampton to All members of the President's Committee on NEPHW, 27 February 1948.

69. Frampton to McIntire and Ramspeck, 12 March 1948, Folder PRESIDENT'S COMMITTEE-1947-51, Box 19, Record Group 220 PCEH, National Archives II.

70. Frank Pace to the President, n.d.; Truman to the Speaker of the House, 7 June 1948; Truman to Schwellenbach, 7 June 1948, Folder PC BUDGET FISCAL YEAR 1948, Box 40, Record Group 220 PCEH, National Archives II.

71. Copy of Senate, *Congressional Record*, 19 June 1948, page 9226, Folder PC BUDGET FISCAL YEAR 1948, Box 40, Record Group 220 PCEH, National Archives II; Memorandum David H. Stowe to Steelman, 30 June 1948, Box 1291, Official File 443-B, President's Committee on Employment of the Physically Handicapped 1952–1953, Truman Papers.

72. Ramspeck to Truman, 2 March 1949, Box 1291, Official File 443-B, President's Committee on Employment of the Physically Handicapped 1952–1953, Truman Papers; McCahill to Gibson, 17 June 1948, Folder Labor Physically Handicapped [2], Box 8, Gibson Papers.

73. Memorandum David H. Stowe to Steelman, 30 June 1948, Box 1291, Official File 443-B, President's Committee on Employment of the Physically Handicapped 1952–1953, Truman Papers.

74. Ramspeck to Truman, 2 March 1949.

75. Harry S. Truman to Maurice J. Tobin, 11 July 1949, Box 1291, Official File 443-B, President's Committee on Employment of the Physically Handicapped 1952–1953, Truman Papers; and Harry S. Truman to Senator George D. Aiken, 16 April 1949; Harry S. Truman to Congressman Augustine B. Kelley, 16 April 1949; Harry S. Truman to Senator John J. Sparkman, 16 April 1949, Box 1291, Official File 443-B, President's Committee on Employment of the Physically Handicapped 1952–1953, Truman Papers.

Chapter 5. Work or Welfare: The Limits of the Body Politic

1. George Meany, "Jobs for the Handicapped," *American Federationist* (April 1947): 3–5, Folder ORGANIZED LABOR AMERICAN FEDERATION OF LABOR OCTOBER 1947–NOVEMBER 30, 1955, Box 63, Record Group 363, National Archives II.

2. Ibid.

3. See also Audra Jennings, "'The Greatest Numbers . . . Will Be Wage Earners': Organized Labor and Disability Activism, 1945–1953," *Labor: Studies in Working-Class History of the Americas* 4 (November 2007): 55–82.

4. See Susan M. Hartmann, *Truman and the 80th Congress* (Columbia: University of Missouri Press, 1971).

5. Sparkman introduced S. 2896 with numerous co-sponsors, including Olin Johnston (D-SC), Lister Hill (D-AL), Arthur Stewart (D-TN), James McGrath (D-RI), Ernest McFarland (D-AZ), George Aiken (R-VT), Ralph Flanders (R-VT), Wayne Morse (R-OR), and Joseph McCarthy (R-WI). Congress, Senate, Senator Sparkman of Alabama introducing S. 2896, 80th Cong., 2nd sess., *Congressional Record* 94, pt. 7 (19 June 1948): 9110.

6. Paul Strachan to John Gibson, 29 December 1948, Folder Labor Physically Handicapped [2], Box 8, Gibson Papers.

7. Congress, House, Committee on Labor, Subcommittee on Aid to the Physically Handicapped, *Hearings, Part 23, H.R. 5206*, 79th Cong., 2nd sess. (Washington, D.C.: GPO, 1946); Congress, House, Committee on Education and Labor, *Hearings: Federal Commission for Physically Handicapped*, 81st Cong., 1st sess. (Washington, D.C.: GPO, 1949); Congress, Senate, Subcommittee of the Committee on Labor and Public Welfare, *Hearings, Vocational Rehabilitation of the Physically Handicapped*, 81st Cong., 2nd sess. (Washington, D.C.: GPO, 1950).

8. Sparkman introduced S. 1066 with Walter George (D-GA), Elbert Thomas (D-UT), Claude Pepper (D-FL), Edwin Johnson (D-CO), Lister Hill (D-AL), Ernest McFarland (D-AZ), Clyde Hoey (D-NC), Olin Johnston (D-SC), Francis Myers (D-PA), James McGrath (D-RI), Matthew Neely (D-WV), Hubert Humphrey (D-MN), Estes Kefauver (D-TN), Ralph Brewster (R-ME), George Aiken (R-VT), Wayne Morse (R-OR), and Joseph McCarthy (R-WI). Congress, Senate, Senator Sparkman of Alabama introducing S. 1066, 81st Cong., 1st sess., *Congressional Record* 95, pt. 2 (25 February 1949): 1533–38.

9. Congress, House, Representative Kelley of Pennsylvania introducing H.R. 3095, 81st Cong., 1st sess., *Congressional Record* 95, pt. 2 (1 March 1949): 1694.

10. House, Subcommittee on Aid to the Physically Handicapped, *Hearings, Part 23, H.R. 5206*; House, Committee on Education and Labor, *Hearings: Federal Commission for Physically Handicapped*; Senate, Subcommittee of the Committee on Labor and Public Welfare, *Hearings, Vocational Rehabilitation of the Physically Handicapped.*

11. Ibid.

12. House, Subcommittee on Aid to the Physically Handicapped, *Hearings, Part 23, H.R. 5206*, 2423.

13. Ibid., 2289–94; House, Committee on Education and Labor, *Hearings: Federal Commission for Physically Handicapped*, 1–7.

14. Ibid.

15. Ibid.

16. Ibid.

17. House, Committee on Education and Labor, *Hearings: Federal Commission for Physically Handicapped*, 3–4, 136–42; House, Subcommittee on Aid to the Physically Handicapped, *Hearings, Part 23, H.R. 5206*, 2421–25.

18. Ibid.

19. See Felicia Kornbluh, "Disability, Antiprofessionalism, and Civil Rights: The National Federation of the Blind and the 'Right to Organize' in the 1950s," *Journal of American History* 97 (March 2011): 1023–47.

20. For a broader discussion of welfare and dependency, see Felicia Kornbluh, *The Battle for Welfare Rights: Politics and Poverty in Modern America* (Philadelphia: University Pennsylvania Press, 2007); Jennifer Mittelstadt, *From Welfare to Workfare: The Unintended Consequences of Liberal Reform, 1945–1965* (Chapel Hill: University of North Carolina Press, 2005); Jennifer Mittelstadt, "'Dependency as a Problem to Be Solved': Rehabilitation and the American Liberal Consensus on Welfare in the 1950s," *Social Politics* 8 (Summer 2001): 228–57; and Nancy Fraser and Linda Gordon, "A Genealogy of Dependency: Tracing a Keyword of the U.S. Welfare State," *Signs* 19 (Winter 1994): 309–36.

21. Douglas C. Baynton, "Disability and the Justification of Inequality in American History," in *The New Disability History: American Perspectives*, ed. Paul K. Longmore and Lauri Umansky (New York: New York University Press, 2001), 45–51; Barbara Young Welke, *Law and the Borders of Belonging in the Long Nineteenth Century United States* (Cambridge: Cambridge University Press, 2010), 32–33.

22. House, Subcommittee on Aid to the Physically Handicapped, *Hearings, Part 23, H.R. 5206*, 2292, 2341.

23. Congress, Senate, Committee on Labor and Public Welfare, Subcommittee on Health, *Hearings: National Epilepsy Act (S. 659)*, 81st Cong., 1st sess. (Washington, D.C.: GPO, 1949); Congress, Senate, Committee on Labor and Public Welfare, Subcommittee on Health, *Hearings: National Cerebral Palsy Act (S. 1538)*, 81st Cong., 1st sess. (Washington, D.C.: GPO, 1949); and Congress, Senate, Committee on Labor and Public Welfare, Subcommittee on Health, *Hearings: National Leprosy Act (S. 704)*, 81st Cong., 1st sess. (Washington, D.C.: GPO, 1949).

24. N. S. Haseltine, "Epileptic Tag Often Harms Victims Most," *Washington Post*, 9 September 1952, 8.

25. Senate, Subcommittee on Health, *Hearings: National Leprosy Act (S. 704)*, 54, 56.

26. "History, Achievements, and Future Program of the American Federation of the Physically Handicapped," Folder Handicapped 2 (supplementary materials), Box 57, John Carmody Papers, Franklin D. Roosevelt Library, Hyde Park, N.Y. (hereafter Carmody Papers); Paul Starr, *The Social Transformation of American Medicine: The Rise of a Sovereign Profession and the Making of a Vast Industry* (New York: Basic, 1982), 342–43.

27. Paul Strachan to William Green, 14 March 1946, #23/11, Record Group 21-001, Meany Archives.

28. Quoted in Craig Phelan, *William Green: Biography of a Labor Leader* (Albany: State University of New York Press, 1989), 5–6.

29. William Green to Paul Strachan, 22 March 1946, #23/11, Record Group 21-001, Meany Archives.

30. Several histories have examined the role of disability in working class politics, unionization campaigns, and individual unions. See Sarah F. Rose, "'Crippled' Hands: Disability in Labor and Working-Class History," *Labor: Studies in Working-Class History of the Americas* 2 (Spring 2005): 27–54; Kim E. Nielsen, *The Radical Lives of Helen Keller* (New York: New York University Press, 2004); and John Williams-Searle, "Cold Charity: Manhood, Brotherhood, and the Transformation of Disability, 1870–1900," in *The New Disability History*, ed. Longmore and Umansky, 157–86.

31. Ernst P. Boas, "Your Health!," *AFL Weekly News Service* (hereafter *AFL WNS*), 19 February 1946; "Cruikshank Exposes Fantastic Claims on Coverage of Voluntary Health Plan," *AFL WNS*, 10 June 1949.

32. Tracy Roof, *American Labor, Congress, and the Welfare State, 1935–2010* (Baltimore: Johns Hopkins University Press, 2011), 69–72.

33. Much has been written about labor's struggle to define and combat occupational hazards, improve workers' health, and provide workers with health care and compensation. See Roof, *American Labor, Congress, and the Welfare State*; Michael J. Broadway and Donald D. Stull, "'I'll Do Whatever You Want, But It Hurts': Worker Safety and Community Health in Modern Meatpacking," *Labor: Studies in Working-Class History of the Americas* 5 (Summer 2008): 27–37; Roger Horowitz, "'That Was a Dirty Job!' Technology and Workplace Hazards in Meatpacking over the Long Twentieth Century," *Labor: Studies in Working-Class History of the Americas* 5 (Summer 2008): 13–25; Rose, "'Crippled' Hands"; Daniel E. Bender, *Sweated Work, Weak Bodies: Anti-Sweatshop Campaigns and Languages of Labor* (New Brunswick, N.J.: Rutgers University Press, 2004); John Fabian Witt, *The Accidental Republic: Crippled Workingmen, Destitute Widows, and the Remaking of American Law* (Cambridge, Mass.: Harvard University Press, 2004); Jennifer Klein, *For All These Rights: Business, Labor, and the Shaping of America's Private Welfare State* (Princeton, N.J.: Princeton University Press, 2003); Williams-Searle, "Cold Charity"; Richard P. Mulcahy, *A Social Contract for the Coal Fields: The Rise and Fall of the United Mine Workers of America Welfare and Retirement Fund* (Knoxville: University of Tennessee Press, 2000); Alan Derickson, *Black Lung: Anatomy of a Public Health Disaster* (Ithaca, N.Y.: Cornell University Press, 1998); Claudia Clark, *Radium Girls: Women and Industrial Health Reform, 1910–1935* (Chapel Hill: University of North Carolina Press, 1997); David Rosner and Gerald Markowitz, "Hospitals, Insurance, and the American Labor Movement: The Case of New York in the Postwar Decades," *Journal of Policy History* 9, 1 (1997): 74–95; Alan Derickson, "Health Security for All? Social Unionism and Universal Health Insurance, 1935–1958," *Journal of American History* 80 (March 1994): 1333–56; David Rosner and Gerald Markowitz, *Deadly Dust: Silicosis and the Politics of Occupational Disease in Twentieth-Century America* (Princeton, N.J.: Princeton University Press, 1991); Gerald Markowitz and David Rosner, "'The Streets of Walking Death': Silicosis, Health, and Labor in the Tri-State Region, 1900–1950," *Journal of American History* 77 (September 1990): 525–52; Gerald Markowitz and David Rosner, "Death and Disease in the House of Labor," *Labor History* 30, 1 (1989): 113–17; Alan Derickson, *Workers' Health, Workers' Democracy: The Western Miners' Struggle, 1891–1925* (Ithaca, N.Y.: Cornell University Press, 1988); David Rosner and Gerald Markowitz, eds., *Dying for Work: Workers' Safety and Health in Twentieth-Century America* (Bloomington: Indiana University Press, 1987); Barbara Ellen Smith, *Digging Our Own Graves: Coal Miners and the Struggle over Black Lung Disease* (Philadelphia: Temple University Press, 1987); Bennett M. Judkins, *We Offer Ourselves*

as Evidence: Toward Workers' Control of Occupational Health (Westport, Conn.: Greenwood, 1986); David Rosner and Gerald Markowitz, "Safety and Health on the Job as a Class Issue: The Workers' Health Bureau of America in the 1920s," *Science & Society* 48 (Winter 1984/1985): 466–82; and Edward D. Berkowitz, "Growth of the U.S. Social Welfare System in the Post-World War II Era: The UMW, Rehabilitation, and The Federal Government," *Research in Economic History* 5 (1980): 233–47.

34. "Dead Bills and Dead Men," *AFL WNS*, 2 January 1952, 8.

35. "Men Dying in Gas-Filled Mine Shaft Wrote Pathetic Letters to Relatives," *AFL WNS*, 1 April 1947; "Mine Owners Fined $1,000 in Disaster," *AFL WNS*, 15 July 1947.

36. "AFL Supports Health Insurance Bill; Hits Poor Conditions in Mine State," *AFL WNS*, 1 July 1947.

37. House, Committee on Education and Labor, *Hearings: Federal Commission for Physically Handicapped*, 8.

38. Ibid., 122–23.

39. Senate, Subcommittee of the Committee on Labor and Public Welfare, *Hearings, Vocational Rehabilitation of the Physically Handicapped*, 379.

40. Ibid., 354.

41. Chief of the Bureau of Statistics, Treasury Department, *Statistical Abstract of the United States* (Washington, D.C.: GPO, 1946), 217.

42. Chief of the Bureau of Statistics, Treasury Department, *Statistical Abstract of the United States* (Washington, D.C.: GPO, 1950), 206.

43. House, Committee on Education and Labor, *Hearings: Federal Commission for Physically Handicapped*, 121.

44. Ibid., 116.

45. Senate, Subcommittee of the Committee on Labor and Public Welfare, *Hearings, Vocational Rehabilitation of the Physically Handicapped*, 343.

46. House, Committee on Education and Labor, *Hearings: Federal Commission for Physically Handicapped*, 7–8.

47. Beth Linker, *War's Waste: Rehabilitation in World War I America* (Chicago: University of Chicago Press, 2011), 1–5; Paul A. Strachan, "Helping Disabled Is Good Business," *Washington Post*, 29 July 1951, B2; Paul Strachan to John W. Gibson, 29 December 1948, Box 1289, Official File 443, The Physically Handicapped (1945–47), Truman Papers; House, Committee on Education and Labor, *Hearings: Federal Commission for Physically Handicapped*, 94; Senate, Subcommittee of the Committee on Labor and Public Welfare, *Hearings, Vocational Rehabilitation of the Physically Handicapped*, 353.

48. Congress, House, Committee on Labor, Subcommittee to Investigate Aid to the Physically Handicapped, *Hearings, Part 5, Pittsburgh, PA.*, 78th Cong., 2nd sess. (Washington, D.C.: GPO, 1945), 778–79.

49. House, Subcommittee on Aid to the Physically Handicapped, *Hearings, Part 23, H.R. 5206*, 2349–51.

50. Senate, Subcommittee of the Committee on Labor and Public Welfare, *Hearings, Vocational Rehabilitation of the Physically Handicapped*, 341, 348.

51. Ibid., 340, 344.

52. Ibid., 355–56.

53. "Information Service Series Number 31," OVR Memorandum to State Boards of Vocational Education; Division of Vocational Rehabilitation; Commissions and Other Agencies for

the Blind, 24 April 1947, folder ORGANIZED LABOR AMERICAN FEDERATION OF LABOR OCTOBER, 1947–NOVEMBER 30, 1955, Box 63, Record Group 363, National Archives II; and "W. Oliver Kincannon Retired U.S. Information Officer, 70," *Washington Post*, 8 September 1969, C4.

54. For more information on the UMWA Health and Retirement Fund, see Mulcahy, *A Social Contract for the Coal Fields*; Berkowitz, "Growth of the U.S. Social Welfare System in the Post-World War II Era"; and Melvyn Dubofsky and Warren Van Tine, *John L. Lewis: A Biography* (New York: Quadrangle, 1977).

55. "Joint Statement of Principles by the United Mine Workers of America Welfare and Retirement Fund and the Office of Vocational Rehabilitation, Federal Security Agency, Applicable to the Vocational Rehabilitation of Disabled Miners," January 1948, folder UNITED MINE WORKERS 1947–1948 (Folder #00), Box 64, Record Group 363, National Archives II.

56. Mulcahy, *A Social Contract for the Coal Fields*, 102–3.

57. Howard Hillhouse to W. P. Snuggs, 2 April 1948; H. D. Hicker to Michael J. Shortley, 18 June 1948, folder UNITED MINE WORKERS 1947–1948 (Folder #00), Box 64, Record Group 363, National Archives II; UMWA Welfare and Retirement Fund, "Vocational Rehabilitation Services," 30 June 1954, folder UNITED MINE WORKERS OF AMERICA PUBLICATIONS AND REPORTS, Box 64, Record Group 363, National Archives II.

58. T. Russell Esken to Kenneth E. Pohlmann, 2 November 1950, folder UNITED MINE WORKERS Folder #4—July 1950–Dec. 1950, Box 64, Record Group 363, National Archives II.

59. Kenneth E. Pohlmann to Donald A. Dablestein, 8 November 1950, folder UNITED MINE WORKERS Folder #4—July 1950–Dec. 1950, Box 64, Record Group 363, National Archives II.

60. M. B. Perrin to Tom G. Rathbone, 24 November 1950, folder UNITED MINE WORKERS Folder #4—July 1950–Dec. 1950, Box 64, Record Group 363, National Archives II.

61. Kenneth E. Pohlmann to Mary E. Switzer, 14 February 1951; T. Russell Esken to Leslie A. Falk, 2 February 1951, folder UNITED MINE WORKERS OF AMERICA January 1, 1951–June 30, 1951, Box 64, Record Group 363, National Archives II.

62. Memorandum, W. C. Hushing to William Green, 1 May 1950, #23/16, Record Group 21-001, Legislative Department, Legislative Reference Files, Meany Archives; Sam Stavisky, "Aid to Handicapped Fight Nears Climax," *Washington Post*, 1 May 1950, 6.

63. Constituent letters, Folders 443 (APR.–NOV. 1949) and 443 (Dec. 1949), Box 1290, Official File 443, Physically Handicapped, Truman Papers.

64. Katherine Fosler to President, 11 August 1949, Folder 443 (Dec. 1949), Box 1290, Official File 443, Physically Handicapped, Truman Papers.

65. M. P. Kayle to Roger Jones, Memorandum, 12 September 1949, Folder 443 (Dec. 1949), Box 1290, Official File 443, Physically Handicapped, Truman Papers.

66. Memorandum, W. C. Hushing to William Green, 1 May 1950, #23/16, Record Group 21-001, Legislative Department, Legislative Reference Files, Meany Archives; Stavisky, "Aid to Handicapped Fight Nears Climax," 6.

67. Ibid.

68. Senate, Subcommittee of the Committee on Labor and Public Welfare, *Hearings, Vocational Rehabilitation of the Physically Handicapped*, 92.

69. Ibid., 90.

70. Ibid., 89. See, Alice Kessler-Harris, *In Pursuit of Equity: Women, Men, and the Quest for Economic Citizenship in 20th-Century America* (Oxford: Oxford University Press, 2001).

71. Senate, Subcommittee of the Committee on Labor and Public Welfare, *Hearings, Vocational Rehabilitation of the Physically Handicapped*, 93.

72. Ibid., 388.

73. House, Committee on Education and Labor, *Hearings: Federal Commission for Physically Handicapped*, 77.

74. OVR supporters included the National Rehabilitation Association, the American Public Welfare Association, the National Council on Rehabilitation, the AMA, the Citizens' Federal Committee on Education, the States' Vocational Rehabilitation Council, the American Foundation for the Blind, the American Association of Workers for the Blind, and the Council of State Executives of State Commissions or Agencies for the Blind (ibid., 76).

75. The Robert Brookings Graduate School of Economics and Government was one of the programs that would merge to become the Brookings Institution. Senate, Subcommittee of the Committee on Labor and Public Welfare, *Hearings, Vocational Rehabilitation of the Physically Handicapped*, 391; "G. Lyle Belsley Dies at 88; Federal Official," *Washington Post*, 17 April 1993, D7.

76. Senate, Subcommittee of the Committee on Labor and Public Welfare, *Hearings, Vocational Rehabilitation of the Physically Handicapped*, 388, 390.

77. Ibid., 338.

78. House, Committee on Education and Labor, *Hearings: Federal Commission for Physically Handicapped*, 116.

79. Paul Strachan to John W. Gibson, 29 December 1948, Folder Labor Physically Handicapped [2], Box 8, Gibson Papers; Senate, Subcommittee of the Committee on Labor and Public Welfare, *Hearings, Vocational Rehabilitation of the Physically Handicapped*, 8–15.

80. The emphasis here has been added for clarity. W. Oliver Kincannon to Michael J. Shortley, 26 April 1949, Folder ORGANIZED LABOR MISCELLANEOUS AUGUST 1, 1944–JUNE 30, 1950, Box 64, Record Group 363, National Archives II.

81. Memorandum, W. C. Hushing to William Green, 11 July 1949, #23/13, Record Group 21-001, Legislative Department, Legislative Reference Files, Meany Archives; Memorandum, W. C. Hushing to William Green, 1 May 1950, #23/16, Record Group 21-001, Legislative Department, Legislative Reference Files, Meany Archives.

82. William Green to Paul Strachan, 21 December 1949, Box 56, Folder American Federation of the Physically Handicapped, Box 56, Carmody Papers.

83. Martin P. Durkin to William Hushing, 2 June 1950, #23/16, Record Group 21-001, Legislative Department, Legislative Reference Files, Meany Archives; Martin P. Durkin, Neil Haggerty, Reubin Soderstrom, and Charles M. Houk to William Green, 13 June 1950, #23/16, Record Group 21-001, Legislative Department, Legislative Reference Files, Meany Archives.

84. Ibid.

85. J. Hank Smith to District Supervisors and Counselors, 7 June 1950, Folder ORGANIZED LABOR MISCELLANEOUS AUGUST 1, 1944–JUNE 30, 1950, Box 64, Record Group 363, National Archives II.

86. W. Oliver Kincannon to David Bernstein, 14 July 1950, Folder ORGANIZED LABOR MISCELLANEOUS JULY 1, 1950–JUNE 30, 1951, Box 64, Record Group 363, National Archives II.

87. Memorandum to Michael J. Shortley, "Analysis of Regional Representatives' Reports on Labor Relations of State Rehabilitation Agencies," 20 September 1950; Marion G. Bowen to Philip Schafer, 31 August 1950; Clifford A. Stocker to Philip Schafer, 8 September 1950; C. F.

Feike to Philip Schafer, 7 September 1950; Tom G. Rathbone to Michael J. Shortley, 16 August 1950; Folder ORGANIZED LABOR MISCELLANEOUS JULY 1, 1950–JUNE 30, 1951, Box 64, Record Group 363, National Archives II.

88. Senate, Subcommittee of the Committee on Labor and Public Welfare, *Hearings, Vocational Rehabilitation of the Physically Handicapped,* 53.

89. Douglas, Lehman, and Aiken along with Elbert Thomas (D-UT), James Murray (D-MT), Claude Pepper (D-FL), Matthew Neely (D-WV), Hubert Humphrey (D-MN), and Wayne Morse (R-OR) sponsored the bill. Congress, Senate, Senator Douglas of Illinois introducing S. 4051, 81st Cong., 2nd sess., *Congressional Record* 96, pt. 9 (15 August 1950): 12478–89; Senate, Committee on Labor and Public Welfare, *Vocational Rehabilitation of the Physically Handicapped,* report prepared by Paul H. Douglas, 81st Cong., 2nd sess., 1950, Committee Print, 1–63.

90. Senate, Committee on Labor and Public Welfare, *Vocational Rehabilitation of the Physically Handicapped,* report, 7–12, 15–18, 27–39; Congress, Senate, Senator Douglas of Illinois introducing S. 4051, 81st Cong., 2nd sess., *Congressional Record* 96, pt. 9 (15 August 1950): 12478–89.

91. Senate, Committee on Labor and Public Welfare, *Vocational Rehabilitation of the Physically Handicapped,* report, 15–39; Senate, Senator Douglas of Illinois introducing S. 4051, 81st Cong., 2nd sess., *Congressional Record* 96, pt. 9 (15 August 1950): 12478–89.

92. Senate, Committee on Labor and Public Welfare, *Vocational Rehabilitation of the Physically Handicapped,* report, 7–8, 16–17, 28–63.

93. Ibid, 9–12.

94. Paul H. Douglas, "The War Risk Insurance Act," *Journal of Political Economy* 26 (May 1918): 474–75; Linker, *War's Waste,* 32.

95. For an in-depth discussion of the power of expertise at midcentury in the United States as well as disability challenges to that authority, see Kornbluh, "Disability, Antiprofessionalism, and Civil Rights," 1023–47, particularly 1024–25 and note 3. See also Mittelstadt, *From Welfare to Workfare*; Mittelstadt, "'Dependency as a Problem to Be Solved.'"

96. Senate, Committee on Labor and Public Welfare, *Vocational Rehabilitation of the Physically Handicapped,* report, 2–3.

97. Congress, Senate, Senator Sparkman of Alabama extending his remarks on employment of people with disabilities, 82nd Cong., 1st sess., *Congressional Record* 97, pt. 14 (27 August 1951): A5407–9.

98. Paul Strachan to Labor Associates of AFPH, 26 August 1950, Folder Mason—Handicapped 1950/08–1950/09, #86/54, Record Group 21-001, Department of Legislation, Staff Working Files, Meany Archives.

99. Congress, Senate, Senator Douglas of Illinois remarking on S. 4051, 81st Cong., 2nd sess., *Congressional Record* 96, pt. 11 (13 September 1950): 14682–91.

100. Representative Emanuel Celler (D-NY) first introduced the AFPH bill on January 3, 1951. Congress, House, Representative Celler of New York introducing H.R. 35, 82nd Cong., 1st sess., *Congressional Record* 97, pt. 1 (3 January 1951): 23. Senators Douglas, James Murray (D-MT), Lister Hill (D-AL), Matthew Neely (D-WV), Hubert Humphrey (D-MN), Herbert Lehman (D-NY), Robert Taft (R-OH), George David Aiken (R-VT), and Wayne Morse (R-OR) sponsored the Douglas compromise bill in 1951, introducing it into the Senate on March 22. Congress, Senate, Senator Douglas of Illinois introducing S. 1202, 82nd Cong., 1st sess., *Congressional Record* 97, pt. 2 (22 March 1951): 2814.

101. Jill Quadagno, *One Nation Uninsured: Why the U.S. Has No National Health Insurance* (New York: Oxford University Press, 2005), 52–55; Edward D. Berkowitz, *Disabled Policy: America's Programs for the Handicapped* (Cambridge: Cambridge University Press, 1987), chapter 2; and Roof, *American Labor, Congress, and the Welfare State*, 67–68.

Chapter 6. Götterdämmerung: Rehabilitating Rights in the 1950s

1. Copy of article, "The Gotterdammerung of the Rehab Gods," *Valor* (December 1950), Folder AMERICAN FEDERATION OF THE PHYSICALLY HANDICAPPED JULY 1, 1950–JUNE 30, 1955, Box 142, Record Group 363, National Archives II.

2. Ibid.; "M. J. Shortley Gets FSA Post," *Washington Post*, 7 November 1950, B1; "FSA Promotes Miss Switzer to New Post," *Washington Post*, 10 November 1950, B1; Ruth O'Brien, *Crippled Justice: The History of Modern Disability Policy in the Workplace* (Chicago: University of Chicago Press, 2001), 71.

3. "The Gotterdammerung of the Rehab Gods."

4. More conservative Republicans would reject a broader role for the federal government in civilian disability policy for numerous reasons that grew out of fiscal concern, a broad state's rights ideology, and a more limited conception of the duties and responsibilities of the federal government than liberal Democrats. For histories of conservatism in the postwar era, see Kari Frederickson, *The Dixiecrat Revolt and the End of the Solid South, 1932–1968* (Chapel Hill: University of North Carolina Press, 2001); Lisa McGirr, *Suburban Warriors: The Origins of the New American Right* (Princeton, N.J.: Princeton University Press, 2001); Jonathan M. Schoenwald, *A Time for Choosing: The Rise of Modern American Conservatism* (New York: Oxford University Press, 2001); Godfrey Hodgson, *The World Turned Right Side Up: A History of the Conservative Ascendancy in America* (Boston: Houghton Mifflin, 1996); Jerome L. Himmelstein, *To the Right: The Transformation of American Conservatism* (Berkeley: University of California Press, 1990); and Susan M. Hartmann, *Truman and the 80th Congress* (Columbia: University of Missouri Press, 1971).

5. Minutes of the American Federation of the Physically Handicapped National Council Meeting, 5–6 December 1952; Memorandum, Ruth Bower to Virginia Tehas, 26 March 1953; George Meany to Paul Strachan, 17 June 1953; Resolution No. 86, 71st Annual Convention of the AFL, 15–23 September 1952; and George Meany to Paul Strachan, 3 December 1952, #36/13, Record Group 1-027 (hereafter Record Group 1-027), Miscellaneous Correspondence, 1952–1960, Meany Archives; George Meany to the Officers and Members of National and International Unions, City and State bodies and Directly Affiliated Unions, 15 May 1956, #36/15, Record Group 1-027, Meany Archives; W. C. Hushing to Augustine Kelley, 26 July 1949, #23/13, Record Group 21-001, Staff Working Files, AFL, AFL-CIO Department of Legislation (hereafter Record Group 21-001), Meany Archives; George Nelson to Members of AFPH Labor Associates Committee, 7 January 1953, Paul Strachan to Members of AFPH Labor Associates Committee, 5 March 1953, #23/19, Record Group 21-001, Meany Archives; George Nelson to George Meany, 10 April 1953, #23/20, Record Group 21-001, Meany Archives; George Nelson to Members of AFPH Labor Associates Committee, 1 June 1954, #23/26, Record Group 21-001, Meany Archives; George Nelson to Charles Rae Jeffrey, 27 September 1957, #23/31, Record Group 21-001, Meany Archives; Report to Members of AFPH National Council, 22 September 1954, Folder American Federation of the Physically Handicapped, Box 56, Carmody Papers.

6. Paul Strachan to Walter Mason, 26 July 1952, #23/18, Record Group 21-001, Meany Archives; "1953 Contributions, Labor (as of Nov. 4)," n.d., #36/13, Record Group 1-027, Meany

Archives; "Contributions, 1952, A.F. of L. Internationals," n.d., #23/18, Record Group 21-001, Meany Archives; Report to AFPH National, State, and Lodge Officers from Mildred Scott, Secretary-Treasurer, September 1952, Folder American Federation of the Physically Handicapped, Box 56, Carmody Papers.

7. Paul Strachan to George Meany, 25 February 1953, folder Physically Handicapped, 1952–1953, #36/13, Record Group 1-027, Meany Archives.

8. Ibid.

9. Paul Strachan to Harry S. Truman, 28 March 1952, Box 1291, Official File 443b, President's Committee on the Employment of the Physically Handicapped, Truman Papers.

10. Ibid.

11. Ibid.

12. Executive Secretary to Chairman, Vice Chairman, 14 April 1952, Folder PRESIDENT'S COMMITTEE—1952–53, Box 19, Record Group 220 PCEH, National Archives II.

13. Paul Strachan to Mary Switzer, 22 April 1952, Folder AMERICAN FEDERATION OF THE PHYSICALLY HANDICAPPED JULY 1, 1950–JUNE 30, 1955, Box 142, Record Group 363, National Archives II.

14. "Ike Signs New Cabinet Post Bill Into Law," *Washington Post*, 2 April 1953.

15. Paul Strachan to George Meany, 27 September 1954, Folder Physically Handicapped, 1954–1955, #36/14, Record Group 1-027, Meany Archives; Memorandum from Stuart Rothman, n. d., Folder A American F–American G 1954, Box 81, Record Group 174, General Records of the Department of Labor, Office of the Secretary, Subject Files of Secretary James P. Mitchell, 1953–60 (hereafter Record Group 174 Mitchell), National Archives II.

16. Kevin Boyle, *The UAW and the Heyday of American Liberalism, 1945–1968* (Ithaca, N.Y.: Cornell University Press, 1995), chapter 4.

17. Craig Phelan, *William Green: Biography of a Labor Leader* (Albany: State University of New York Press, 1989), 168–72.

18. Paul Strachan to George Meany, 12 March 1954, Folder Physically Handicapped, 1954–1955, #36/14, Record Group 1-027, Meany Archives.

19. Paul Strachan to George Meany, 21 November 1959, Folder Physically Handicapped, 1956–1960, #36/15, Record Group 1-027, Meany Archives.

20. Congress, House, Special Subcommittee of the Committee on Education and Labor, *Hearings: Assistance and Rehabilitation of the Physically Handicapped*, 83rd Cong., 1st sess. (Washington, D.C.: GPO, 1953), 108–11, 113–14.

21. Russell J. W. Dean to Mr. Collier, 30 April 1954, Folder AMERICAN FEDERATION OF THE PHYSICALLY HANDICAPPED JULY 1, 1950–JUNE 30, 1955, Box 142, Record Group 363, National Archives II.

22. Paul S. Barrett to H. B. Cummings, 2 September 1953, Folder AMERICAN FEDERATION OF THE PHYSICALLY HANDICAPPED JULY 1, 1950–JUNE 30, 1955, Box 142, Record Group 363, National Archives II.

23. Ibid; Robert L. Thornton to Paul Barrett, 29 August 1953, Folder AMERICAN FEDERATION OF THE PHYSICALLY HANDICAPPED JULY 1, 1950–JUNE 30, 1955, Box 142, Record Group 363, National Archives II; "Governor Talmadge, of Georgia, Receives AFPH 'Commendation,'" *Valor* (October 1951): 27.

24. "Cooke Leaves Today For House Committee Hearing," *Atlanta Daily World*, 15 July 1953, 1; "Churches Asked to Assist the Handicapped," *Atlanta Daily World*, 12 July 1953; "Testimony For the Handicapped," *Atlanta Daily World*, 7 July 1953, 6; Rev. Tashereau Arnold, "On

the Reel," *Atlanta Daily World*, 4 July 1953, 3; "Cooke To Speak on Proposal To Start Fed. Agency," *Atlanta Daily World*, 4 July 1953, 1; J. Rosemond Cooke, Letter to the Editor, *Atlanta Daily World*, 28 June 1953, 4.

25. Hartmann, *Truman and the 80th Congress*, 151–54; James T. Patterson, *Grand Expectations: The United States, 1945–1974* (New York: Oxford University Press, 1996), 375–406.

26. For more on the "Right to Organize" campaign, see Felicia Kornbluh, "Disability, Antiprofessionalism, and Civil Rights: The National Federation of the Blind and the 'Right to Organize' in the 1950s," *Journal of American History* 97 (March 2011): 1023–47.

27. Michael J. Shortley, "Rehabilitation of the Civilian Disabled," *Annals of the American Academy of Political and Social Science* 239 (May 1945): 101–8.

28. House, Special Subcommittee of the Committee on Education and Labor, *Hearings: Assistance and Rehabilitation of the Physically Handicapped*, 90–108, 181–90, 199–221, 300–302.

29. "Eisenhower Outlines Program in Message to Congress," *Chicago Daily Tribune*, 8 January 1954, 8.

30. Jill Quadagno, *One Nation Uninsured: Why the U.S. Has No National Health Insurance* (Oxford: Oxford University Press, 2005), 44–46.

31. Howard A. Rusk, "'Human' U.S.-Budget Item Asks Rise in Aid to Disabled," *New York Times* 24 January 1954, 59; Shortley, "Rehabilitation of the Civilian Disabled," 101–8.

32. Senate, Committee on Labor and Public Welfare, *Vocational Rehabilitation of the Disabled*, report prepared by William Purtell, 83rd Cong., 2nd sess., 1954, Committee Print, 48–49; Senate, Committee on Labor and Public Welfare, *Vocational Rehabilitation of the Physically Handicapped*, report prepared by Paul H. Douglas, 81st Cong., 2nd sess., 1950, Committee Print, 27.

33. Smith was joined by Homer Ferguson (R-MI), Leverett Saltonstall (R-MA), Robert Upton (R-NH), Lister Hill (D-AL), and Irving Ives (R-NY) in introducing S. 2758, a bill designed to expand the Hill-Burton Act to provide federal funds for the construction of hospitals for people with chronic illnesses, nursing care and diagnostic centers, and rehabilitation facilities. Upton and Ives joined Smith in co-sponsoring S. 2759, a bill designed to strengthen the rehabilitation service. Congress, Senate, Senator Smith of New Jersey introducing S. 2758 and S. 2759, 83rd Cong., 2nd sess., *Congressional Record* 100, pt. 1 (19 January 1954): 413; Joseph A. Loftus, "Eisenhower Urges Health Insurers Get Federal Help," *New York Times* 19 January 1954, 1.

34. Senate, Committee on Labor and Public Welfare, *Vocational Rehabilitation of the Disabled*, report prepared by Purtell, 3–12.

35. Ibid.; Senate, Committee on Labor and Public Welfare, *Vocational Rehabilitation of the Physically Handicapped*, report prepared by Douglas, 5–6.

36. Ibid.; Congress, Senate, Senator Douglas of Illinois introducing S. 4051, 81st Cong., 2nd sess., *Congressional Record* 96, pt. 9 (15 August 1950): 12478–79.

37. Senate, Committee on Labor and Public Welfare, *Vocational Rehabilitation of the Disabled*, report prepared by Purtell, 3–12; Senate, Committee on Labor and Public Welfare, *Vocational Rehabilitation of the Physically Handicapped*, report prepared by Douglas, 32.

38. House, Committee on Education and Labor, *Vocational Rehabilitation of the Physically Handicapped*, report prepared by Samuel K. McConnell, Jr., 83rd Cong. 2nd sess., 1954, Committee Print, 1–15.

39. Congress, Senate, Senator Murray of Montana remarks on amendments to S.2759, 83rd Cong., 2nd sess., *Congressional Record* 100, pt. 7 (7 July 1954): 9901–8.

40. Ibid.

41. Ibid; "Workmen's Compensation: Encouraging Employment of the Handicapped in Michigan: A Proposal for Revision of the Michigan Second Injury Fund," *Michigan Law Review* 67 (December 1968): 393–406; Arthur Williams, Jr., "Workmen's Compensation and the Handicapped," *American Risk and Insurance* 26 (Summer 1959): 13–27.

42. "Supplemental Views of Senators Lehman, Murray, Hill, Neely, and Douglas," in Senate, Committee on Labor and Public Welfare, *Vocational Rehabilitation of the Disabled*, report prepared by Purtell, 48–50; Congress, Senate, Senator Lehman of New York remarks on S.2759, 83rd Cong., 2nd sess., *Congressional Record* 100, pt. 7 (7 July 1954): 9899.

43. George Nelson to AFPH Labor Associates Committee, 1 June 1954, Folder Handicapped 1954/05–1954/06, #23/26, Record Group 21-001, Meany Archives; Congress, Senate, Senator Murray of Montana remarks on amendments to S.2759, 83rd Cong., 2nd sess., *Congressional Record* 100, pt. 7 (7 July 1954): 9901–8.

44. Paul Strachan to Edwin Johnson, 25 June 1954; Paul Strachan to Guy Gillette, 25 June 1954; Paul Strachan to Warren Magnuson, 25 June 1954; Paul Strachan to Estes Kefauver, 25 June 1954; Paul Strachan to George Smathers, 25 June 1954; Paul Strachan to Wayne Morse, 25 June 1954; Paul Strachan to Richard Russell, 26 June 1954; and Paul Strachan to John J. Sparkman, 25 June 1954, Folder Handicapped 1954/05–1954/06, #23/26, Record Group 21-001, Meany Archives.

45. Paul Strachan to Harley Kilgore, 25 June 1954, folder Handicapped 1954/05–1954/06, #23/26, Record Group 21-001, Meany Archives.

46. Paul Strachan to Edwin Johnson, 25 June 1954; Paul Strachan to Guy Gillette, 25 June 1954; Paul Strachan to Warren Magnuson, 25 June 1954; Paul Strachan to Estes Kefauver, 25 June 1954; Paul Strachan to George Smathers, 25 June 1954; Paul Strachan to Wayne Morse, 25 June 1954; Paul Strachan to Richard Russell, 26 June 1954; and Paul Strachan to John J. Sparkman, 25 June 1954, Folder Handicapped 1954/05–1954/06, #23/26, Record Group 21-001, Meany Archives.

47. Paul Strachan to Franklin D. Roosevelt, Jr., 25 June 1954; Paul Strachan to Clyde Doyle, 25 June 1954; Paul Strachan to Homer Angell, 25 June 1954; Paul Strachan to John Dingell, 25 June 1954; Paul Strachan to Emanuel Celler, 25 June 1954; Paul Strachan to John McCormack, 25 June 1954; Paul Strachan to George Rhodes, 25 June 1954; and Paul Strachan to John Fogarty, 25 June 1954, Folder Handicapped 1954/05–1954/06, #23/26, Record Group 21-001, Meany Archives.

48. Paul Strachan to George Nelson, 26 June 1954, Folder Handicapped 1954/05–1954/06, #23/26, Record Group 21-001, Meany Archives.

49. Congress, Senate, Senator Lehman of New York remarks on S.2759, 83rd Cong., 2nd sess., *Congressional Record* 100, pt. 7 (7 July 1954): 9896–9901.

50. Congress, Senate, Senator Murray of Montana remarks on amendments to S.2759, 83rd Cong., 2nd sess., *Congressional Record* 100, pt. 7 (7 July 1954): 9901–9.

51. Congress, Senate, Senator Johnson of Colorado remarks on amendments to S.2759, 83rd Cong., 2nd sess., *Congressional Record* 100, pt. 7 (7 July 1954): 9920–22.

52. Congress, Senate, Senator Humphrey of Minnesota remarks on amendments to S.2759, 83rd Cong., 2nd sess., *Congressional Record* 100, pt. 7 (7 July 1954): 9922–23.

53. Congress, Senate, Senator Sparkman of Alabama remarks on amendments to S.2759, 83rd Cong., 2nd sess., *Congressional Record* 100, pt. 7 (7 July 1954): 9923–24.

54. Congress, Senate, Senator Morse of Oregon remarks on amendments to S.2759, 83rd Cong., 2nd sess., *Congressional Record* 100, pt. 7 (7 July 1954): 9910–17.

55. Congress, Senate, Roll Call Vote on S. 2759, 83rd Cong., 2nd sess., *Congressional Record* 100, pt. 7 (7 July 1954): 9926.

56. Congress, House, Debate over an amendment to H. R. 9640 offered by Representative Rhodes of Arizona, 83rd Cong. 2nd sess., *Congressional Record* 100, pt. 7 (7 July 1954): 9955–56.

57. Congress, House, Debate over amendments to H. R. 9640 offered by Representative Kelley of Pennsylvania, 83rd Cong. 2nd sess., *Congressional Record* 100, pt. 7 (7 July 1954): 9957–58, 9962–63.

58. Congress, House, Debate over an amendment to H. R. 9640 offered by Representative Sheppard of California, 83rd Cong. 2nd sess., *Congressional Record* 100, pt. 7 (7 July 1954): 9960–62.

59. Congress, House, Debate over an amendment to H. R. 9640 offered by Representative Bennett of Florida, 83rd Cong. 2nd sess., *Congressional Record* 100, pt. 7 (7 July 1954): 9963–64.

60. Congress, House, Roll Call Vote on H. R. 9640, 83rd Cong., 2nd sess., *Congressional Record* 100, pt. 8 (8 July 1954): 10060–61; Congress, House, Consideration of S. 2759, 83rd Cong., 2nd sess., *Congressional Record* 100, pt. 8 (8 July 1954): 10096–99.

61. "Rehabilitation Act Signed by President," *New York Times*, 4 August 1954, 19; House, Committee on Education and Labor, *Vocational Rehabilitation of the Physically Handicapped*, conference report, prepared by McConnell.

62. Paul Strachan to AFPH National and Lodge Officers, September 1954, Folder Handicapped 1954/07–1954/09, #23/27, Record Group 21-001, Meany Archives.

63. "President Signs 3-Year Bill for Specialized Medical Care," *Washington Post*, 13 July 1954, 38.

64. Statement of Income and Expenses, AFPH, Year ended June 30, 1955, Folder Handicapped 1955–, #23/30, Record Group 21-001, Meany Archives; Financial Statement of the AFPH, Fiscal Year July 1, 1953–June 30, 1954, Folder Handicapped 1954/07–1954/09, #23/27, Record Group 21-001, Meany Archives.

65. Paul Strachan to George Meany, 4 June 1955, Folder Physically Handicapped, 1954–1955, #36/14, Record Group 1-027, Meany Archives.

66. Patrick Gorman to Paul Strachan, 11 July 1955; and Paul Strachan to Patrick Gorman, 13 July 1955, Folder Physically Handicapped, 1954–1955, #36/14, Record Group 1-027, Meany Archives.

67. Walter Mason to Paul Strachan, 5 January 1955, Folder Handicapped 1955–, #23/30, Record Group 21-001, Meany Archives.

68. George Meany to Paul Strachan, 27 December 1955, Folder Handicapped 1955–, #23/30, Record Group 21-001, Meany Archives.

69. Quadagno, *One Nation Uninsured*, 52–55; Edward D. Berkowitz, *Disabled Policy: America's Programs for the Handicapped* (Cambridge: Cambridge University Press, 1987), chapter 2; and Tracy Roof, *American Labor, Congress, and the Welfare State, 1935–2010* (Baltimore: Johns Hopkins University Press, 2011), 67–68.

70. George Meany to the Officers and Members of national and International Unions, City and State Bodies and Directly Affiliated Unions, 15 May 1956, Folder Physically Handicapped, 1956–1960, #36/15, Record Group 1-027, Meany Archives.

71. Paul Strachan to National and International Unions, State Federations and Councils, and City Bodies, AFL-CIO, 27 November 1956, Folder Physically Handicapped, 1956–1960, #36/15, Record Group 1-027, Meany Archives.

72. Mildred Scott to John Carmody, 2 April 1959, Folder the American Federation of the Physically Handicapped, Box 185, Carmody Papers.

73. Paul Strachan to Mary Switzer, 11 July 1957, Folder AMERICAN FEDERATION OF THE PHYSICALLY HANDICAPPED JULY 1, 1955–JUNE 30, 1960, Box 142, Record Group 363, National Archives II.

74. Paul Strachan to All Actual Members, AFPH, 3 September 1957; George Nelson to Charles Rae Jeffrey, 27 September 1957, Folder Handicapped 1956/01–1957/12, #23/31, Record Group 21-001, Meany Archives.

75. Mildred Scott to John Carmody, 2 April 1959, Folder the American Federation of the Physically Handicapped, Box 185, Carmody Papers.

76. Ralf Peckham to Mary Switzer, 7 April 1958, Folder AMERICAN FEDERATION OF THE PHYSICALLY HADNICAPPED JULY 1, 1955–JUNE 30, 1960, Box 142, Record Group 363, National Archives II.

77. Mildred Scott to John Carmody, 2 April 1959, Folder the American Federation of the Physically Handicapped, Box 185, Carmody Papers.

78. Paul Strachan to Mary Switzer, 13 July 1967; Paul Strachan to Mary Switzer, 11 August 1967; Henry Redkey to Joseph Hunt, 26 July 1967; Paul Strachan to Mary Switzer, 26 June 1967; Mary Switzer to Paul Strachan, 21 June 1967; Paul Strachan to Mary Switzer, 7 June 1967, Folder AMERICAN FEDERATION OF THE PHYSICALLY HANDICAPPED JULY 1, 1966–JUNE 30, 1968, Box 142, Record Group 363, National Archives II.

79. Jean R. Hailey, "Paul A. Strachan, 83, Fought for Physically Handicapped," *Washington Post*, 19 September 1972, C4.

80. Chief of the Bureau of Statistics, Treasury Department, *Statistical Abstract of the United States* (Washington, D.C.: GPO, 1955), 276; Chief of the Bureau of Statistics, Treasury Department, *Statistical Abstract of the United States* (Washington, D.C.: GPO, 1962), 275, 303; Chief of the Bureau of Statistics, Treasury Department, *Statistical Abstract of the United States* (Washington, D.C.: GPO, 1956), 254, 283; and Chief of the Bureau of Statistics, Treasury Department, *Statistical Abstract of the United States* (Washington, D.C.: GPO, 1960), 263.

81. Kornbluh, "Disability, Antiprofessionalism, and Civil Rights," 1024–25.

Epilogue

1. J. Rosemond Cook, Jr., "The Work of the Federation of the Physically Handicapped," *Atlanta Daily World*, 18 November 1952, 3.

2. Ibid.

3. See, for example, "Wickert, Mrs. Nina E., Saginaw, Michigan," *Saginaw News*, 9 February 2002, C7; "Leiner, Florence B., Bay City, Michigan," *Saginaw News*, 14 September 1998, C7; and "Leiner, Harry J., Bay City, Michigan," *Saginaw News*, 31 August 1987, D7. See also Lindsey Patterson, "The Right to Access: Citizenship and Disability, 1950–1973" (Ph.D. dissertation, Ohio State University, 2012).

4. Ralf Hotchkiss and Judy Heumann, "The Handicapped: Issues on Employment, Civil Rights and a Slogan . . . ," *Washington Post*, 20 May 1973, C7.

5. "Proceedings," Annual Meeting, The President's Committee on Employment of the Physically Handicapped, 4 September 1952, Box 1291, Official File 443-B, President's Committee on Employment of the Physically Handicapped 1952–1953, Truman Papers.

6. Ruth-Ellen Ross, *The President's Committee on Employment of People with Disabilities: 50*

Years of Progress (Washington, D.C.: President's Committee on Employment of People with Disabilities, 1997).

7. Patterson, "The Right to Access," 12–49; Richard K. Scotch, *From Goodwill to Civil Rights: Transforming Federal Disability Policy*, 2nd ed. (Philadelphia: Temple University Press, 2001), 28–31, 55–57; Fred Pelka, *The ABC-Clio Companion to the Disability Rights Movement* (Santa Barbara, Calif.: ABC-Clio, 1997), 25–26.

8. Patterson, "The Right to Access," 61–77.

9. Jules Asher, "Disabled Protest U.S. Bias," *Washington Post*, 6 May 1972, B2; "Vigil Ends Protest by Handicapped," *Washington Post*, 4 May 1973, C2.

10. Patterson, "The Right to Access," 126–29.

11. Richard W. Stevenson, "Justin Dart, Jr., 71, Advocate for Rights of Disabled People," *New York Times*, 24 June 2002, B8; Louie Estrada, "Justin Dart, Jr. Dies; Activist Battled for Rights of Disabled," *Washington Post*, 23 June 2002, C6; Fred Fay and Fred Pelka, "Justin Dart Obituary," *Ability Magazine*, 22 June 2002; William J. Eaton, "Disabled People Rally, Crawl Up Capitol Steps," *Los Angeles Times*, 13 March 1990, OCA27; Maralee Schwartz, "The New Regime: Dart to Chair Board on Disabled Workers," *Washington Post*, 9 August 1989, A19; Barbara Vobejda, "Rehabilitation Commissioner Resigns After Test of Wills," *Washington Post*, 2 December 1987, A23; Maralee Schwartz, "The New Regime: Dart to Chair Board on Disabled Workers," *Washington Post*, 9 August 1989, A19.

Index

Acknowledgments

This book began with a story. Near the end of his shift at the East Diamond Mine in Kentucky in the winter of 1938, a roof fall trapped Robert Henry Jennings, my grandfather, in the mines. He was only twenty-five years old at the time. In the hospital, he was wrapped in a heavy plaster cast, and doctors told him he would never walk again.

My grandfather left the hospital using two canes, a bit sorry that his stubbornness had led him to refuse a wheelchair. By the time he was called to report to his local draft board, my grandfather still needed his canes. To get to his examination, he struggled up some thirty steps only to meet the same doctor who had treated him after his accident. My grandfather explained that he was reporting for duty, but the doctor told him to hobble back down those stairs and go home because Uncle Sam would not be sending him anywhere.

The experience did little to dampen my grandfather's feelings that he should do something for the war effort. So in the fall of 1941 he went to look for a job at the newly founded Republic Aviation plant in Evansville, Indiana. He was hired as a troubleshooting mechanic for the plant. As a production soldier, my grandfather fought the war at home, building P-47 fighter planes.

Disability was central to many of the stories I heard about World War II as a child. My grandfather shared story after story of his experience at Republic. He talked about blind people who sorted and inspected parts, little people working on planes from the inside, and every manner of "crippled and hobbled walking," as he put it, that was commonplace at Republic. This research first grew out of a desire to understand and place my grandfather's experience in the broader narrative of U.S. history.

While my grandfather's World War II experiences led me to some of the specific questions I ask here, his stories and the stories of my other grandparents, parents, aunt and uncle, siblings, nieces and nephews, cousins, friends, and the people of my home community inspired my love of history. Rural western Kentucky is rich with stories and gifted storytellers. This community of storytellers taught me to appreciate the past, to search for wisdom in others' experiences, and to value the experience of being absorbed into someone else's narrative.

As this book moved from curiosity to final product, I have benefited from unbelievable generosity, kindness, and support. I will forever be indebted to Susan M. Hartmann, my mentor and friend. Her example shapes almost every interaction I have with students and colleagues and provides a constant guide of how to be engaged and exacting and kind, caring, and supportive all the while. I am grateful for her insightful critiques of my work, for her continual intellectual encouragement and support, and her willingness to give so much of her time to push me to be a better writer and researcher. Kevin Boyle and Warren Van Tine also read chapters and provided advice and support along the way. Birgitte Søland read numerous chapters over the years. Her kindness, support, critiques, and advice made me a better scholar and this a better book. I benefited and continue to benefit from David J. Staley's mentorship, encouragement, and willingness to talk about ideas, methods, research, and teaching. Many thanks also to Judy Tzu-Chun Wu, Lucy Eldersveld Murphy, William R. Childs, and Brenda Brueggemann for helping to shape my education. I am grateful for John C. Burnham's critique of an earlier draft as well as feedback from many members of the Modern U.S. Seminar at Ohio State University.

Susan and the broader women's history faculty created a community of care among the women's history department at OSU. My colleagues in several women's history seminars offered critiques of nearly every chapter, encouragement, and many thoughtful suggestions for navigating research, writing, and teaching. Many thanks to Stephanie Gilmore, for her willingness to train her critical eye on my work and her kindness and support—then and now. Through many seminars, writing groups, and long conversations, I gained much from Jane Berger, Karen Huber, Caryn Neumann, and Ellen Fout. I am grateful to Michelle Wolfe for reading numerous drafts, keeping me accountable along the way, listening to me talk through various ideas, and being a friend. While not a member of the women's history community, Alison Efford shaped my experience at OSU. I am grateful for her friendship.

My work would not be what it is today without the suggestions and insight of many gifted and wonderful scholars in the disability history community. When I first began working on this project, I met Paul K. Longmore through the H-Disability listserv. Paul was a tremendous and generous scholar, who guided my research, writing, and thinking about disability. He introduced me to many other scholars in the field and provided constant encouragement. He is greatly missed. I would like to thank Susan Burch, who I also met in the early stages of this project. Like Paul, Susan is an incredibly talented and giving scholar, who not only read chapters and offered keen insights along the way but also provided research and career advice and continual support. Many thanks to Mike Rembis, whose editorial guidance helped to shape my thoughts on the connections between disability and gender as well as disability and organized labor. I also benefited from the encouragement and support of Sandy Sufian, Penny Richards, and Cathy Kudlick. I count myself tremendously lucky that Felicia Kornbluh and Kim Nielsen peer reviewed my manuscript, as I would later learn when both of these talented and generous scholars offered kind words and additional support. Their thoughtful critiques helped me to clarify my central arguments and sharpen my ideas. I am grateful for their investment in making this a better book. Felicia and I have since begun a collaboration on a new project. Our work has expanded my thinking about disability rights, and I am grateful to Felicia for her incredible support as I finished revisions on this book.

Beyond the disability history community, Stephen Ortiz encouraged me to write an essay on disabled veterans for his edited collection. His feedback on that essay was tremendously helpful as I revised this manuscript and honed my thinking on disabled veterans. I am also grateful for Edward Berkowitz's feedback on an earlier draft of the manuscript. Many thanks to Jon Free, whose research assistance proved critical as I made final revisions.

Since I began working at Western Kentucky University, Craig T. Cobane has been a mentor, supporter, and friend. Thanks to him for his encouragement and willingness to give me the time and space to work on this project. I am grateful for my colleagues in the Honors College at WKU. The college has been a wonderful place to work, in large measure because of its kind, caring, and committed people. While the college has grown so much in the past few years that I cannot name you all here, thank you for being tremendous colleagues and friends. To the folks in the PUMA, Melinda Grimsley-Smith, Melinda Edgerton, and Cheryl Kirby-Stokes especially, thank you for your support, encouragement, and friendship these last few years and for making the PUMA a great place to work. To my colleagues in the Honors Academy—Yufen Chang, Elizabeth Gish, Alexander Olson, and Leila Watkins—I feel lucky to be part of a department with such talented and supportive colleagues. I am grateful to Clay Motley, who served as department chair until recently, for his support of my research. I would like to thank Stephanie Hammons especially for being incredibly helpful and supportive. Many thanks to my writing group, especially Kristi Branham and Tiara Na'puti, for creating a supportive and encouraging space to write and think. I am thankful for the community of friends I have found in Bowling Green—Kristi, Addie Cheney, Elizabeth, Melinda Grimsley-Smith, Grayson Hunt, Tiara, and Judy Rohrer. I am grateful to Judy for listening, caring, and encouraging and to Judy and her partner Dorrie Mazzone for hosting me in the Bay Area and providing a much needed break before I began the final revisions. Thanks to Elizabeth for being one of the most caring people I know and to Kristi for keeping me accountable and always making me laugh. Many thanks to Addie, whose friendship, wit, care, and love of laughter and baking has sustained me. I would also like to thank Beth Plummer, one of the first people I met at WKU, for her guidance, encouragement, and friendship along the way. While she is no longer at WKU, Jeanne Sokolowski has been and continues to be a wonderful friend. Finally, I count myself fortunate to work with such amazing students, who daily remind me through their fierce commitment to making the world better, tremendous abilities, and good work that there is indeed hope for a better tomorrow. While I cannot possibly name them all here and am sure I will fail to mention a few I should, Drew Mitchell, Cassie Warren, Lindsey Filiatreau, Cory Dodds, Sarah Schrader, Clarice Esch, Chad Coomer, Bailey Mack, Paul Fleischmann, Sarah Fox, and Jarred Johnson, you are wonderful.

I have benefited greatly from the help and support of many amazing archivists and librarians. I would like to thank the archivists and staff of the Truman Library, particularly Liz Safly, who is missed, for patiently answering my many questions, for their kindness and consideration, and for their support of my research. I am also grateful for the assistance of archivists at the Roosevelt Library and National Archives at College Park and in Washington, D.C. Many thanks to David Lincove and Laura DeLancey, both outstanding librarians who helped me along the way, one at the beginning and the other at the end. This book is better because of the financial support that made much of my research possible and gave me the time to focus on writing. Thanks to the Harry S. Truman Library Institute; the Franklin and Eleanor Roosevelt Institute; the Department of History and Department of Economics at OSU; and both University College and the Honors College at WKU.

At University of Pennsylvania Press, I am grateful to the editors of the Politics and Culture in Modern America series (Margot Canaday, Glenda

Gilmore, Michael Kazin, Stephen Pitti, and Thomas Sugrue) for deciding to include this book among such outstanding work. Many thanks to my editor Robert Lockhart for guiding me and this project along the way. He helped to sharpen my writing and clarify my thinking, patiently answered my seemingly endless questions, and always believed in this project. Thanks also to Glenda Gilmore, who invested considerable time in providing keen insight and thoughtful critique that has made this book much stronger.

Portions of this book were published elsewhere in different forms. My analysis of gender and disability first appeared in *Disability Histories*, ed. Susan Burch and Michael Rembis (Urbana: University of Illinois Press, 2014), 345–63, while some of my work on disabled veterans appeared in *Veterans' Policies, Veterans' Politics: New Perspectives on Veterans in the Modern United States*, ed. Stephen R. Ortiz (Gainesville: University Press of Florida, 2012), 94–116. Finally, an earlier piece, which appeared in *Labor: Studies in Working-Class History of the Americas* 4 (November 2007): 55–82, analyzed organized labor's role in supporting disability activism.

This book has been a significant part of my life for many years and has created many burdens for who have lived closest to it. Words cannot express how grateful I am for my dearest friend Jessica R. Pliley. Jessica once wrote that we were intellectual sisters, a fitting description. She has trained her critical eye on countless drafts across many years, shared scores of hotel rooms and tables at the National Archives, pushed me to see the forest when I was enamored with the trees, listened patiently, and always believed in this book. Thanks to Donovan Pierce, who served as a surrogate Jessica from time to time when she was out of the country and a true friend in his own right. A number of history professors and wonderful people at Murray State University contributed much to my development as a scholar. I am grateful to William Schell, Jr., the late T. Wayne Beasley, and Stephanie A. Carpenter. Stephanie directed my undergraduate honors thesis in which I first began to examine disability during World War II and taught me about research. I am grateful too for my family and their endless faith. Many thanks to my father Robert A. Jennings, whose love of politics and sense of justice, no doubt shaped my interest in political history, and to my mother Renee Bliznick, whose art, creativity, and sense of wonderment, molded my commitment to writing and learning. Thank you, Pam Jennings, Bill Bliznick, Bridget Noffsinger, Mary Sublett, and Robert K. Jennings, for all the love and support. I am fortunate to have had such wonderful grandparents. Thanks to the late Robert H. Jennings and Marjorie Jennings and to Tunney and Clemmie

Noffsinger. Then there is Sion Sublett, my partner, who has had to endure long periods when I was away researching, bad moods brought on by long days spent writing, proofreading numerous drafts, and books and papers spread from one end of our house to the other. Thank you for the laughter and the love.